ESSAYS IN RUSSIAN SOCIAL AND ECONOMIC HISTORY

Imperial Encounters in Russian History

Series Editor:

Gary Marker (State University of New York, Stony Brook)

ESSAYS IN RUSSIAN SOCIAL AND ECONOMIC HISTORY

STEVEN L. HOCH

BOSTON
2015

Library of Congress Cataloging-in-Publication Data:
A catalog record for this title is available from the Library of Congress.

ISBN 978-1-61811-428-0 (cloth)
ISBN 978-1-61811-429-7 (electronic)
Book design by Ivan Grave

Published by Academic Studies Press in 2015
28 Montfern Avenue
Brighton, MA 02135, USA
press@academicstudiespress.com
www.academicstudiespress.com

To A., C., E., N., and especially T.

Contents

1

Did Russia's Emancipated Serfs Really Pay Too Much for Too Little Land? Statistical Anomalies and Long-Tailed Distributions

> Where can I find in English a correct history of the emancipation of the Russian serfs, and the terms of their liberation? When that wise man the Emperor of Russia set free twenty-two million serfs, he compelled their masters to give them homesteads upon the very soil which they had tilled ... for they have earned this, they have worked upon the land for ages, and they are entitled to it. The experiment has been a perfect success.
>
> -Thaddeus Stevens,
> U.S. Congressman and radical Republican[1]

Contemporaries and scholars, bureaucrats and critics, revolutionaries and historians have produced volumes of tables and charts seeking to assess the impact of emancipation and land reform on late Imperial Russia. The story they tell, with rare exception, is essentially the same. Extremely influential, especially as regards government policy in the late nineteenth century, was the study of Iu. E. Ianson, who first detailed in 1877 what still remains the standard view: when freed in 1861, Russian serfs received too little land to ensure their livelihood and were forced to pay an inflated price. "The allotment did not guarantee peasant well-being.... Payments and dues on the land were not at all in accord with the allotment received, let alone the income from it."[2] Ianson's stature and importance were such that in 1895 the preeminent encyclopedia

---

This article was originally published in *Slavic Review* 63, no. 2 (Summer 2004): 247-274.

[1] Epigraph taken from Thaddeus Stevens to Charles Sumner, October 7, 1865, in Charles Sumner Papers, cited in Eric Foner, *Nothing but Freedom: Emancipation and Its Legacy* (Baton Rouge, 1983), 8.

[2] Iu. E. Ianson, *Opyt statisticheskago izsledovaniia o krest'ianskikh nadelakh i platezhakh* (St. Petersburg, 1877), 123-25.

of late Imperial Russia, the *Entsiklopedicheskii slovar'* by F. A. Efron and I. A. Brokgauz, would state that he "had established beyond a doubt the inadequacy of peasant land allotments and their excessively high assessment." In complete acceptance of Ianson's views, the encyclopedia, in a lengthy essay on the Russian peasantry, concluded: "The inadequate size of land allotments and the inordinately high dues—these are the two basic reasons why the 1861 peasant reform did not justify economically the hope that was placed in it."[3] Seventy years later, in *The Cambridge Economic History of Europe*, Alexander Gerschenkron would claim: "The peasantry released from serfdom received insufficient allotments of land for which it had to pay a disproportionately high purchase price."[4] Identical views have been advanced by Geroid Robinson, M. N. Pokrovskii, P. I. Liashchenko, P. A. Zaionchkovskii, Jerome Blum, R. Philippot, Basil Kerblay, P. A. Khromov, Lazar Volin, N. M. Druzhinin, Peter Gatrell, Arcadius Kahan, Paul Gregory, and, I presume, others.[5] After 1861, the story continues, the emancipated serfs sank into a state

---

3 F. A. Brokgauz and I. A. Efron, eds., "Krest'iane," *Entsiklopedicheskii slovar'* (St. Petersburg, 1895), 32:723-24.

4 Alexander Gerschenkron, "Agrarian Policies and the Industrialization of Russia, 1861-1917," in *The Cambridge Economic History of Europe* (Cambridge, 1965), vol. 6, pt. 2, pp. 741-43 (emphasis in the original).

5 Geroid T. Robinson, *Rural Russia under the Old Regime: A History of the Landlord-Peasant World and a Prologue to the Peasant Revolution of 1917* (New York, 1932), 88; M. N. Pokrovskii, *Russkaia istoriia s drevneishikh vremen* (Moscow, 1934), 4:93; P. I. Liashchenko, *Istoriia narodnogo khoziaistva SSSR* (Moscow, 1956), 1:584; P. A. Zaionchkovskii, *Provedenie v zhizn' krest'ianskoi reformy 1861 g.* (Moscow, 1958), 138-39, 305-7; P. A. Zaionchkovskii, *Otmena krepostnogo prava v Rossii*, 3rd ed. (Moscow, 1968), 232-59, 299; Jerome Blum, *Lord and Peasant in Russia from the Ninth to the Nineteenth Century* (Princeton, 1961), 597; Jerome Blum, *The End of the Old Order in Rural Europe* (Princeton, 1978), 390; R. Philippot, "L'application de la Réforme dans la province de Kharkov," in *Le Statut des paysans libérés du servage, 1861-1961*, ed. Roger Portal (Paris, 1963), 245; Basile Kerblay, "La vie rurale dans la province de Smolensk vers 1875, d'apres A. Engel'gardt," in Portal, *Le Statut*, 272-77; P. A. Khromov, *Ekonomicheskoe razvitie Rossii* (Moscow, 1967), 321; Lazar Volin, *A Century of Russian Agriculture: From Alexander II to Khrushchev* (Cambridge, MA, 1970), 51; N. M. Druzhinin, *Russkaia derevnia na perelome 1861-1880 gg.* (Moscow, 1978), 114-33; Peter Gatrell, *The Tsarist Economy, 1850-1917* (London, 1986), 196-98; Arcadius Kahan, "The Russian Economy, 1860-1913," in his *Russian Economic History: The Nineteenth Century*, ed. Roger Weiss (Chicago, 1989), 5; and Paul R. Gregory, *Before Command: An Economic History of Russia from Emancipation to the First Five-Year Plan* (Princeton, 1994), 40.

of debt peonage, forced to labor on the estates of former or neighboring lords under disadvantageous terms, to enter the harsh world of migratory or seasonal labor, or to engage in nonagricultural pursuits to meet subsistence needs. As a result, the ex-serfs fell victim to economic underdevelopment and Malthusian population checks.

The sheer weight of comment is seemingly so heavy that few may be prepared to entertain contrasting views. In reality, however, the emancipation legislation, voluminous though it was, said little about the new market relations that were to exist between landlords and their former serfs. No Draconian labor code was put in place in Russia to compel the liberated serfs to work for their former lords. No regulations prohibited the transfer of noble land to the peasants, and ex-serfs were not expected to survive solely by selling their free labor on the market. With property rights in man abrogated, emancipation embodied the small peasant land-holder, tied to family and often commune. But, most important, as regards the actual distribution of land to the peasants and the price they were required to pay for it, the reform legislation of 1861 was tilted more favorably toward the serfs than has been appreciated.

The land allotments provided to the overwhelming majority of peasants resulted in the creation of a vibrant, self-sufficient peasant economy, one virtually immune to seigneurial or capitalist intrusion, as subsequently theorized by A. V. Chaianov.[6] The fear on the part of merchants, former slaveholders, and governments, common in the postbellum American South and the Caribbean, that emancipation would result in a decommercialization of the economy as free peasants focused on subsistence agriculture was not an issue in Russia. Quite the contrary, the autocracy forced most emancipated serfs to accept a subsistence plot. To these peasants, this comported with their sense of familial autonomy, if not freedom. In the end, it needs to be considered that the abolition of serfdom may well have stripped lords of the ability to exact labor and money rents, ensuring peasant well-being. The destruction of serfdom may well have come to mean the predominance of the

[6] While not taking issue with Chaianov's actual *Theory of Peasant Economy*, the findings to be presented here place the peasant family farm in a more favorable economic setting, suggesting that peasants were more autonomous, with greater capital and fuller control over their labor output. Daniel Thorner, Basile H. Kerblay, and R. E. F. Smith, eds., *A. V. Chayanov on the Theory of Peasant Economy* (Madison, 1986), 1-28.

unrestrained peasant family farm. The numbers asserting the harmful effects of emancipation on the peasantry, used in support of the standard view, have become quite well known, but none more so than those compiled by A. E. Lositskii. Since 1906, when he published a fifty-six-page pamphlet entitled *The Redemption Operation*, Lositskii's work has been the source for the overcharge half of the argument for all those cited above. And so, unfortunately, I must begin with him.[7] Much, of course, had been written before Lositskii. But the early studies produced by Ianson, along with those of I. Vil'son and L. V. Khodskii, who offered a quite divergent view, were based upon official information subsequently deemed unreliable and unverifiable. The importance of Lositskii's very brief work was that it seemed to place Ianson's conclusions on a much firmer footing.[8] The defects of these early works, those prior to Lositskii, were many. First, the authors did not have access to the complete works of the Editing Commission that drafted the emancipation legislation—the thirty-eight volumes of information and data it assembled and the arguments it put forth. In fact, with the information available to Ianson, all he could really show was that the terms of land reform were less favorable for serfs than for state or crown peasants. But with respect to land allotments and peas-ant dues, such had been the case prior to emancipation as well. Second, P. Kovan'ko, author of the only comprehensive analysis of the financial aspects of emancipation, noted in 1914 that until the end of the nineteenth century, "the accounts of the state comptrollers on the redemption operation were so incomplete that the comptrollers themselves decided not to draw any conclusions based upon the data at their disposal."[9] But Ianson and Vil'son, writing in 1877 and 1878 respectively, decades before Ko-van'ko's findings, used the information from the state comptrollers. From the late 1870s until the early 1890s, the government did make numerous attempts to balance the confused books of the redemption operation. But in 1893 the

7 A. E. Lositskii, *Vykupnaia operatsiia* (St. Petersburg, 1906).

8 I. Vil'son, "Vykupnye za zemli platezhi krest'ian-sobstvennikov byvshikh pomeshchich'ikh 1862-1876," in *Zapiski Imperatorskago russkago geograficheskago obshchestva po otdeleniiu statistiki* (1878), 5: 259-318 and 325-80; and L. V. Khodskii, *Zemlia i zemledelets: Ekonomicheskoe i statisticheskoe izsledovanie* (St. Petersburg, 1891).

9 P. L. Kovan'ko, *Reforma 19 fevralia 1861 goda i eia posledstviia s finansovoi tochki zreniia (Vykupnaia operatsiia 1861g.-1907g.)* (Kiev, 1914), 4.

State Bank was forced to admit that the failure to establish uniform, consolidated accounting procedures from the outset had resulted in "general confusion in the accounts of the redemption operation."[10]

Four publications appearing between 1893 and 1903 made clear that much of the early research on peasant land reform and especially the redemption operation was so flawed that Ianson and others could no longer be cited as authoritative, if at all. Hence the significance of Lositskii's work when it was published in 1906 and why it has been so widely cited. The first of these four studies, a detailed analysis of the land redemption operation, was published in 1893, after seven years of research, under the title *The Report of the State Bank on the Redemption Operation from its Beginning through January 1, 1892.*[11] It was received as the best work that could be produced under the circumstances, and it is the best we are likely to ever get.[12] Thereafter, the State Bank published annual reports. Second, in 1895, attendant to drafting a new charter for the Peasant Land Bank, the government attempted to analyze land price data recorded by notaries in assessing the transfer tax on the sale of land. Having never compiled a cadastre for the empire nor instituted an effective system of property assessment, the autocracy lacked reliable data on land prices and rates of turnover, now deemed essential for reorganizing this mortgage land bank. Under the direction of A. Ia. Reinbot, and with Lositskii as a member of the staff, the Ministry of Finance published land price data based upon notarial records for the period from 1893 to 1895. In 1901 and 1903, retrospective data on land prices were published for the years from 1863 to 1892.[13] Third, as part of

---

10 *Otchet gosudarstvennago banka po vykupnoi operatsii s otkrytiia vykupa po 1 ianvaria 1892* (St. Petersburg, 1893), 1-4.

11 Ibid. Thereafter, annual reports were published though 1907. See *Otchet gosudarstvennago banka po vykupnoi operatsii za 1892* ... through ... *za 1907* [titles vary] (St. Petersburg, 1893-1908), and Kovan'ko, *Reforma*, 20-22.

12 P. P. Migulin, *Vykupnye platezhi: K voprosu o ikh ponizhenii* (Khar'kov, 1904), 18; and Kovan'ko, *Reforma*, 278-79.

13 Departament okladnykh sborov, *Materialy po statistike dvizheniia zemlevladeniia v Rossii*, 25 vols. (St. Petersburg, 1896-1917); *Svod dannykh o kuple-prodazhe zemel' v 45 guberniiakh Evropeiskoi Rossii za tridtsatiletie 1863-1892 gg.* (1901-1903), vol. 4, pt. 1, and vol. 7, pt. 2 (see also vols. 1-3); *Materialy po statistike dvizheniia zemlevladeniia v Rossii* [v 1893 g.] (1896); *Kuplia-prodazha zemel' v Evropeiskoi Rossii v 1894 g.* (1898); and *Kuplia-prodazha zemel' v Evropeiskoi Rossii v 1895 g.* (1898).

this project, researchers came across a study of land prices undertaken by the Land Division of the Ministry of Internal Affairs at the request of the Editing Commission. Prior to drafting the emancipation legislation, the Land Division analyzed land prices using notarial records for 1854-1858.[14] Using this data, D. I. Rikhter presented a paper in 1897 to the Imperial Free Economic Society entitled "Forgotten Material on the Statistics of Sale Prices on Land," which was published in the society's proceedings.[15] Finally, in 1903, the fourth publication, issued for the Special Conference on the Needs of Agriculture, included a summary report entitled "The General Balance of the Redemption Operation." It provided updated financial information on the redemption operation to January 1, 1902.[16]

Lositskii's widely cited but regrettable table (Table 1) used data from these four sources. This table forms the basis for the argument that the serfs were so overcharged for their land allotments that redemption in effect included considerable compensation to serf-owners, not only for the lands they lost but for their loss of servile labor as well. Comparing the price of land from notarial records for 1863-1872 with land redemption prices under the terms of the emancipation settlement, the overcharge appears to be 90 percent in the non-black earth provinces and 20 percent in the black earth provinces. Only in the western provinces did peasants apparently pay prices current at the time. This is the comparison that is usually made. If 1854-1858 notarial prices are used, the overcharge is universal and even greater. Surprisingly, Lositskii's conclusions have been subjected to careful scrutiny only once, in 1989, in a short article by Evsey Domar, then Ford Professor of Economics Emeritus at the Massachusetts Institute of Technology.[17] Domar thought Lositskii's work

14 Land sold by deeds of purchase excluded all transfers by inheritance, escheat, or public auction for nonpayment of state debts, or as a result of confiscation for criminal activity or disloyalty.

15 D. I. Rikhter, "Zabytyi material po statistike prodazhnykh tsen na zemliu," *Trudy Imperatorskago Vol'nago Ekonomicheskago Obshchestv*a (September 1897), vol. 2, bk. 4, 1-28.

16 "Obshchii balans vykupnoi operatsii," *Vestnik Finansov, Promyshlennosti i Torgovli* (June 8, 1903), prilozhenie no. 23.

17 Evsey Domar, "Were Russian Serfs Overcharged for Their Land by the 1861 Emancipation? The History of One Historical Table," *Research in Economic History*, supplement 5B (1989): 429-39.

Table 1
Lositskii's Original Table

Provinces	Total area of Land Allotments (in 1000s of *desiatinas*)	Total Value of Allotments (in millions of rubles)		
		According to Notarial Sale Prices		Under the Terms of Redemption
		1854-1858	1863-1872	
Non-Black Earth	12,286	155	180	342
Black Earth	9,841	219	284	342
Western	10,141	170	184	183
All	32,268	544	648	867

Source: A. E. Lositskii, *Vykupnaia operatsiia* (St. Petersburg, 1906), 16.

"sloppy" and was highly critical of those who have relied upon his numbers. "They accepted his figures on faith, without examining the origin of his data and the nature of his assumptions. They did not even check his arithmetic."[18] Domar first made minor revisions to Lositskii's table based upon more recent information from Zaionchkovskii, which resulted in a modest downward revision of the apparent overcharge. But, second and more important, he sought to determine "those 'free market prices' that the peasants should have paid." Domar still relied upon official (notarial) price data. Two different measures were used, and the results suggested an overcharge so high, 3.4 times the estimated market price, that Domar felt "it is unlikely that even the tsarist government, acting as it did in the interest of the serf-owners (pomeshchiki) could have perpetrated such a fraud. There must be some other explanations of these fantastic ratios."[19] Ultimately, it all amounted to the same thing: "Any calculation based upon official prices may simply be wrong." Amused by this brief exercise, Domar concluded, "Were the peasants overcharged for their land? They most probably were. Perhaps they were overcharged much more than anyone has ever suggested. And perhaps much less, or not at all."[20]

Domar certainly succeeded in casting doubt on Lositskii's conclusions. But with the anticipated clarity of an economist, he has not helped

[18] Ibid., 430 and 437.
[19] Ibid., 436.
[20] Ibid., 437.

us very much. Domar was also unable to ferret out Lositskii's sources and examine the defects in the original data. In contrast to previous scholars, however, this at least seems to have disturbed him.[21] Nor was Domar able to shed much light on the seemingly even higher overcharge his own alternate approaches produced. Finally, he was incorrect regarding the origin of the 1863-1872 land price data used by Lositskii (Table 1, column 3) and misunderstood the potential value and use of these figures.

Lositskii's table and the entire discussion surrounding it comprise less than six pages, four of text and two of appended tables. Although nobody's figures agree, discrepancies in the total amount of land allotted to the serfs do not appear to be considerable (see Table 2). Neither is there any significant difference in the total compensation the peasants were to pay the lords under the terms of the redemption law (Table 1, column 4). The Report of the State Bank published in 1893 (excluding Tiflis and Stavropol' provinces and Bessarabia, which were not included in Lositskii's data) gives a total redemption cost of 340.8 million rubles for the non-black earth provinces; exactly the same amount for the black earth provinces, and 185.6 million rubles for the western provinces, for a total of 867.2 million rubles. Lositskii's figures are 342.0, 341.5, and 183.1 million rubles, respectively, for a total of 866.6 million rubles. The difference is largely attributable to a minor discrepancy in the data reported for Kovno province. In other words, the problem with Lositskii's analysis is solely in his use of land price data drawn from notarial records that served as a basis of comparison.

The land prices for 1854-1858 in Lositskii's table (Table 1, column 2) came directly from Rikhter's 1897 article, which is acknowledged. The importance of Rikhter's article at the time was that there were only three other sources of information on land prices for Russia as a whole. First were the notarial price data for 1893, published in 1896, in which Lositskii had a part. Second, in 1889, the Central Statistical Committee published land price data based upon notarial records for the years 1882 and 1887.[22] Third, in 1891, the Ministry of State Domains published

---

21 Ibid., 430.

22 Tsentral'nyi statisticheskii komitet, Ministerstvo vnutrennikh del, *Tseny na zemliu v Evropeiskoi Rossii po prodazham, sdelannym v 1882 i 1887 godakh*, in *Vremennik Tsentral'nago statisticheskago komiteta Ministerstva vnutrennikh del*, no. 11 (St. Petersburg, 1889).

Table 2
Total Area of Land Allotments (in 1000s of *desiatinas*)

Provinces	Report of State Bank (1893)	Lositskii (1906)	Domar (1989)
Non-Black Earth	12,434.8	12,286.5	13,002.6
Black Earth	9,814.3	9,840.9	10,771.1
Western	10,995.0	10,141.1	10,133.5
All	33,244.1	32,268.5	33,887.2*

Source: *Otchet gosudarstvennago banka po vykupnoi operatsii s otkrytiia vykupa po 1 ianvaria 1892* (St. Petersburg, 1893); A. E. Lositskii, *Vykupnaia operatsiia* (St. Petersburg, 1906), 16; Evsey Domar, "Were Russian Serfs Overcharged for Their Land by the 1861 Emancipation? The History of One Historical Table," *Research in Economic History*, supplement 5 (1989), 439.
*Domar's explanation for his adjusted figures explains why the column does not add up. See Domar, "Were Russian Serfs Overcharged," 437, note 3.

information on land prices for 1860-1889 as reported by respondents to written surveys conducted in 1883 and 1889.[23] The ministry undertook this project as it believed that the prices given in deeds of purchase (notarial records) had been falsely reported in order to evade transfer taxes. In fact, the ministry described as a "failure" the Central Statistical Committee's project of using notarial records.[24] Rikhter, in turn, was critical of this work and thus felt the need to publish this forgotten material from the works of the Editing Commission. He recognized that the 1882 and 1887 price data of the Central Statistical Committee, based as they were on notarial records, were "underestimates, since during the completion of the sale documents the price for the land is often registered below the actual, with the intent to reduce state duties," that is, the 4 percent property transfer tax.[25] The same held true for the 1854-1858 land prices of the Land Division he was republishing. Yet, in

[23] Ministerstvo gosudarstvennykh imushchestv, *Prodazhnye tseny na zemliu*, in *Sel'skokhoziaistvennye i statisticheskie svedeniia po materialam, poluchennym ot khoziaev* (St. Petersburg, 1891), vol. 4. Summary data from these two sources were published in 1894 by the Chancellery of the Council of Ministers, *Svod statisticheskikh materialov, kasaiushchikhsia ekonomicheskago polozheniia sel'skago naseleniia Evropeiskoi Rossii* (St. Petersburg, 1894).

[24] Ministerstvo gosudarstvennykh imushchestv, *Prodazhnye tseny na zemliu*, 4:1-10.

[25] Ibid., 4:2; Rikhter, "Zabytyi material," 2.

spite of this problem, Rikhter felt these data to be far superior to those gathered by the Ministry of State Domains.

Although the data compiled by the Ministry of State Domains covered the entire period from 1860 to 1889 and would thus seem to be more valuable for studying long-term movements in land prices, Rikhter argued that these data should not be trusted. He noted that the data from respondents were not based on actual recorded transactions; the data were instead simply the respondents' recollection of prevailing land prices some twenty to twenty-five years earlier. Moreover, for the forty-four provinces included in the survey, respondents provided only 879 cases for the entire decade of the 1860s, hardly an adequate database for use in comparing with redemption land prices. In further support of his view, Rikhter quoted from the compilers of the ministry's data who noted: "The data received from landlords is extremely fragmentary and incomplete for many places, and therefore for practical purposes, as regards the purchase and sale of land, is poorly suited."[26]

According to Rikhter, the works of the Editing Commission, especially its statistical supplements, were bibliographic rarities, thereby explaining why the land price data assembled by the Land Division of the Ministry of the Interior for 1854-1858 had been overlooked for almost forty years. In his article of 1897, Rikhter reiterated almost verbatim the inadequacies of these data as detailed in the introduction to the original publication, especially the well-recognized problem of tax evasion.[27] Nevertheless, as information on land prices for these five years was based upon 12,132 actual sales in thirty-seven provinces, Rikhter felt, in contrast to the compilers, that the data could be used to assess the impact of emancipation on the peasantry.

But Rikhter's optimism was not shared by the Editing Commission when it initially published the data in 1860, and the commission issued

---

26 Rikhter, "Zabytyi material," 2. Domar assumed these were the data used by Lositskii for the 1860s, and, not surprisingly, "lost further interest in them." Domar, "Were the Russian Serfs Overcharged," 433.

27 Russia, Redaktsionnye Kommissii dlia sostavleniia polozhenii o krest'ianakh, vykhodiashchikh iz krepostnoi zavisimosti, *Prilozheniia k trudam Redaktsionnykh Kommissii dlia sostavleniia polozhenii o krest'ianakh vykhodiashchikh iz krepostnoi zavisimosti*, vol. 14, *Svedeniia o tsenakh na zemli naselennyia i nenaselennyia* (St. Petersburg, 1860), 7-9; Rikhter, "Zabytyi material," 6-7.

warnings few have subsequently heeded.[28] The commission noted that the data recorded in deeds of purchase included both agricultural and waste lands, although under the terms of the emancipation the serfs were to purchase only usable land. This would tend to push the average price of land based upon the deeds of purchase down relative to the land the emancipated serfs were to acquire. In addition, transfers by deed of purchase included properties with valuable noble residences and other structures or land with special sources of revenue. This could result in prices higher than the mean value of the household plot and arable lands the peasants were to redeem.

A far more serious problem, as has been suggested, was that the transfer of land by deed of purchase, including serf estates, required the payment of a 4 percent tax. Landowners, not surprisingly, misrepresented the prices they reported to the state. In 1840, to limit widespread abuse, the government established, for the purposes of tax assessment, an official, minimum sale price for each province for all land transferred by deed of purchase.[29] A huge percentage of sales were then recorded as taking place at the minimum price, which the commission noted "almost everywhere was significantly below the actual price."[30] In fact, an independent study by the Ministry of State Domains on land prices as recorded in deeds of purchase for Kostroma province between 1831 and 1857 concluded: "out of 800 deeds of purchase, only 26 turned out to be trustworthy ... a large portion of the prices indicated in the deeds of purchase are so low that they do not in the least correspond to the actual value of the land."[31] After considering all the factors affecting the reporting of land prices to the state, the Editing Commission concluded that "the circumstances that have an influence on underestimating prices

---

28 Russia, Redaktsionnye Kommissii, Prilozheniia k trudam, vol. 14, *Svedeniia o tsenakh na zemli naselennyia i nenaselennyia*, 5.

29 *Polnoe sobranie zakonov Rossiiskoi Imperii, Sobranie vtoroe*, 55 vols. (St. Petersburg, 1830-1894), vol. 15, no. 13,750 (31 August 1840). See also *Svod zakonov Rossiiskoi imperii*, 1857 edition (St. Petersburg, 1857), 5:156-57.

30 Russia, Redaktsionnye Kommissii, *Prilozheniia k trudam*, vol. 14, *Svedeniia o tsenakh na zemli naselennyia i nenaselennyia*, 6. See also *Zemledel'cheskaia gazeta* 57 (July 17, 1859).

31 Ministerstvo gosudarstvennykh imushchestv, *Materialy dlia statistiki Rossii, sobiraemye po vedomstvu ministerstva gosudarstvennykh imushchestv* (St. Petersburg, 1858) 1:145.

have a more widespread and decisive effect, and thus outweigh those circumstances that serve only occasionally as a basis for inflating the sale price of land."[32]

If this were not enough, the Editing Commission report of 1860 then discussed how the original flawed data were analyzed. It is enough to distress any statistician. The Land Division eliminated all outliers from its analysis, whether it had reason to or not. Cases were excluded in which a clear intent to evade transfer taxes appeared. Sales that involved large amounts of land were discarded, as they had too great an influence on the mean. Having done all this, mean sale prices were then computed. In some cases, mean sale prices by district (*uezd*) were calculated by dividing the total value of the land sold by total land area. In other instances, individual sales were weighted equally, and an average of averages computed. The first method was generally used at the provincial level, but, on occasion, district averages were averaged.[33] In September 1860 the commission wrote that its analysis "serves only as a starting point for further research on the important problem of land prices in Russia."[34] With respect to policy-making and the development of the emancipation legislation, the commission rejected all the data on land prices that it had at its disposal.[35]

The data from notarial records for 1854-1858 republished and analyzed by Rikhter included separate prices for the sale of settled land (serf estates) and for unsettled or unpopulated land. After emancipation, of course, land could not be sold with a servile population attached. As a consequence and of considerable import, Lositskii used only Rikhter's prices for unsettled (unpopulated) land, as he had no way to disaggregate the various components included in the sale of a serf estate, that

---

32 Russia, Redaktsionnye Kommissii, *Prilozheniia k trudam*, vol. 14, *Svedeniia o tsenakh na zemli naselennyia i nenaselennyia*, 7.

33 Russia, Redaktsionnye Kommissii, *Prilozheniia k trudam*, vol. 14, *Svedeniia o tsenakh na zemli prodannyia s publichnago torga s 1 ianvaria 1854 do 1 ianvaria 1859g.* (St. Petersburg, 1859), 1-3.

34 Russia, Redaktsionnye Kommissii, *Prilozheniia k trudam*, vol. 14, *Svedeniia o tsenakh na pustoporozhniia zemli (v vol'noi prodazhe v 1856-1858 gg.)* (St. Petersburg, 1860).

35 *Pervoe izdanie materialov Redaktsionnykh Kommissii, dlia sostavleniia "Polozhenii o krest'ianakh vykhodiashchikh iz krepostnoi zavisimosti,"* 18 vols. (St. Petersburg, 1859-1860), 3: 98 (Report of the Economic Division, no. 17).

is, the land, serfs, livestock, outbuildings, tools, inventory, and other assets. In so doing, Lositskii adopted a method of disaggregation that assumed that the value of the land alone (apart from all the assets on or legally attached to it) was equal to the local price of unpopulated land.[36]

There are many problems with this assumption. The legal distinction between populated and unpopulated lands derived from Russia's administrative underdevelopment. As has been stated, the autocracy had never undertaken to compile a cadastre for the empire. In fact, prior to emancipation, male serfs were the only asset that the state had reliably measured. Therefore, the only distinction that could be made in assessing immovable property to levy land transfer taxes was between populated serf estates and unsettled or vacant lands. The crudeness of the measure is evident in the law itself: "In deeds of transfer for populated estates, the price is to be determined by the number of male revisional souls on them, using a price for them not less than that given in the attached table by class of province, independent of the amount of land which is found on the settled estate, and without any calculation of its proportion per soul."[37] Thus, all provinces were placed in one of six categories. The minimum assessed value of a serf estate varied from a low of 60 rubles to a high of 150 rubles per male serf registered in the previous tax census. Oddly enough, for male serfs sold without land, the same rates applied.[38]

For unpopulated lands, the price data that Lositskii used, six categories were also established. Sixteen provinces wound up in different groups, however. The minimum assessed sale price fluctuated from 1.50 to 10.50 rubles per *desiatina* (2.7 acres), a considerably greater variance than for populated estates. In addition, the law stated: "In deeds of transfer for unsettled land ... when an unknown amount of land is transferred, then this is to be declared in the completed deed, showing its price honestly."[39] Given Lositskii's use of these data, none of this inspires confidence, although the notarial system (deeds of transfer) may have proved adequate for the purposes of revenue collection and land registration for which it was designed.

---

36 See also Domar, "Were the Russian Serfs Overcharged," 433.

37 *Svod zakonov Rossiiskoi imperii*, vol. 5, *Ustav o poshlinakh*, 1857 edition (St. Petersburg, 1857), 87 (article 399, emphasis added).

38 Ibid. (article 400).

39 Ibid. (article 402).

Problems of measurement aside, the legal distinction between populated and unpopulated land masked an economic reality that greatly affected prices. In the vast majority of cases, the difference was between developed, populated land and undeveloped, vacant land. Land on serf estates had all the appurtenances of agricultural development—cleared, often manured fields; gardens, meadows, and hayfields; access to water and roads; estate and peasant infrastructure. Although some sales of unpopulated lands included particularly valuable orchards or meadows, far more often they were undeveloped lands that would have required considerable investment before yielding a return. Many were also marginal sales at low prices to resolve property disputes.

A variety of other factors contribute to making Lositskii's use of the price for unsettled land problematic. Unpopulated land was only a quarter of the total land sold between 1854 and 1858, but it accounted for almost three-quarters of all transactions. Unsettled land was generally sold in small amounts, averaging 56 desiatinas per sale; sales of serf estates averaged more than eight times that amount. By law the market for populated estates was limited to a small number of buyers—hereditary nobles—while vacant land could be acquired by most persons of non-servile status. The precise impact of these factors on prices, some working at cross-purpose, is impossible to assess. But, at a minimum, these aspects raise significant questions regarding comparability, that is, using vacant, undeveloped land prices as a proxy for those of settled, developed land, which is what Lositskii did in his table (see Table 1, column 2). On balance, it is certain that his use of unpopulated land prices underestimated the value of the land actually redeemed by the freed serfs.

In his table, Lositskii also used data from the 107,983 land transactions recorded by notaries on deeds of purchase between 1863 and 1872, the period when most serfs entered into redemption settlements with their lords (Table 1, column 3). As he sought to determine whether the former serfs had paid a fair price for their lands, these data, which he had helped assemble and publish, seemed the best basis of comparison. Lositskii had a lot of difficulty adding and subtracting, however. His calculations of average prices per desiatina of land are shown in Table 3, column 3. But the actual 1863-1872 prices were 10.78 rubles per desiatina for the non-black earth provinces; 22.08 rubles for the

Table 3
Average Price of Land (from Lositskii)

Provinces	Total area of Land Allotments (in 1000s of desiatinas)	Average Price of Land per Desiatina (in rubles)		
		According to Notarial Sale Prices		Under the Terms of Redemption
		1854-1858	1863-1872	
Non-Black Earth	12,286	12.61	14.65	27.84
Black Earth	9,841	22.25	28.86	34.75
Western	10,141	16.76	18.14	18.05
All	32,268	16.86	20.08	28.87

Source: A. E. Lositskii, *Vykupnaia operatsiia* (St. Petersburg, 1906), 38-39.

black earth provinces; and 18.23 rubles for the western provinces.[40] How Lositskii arrived at his figures remains unknown. Nevertheless, the adjusted figures, although significantly different, only strengthen his argument, as they produce an even greater overcharge. Indeed, it appears we are headed down the same road as Domar.

In reality, little of this matters, although it hardly inspires confidence in Lositskii's work. The more serious problem is how useful are these average sale prices, whether calculated correctly or not. As can be seen in Tables 4-7, an analysis of the 107,983 transactions between 1863 and 1872 used by Lositskii reveals that the distribution of sale prices is not normal; it has a long left-hand tail. The mean (average) sale price is considerably smaller than the median. "Statisticians often use the median rather than the average when dealing with long-tailed distributions, the reason being that in some cases the average pays too much attention to a small percentage of cases in the extreme tail of the distribution."[41] This is the situation that presents itself here. Between 1863 and 1872, 7 percent of all transactions, those involving more than 500 desiatinas, accounted for 62 percent of the total value of land sold. This land sold for an average price of 14.52 rubles. In contrast, the majority of all sales, almost 57 percent, entailed transfers of fewer than 25 desiatinas but accounted for only slightly more than 7 percent of the total land value.

[40] *Svod dannykh o kuple-prodazhe zemel' v 45 guberniiakh Evropeiskoi Rossii za tridtsatiletie 1863-1892 gg.* (St. Petersburg, 1903), 38-49, 74-85, and 112-33.

[41] David Freedman et al., *Statistics*, 2nd ed. (New York, 1991), 60.

Table 4
Average Annual Land Sales in Forty-Five Provinces (1863-1872)

Amount of Land Sold	Number of Sales	Total Area (desiatinas)	Total Value (rubles)	Average Area per Sale (desiatinas)	Average Price per Desiatina (rubles)
<25 desiatinas	6,109	46,538	2,565,014	7.6	55.11
25-500 desiatinas	3,940	467,992	10,608,186	118.7	22.67
>500 desiatinas	749	1,462,509	21,235,026	1,952.6	14.52
Total	10,798	1,977,039	34,408,226	183.1	17.40

Sources: Departament okladnykh sborov, *Materialy po statistike dvizheniia zemlevladeniia v Rossii*, vol. 4, pt. 1, and vol. 7, pt. 2, *Svod dannykh o kuple-prodazhe zemel' v 45 guberniiakh Evropeiskoi Rossii za tridtsatiletie 1863-1892 gg.* (St. Petersburg, 1901-1903); V. V. Sviatlovskii, *Mobilizatsiia zemel'noi sobstvennosti v Rossii (1861-1908 g.)* (St. Petersburg, 1911), 89, 90, and 92.

Table 5
Average Annual Land Sales in Fifteen Non-Black Earth Provinces (1863-1872)

Amount of Land Sold	Number of Sales	Total Area (desiatinas)	Total Value (rubles)	Average Area per Sale (desiatinas)	Average Price per Desiatina (rubles)
<25 desiatinas	1,945	17,326	965,367	8.9	55.72
25-500 desiatinas	1,705	187,660	3,162,356	110.1	16.85
>500 desiatinas	230	494,310	3,411,751	2,149.2	6.90
Total	3,880	699,296	7,539,474	180.2	10.78

Sources: Departament okladnykh sborov, *Materialy po statistike dvizheniia zemlevladeniia v Rossii*, vol. 4, pt. 1, and vol. 7, pt. 2, *Svod dannykh o kuple-prodazhe zemel' v 45 guberniiakh Evropeiskoi Rossii za tridtsatiletie 1863-1892 gg.* (St. Petersburg, 1901-1903); V. V. Sviatlovskii, *Mobilizatsiia zemel'noi sobstvennosti v Rossii (1861-1908 g.)* (St. Petersburg, 1911), 89, 90, and 92.

These lands were considerably more expensive, however, averaging 55.11 rubles per desiatina.

Simply adding soil quality to the equation complicates matters even further. In the non-black earth provinces, the average price of land per desiatina involving sales of fewer than 25 desiatinas was 8.1 times higher than large-scale sales of more than 500 desiatinas. In the black

Table 6
Average Annual Land Sales in Twenty-One Black Earth Provinces (1863-1872)

Amount of Land Sold	Number of Sales	Total Area (desiatinas)	Total Value (rubles)	Average Area per Sale (desiatinas)	Average Price per Desiatina (rubles)
<25 desiatinas	3,791	25,908	1,449,647	6.8	55.95
25-500 desiatinas	1,908	235,938	6,499,892	123.7	27.55
>500 desiatinas	388	665,031	12,523,278	1,714.0	18.83
Total	6,087	926,877	20,472,817	152.3	22.08

Sources: Departament okladnykh sborov, *Materialy po statistike dvizheniia zemlevladeniia v Rossii*, vol. 4, pt. 1, and vol. 7, pt. 2, *Svod dannykh o kuple-prodazhe zemel' v 45 guberniiakh Evropeiskoi Rossii za tridtsatiletie 1863-1892 gg.* (St. Petersburg, 1901-1903); V. V. Sviatlovskii, *Mobilizatsiia zemel'noi sobstvennosti v Rossii (1861-1908 g.)* (St. Petersburg, 1911), 89, 90, and 92.

Table 7
Average Annual Land Sales in Nine Western Provinces (1863-1872)

Amount of Land Sold	Number of Sales	Total Area (desiatinas)	Total Value (rubles)	Average Area per Sale (desiatinas)	Average Price per Desiatina (rubles)
<25 desiatinas	373	3,303	150,024	8.9	45.42
25-500 desiatinas	327	44,394	945,938	135.9	21.31
>500 desiatinas	131	303,168	5,299,970	2,314.3	17.48
Total	831	350,865	6,395,932	422.2	18.22

Sources: Departament okladnykh sborov, *Materialy po statistike dvizheniia zemlevladeniia v Rossii*, vol. 4, pt. 1, and vol. 7, pt. 2, *Svod dannykh o kuple-prodazhe zemel' v 45 guberniiakh Evropeiskoi Rossii za tridtsatiletie 1863-1892 gg.* (St. Petersburg, 1901-1903); V. V. Sviatlovskii, *Mobilizatsiia zemel'noi sobstvennosti v Rossii (1861-1908 g.)* (St. Petersburg, 1911), 89, 90, and 92.

earth region, the range varied by a factor of only 3.0. In the nine western provinces, a mixture of black earth and non-black earth, the range was even smaller. Excluding the nine western provinces, the average price for small parcels of land in both the black earth and non-black earth region was not substantially different, 55.72 rubles versus 55.95. But

Table 8
Average Land Sale Prices in Rubles (1863-1872)
(excluding sales of less than 1 desiatina)

Amount of Land Sold	Total Number of Annual Sales (All Provinces)	Non-Black Earth Provinces	Black Earth Provinces	Western Provinces	All provinces
<25 desiatinas	5,176	48.70	49.21	39.71	48.20
25-500 desiatinas	3,940	16.85	27.55	21.31	22.67
>500 desiatinas	749	6.90	18.83	17.48	14.52

Sources: Departament okladnykh sborov, *Materialy po statistike dvizheniia zemlevladeniia v Rossii*, vol. 4, pt. 1, and vol. 7, pt. 2, *Svod dannykh o kuple-prodazhe zemel' v 45 guberniiakh Evropeiskoi Rossii za tridtsatiletie 1863-1892 gg.* (St. Petersburg, 1901-1903); V. V. Sviatlovskii, *Mobilizatsiia zemel'noi sobstvennosti v Rossii (1861-1908 g.)* (St. Petersburg, 1911), 89, 90, and 92.

for large-scale transactions, land in the black earth provinces sold for 18.83 rubles per desiatina, almost three times the price of the non-black earth provinces, which averaged 6.90 rubles per desiatina. According to V. V. Sviatlovskii, who analyzed these data for the Ministry of Finance, most transfers of land of less than 1 desiatina involved the sale of particularly valuable assets—factories, taverns, market squares, gardens, orchards, or noble country houses.[42] Eliminating such sales lowers the average price for transfers under 25 desiatinas but provides a more realistic estimate for land under cereal cultivation, pasture, meadow, or peasant homestead. The corrected results are given in Table 8.

So, to return to Lositskii, the problem of finding comparable prices is not simply a matter of overcoming the limitations in the original data, of which there are many indeed, but of determining which number best describes the center. Lositskii, unfortunately, used the mean, an extremely poor descriptive statistic in this situation. But he was not so unusual in this regard. Early statisticians idealized the average and failed to appreciate its limitations as an indicator. Quite simply, Lositskii's exclusive reliance on the mean (or average) as a measure of central tendency is misleading. The median would have been a far better choice.

[42] *Svod dannykh o kuple-prodazhe zemel'* and V. V. Sviatlovskii, *Mobilizatsiia zemel'noi sobstvennosti v Rossii (1861-1908 g.)* (St. Petersburg, 1911), viii.

From the published data it is not possible to calculate the median directly, but it is possible to approximate it by weighting the available data, taking into consideration the frequency of land transactions occurring at the reported price. Between 1863 and 1872, merchants and nobles together purchased 72 percent of the total ruble value of land sold. The average amount of land they acquired per transaction was 333 desiatinas; in contrast, peasants of all legal statuses bought land in comparatively small parcels, as is to be expected. Their average purchase was almost eight times smaller. Nevertheless, peasant participation in the market (whether individually, communally, or in groups) was substantial; they constituted one-third of the total number of buyers.[43]

The distribution of peasant purchases also reflects a left-hand tail distribution. Peasants buying land on the open market between 1863 and 1872 were most likely to be involved in purchases of fewer than 25 desiatinas and very unlikely to be engaged in buying more than 500 desiatinas. Over three-quarters of all peasant acquisitions on the open market were by individuals. But even when peasant communes bought land, which were the largest peasant acquisitions, the average amount of land per transaction was only 192.9 desiatinas in the fifteen non-black earth provinces and 96.5 desiatinas in the twenty-one provinces in the black earth zone.

Tables 4 through 8 suggest that the overall median sale price of land is closer to 48.20 rubles, the corrected average for sales under 25 desiatinas (excluding sales under 1 desiatina), than to 22.67 rubles, the average for sales between 25 and 500 desiatinas. In the non-black earth region, given that the average peasant purchase was approximately 50 desiatinas, the most appropriate weights suggest that 60 percent of all peasant purchases involved fewer than 25 desiatinas and 40 percent involved parcels between 25 and 500 desiatinas. In the black earth provinces, with an average peasant purchase of 38 desiatinas per transaction, the most suitable weights result in 73 percent of all peasant purchases involving fewer than 25 desiatinas and 27 percent involving between 25 and 500. In the nine western provinces, the average peasant purchase was 54.9 desiatinas, implying that 64 percent of all peasant purchases were for fewer than 25 desiatinas. These would result in weighted average purchase prices between 1863 and 1872 of 38.51 rubles per desiatina

---

[43] *Svod dannykh o kuple-prodazhe zemel'*, pt. 1, 8-14.

in the fifteen non-black earth provinces, 48.96 rubles in the black earth provinces, and 36.74 rubles in the western provinces. The advantage of using weights is that they allow for a direct comparison of notarial prices for land actually bought by peasants on the open market between 1863 and 1872 with the prices for their land allotments established under the terms of the redemption operation.

Comparing these prices to the imputed value of the land by capitalizing the quitrent (*obrok*), which was the redemption price as determined by the emancipation legislation, yields quite startling results and suggests a very considerable undercharge.[44] And these weights only serve to provide a better description of the center for the data as recorded in the deeds of purchase. The weights do not correct for distortions in the original data, that is, the false reporting of prices to evade transfer taxes. Thus, the amount of the undercharge observed below (see Table 9), based upon weighted prices, still remains an underestimate.

When correctly evaluated, the numbers certainly do not tell the story Lositskii and so many others have made them tell. Indeed, assertions that "the authorities in charge of the redemption operation placed a much inflated valuation on the allotment land" no longer appear tenable.[45] It is not apparent that "the price of land was fixed at a level that

---

44 Various weights were tested, but the results did not substantially differ. To give but one example, for the black earth provinces, assuming that 60 percent of all peasant purchases on the open market between 1863 and 1872 involved fewer than 25 desiatinas, 30 percent between 25 and 500 desiatinas, and 10 percent more than 500 desiatinas (as opposed to the weights of 73, 27, and 0 used in Table 8 above), the weighted average price is 39.67 rubles per desiatina. Weights of 50, 30, and 20 percent for the non-black earth provinces (as opposed to the weights of 60, 40, 0 used above) yield a weighted average of 30.78 rubles. Using similar weights for the western provinces (as opposed to 64, 36, and 0) produces a weighted average sale price of 29.74 rubles per desiatina.

With these weights, the total market value of the non-black earth land allotted to the peasants would be 378 million rubles, 390 million rubles in the black earth provinces, and 302 million rubles in the western provinces for a total of 1,070 million rubles. This would still imply a very substantial undercharge, as the peasants paid a total of 867 million rubles under the terms of redemption. And given the average size in desiatinas of peasant purchases, these weights are quite inappropriate as they imply average peasant purchases (in area) considerably above observed levels.

45 Blum, *End of the Old Order*, 391.

Table 9
Revised Estimates of Peasant Land Allotment Values

Provinces	Total area of Land Allotments (in 1000s of desiatinas)	Total Value of Allotments(in millions of rubles) According to Notarial Sale Prices			
		1854-1858 (Lositskii from Rikhter)	1863-1872 (Lositskii's Figures)	1863-1872 (Weighted Prices)	Under the Terms of Redemption
Non-Black Earth	12,286	155	180	442	342
Black Earth	9,841	219	284	427	342
Western	10,141	170	184	336	183
All	32,268	544	648	1,025	867

would satisfy the formers serf-owners by including implicit compensation payment for the former serfs themselves," in spite of how often Lositskii's original claim is reiterated.[46] A more careful and detailed analysis of land prices as recorded in the deeds of purchase suggests the need to consider that the Editing Commission wrote a law considerably more favorable to the serfs than has been perceived to date, whether intended or not.

It needs to be emphasized that the Editing Commission repeatedly claimed when drafting the emancipation legislation that it made no attempt to equate the real value of the land the peasants received with the capitalized value of their prereform quitrents (or the imputed value of their labor obligations). Under the law peasants redeemed a portion of their former dues, not the land they received. This was done because the Editing Commission could not determine, although not for lack of trying, the market value of the land to be allotted to the peasants.

Half a century later, the autocracy still found itself without reliable data on the market prices of land. The best the government could manage, even then, as it sought to reformulate its fiscal policies, was to assemble notarial data retrospectively. This was the purpose of the project undertaken by the Ministry of Finance under Reinbot's direction and with Lositskii's participation. But Imperial Russia remained administratively underdeveloped, an aspect well reflected in the

46 Kahan, "Russian Economy, 1860-1913," 5.

numerical description the autocracy produced of itself. Clearly, with the information available, the autocracy remained hampered in its ability to analyze the consequences of its own policies, which is the heart of the problem here.

The story on changes in peasant land use across emancipation and reform is also seemingly well known. Received wisdom has it that, prior to 1861, approximately 35.2 million desiatinas were under peasant use. Freedom resulted in a 4.1 percent loss, to roughly 33.8 million desiatinas.[47] But, as we have repeatedly been informed, this overall reduction "disguises the fact that the subtractions and additions were very unequally distributed as among the various areas of the country."[48] Over 90 percent of the increase occurred in the western provinces, as the autocracy sought to impose discriminatory legislation against the region's primarily Polish gentry. In contrast, in the thirty-six non-western provinces, the overall loss was 13 percent. But, as we are told, the reduction in the black earth provinces was even greater. "In the black-soil belt where land was worth keeping, the landlords cut the peasants off with reduced allotments."[49] In the six central black earth provinces of Voronezh, Kursk, Riazan', Tula, Tambov, and Orel, the total amount of land allotted for the emancipated serfs' use was reduced by 16.2 percent.[50] Peasants in New Russia and the lower Volga suffered losses in excess of 25 percent.[51] In the non-black earth provinces, where land was considerably less valuable, according to the standard interpretation, lords "were not interested in reducing allotments, but in receiving the most amount of money for the land granted to the peasants."[52] Here, it is claimed, lords succeeded in saddling their former serfs with land of limited value. Echoing views dating back to the 1880s, Robinson, Gerschenkron, and Zaionchkovskii, to mention just a few, saw large allotments here as a ruse lords employed to receive the maximum compensation under the

47 V. I. Anisimov," Nadely," in A. K. Dzhivelegov, S. P. Mel'gunov, and V. I . Picheta, eds., *Velikaia reforma; russkoe obshchestvo i krest'ianskii vopros v proshlom i nastoiashchem*, 6 vols. (Moscow, 1911), 6:92-96; Robinson, *Rural Russia*, 87.

48 Gerschenkron, "Agrarian Policies," 729-30; Blum, *End of the Old Order*, 395.

49 Robinson, *Rural Russia*, 88.

50 B. G. Litvak, *Russkaia derevnia v reforme 1861 goda: Chernozemnyi tsentr 1861-1865 gg.* (Moscow, 1972), 196.

51 Zaionchkovskii, *Otmena krepostnogo prava*, 240.

52 Zaionchkovskii, *Provedenie v zhizn'*, 181.

terms of redemption.[53] In seventeen provinces emancipation resulted in an increase in the total area of peasant allotments. In twenty-seven provinces, peasants lost land. Nevertheless, "North and South, the scales were weighted against the peasant."[54] But, summarizing the data in this way, as has been done so often, is deceptive and misleading. The problem, again, is statistical-using excessively simple measures for describing central tendencies and failing to understand the distribution in the size of prereform and postreform peasant land allotments. Not only were changes in the amount of land allotted to former serfs not evenly distributed by region, they were not equally distributed among peasants living on different estates. It is not simply a question of how much total land the serfs lost, which is how the data are most often represented, but how these losses were distributed among the peasants.[55]

Due solely to the efforts of Sergei G. Kashchenko, historians now have a more complete understanding of the impact of emancipation on peasant land allotments. Kashchenko was aware of the many limitations of the available data, but his cautious use of this information and his sophisticated understanding of quantitative concepts and statistical measures allow quite a different story to be told. Unfortunately, Kashchenko, in his early scholarship, was trapped within a Soviet historiographical paradigm that necessitated a negative assessment of emancipation and land reform, an influence that persists even in his more recent works. But Kashchenko's three major studies include lengthy statistical appendices, providing more than one hundred twenty-five pages of data.[56] Analyzing this new information makes it possible to draw conclusions that Kashchenko himself was either unable or unwilling to make.

---

53 Robinson, *Rural Russia*, 88; Zaionchkovskii, *Provedenie v zhizn'*, 181; Gerschenkron, "Agrarian Policies," 729; "Finansovaia politika v period 1861-1880 gg.," *Otechestvennye zapiski* 11, pt. 2 (1882): 1-34.

54 Robinson, *Rural Russia*, 88.

55 Zaionchkovskii, *Otmena krepostnogo prava*, 241; Litvak, *Russkaia derevnia*, 152-321; Gerschenkron, "Agrarian Policies," 729.

56 A. Ia. Degtiarev, S. G. Kashchenko, and D. I. Raskin, *Novgorodskaia derevnia v reforme 1861 goda: Opyt izucheniia s ispol'zovaniem EVM* (Leningrad, 1989); S. G. Kashchenko, *Reforma 19 fevralia 1861 goda v Sankt-Peterburgskoi gubernii* (Leningrad, 1990); and S. G. Kashchenko, *Otmena krepostnogo prava v Pskovskoi gubernii: Opyt komp'iuternogo analiza uslovii realizatsii krest'ianskoi reformy 19 fevralia 1861 g.* (St. Petersburg, 1996).

The data on peasant land allotments as recorded in the land charter agreements (*ustavnye gramoty*) and redemption deeds (*vykupnye akty*) that were compiled attendant to emancipation and land reform are the principal sources on peasant land use and ownership. The emancipation law required that land charter agreements be drafted and approved for every serf estate between 1861 and 1863. In contrast, redemption deeds were written only when the peasants purchased all or part of their allotments, and they included any subsequent changes or amendments to the original land charters. Both these sources present problems, although not as serious as those for land prices. The main difficulty is not misrepresentation. All peasants, whether on quitrent or corvee, knew quite well which lands they used. Rather, many estates prior to emancipation had not been properly surveyed. If it were obvious that an estate's prereform allotments were well in excess of the maximum or well below the minimum (or, in some regions, substantially different from the single fixed norm) established by the emancipation law for the locality, there was no need to determine their size, either to implement the land charters between 1861 and 1863 or later at the time of redemption. These allotments would simply be reduced or raised to the statutory level.

Kashchenko reports that, in documents for Novgorod and Pskov provinces, especially on quitrent estates, as lords did not engage in direct farming, it was not unusual to find the comment in the land charters that "how much land was in the hands of the peasants prior to promulgation of the [emancipation] statutes ... is impossible to determine." Elsewhere, the preemancipation figures recorded in the land charters often included land of little or no use or value.[57] Moreover, the open field rotation systems that predominated throughout all of Russia meant estate and peasant fields were often intermingled and poorly demarcated, while other lands, especially pastures and meadows, were frequently held in common. In 1837, on the comparatively well-managed estate of Petrovskoe in Tambov, the bailiff informed his superiors in Moscow: "A surveyor is vitally needed on this estate, for the estate fields are so mixed up with those of the peasants that even the very sowers of estate cereals scarcely know what's what." Twenty years later,

[57] Degtiarev, Kashchenko, and Raskin, *Novgorodskaia derevnia*, 24, and Kashchenko, *Otmena krepostnogo prava*, 19.

another surveyor was requested for the same reason.[58] Only if prereform allotments on an estate were between the statutory minimum and maximum established by the emancipation legislation (or close to them or to the fixed norm where it applied) would lords and peasants have a compelling interest in an accurate survey of these land holdings, as under the law these peasant allotments generally remained unchanged. Overall, Kashchenko found that "for Novgorod province in only 60 percent of the land charter agreements were the data on prereform land use given with sufficient accuracy" that they were suitable for subsequent analysis. A similar situation prevailed in Pskov. The data on prereform allotment size for St. Petersburg province proved to be somewhat better (85 percent accurate).[59]

The distributions of prereform allotments analyzed by Kashchenko for Pskov, Novgorod, and St. Petersburg provinces, all in the non-black earth zone, all have long right-hand tails; the mean allotment is larger than the median. In Figure 1, a logarithmic scale is used to make the tails more visible. In Pskov province, 4.3 percent of the serfs had prereform allotments more than double the median size; in St. Petersburg province, 5.9 percent, and in Novgorod province, 8.5 percent. In other words, in these three non-black earth provinces, a handful of peasants with very large allotments skewed the distribution and unduly influenced the mean. In contrast, my own analysis of Borisoglebsk district in the heart of the black earth zone in Tambov province reveals a more normal distribution in the size of prereform serf allotments, with the mean considerably closer to the median (see Figure 2 and Table 10).

This difference in prereform distribution patterns is due primarily to the geographic distribution of peasant dues. As previously mentioned, on quitrent estates, most prevalent in the northern provinces that Kashchenko researched, lords generally turned all their land over to the peasants, which resulted in a wide variation in allotment sizes with a bias toward the high end. This accounts for the long right-hand tail distribution. In contrast, lords maintaining a demesne, as was more common in

58 Rossiiskii gosudarstvennyi arkhiv drevnikh aktov (RGADA), f. 1262, op. 4, ch. 1, ed. khr. 558, 14June 1837; and ch. 2, ed. khr. 846, October 15, 1857 and May 20, 1858.

59 Degtiarev, Kashchenko, and Raskin, *Novgorodskaia derevnia*, 24; Kashchenko, *Otmena krepostnogo prava*, 19, and Kashchenko, *Reforma 19 fevralia 1861 goda*, 21-23, 129.

the black earth provinces such as Tambov, had a strong incentive to restrict the size of peasant allotments to maximize the land area cultivated directly by the estate. This is best seen in a comparison of coefficients of variation (the standard deviation divided by the arithmetic mean). This summary measure provides a simple "means of comparing the degree to which two sets of variables differ from their respective means. It is often used to know which of two or three variables is most dispersed around its mean."[60] Within all the districts of Pskov province and within all but one in Novgorod province, the coefficient of variation for peasant allotment size, that is, its extent of variation around the mean, was higher, often considerably higher, on quitrent estates than on those in which peasants carried obligatory labor obligations.[61] Similarly, in Borisoglebsk district (Tambov), the coefficient of variation for quitrent peasants (1.301) was almost double that found on corvee estates (0.688). St. Petersburg province presents a less clear picture, largely due to atypical circumstances effecting corvee peasants in two districts adjacent to the Baltic provinces.[62] Nevertheless, on the whole, as the percentage of serfs on quitrent within a district or province increased, the overall variation in peasant allotment sizes also grew.[63] And, this was well known to the Editing Commission, which is why it had imposed maximum sizes on peasant allotments, citing, in particular, the high incidence of land-rich quitrent estates in the northern, non-black earth provinces of Russia.[64]

Figures 1 and 2 clearly illustrate the effect of the maximums imposed by the emancipation statutes on postreform peasant allotment size. In all four provinces, north and south, the pattern of change was the same

---

60 Roderick Floud, *An Introduction to Quantitative Methods for Historians*, 2nd ed. (London, 1979), 82.

61 Degtiarev, Kashchenko, and Raskin, *Novgorodskaia derevnia*, 79-80, 86-87, 92-93, 98-99, 102-3, 106-7, 113, 121, and 125; Kashchenko, *Otmena krepostnogo prava*, 37, 44, 56, 60, 64, 69-70, and 74.

62 Kashchenko, *Reforma 19 fevralia 1861 goda*, 129.

63 Degtiarev, Kashchenko, and Raskin, *Novgorodskaia derevnia*, 134; Litvak, *Russkaia derevnia*, 150-51.

64 *Pervoe izdanie materialov*, 3:27, 34 (Report of the Economic Division, no. 15). The coefficients of variation for serfs on mixed dues, that is, those carrying both labor obligations and money payments, varied considerably, at times closer to pure quitrent peasants, at times closer to serfs only on corvée. In all likelihood, this depended on whether the quitrent was primarily a supplement to barshchina or whether the reverse held true.

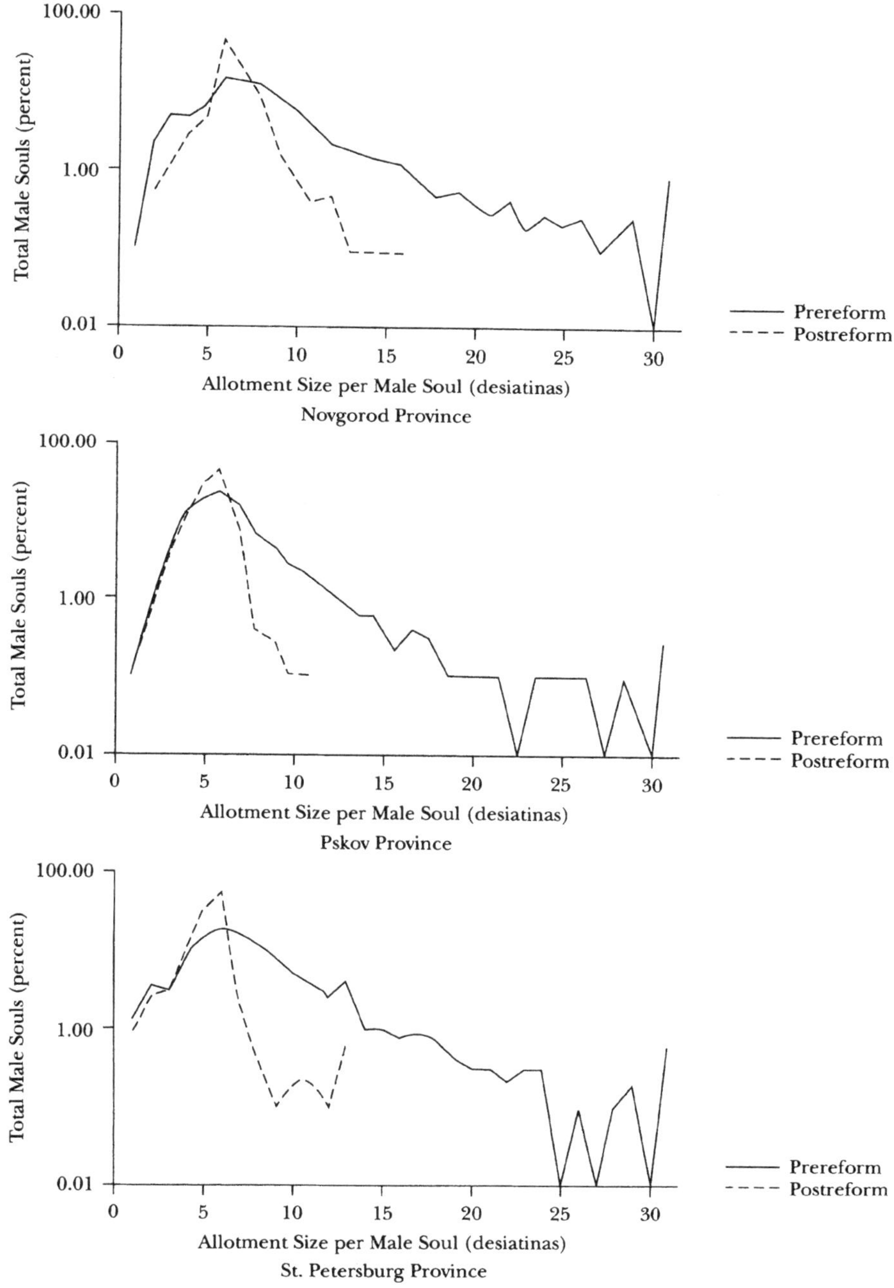

Figure 1. Distribution of Peasant Land Allotments per Male Soul (logarithmic scale).

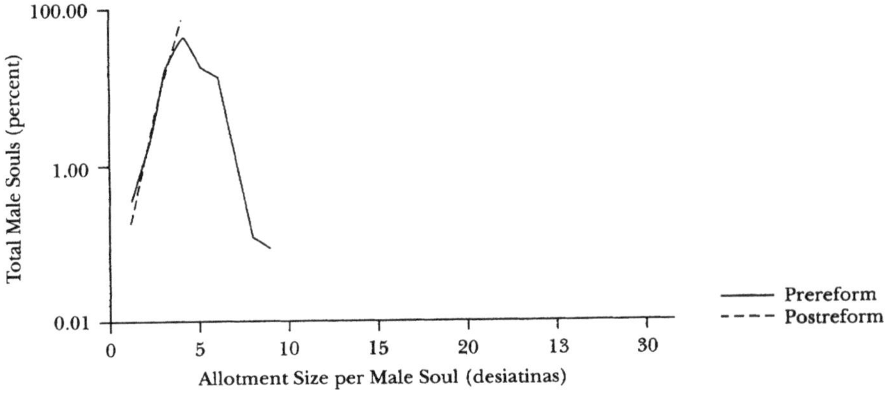

Figure 2. Distribution of Peasant Land Allotments per Male Soul for Borisoglebskii uezd (logarithmic scale).

Table 10
Distribution of Peasant Land Allotments
Borisoglebsk District, Tambov Province

Allotment Size (desiatinas)	Prereform		Postreform	
	Male Souls	Percent Total	Male Souls	Percent Total
<1	53	0.4	23	0.2
1-2	238	1.6	257	1.7
2-3	2,625	17.5	2,559	16.5
3-4	6,987	46.5	12,545	81.5
4-5	2,822	18.8	0	0.0
5-6	2,084	13.9	0	0.0
6-7	168	1.1	0	0.0
7-8	24	0.2	0	0.0
8+	13	0.1	0	0.0
Total	15,015	100	15,389	100.0

Source: Rossiiskii gosudarstvennyi istoricheskii arkhiv, St Petersburg (RGIA), f. 577 (Ministerstvo finansov, Glavnoe vykupnoe uchrezhdenie), op. 40 (Tambovskaia guberniia), d. 1-102.

and, in fact, would be the same for all serfs governed by the first two regional emancipation statutes, which affected 73 percent of all serfs in the empire, that is, primarily those not covered by the inventories in the western provinces. As a result of peasant land reform, the most common prereform allotment size (the mode) became even more common. Essentially, the right-hand tail in the distribution was pushed left, greatly increasing the frequency of the modal size. In Novgorod, Pskov, and St. Petersburg provinces both before and after reform, the modal allotment fell between 5.0 and 6.0 desiatinas (13.5-16.2 acres) of land. In Novgorod, prior to reform, 17.1 percent of all serfs held the modal allotment, after reform 57.0 percent did. In Pskov, prior to 1861, 24.9 percent of all serfs held between 5.0 and 6.0 desiatinas, after reform 47.1 percent held the modal allotment. The figures for St. Petersburg province are 16.7 and 49.8 percent, respectively. In Borisoglebsk district, prior to reform, 46.3 percent of the serfs held the modal allotment (3.0-4.0 desiatinas); just as the Editing Commission thought, allotment sizes here varied substantially less than those in the non-black earth provinces, as evidenced by Kashchenko's data. After reform, 81.5 percent of all allotments in Borisoglebsk district conformed to the mode.

The statistical problems inherent in describing the central tendencies of change in peasant allotments across emancipation and land reform are clearly illustrated by Tables 11-13. In all twenty-seven districts of Novgorod, Pskov, and St. Petersburg provinces, average (mean) allotment sizes—the measure always cited by critics and historians of Russian land reform and the least helpful—declined, in most cases quite considerably. But the median allotment size remained unchanged in twelve districts. In the fourteen districts where the postreform median allotment was smaller, it declined by substantially less than the mean. Of even greater import, the modal allotment was unchanged in twenty-three districts, declined in only three, and increased in one. The same pattern is in evidence for Borisoglebsk district in Tambov (see Table 14). Here, emancipation resulted in scarcely any change in median allotment size regardless of the form of dues peasants had paid as serfs. But the mean for all estates dropped significantly, by 19.1 percent, with the greatest decline, as is to be expected, experienced by serfs with pure quitrent obligations, that is, peasants living on estates that did not maintain a demesne or engage in activities supported by corvee labor.

The compression in the distribution of peasant allotments across reform and the considerable increase in the frequency of the modal allotment can be seen more clearly by presenting the same data shown in Figures 1 and 2 on normal linear rather than logarithmic scales (see Figures 3 and 4). Put in statistical terms, Kashchenko found a significant

Table 11
Change in Prereform to Postreform Allotment Size per Male Soul, Novgorod Province (in percent)

District	Mean	Median	Mode
Novgorodskii	-24.2	-15.4	unchanged
Starorusski	-28.1	-15.4	unchanged
Krestetskii	-37.2	-26.7	unchanged
Dem'ianskii	-22.8	unchanged	unchanged
Valdaiskii	-36.8	-26.7	-26.7
Borovichskii	-31.6	-15.4	unchanged
Tikhvinskii	-8.3	unchanged	unchanged
Ustiuzhenskii	-37.3	-13.3	unchanged
Cherepovetskii	-5.4	+22.0	+120.0
Belozerskii	-28.8	unchanged	unchanged
Kirillovskii	-34.1	-21.0	-21.0
Novgorod Province	-26.9	-15.4	unchanged

Source: A. Ia. Degtiarev, S. G. Kashchenko, and D. I. Raskin, *Novgorodskaia derevnia v reforme 1861 goda: Opyt izucheniia s ispol'zovaniem EVM* (Leningrad, 1989).

Table 12
Change in Prereform to Postreform Allotment Size per Male Soul, St. Petersburg Province (in percent)

District	Mean	Median	Mode
Peterburgskii	-17.1	unchanged	unchanged
Shlissel'burgskii	-22.6	-15.4	-15.4
Tsarskosel'skii	-32.5	-18.2	unchanged
Petergofskii	-35.3	-18.2	unchanged
Novoladozhskii	-39.3	-15.4	unchanged
Iamburskii	-28.8	-18.2	unchanged
Gdovskii	-36.7	-26.7	unchanged
Luzhskii	-36.1	-26.7	unchanged
St. Petersburg Province	-34.1	-15.4	unchanged

Source: S. G. Kashchenko, *Reforma 19 fevralia 1861 goda v Sankt-Peterburgskoi gubernii* (Leningrad, 1990).

Table 13
Change in Prereform to Postreform Allotment Size per Male Soul, Pskov Province
(in percent)

District	Mean	Median	Mode
Pskovskii	-20.5	unchanged	unchanged
Ostrovskii	-20.2	unchanged	unchanged
Porkhovskii	-24.1	unchanged	unchanged
Novorzhevskii	-16.1	unchanged	unchanged
Opochetskii	-13.9	unchanged	unchanged
Velikolukskii	-18.0	unchanged	unchanged
Kholmskii	-23.4	unchanged	unchanged
Toropetskii	-35.1	unchanged	unchanged
Pskov Province	-22.6	unchanged	unchanged

Source: S. G. Kashchenko, *Otmena krepostnogo prava v Pskovskoi gubernii: Opyt komp'iuternogo analiza uslovii realizatsii krest'ianskoi reform 19 fevralia 1861 g.* (St. Petersburg, 1996).

decrease in the coefficients of variation across emancipation in all the districts of Novgorod, Pskov, and St. Petersburg provinces, often by a factor of three or four.[65] In other words, emancipation and land reform resulted in a greatly increased clustering in allotments around what had been the most common prereform allotment size. In a sense, this should be obvious, for it is the logical consequence of any policy imposing minima and maxima on a previously broader distribution. But historians have failed to appreciate that this very considerable clustering occurred around the prereform mode. And, as a result of relying solely on average changes in allotment size and not understanding the distribution of prereform allotments, which peasants lost land has not been fully appreciated.

With emancipation, from a rural reality dictated by the vagaries of servile practices on thousands of individual estates in Russia, the autocracy imposed a massive leveling. Those serfs whose allotments exceeded the maximum for their locality had them reduced to the maximum, and

[65] Degtiarev, Kashchenko, and Raskin, *Novgorodskaia derevnia*, 79-80, 86-87, 92-93, 98-99, 102-3, 106-7, 113, 121, and 125; Kashchenko, *Otmena krepostnogo prava*, 37, 44, 56, 60, 64, 69-70, and 74; and Kashchenko, *Reforma 19 fevralia 1861 goda*, 43-44, 68-70, 78-80, 90-92, 97-98, 102, 107-8, 116 and 123-25.

Table 14
Change in Prereform to Postreform Allotment Size by Estate
Borisoglebsk district, Tambov Province

	All Peasants		Quitrent Peasants		Corvée Peasants		Mixed Dues		Unknown	
	Prereform	Postreform	Prereform	Postreform	Prereform	Postreform	Prereform	Postreform	Prereform	Postreform
Number of Soul Allotments	15,015	15,389	1,984	2,050	7,841	8,140	2,991	2,995	2,199	2,024
Mean (desiatinas)	3.736	3.021	4.302	2.845	3.599	3.051	3.380	3.251	3.811	3.144
Median (desiatinas)	3.256	3.250	3.157	3.180	3.477	3.340	3.476	3.500	3.168	3.160
Coefficient of Variation	0.871	0.198	1.301	0.260	0.688	0.185	0.174	0.153	0.326	0.117

Source: Rossiiskii gosudarstvennyi istoricheskii arkhiv, St. Petersburg (RGIA), f. 577 (Ministerstvo finansov, Glavnoe vykupnoe uchrezhdenie), op. 40 (Tambovskaia guberniia), d. 1-102.

these were, with limited exceptions, the only peasants who suffered. But it needs to be emphasized that they were left with an amount of land many of their neighbors had held prior to reform, and that many more would hold after reform. To quote Kashchenko, in Novgorod: "After reform, an equalization of allotments for all categories of peasants [according to their form of servile dues] took place close to the maximum size for the district, the result of which peasants better provided with land before reform were cut the most." And this "leveling" (*nivelirovka*) of holdings among serfs living on different estates had a greater impact on quitrent serfs, as their prereform allotments were more dispersed around the mean.[66] Similarly, in St. Petersburg province, emancipation resulted in a "leveling of allotments that varied significantly from village to village prior to reform."[67] In all three provinces, including Pskov, "a leveling [*vyravnivanie*] of allotments around the maximum for the district occurred and, as a consequence, there was a reduction in the range of fluctuations (very large and tiny allotments disappeared)."[68]

The highly concentrated effect of emancipation on peasant allotment sizes can be clearly illustrated using data I have collected from the land charters and redemption agreements for Borisoglebsk district in Tambov. There, 6,947 desiatinas of land were taken away from 7,501 peasants. But 60 percent of this reduction (4,181 desiatinas) affected only 9 percent of all estates and only 16.5 percent of all serfs (2,544 peasants). In the three northern provinces studied by Kashchenko, this postreform concentration would be even higher as the prereform variance was considerably greater. In fact, in all of Russia covered by the first two regional statutes, regardless of the locality or local terms of servitude, the vast majority of serfs upon being freed either kept their existing allotment or had their allotment reduced to the prereform modal (most common) size. Surely, this was neither an unreasonable state policy nor an undesirable social and economic outcome. And it was well in line with emancipation settlements throughout Europe over the previous seventy-five years.[69]

---

66 Degtiarev, Kashchenko, and Raskin, *Novgorodskaia derevnia*, 135-39; see also 64-65.

67 Kashchenko, *Reforma 19 fevralia 1861 goda*, 135-36, 145.

68 Kashchenko, *Otmena krepostnogo prava*, 113.

69 Blum, *End of the Old Order*, 383-400.

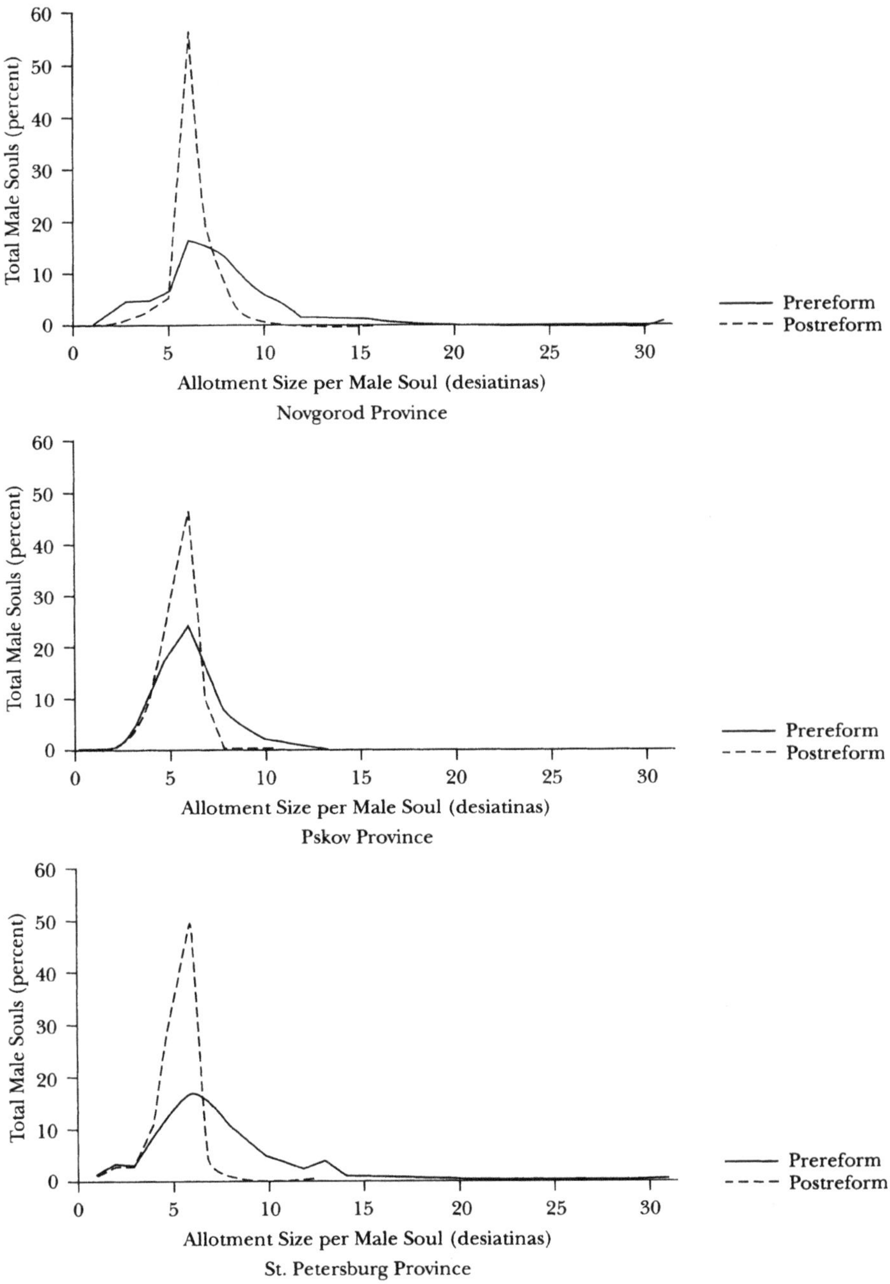

Figure 3. Distribution of Peasant Land Allotments per Male Soul (normal linear scale).

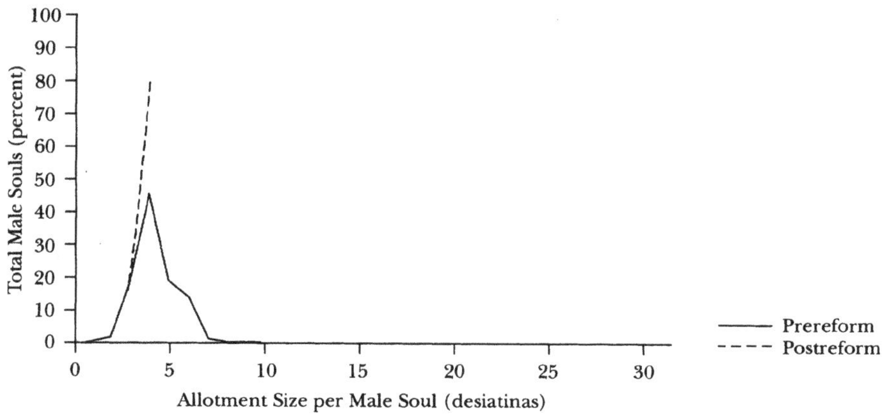

Figure 4. Distribution of Peasant Land Allotments per Male Soul for Borisoglebskii uezd (normal linear scale)

It should now be apparent that the land reform legislation of 1861 was tilted more favorably toward the serfs than has been appreciated. Emancipation dispossessed serf-owners of their labor supply and stripped them of assets whose value, in very large part, had been expended decades before through consumption. State power had not been mobilized in the interest of the lords to guarantee their financial well-being. Unlike slaves in the American South, serfs in Russia got a whole lot more than freedom. Potentially, we have the beginnings of a different story. In paying a fair, if not below, market price for a viable subsistence plot, emancipated peasants were well positioned to resist external attempts to restructure their terms of production, as Chaianov demonstrates.[70] The landed nobility may not have possessed the economic hegemony to ensure the survival of the manor or estate even in a much attenuated form, as is often thought. The resources provided to most serfs under the terms of land reform were more likely to have resulted in a considerable strengthening of a self-sufficient peasant economy. As a consequence, emancipation is unlikely to have fostered the creation of a capitalist wage-labor economy, a dependent labor force, or new forms of manorialism, but it did allow the serfs to travel even further down the road of autonomous, peasant family farmer.

[70] Steven L. Hoch, "The Serf Economy and the Social Order in Russia," in *Serfdom and Slavery: Studies in Legal Bondage*, ed. M. L. Bush (Longman, 1996). See Thorner, Kerblay, and Smith, eds., *A. V. Chayanov on the Theory of Peasant Economy*, 16-28, 224-41.

2

On Good Numbers and Bad: Malthus, Population Trends, and Peasant Standard of Living in Late Imperial Russia

Historians have not been at their finest in attempting to measure standard of living, and late Imperial rural Russia is no exception. Given the absence of reliable measures for personal or household income or even of real wage trends—the most common proxy for the standard of living—scholars have been forced to employ a variety of other surrogates, often with unfortunate results. For Russia, recourse has been made to peasant tax arrears, mass consumption of "luxury" or non-food items, and rye-wages. Shifts in the size of land allotments, numbers of livestock, and patterns of land tenure often have been the focus of study; others have emphasized trends in net national product, grain retained in the village, or grain yields generally. Diet has been assessed both quantitatively, in terms of caloric intake or protein derived from meat products, and qualitatively, underscoring harvest variability. Still other studies have looked at population trends, at times addressing the malthusian dilemma and suggesting that Russia was overpopulated. And frustration has recently led one historian to suggest we give up.[1]

The intent of this article is to critique much that has been written on the peasant standard of living debate and to place population theory and demographic issues at the center of discussion. The first part of the essay will evaluate various surrogate measures that have been used to assess rural living standards; it finds most of them wanting. Particular attention will be paid to land redemption payments, shifting patterns of consumption, rural wage-labor trends, and cereal production and retention. My wider purpose, however, and the focus of the second part

This article was originally published in *Slavic Review* 53, no. 1 (Spring 1994): 41-75.

1 H. S. Vasudevan, "Peasant Land and Peasant Society in Late Imperial Russia," *The Historical Journal* 31, no. 1 (1988): 208-9.

of this article, is to call into question the implicit malthusian paradigm linking rapid population growth to economic and social distress that underscores much of our understanding of the late Imperial period. My findings will place the secular decline in mortality in Russia as far back as the immediate post-emancipation period, and raise the heretical possibility that the reforms of the 1860s might have actually bettered the peasants' lot. The mechanism for this mortality decline has yet to be determined, but there is strong evidence suggesting that an improved level of rural nutrition and a resultant decrease in deaths from specific infectious diseases were more significant factors in Russia than elsewhere in Europe.

First, much that has been said about peasant tax arrears—certainly the most widely cited surrogate measure of rural living standards for Russia—is in need of correction. The figures most often used are total accumulated arrears (usually dating back to the early 1860s), expressed as a percentage of the current year tax assessment. It is frequently noted that by the turn of the century cumulative tax arrears (even after deducting those officially forgiven) exceeded total annual tax revenues. "In other words, the total accumulation of arrears (118,695,000 rubles) in payments due to the State had finally come to exceed by a substantial margin the average amount of current assessments (99,341,000 per year in the period 1896-1900) which the State was attempting to collect." Initially, quoting of tax figures in this manner was politically motivated by those favoring a reduction in rural taxes: the intent was to show that tax arrears amounted to a considerable sum, and citing them in relation to annual tax revenues gave a sense of proportion. Despite their tendentious purpose, the figures on arrears have entered historical literature in this form. To Robinson, arrears presented "perhaps the best of all indices of the peasants' economic situation" and were indicative of "widespread and increasing distress" in rural Russia, a view shared by many.[2]

[2] Geroid T. Robinson, *Rural Russia under the Old Regime* (London, 1932), 96 and 111; N. Brzheskii, *Nedoimochnost' i krugovaia poruka sel'skikh obshchestv* (St. Petersburg, 1897), 393-413; P. P. Migulin, *Vykupnye platezhi: K voprosu o ikh ponizhenii* (Kharkov, 1904), 46; P. I. Liashchenko, *History of the National Economy of Russia to the 1917 Revolution*, trans. L. M. Herman (New York, 1949), 447; Alexander Gerschenkron, "Agrarian Policies and Industrialization, Russia 1861-1917," *The Cambridge Economic History of Europe* (London, 1965) 6:768-70; N. M. Druzhinin, *Russkaia derevnia na perelome,*

Contemporaries and subsequent historians have focused primarily on land redemption receipts attendant to the 1861 emancipation settlement because these constitute one of the longest series of published revenue data and cover a substantial portion of the empire. These figures, though, as the compilers themselves admitted, leave much to be desired. But information on village and zemstvo tax compliance is either unavailable or unreliable; data for other direct state taxes, such as the soul tax, though accessible, are also troublesome. In any case, they were a much smaller proportion of total peasant assessments than redemption dues. Virtually all historians hold that ex-serfs did not make their land redemption payments properly. Simms states: "Peasant land redemption arrears grew not because of an inability to pay, but because of an unwillingness to pay."[3] In contrast, echoing Robinson, Gerschenkron and numerous others, Sanders concludes: "The starkest indicator of peasant distress was the mounting arrears in redemption payments.... The peasants' arrears in redemption payments were grounded in economic reality."[4] And Hamburg is squarely in between: peasants "either could not or would not make their redemption payments."[5] In fact, it is

1861-1880 gg. (Moscow, 1978), 76-77; Dorothy Atkinson, *The End of the Russian Land Commune, 1905-1930* (Stanford, 1983), 33; Hans Rogger, *Russia in the Age of Modernization and Revolution, 1881-1917* (New York, 1983), 77; Boris Mironov, "The Peasant Commune after the Reforms of the 1860s," *Slavic Review* 44, no. 3 (Fall 1985): 453; Peter Gatrell, *The Tsarist Economy, 1850-1917* (London, 1986), 197. Neither Lazar Volin (*A Century of Russian Agriculture from Alexander II to Khrushchev* [Cambridge, 1970], 52-56) nor Stephen G. Wheatcroft ("Crises and the Condition of the Peasantry in Late Imperial Russia" in *Peasant Economy, Culture, and Politics of European Russia, 1800-1921*, ed. Esther Kingston-Mann and Timothy Mixter [Princeton, 1991], 166) cite arrears figures in this manner. They see them, however, as indicative of the heavy fiscal burden on Russian peasants and evidence of their depressed standard of living, if not desperation.

3 James Y. Simms, Jr., "The Crisis in Russian Agriculture at the End of the Nineteenth Century: A Different View," *Slavic Review* 36, no. 3 (September 1977): 385. See also Robert Bideleux, *Communism and Development* (London, 1985), 16.

4 John Thomas Sanders, " 'Once More into the Breach, Dear Friends': A Closer Look at Indirect Tax Receipts and the Condition of the Russian Peasantry, 1881-1899," *Slavic Review* 43, no. 4 (Winter 1984): 664-65.

5 Gary M. Hamburg, "The Crisis in Russian Agriculture: A Comment," *Slavic Review* 37, no. 3 (September 1978): 485.

likely all are wrong. At least, I can say with surety that the numbers that are available support none of these views.

Hoping to discount tax arrears as a measure of peasant distress and challenging the widely held view, Simms has asserted that:

> An examination of available evidence indicates that the "army of tax collectors" [a reference to Robinson] did not extract from the peasantry all the available money for the payment of taxes, which in turn makes possible a reinterpretation of the significance of increasing tax arrears.... There was, for example, a marked increase in redemption payments in 1887, the first full year of Vyshnegradskii's tenure, as compared to 1886. A similar significant increase took place in the receipts of indirect taxes. It has been assumed that the increase in receipts and the promptness of payment were the result of ruthless and more efficient methods of tax collection. But, on the contrary, the fact of excellent harvests in these years and the obvious relationship between good harvests and the ability to pay renders the above assumption somewhat otiose.[6]

To buttress his argument, Simms quotes figures from the late Soviet historian P. A. Khromov which seemingly reflect sharp fluctuations in annual redemption receipts: for example, 48.8 million rubles in 1886 and 89.0 million rubles in 1887.[7] To Simms, "the evidence shows ... that income was retained in the village—held back from the tax collector—and spent to purchase consumer goods."[8] In other words, "the peasantry acknowledged the demands of the tax collector only up to a point," one which varied with harvest size.[9]

While it remains to be demonstrated whether such a moral economy existed in late Imperial Russia, as is evidenced elsewhere,[10] Simms is quite simply wrong. In the mid-1880s, former serfs were redeeming approximately 850 million rubles of serf-owner (*pomeshchik*) land. Paying

---

6 Simms, "Crisis in Russian Agriculture," 381.

7 Ibid., 382, note 27; and P. A. Khromov, *Ekonomicheskoe razvitie Rossii v XIX-XX vekakh* (Moscow-Leningrad, 1950), 498-99.

8 Simms, "The Crisis in Russian Agriculture," 383.

9 Ibid., 385. Wheatcroft also holds that "the many defaults on direct tax payment offered a greater degree of compensation than is often realized ("Crises and the Condition," 166).

10 J. C. Scott, *The Moral Economy of the Peasant: Rebellion and Subsistence in Southeast Asia* (New Haven, 1976).

six percent interest on such loans minus officially legislated payment reductions resulted in total annual payments owed the state in 1887 of approximately 40.9 million rubles. The seemingly huge jump in redemption receipts in 1887 cited by Simms—to 89.0 million rubles—was nothing more than an accounting change: state peasants were for the first time included in the redemption operation. A law promulgated 12 June 1886 which took effect on January 1, 1887 converted former state peasant quitrents into redemption payments; state peasants were to redeem their lands over the next 44 years.[11]

Simply put, the huge increase between 1886 and 1887 is not attributable to harvest fluctuations. Neither can it be explained by a peasant unwillingness nor inability to pay. Equally, one should not necessarily conclude, as Simms later does, that there existed a substantial reserve of peasant purchasing power with which various items subject to indirect state taxes could be acquired (a point to which I shall return).[12] It appears that redemption receipts in the late 1880s do indeed testify to the efficacy of finance minister I. A. Vyshnegradskii's short-lived policy to improve arrears collection: during the three-year period 1887-1889, ex-serfs paid an average of 104.5 percent of their annual assessment, in the process paying off a small amount of their redemption arrears. During the previous three years (1884-1886) under N. Kh. Bunge, the figure was 95.1 percent (see Table 1). These figures, reflecting a ten-percent increase in receipts, seem more in line with what one might expect from a concerted government campaign to collect current and delinquent redemption payments than a single-year increase of 117 percent, as suggested by Simms.

Numerous attempts were undertaken to balance the confused books of the redemption operation—by the government in the early 1880s, again in 1893 and annually thereafter, and one by the historian Kovan'ko

---

11 *Otchet gosudarstvennago banka po vykupnoi operatsii s otkrytiia vykupa po 1 ianvaria 1892 goda* (St. Petersburg, 1893), 23; P. Kovan'ko, *Reforma 19 fevralia 1861 g. i ee posledstviia s finansovoi tochki zreniia (Vykupnaia operatsiia 1861g.-1907g.)* (Kiev, 1914), appendices no. 4 and 5, 54 and 59-60; and *Polnoe sobranie zakonov Rossiiskoi Imperii, Sobranie tretie* (St. Petersburg, 1885-1917), VI: 3,807 (June 12 1886) (hereafter PSZ).

12 Simms, "The Crisis in Russian Agriculture," 382-83. Wheatcroft ("Crises and the Condition," 157) makes the same error as Simms in interpreting the huge increase in redemption receipts.

in 1914.[13] They are in general accord: in spite of all that has been alleged about redemption payments, it appears that ex-serfs paid 94.9 percent of their total redemption assessments, 1.540 of the 1.623 billion rubles due.[14] During the period 1886-1899, focus of much of the debate on the crisis in Russian agriculture and peasant standard of living, former serfs paid 95.9 percent of the total redemption sum due the state, 552.0 million of the 575.4 million rubles owed.[15]

Redemption arrears mounted, of course. Agriculture, even today, involves considerable risk and over a period of 45 years (1862-1906) no region of the empire escaped crop failure. Unless one is to assume total tax compliance, figures on cumulative arrears would logically grow. But the redemption law of 1861 provided for a considerable reserve fund to cover all administrative costs and arrears. In fact, only 92 percent of the total redemption assessment was required to pay the interest and principal on peasant debt.[16] The State Bank calculated the size of the reserve fund at 5.2 million rubles on January 1, 1885, after deducting all administrative costs, all arrears forgiven and all current arrears. For the same year, Kovan'ko figured the size of the redemption capital reserve fund at 8.8 million rubles. At the time of the abolition of the redemption

13 *Otchet gosudarstvennago banka*; [no author] "Obshchii balans vykupnoi operatsii," *Vestnik finansov, promyshlennosti i torgovli*, 23 (1903); Kovan'ko, *Reforma*. See also I. Vil'son, "Vykupnye za zemli platezhi krest'ian-sobstvennikov byvshikh pomeshchich'ikh, 1862-1876," *Zapiski Imperatorskago Russkago Geograficheskago Obshchestva po otdeleniiu statistiki* (St. Petersburg, 1878), 5:259-318 and 326-73. Beginning in 1893, the government issued annual financial reports on the redemption operation.

14 *Otchet gosudarstvennago banka*, 23; "Obshchii balans," appendix; and Kovan'ko, *Reforma*, appendix 4, table 4 and appendix 5, table 1, 54-65.

15 Kovan'ko, *Reforma*, appendix 4, table 4 and appendix 5, table 1, 54-65. The *Otchet gosudarstvennago banka*, which covers 1862-1891, shows that ex-serfs paid 988.9 million rubles in redemption payments over this period, 96% of the total due. In particular, between 1886-1891, peasants paid 97% of the total due.

The figures for the years after 1885 are considered more reliable than those of the earlier period. With the inclusion of the redemption operation in the general state budget that year, accounting procedures improved markedly (*Otchet gosudarstvennago banka*, 3; and Kovan'ko, *Reforma*, 261-85).

16 Steven L. Hoch, "The Banking Crisis, Peasant Reform, and Economic Development in Russia, 1857-1861," *The American Historical Review* 96, no. 3 (1991): 811.

Table 1
Ex-Serf Redemption Payments and Arrears (1862-1906)

Year	Annual redemption assessment (rubles in thousands)	Total peasant payments (rubles in thousands)	Percent paid of assessment (%)	Yearly arrears	Arrears forgiven (rubles in thousands)	Cumulative arrears
1862	159.2	65.1	40.9	94.1	—	94.1
1863	2,611.2	1,415.2	54.2	1,196.0	—	1,290.2
1864	7,958.0	5,543.1	69.7	2,414.9	—	3,705.0
1865	14,974.2	12,535.1	83.7	2,439.1	—	6,144.0
1866	21,130.2	19,414.3	91.9	1,715.9	—	7,859.9
1867	27,581.1	27,162.3	98.5	418.8	—	8,278.8
1868	34,433.3	32,421.8	94.2	2,011.5	—	10,290.3
1869	35,927.9	35,316.6	98.3	611.3	—	10,901.7
1870	33,648.2	33,055.5	98.2	592.7	—	11,494.3
1871	36,474.6	35,156.3	96.4	1,318.3	—	12,812.6
1872	37,841.2	36,869.9	97.4	971.3	1.0	13,782.7
1873	39,154.6	39,712.1	101.4	(557.5)	1.0	13,224.3
1874	39,790.0	39,610.7	99.5	179.3	1.0	13,402.5
1875	40,520.9	39,957.3	98.6	563.6	1.0	13,964.6
1876	41,015.5	38,622.9	94.2	2,392.6	5.3	16,351.8
1877	41,681.1	40,200.3	96.4	1,480.8	9.6	17,822.9
1878	42,907.3	43,741.5	101.9	(834.2)	77.5	16,911.3
1879	43,306.2	43,173.5	99.7	132.7	151.5	16,892.4
1880	43,951.0	40,301.3	91.7	3,649.7	46.6	20,495.5
1881	44,721.1	41,122.6	92.0	3,598.5	644.9	23,449.1
1882	42,664.3	39,508.3	92.6	3,156.0	372.9	26,233.2
1883	43,597.9	41,216.9	94.5	2,381.0	13,769.1	14,844.1
1884	36,393.0	37,073.0	101.9	(680.0)	2,273.8	11,890.3
1885	40,890.1	36,549.2	89.4	4,340.9	28.6	16,202.6

1886	40,917.9	38,473.9	94.0	2,444.0	26.6	18,619.9
1887	40,860.9	43,341.5	106.1	(2,480.6)	32.5	16,106.9
1888	40,924.8	44,038.5	107.6	(3,113.7)	49.1	12,944.1
1889	41,424.8	41,316.5	99.7	108.3	33.1	13,019.3
1890	41,418.0	39,860.7	96.2	1,557.3	35.1	14,541.5
1891	41,279.2	33,530.9	81.2	7,748.3	20.9	22,268.8
1892	41,185.1	34,416.9	83.6	6,768.2	21.1	29,015.9
1893	41,290.1	41,479.2	100.5	(189.1)	68.3	28,758.5
1894	41,080.5	39,469.3	96.1	1,611.2	31.5	30,338.3
1895	40,975.9	41,642.3	101.6	(666.4)	—	29,671.9
1896	41,069.3	40,262.2	98.0	807.1	—	30,479.1
1897	41,052.7	37,022.6	90.2	4,030.1	—	34,509.2
1898	41,060.3	37,360.8	91.0	3,699.5	—	38,208.7
1899	40,836.7	39,803.5	97.5	1,033.2	—	39,241.9
1900	40,237.5	39,937.1	99.3	300.4	—	39,542.4
1901	38,683.9	38,236.4	98.8	447.5	—	39,989.8
1902	39,180.6	38,068.2	97.2	1,112.4	—	40,710.0
1903	38,923.8	37,384.0	96.0	1,539.8	—	42,010.4
1904	38,768.5	34,252.0	88.4	4,516.5	16,280.2	30,086.5
1905	38,648.1	23,938.4	61.9	14,709.7	23,303.4	21,354.9
1906	19,991.5	16,745.1	83.8	3,246.4	1,173.6	22,674.7
Total	1,623,142.2	1,540,326.8	94.9	82,817.4	58,459.7	

Note: Data in parenthesis are for years when the peasants paid in excess of their annual assessment, either paying off prior arrears or making advance payments. An error of 0.4 million rubles appears in 1902. By 1906, the error has grown to 0.8 million rubles. In addition, the total of yearly arrears does not equal the combined total of forgiven and cumulative arrears due to the above noted error and to legislation that rescheduled rather than forgave some arrears beginning in 1899. The net result of both is a discrepancy of only 1.7 million rubles. *Sources: Otchet Gosudarstvennago banka po vykupnoi operatsii s otkrytiia vykupapo 1 lanvaria 1892 goda* (St. Petersburg, 1893), 23; [no author] "Obshchii balans vykupnoi operatsii," *Vestnik Finansov, Promyshlennosti i Torgovli* (8 June 1903): 23, appendix; and P. Kovan'ko, *Reforma 19 fevralia 1861 goda i ee posledstviia s finansovoi tochki zreniia (Vykupnaia operatsiia 1861 g.-1907g.)* (Kiev, 1914), appendix no. 4, table 4 and appendix 5, table 1.

operation in 1906, the reserve fund stood at 25.5 million rubles.[17] To quote Kovan'ko:

> During the entire course of the redemption operation, arrears were a normal occurrence.... However, the existence of large arrears did not undermine the redemption operation as a whole. Annually, the entire sum of peasant payments more than covered the payment on government obligations.... The peasants never had the ability to pay the full sum into the reserve fund; but their arrears (as a whole, and not in individual cases) were arrears not in the [redemption] operation, but in its reserve capital.[18]

Other factors also have to be taken into consideration when assessing redemption arrears. They continued to increase not merely because the government kept adding them up but also because more temporarily obligated peasants were entering redemption agreements. And, although mandatory redemption was ordered on December 28, 1881, many landowners did not proceed expeditiously; between 1885 and 1891, 48.3 million rubles in new redemption agreements were authorized. If these peasants, who mostly lived on smaller estates, paid their redemption obligations at the same rate as other ex-serfs, then their inclusion in the redemption operation would by itself account for a six percent increase in the rate of arrears accumulation.[19] If the peasants, entering these agreements, had higher default rates either because they were poorer or unused to redemption payments, then their weight in the increase in arrears would be even greater.

It should also be emphasized that the figures on peasant redemption payments cannot be verified independently nor readily corrected. But the numbers cited by contemporaries and subsequent historians (with the exception of Simms's accounting error) are essentially in accord and have not been a source of dispute. While total accumulated arrears were indeed more than annual tax receipts, this is a strange, if not polemical, measure of tax compliance and economic distress. It makes far more sense to compare total payments due with what ex-serfs actually paid. The best evidence we have available, in fact the only evidence, such as it

17 *Otchet gosudarstvennago banka*, 60-2; Kovan'ko, *Reforma*, 467.
18 Kovan'ko, *Reforma*, 480-1.
19 *Otchet gosudarstvennago banka*, 6-7.

is, suggests that ex-serfs defaulted on only five percent of their obligations (about what the government anticipated when it drafted the original legislation). While over the years arrears accumulated, we should not lose sight of what it seems the peasants did pay: about nineteen times more. Moreover, one needs to take into consideration the expansion of the redemption operation itself. To restate the point, redemption payments, however burdensome, and their arrears tell us only that the peasants paid their obligations; they provide no information to assess peasant standard of living. We may not want to believe the figures; but they do not tell the story so many have made them tell.

The rest of Simms's argument—that increased indirect tax receipts in the last decades of the nineteenth century are necessarily evidence of increased overall peasant consumption—can be refuted on the basis of neo-classical economic theory, which Simms himself utilizes. According to Simms:

> Given the fact that the consumption of cotton, tea, sugar, matches, kerosene, tobacco and so forth was growing absolutely, it is hardly likely that the overall standard of living of the peasant was dropping.... Assuming that the peasant acted rationally in making his economic decisions, would the peasant reduce his consumption of an absolute necessity—food—relative to consumption of cotton or matches?

Elsewhere, he states that "one would hardly want to argue that the peasantry taken as a whole was consuming more matches and less grain!"[20] Why not? It actually depended on how much peasants valued their marginal loaf of bread relative to their first box of matches. The fundamental flaw in Simms's argument is his inability to appreciate what a market means. A developing market could bring about substantial changes in consumption patterns, whether peasants were experiencing an improved, stable, or lower standard of living, as is evidenced by the recent history of the Third World. Only if Russian peasants were at a rigid or absolute subsistence level (definable as a point below which no life is possible, where even the slightest change in consumption patterns would result in an immediate increase in mortality) would market relations not penetrate the economy and provide choice. Yet, Simms admits

[20] Simms, "Crisis in Russian Agriculture," 391 and 397.

that peasants were not being forced to part with all their produce beyond what was needed to subsist in the most literal sense. He is correct that food was an "absolute necessity," but he forgets that the demand for food was not absolutely inelastic.[21]

Rejecting tax, livestock, and land price data, Stephen Wheatcroft relies heavily on two other measures in a recent attempt to assess the crisis in Russian peasant living standards.[22] To Wheatcroft, it is important to examine "relative price levels and, in particular, the real rural wage levels of different groups of producers measured in terms of their command over the purchasing power of basic foodstuffs (i.e., their rye equivalent)."[23] In other words, he deflates nominal, money wages into rye wages, using prevailing rye prices, and concludes that "between 1882 and 1914 the rise in [nominal, money] wages is largely but not completely offset by the rise in prices of rye."[24] And here the problems begin.

How good a proxy is this for peasant standard of living? Wheatcroft himself is aware of one potential objection—that few peasants engaged in rural day labor and the short-term nature of their employment may not be indicative of annual wage levels and thus the real value of rural labor. This concern he then summarily dismisses. But to the noted economic historian Jan de Vries, "for most preindustrial economies, the

---

21 Ibid., 380 and 397. Boris Mironov ("The Peasant Commune," 460-1) makes a similar error, but with opposite results, when he tries to argue that a decrease in per capita consumption of vodka—"a necessity, not a luxury"—during the 1870s makes "graphically apparent" the "deteriorating condition of the peasantry." Another critique of Simms is that he significantly underestimates urban consumption of newly taxed items (Sanders, "Once More into the Breach," 661 and 663). Wheatcroft, in contrast ("Crises and the Condition," 161), finds this argument wanting. My own recalculation of Sanders's figures reveals that peasants accounted for 57% of the sugar, 67% of the vodka, and 37% of the tobacco indirect tax receipts, which hardly comports with his views, assuming his numbers are accurate.

22 Wheatcroft, "Crises and the Condition," 142, 151, and 153.

23 Ibid., 129.

24 Oddly, in the very next sentence Wheatcroft appears to contradict himself when he writes that "the rye equivalent of wages rose from 10 to 15 kilograms per day in 1882 to 15 to 20 kilograms per day in 1914" ("Crises and the Condition," 147). This would be a not insignificant 40% increase, even if marked by periods of unevenness and decline.

proposition that the real wages of day laborers adequately reflect the trends in personal income must be regarded as dubious." The exceptions de Vries had in mind were economies with high levels of urbanization and commercially oriented agriculture, which hardly seems to describe late Imperial Russia.[25] In addition, real day wage data give no indication of how much labor is available at the current wage. As Schofield has pointed out, they may be an especially poor indicator of female and child employment.[26]

To be more specific, how much of Wheatcroft's index of "rural real daily wages expressed in rye equivalents" would figure in a total basket of consumables comparable, for example, to the Phelps Brown and Hopkins index so central to the English standard of living debate?[27] In the latter index 80 percent of household expenditures was attributed to food: 20 percent to farinaceous foods, 25 percent to meat and fish, 12.5 percent to dairy products, and 22.5 percent to drink. Rural household budget studies for Russia in the late Imperial period often failed to include information on housing. Nevertheless, they suggest in very rough terms that, excluding shelter, between half and four-fifths of total expenditures (in money and in kind) were on food: approximately one third of total expenditures was on cereals, of which two thirds was rye.[28]

---

[25] Jan de Vries, "The Population and Economy of the Preindustrial Netherlands" in *Population and Economy: Population and History from the Traditional to the Modern World*, ed. Robert I. Rotberg and Theodore K. Rabb (Cambridge, 1986), 111. See also William W. Hagen, "Working for the Junker: The Standard of Living of Manorial Laborers in Brandenburg, 1584-1810," *Journal of Modern History* 58, no. 1 (March 1986):151.

[26] Roger S. Schofield, "Through a Glass Darkly: *The Population History of England* as an Experiment in History," *Population and Economy*, 26. Similar concerns regarding day wage rates can be found in Peter H. Lindert and Jeffrey G. Williamson, "English Workers' Living Standards During the Industrial Revolution: A New Look," *The Economic History Review*, second series 36, no. 3 (February 1983): 3.

[27] E. Henry Phelps Brown and Sheila V. Hopkins, "Seven Centuries of Building Wages," *Economica* 22, no. 87 (August 1955): 195-206; idem, "Seven Centuries of the Prices of Consumables, Compared with Builders' Wage-rates," ibid., 23, no. 92 (November 1956): 296-314.

[28] S. A. Klepikov (*Pitanie russkogo krest'ianstva* [Moscow, 1920], 3 and 12) notes on the basis of budget studies for European Russia that cereals accounted for approximately 63% of total adult caloric intake, two thirds of which was rye. And, with cereal calories among the cheapest source of nutrition, the rough estimations for expenditures presented here do not seem unreasonable.

If to be overly cautious we assume that 90 percent of Russian peasant household expenditures were on food (as much as 50 percent of which was on cereals, 75 percent being rye) then the Wheatcroft rye index makes up only one third of a basket of consumables. If more realistic, but still conservative figures are used (80 percent on food, of which 40 percent is on cereals, with two-thirds rye), then rye makes up only slightly more than one-fifth of likely consumables or the cost of living. Another difficulty with Wheatcroft's measure of standard of living is that it cannot be assumed that the proportion of rye in the Russian peasant diet remained constant over the period under consideration (1882-1916): there is considerable evidence that both potatoes and wheat became larger components.[29] Increased market development clearly led to changed consumption patterns, as Wheatcroft himself acknowledges.[30] In other words, over time, a rye index becomes an increasingly poor indicator.

The other component of the Wheatcroft rye-wage index is money wages. Here, it needs to be noted that nominal (money) wages are often sticky, even in the face of sharp price fluctuations, and thus real wage trends depend to a large degree on the price index chosen, in this case a rye price index.[31] Consequently, a rye-wage series tends to reflect the size of the rye harvest more than a standard of living. And how well did rye prices correlate, for example, with those of other cereals, let alone other consumables? According to recent price data assembled by B. N. Mironov, while cereal prices had a strong positive correlation (r = 0.8), they did not move completely in tandem. In other words, only 64 percent of the variation in the price of other cereals is explained by the influence of rye prices. This adds yet another dimension of uncertainty

[29] Smith and Christian, *Food and Drink*, 278-87; and Paul R. Gregory, "Grain Marketings, and Peasant Consumption, Russia, 1885-1913," *Explorations in Economic History* 17, no. 2 (1980): 151. See also Joan Thirsk, "The Horticultural Revolution: A Cautionary Note on Prices" in *Hunger and History: The Impact of Changing Food Production and Consumption Patterns on Society*, ed. Robert I. Rotberg and Theodore K. Rabb (Cambridge, 1983), 102-3.

[30] Wheatcroft, "Crises and the Condition," 158-61.

[31] Robert W. Fogel et al., "Secular Changes in American and British Stature and Nutrition," in *Hunger and History*, 248; and Peter H. Lindert, "English Population, Wages, and Prices: 1541-1913," in *Population and Economy*, 49-58.

Table 2
Correlations Among Cereal Prices in European Russia (1861-1914)

	Rye	Wheat	Oats	Buckwheat	Barley
Rye	1.000				
Wheat	0.792	1.000			
Oats	0.844	0.926	1.000		
Buckwheat	0.781	0.380	0.387	1.000	
Barley	0.824	0.988	0.958	0.437	1.000

Source: B. N. Mironov, *Khlebnye tseny v Rossii za dva stoletiia (XVIII-XIX vv.)* (Leningrad, 1985), table 5 and 46-50.

to a rye-price index (see Table 2). And there is every reason to expect a more complete basket of consumables would be less well correlated with rye prices. A final drawback with the wage data that Wheatcroft used was that he was forced to confine his analysis to day workers hiring themselves out without a horse and receiving no food or meals as partial wages, presumably because it would have been difficult, if not impossible, to disaggregate the components of draft labor and in-kind compensation. Thus, he analyzed only a portion, perhaps a narrow portion, of an already small, day-wage labor market, and possibly its poorest stratum.[32]

We can now more fully appreciate how inadequate a proxy Wheatcroft's index really is. In all likelihood, it encompasses no more than one fifth of what was included in the Phelps Brown and Hopkins index, which itself has been described as "crude."[33] Add to this all the limitations given above, and Wheatcroft's conclusion, even if true, is not

32 Teodor Shanin (*Russia as a 'Developing Society': The Roots of Otherness: Russia's Turn of the Century* [New Haven, 1985], 1:94-102) has recently estimated that the agricultural wage labor work force was between 2.3% and 6.0% of the total rural population. These figures include annual and seasonal as well as day- wage workers. See also Robert Bideleux, "Agricultural Advance Under the Russian Village Commune System," in *Land Commune and Peasant Community in Russia: Communal Forms in Imperial and Early Soviet Society*, ed. Roger Bartlett (London, 1990), 200; and Hagen, "Working for the Junker," 151.

33 Thirsk, "The Horticultural Revolution," 101.

very meaningful. In all, it remains uncertain if Wheatcroft has given us a best estimate or even one that can be described as helpful.[34]

The evidence is now overwhelming regarding long-term trends in peasant grain production and yields—leaving little life in the pessimist view. Increased per capita cereal production during the last 30 years of the empire has been demonstrated by Goldsmith, Nifontov, Gregory, Löwe, and Wheatcroft. Their findings are supported by Kahan, Bideleux, and Gatrell, though these studies are not based upon original analysis. The position of Gerschenkron and Volin among others is no longer tenable, and the recent attempt by Shanin to resurrect it has been properly criticized by Bushnell. Nor is the seemingly more optimistic view new. As many of the above scholars have pointed out, both V. M. Obukhov and V. G. Mikhailovskii, writing in the 1920s, were in accord. However, on livestock production, opinion remains distinctly split.[35] But cereal

34 Gregory ("Grain Marketings," 153) found real wages rose at a rate "well below the rates of growth of peasant grain consumption," calculated on the basis of peasant grain retained in the village. He attributed the discrepancy to the fact that "wages figures are quite inexact." Six years before Wheatcroft, Gregory also wrote that "official series of wages of hired farm labor are available ... but a wage series such as this would be a quite unreliable guide to rural living standards" ("The Russian Agrarian Crisis Revisited" in *The Soviet Rural Economy*, Robert C. Stuart, ed. [Totowa, 1983], 22). In neither essay does Gregory detail his criticisms. I have not chosen to address a note by Simms ("More Grist for the Mill: A Further Look at the Crisis in Russian Agriculture at the End of the Nineteenth Century," *Slavic Review* 50, no. 4 [Winter 1990]: 999-1009), as it suffers from the same weaknesses as Wheatcroft, on whom he relies heavily.

The essay by Elvira Wilbur ("Peasant Poverty in Theory and Practice: A View from Russia's 'Impoverished Center' at the End of the Nineteenth Century," *Peasant Economy*, 101-27) is not discussed because her analysis is essentially static and because the data sample upon which she bases her calculations is unscientific and flawed. See Herman H. Freudenberger, "Discussion," *Journal of Economic History* 43, no. 1 (March 1983): 146.

35 Raymond W. Goldsmith, "The Economic Development of Tsarist Russia 1860-1913," *Economic Development and Cultural Change* 9, no. 3 (April 1961): 442-53; A. S. Nifontov, *Zernovoe proizvodstvo Rossii vo vtoroi polovine XIX veka po materialam ezhegodnoi statistiki urozhaev evropeiskoi Rossii* (Moscow, 1974), 285-88; Paul R. Gregory, "Russian Agrarian Crisis," 22-31; ibid., *Russian National Income, 1885-1913* (New York, 1982), 89-91 and 264-70; Heinz-Dietrich Löwe, *Die Lage der Bauern in Russland 1880-1905* (St. Katharinen, 1987); Wheatcroft, "Crises and the Condition," 133; Gatrell, *The Tsarist Economy*, 43-7; Bideleux, *Communism*, 13-14; Arcadius Kahan, *Russian Economic History: The Nineteenth*

output—even if disaggregated by region, net of exports, or wealth per capita (number of acres, livestock holdings or ruble income)—is a questionable determinant of standard of living. For food, the problem is not what came out of the ground or walked around on hoof, but what went into the stomach.[36] Increased per capita cereal production, even if reflective of consumption patterns, may be evidence of a poorer diet, especially if higher quality foods such as protein-rich meats were being replaced by inferior grains. This, at least, needs to be considered because a long period of growing meatlessness characterized much of Europe after the sixteenth century. Marked increases in potato consumption, as occurred in Russia in the 1890s, have also been interpreted as evidence of a "certain relative pauperization."[37] Moreover, "adequate or surplus mean per capita availability is no indicator of satisfactory food intake and good nutritional status, except when income and purchasing power show a normal distribution and do not become constraints."[38]

In attempting to resolve a few of these dilemmas, Paul Gregory tried to assess levels of grain retained in the village, in order to find a more reliable indicator of rural living standards. He was aware of the difficulty of going from "retained food grains to general peasant living standards," but he did not expect the relationship between them to be weak.[39] In all, retained grain products accounted for only half of retained farm consumption, and Gregory admitted that little is known about the other half. Moreover, his results were obviously more indicative of consumption in grain-surplus provinces. Gregory omitted from his analysis corn and oats, contending that they were not for human consumption, and

---

Century (Chicago, 1989), 11; Shanin, *Russia*, 1:140-44; and John Bushnell, "Peasant Economy and Peasant Revolution at the Turn of the Century: Neither Immiseration nor Autonomy," *The Russian Review* 47, no. 1 (January 1988): 75-82. See also S. A. Klepikov, *Atlas diagramm i kartogramm po agrarnomu voprosu* (Moscow, 1917), 25. On livestock herds, Gregory finds constant per capita livestock holdings between 1890-1913; Kahan a decline of over 40%.

36 Santhebachahalli G. Srikantia, "Better Nutrition and India: A Comment," in *Hunger and History*, 171; Gregory, "Grain Marketings," 138.

37 J. Hémardinquer, "The Family Pig of the Ancien Regime: Myth or Fact?" in *Food and Drink in History*, ed. R. Forster and O. Ranum (Baltimore, 1979), 58-59 and 66-72; and M. Morineau, "The Potato in the Eighteenth Century," in ibid., 31-32, originally published in *Annales, E.S.C.* (November-December 1970).

38 Srikantia, "Better Nutrition," 171.

39 Gregory, "Grain Marketings," 138.

the minor grains (buckwheat and millet), as the data are poor and they comprise a small portion of food-grain production. In doing so, he underestimated retained levels, for oats were certainly consumed by peasants in large quantities. Finally, he agreed with Simms on tax arrears, suggesting that peasants "treated direct tax obligations rather casually" because the state did not possess "sufficient power ... to force peasants to part involuntarily with their output." Gregory was straightforward about the many limitations of his analysis, but his results were startling. Between 1885 and 1913, retained food grains grew far more rapidly than the population: "The picture is one of an agricultural population that was experiencing rising per capita income and living standards." Retained food grains were growing at rates "well above," in fact more than double, those of population growth.[40] These findings contrast sharply with those of Goldsmith, who found that between 1860 and 1914, "it is unlikely that there could have been a noticeable increase in the supply of agricultural products consumed per head of the population. Indeed, a small decline cannot be ruled out."[41]

I shall return to this controversy later. For now, it is important to reiterate that, in assessments of Russian rural standard of living, even benchmark statistics on non-food consumption (especially housing) in late Imperial Russia are wholly lacking. Similarly, times series data on livestock and non-grain food consumption (meat, fish, poultry, vegetables, fruits, drink, dairy produce, sugar, and oils) are nonexistent or problematic. Attempts to measure real wage trends or to interpret the available figures on direct and indirect tax payments have proven unsuccessful, and Gregory's revisionist view essentially stands alone.[42] At a minimum, it should be clear that many of the numbers employed on both sides of the debate are deficient.

---

40 Gregory, "Russian Agrarian Crisis," 26 and 28-9; and idem, "Grain Marketings," 148.

41 Goldsmith, "Economic Growth," 454.

42 Gatrell, *The Tsarist Economy*, 46 and 137-38; Vasudevan, "Peasant Land," 208; and Gregory, *Russian National Income*, 138. Bideleux (*Communism*, 12-18), relying heavily on the work of Simms and Gregory and on earlier research by Wheatcroft, supports Gregory's position. In particular, Bideleux rejects the "dismal portrayal of the plight of the Russian peasantry" put forth by Marx and Engels, an interpretation "most Soviet and Western historians of Russia have gone along with ..."(27).

But nothing has done more to befuddle assessments of late Imperial, rural Russia than population issues and demographic measures. And with such ideas, (Thomas) Robert Malthus, that much maligned English minister, comes to mind. To Shanin, "Russian ruralities seemed caught in a 'Malthusian cycle' of more and more population chasing after produce." In an odd metaphor, he writes, "a 'population explosion' was beginning to build up." Without a decline in rural natural growth rates, "without what Gerschenkron referred to as the 'Malthusian corrective'," or without a way to absorb the rural surplus population, crisis loomed. To others, "the central fact of the period was the demographic revolution that threatened to overrun land resources and to outstrip food production." "The gains achieved by the peasantry as a whole were nullified by demographic pressures." "Much of what happened was a consequence of land hunger and a large increase in the rural population." "The gains made by the peasantry as a class ... were not enough to satisfy those who hungered most for land, or to keep pace with the explosive pressure of population."[43] Russia has repeatedly been described as "overpopulated" or relatively land-short, in spite of the ambiguity of these terms.[44] In Robinson's portrayal of the hungry village, we find "the fecundity of the peasant families was prodigious.... For every new worker in the field, there had to be also a new place at the table, but too often the place could

---

[43] Shanin, *Russia*, 1:141 and 188; Hamburg, "Crisis," 485; Robert Edelman, *Proletarian Peasants: The Revolution of 1905 in Russia's Southwest* (Ithaca, 1987), 83; Vasudevan, "Peasant Land," 212; and Rogger, *Russia in the Age*, 76. See also Sanders, "Once More into the Breach," 666.

[44] Ambiguity in the use of the term "overpopulation" is evidenced by the fact that some place the word within quotes (Gatrell, *The Tsarist Economy*, 56 and 66; and Shanin, *Russia*, 1:83). Similarly, Robinson speaks of a "comparatively dense population" (*Rural Russia*, 245). Overpopulation is also asserted by Gerschenkron ("Agrarian Policies," 755 and 771); George Pavlovsky (*Agricultural Russia on the Eve of the Revolution* [New York, 1930], 84-8); Liashchenko (*History of the National Economy*, 11:66-69); Rogger (*Russia in the Age*, 76, 84, 86, 100, and 127); Sanders ("Once More Into the Breach," 666); Atkinson, (*End*, 104); and Chaianov (*Theory of Peasant Economy*, 235). See also Esther Kingston-Mann, "Peasant Commune and Economic Innovation: A Preliminary Inquiry," in *Peasant Economy*, 44; Volin, *Century*, 48; Mironov, "The Peasant Commune," 460; Maureen Perrie, "The Russian Peasant Movement of 1905-1907: Its Social Composition and Revolutionary Significance," *Past and Present* 57 (November 1972): 123-24; Vasudevan, "Peasant Land," 212.

not be found." And the usual figures are rounded up: from emancipation to 1897, the population grew by over fifty percent, while the increase in land available to the peasantry failed to keep pace. "In other words, there was an increasing dearth of the peasant's chief source of subsistence."[45] To one skeptical outsider, "the tale is Malthusian with a vengeance: all the economic progress eaten up by additions to population."[46]

This portrayal of Russia as overpopulated is somewhat surprising, as nineteenth-century Russian marxists, populists, liberals, and conservatives felt little sympathy with malthusian ideas.[47] For them, unlike many subsequent Russian historians, population pressure was not an exogenous variable placing excessive demand on limited resources and was unlikely to result in a malthusian homeostatic response. With population densities in European Russia considerably below those found elsewhere in Europe, other issues came to the fore. For marxists, agrarian class structures were the root of the problem; for populists, government fiscal policies; for both liberals and conservatives, peasant backwardness, indolence, and ignorance, coupled with traditional patterns of land tenure; and for liberals alone, constraints on the movement of labor. Moreover, the view of Russia suffering from overpopulation is complicated by the ambiguity of the concept itself. What precisely do we have in mind when we raise the specter of overpopulation? Is it really Malthus, with declining fertility or increasing mortality? Or is it movement away from optimal use of available resources? Or is it to be found somewhere in between, where the marginal productivity of labor equals zero?[48] Attempts

45 Robinson, *Rural Russia*, 94.

46 Freudenberger, "Discussion," 146.

47 Daniel P. Todes, *Darwin without Malthus: The Struggle for Existence in Russian Evolutionary Thought* (New York, 1989), 166-72; Yves Charbit, "The Fate of Malthus's Work: History and Ideology," in *Malthus: Past and Present*, ed. D. Dupaquier et al. (London, 1983), 26; Etienne van de Walle, "Malthus Today," in ibid., 242; Esther Kingston-Mann, "Marxism and Russian Rural Development: Problems of Evidence, Experience and Culture," *The American Historical Review* 86, no. 4 (October 1981): 738; Volin, *Century*, 92; and Gatrell, *The Tsarist Economy*, 1-28. Notable exceptions were the "legal marxists," such as Struve and Bulgakov, who were criticized by Lenin for attributing rural impoverishment to malthusian population pressures. On this, see Bideleux, *Communism*, 73.

48 David Grigg, *Population Growth and Agrarian Change: An Historical Perspective* (New York, 1980) 11-19.

to measure overpopulation in terms of rural surplus population, that is, in non-malthusian terms, were undertaken in Russia at the turn of the century. The results indicated that anywhere from 21 to 42 percent of the adult males in European Russia were under-employed.[49] The variance itself is suggestive of methodological problems. Similar, though far more sophisticated, attempts to assess rural poverty for the underdeveloped world based upon production approaches have been subjected to criticism, much of which is relevant here. First, it is not easy to measure the available labor of men, women, and children, and even more difficult to assess labor needs. In particular, efforts to measure the underemployment of family labor have been unsuccessful, while calculating the labor requirements of a traditional agrarian economy have proven virtually impossible. The seasonal nature of agricultural labor and the weighting of different land uses (arable, meadow, garden, pasture and forest) greatly complicate the analysis. There are also difficulties with consumption-related attempts to define rural overpopulation. For example, even in the 1910s and 1920s key agrarian specialists in Russia could still not agree on consumption norms in order to postulate an adequate standard of living.[50] Of all such efforts, Grigg has concluded that they "may greatly overestimate rural overpopulation."[51] The malthusian variant of overpopulation presents fewer difficulties for measurement (assuming the data are available): falling real incomes would cause mortality to rise or fertility to decline, the latter by moral restraint, that is, by delayed marriage or increased celibacy. Among modern Russian historians, malthusian population questions have never been at the center of discussion, though much of the rhetoric on the crisis in rural living standards has been couched in these terms. But mortality was subject to considerable analysis and debate in the latter half of the nineteenth century, and many of the negative assessments of rural Russian society emerged from this early literature.

Most pre-census research (1897) suggested that Russia suffered from extraordinarily high and even increasing mortality levels. The influential studies and reports of Dr. Nikolai Ekk, alleging worsening mortality

---

49 Shanin, *Russia*, 1:140. See also Bideleux, "Agricultural Advance," 198.

50 A. V. Chaianov, "Predislovie," in Klepikov, *Pitanie*, vii-xxiv; Klepikov, *Pitanie*, 26; and S. G. Wheatcroft, "The Reliability of Russian Prewar Grain Output Statistics," *Soviet Studies* 26, no. 2 (April 1974): 167-68.

51 Grigg, *Population Growth*, 13-18.

conditions, actually led to the establishment of a special government commission in 1886 to investigate reducing mortality in Russia. Similar pessimistic results were subsequently obtained by Bortkevich (1890-1891), Besser and Ballard (1897) and a number of others attempting to examine mortality trends in specific provinces and districts.[52] Only later, as a consequence of a better understanding of demographic theory and the publication of census data (1899-1905), did views begin to change. The reasons for the shift are clear: early, pre-census researchers, unable to estimate the population at risk, were forced to rely on a number of complicated, indirect methods which turned out to be quite inexact.[53] Difficulties in evaluating demographic trends in late Imperial Russia derive less from problems in the system of vital registration—the recording of births, marriages, and deaths—than in the lack of appropriate census data on the age structure of the population and population totals in general, especially prior to the first census of 1897. As relates to European Russia, the most prominent contemporary demographer, S. A. Novosel'skii, held that "a more or less correct and accurate registration of births and deaths can be found." This view has been affirmed

---

[52] Nikolai Ekk, *Opyt obrabotki statisticheskikh dannykh o smertnosti v Rossii* (St. Petersburg, 1888), 83; Vladislav Bortkevich, *Smertnost' i dolgovechnost' muzhskago pravoslavnago naseleniia Evropeiskoi Rossii*, in *Zapiski Imperatorskoi akademii nauk* LXIII, no. 8 (1890), appendix; and idem, *Smertnost' i dolgovechnost' zhenskago pravoslavnago naseleniia Evropeiskoi Rossii*, in *Zapiski Imperatorskoi akademii nauk* LXVI, no. 3 (1891), appendix; and L. Besser and K. Ballod, *Smertnost', vozrastnoi sostav i dolgovechnost' pravoslavnago narodonaseleniia oboego pola v Rossii za 1851-1890 gody* in *Zapiski Imperatorskoi akademii nauk* (1897), VIII series, I, no. 5, (1897):21 and 67. D. A. Sokolov and V. I. Grebenshchikov (*Smertnost' v Rossii i bor'ba s neiu* [St. Petersburg, 1901], 25) argued that mortality was flat between 1886 and 1901. Although there was one prominent early critic of Ekk's negative assessment, E. E. Eikhval'd ("Kriticheskiia prilozheniia k stat'e: K voprosu ob umen'shenii smertnosti v Rossii," *Prakticheskaia meditsina* [November 1887, July and August-September 1888]), this view found little acceptance. See S. A. Novosel'skii, "Statisticheskii material po voprosu o vysokoi smertnosti v Rossii," *Vestnik obshchestvennoi gigieny* (January 1908):19-20. Even Eikhval'd, however, admitted that infant mortality in Russia was increasing ([July 1888]: 59-60).

[53] For a detailed critique of pre-census research on mortality, see S. A. Novosel'skii, *Smertnost' i prodolzhitel'nost' zhizni v Rossii* (Petrograd, 1916), 21-22 and 52-97. See also E. A. Osipov, "Statisticheskii ocherk Rossii i eia sanitarnago sostoianiia," in *Russkaia zemskaia meditsina* (Moscow, 1899), 37.

by more recent scholarship. The French demographer Jean-Noel Biraben has described the registration data between 1862 and 1913 for European Russia as "relatively good" and "close enough to reality." David Heer has noted that Russian registration data are "far superior" to that of "contemporary underdeveloped nations." Tests by Ansley Coale and his associates at the Office of Population Research at Princeton raised the possibility that registration data were "more nearly complete" than the census of 1897.[54]

During the last fifty years of the old regime, Russia was clearly experiencing a high rate of natural population growth: an average of 1.5 percent per annum between 1867 and 1913.[55] Some have suggested that this rate of growth was double that of the previous fifty years,[56] but there is considerable reason for doubt. Such estimations have been calculated on the basis of the five tax-censuses taken between 1811 and 1858. But these censuses were conducted immediately following demographic crises, so that their use to measure growth rates extrapolates between troughs and does not necessarily indicate actual trends.[57] While it is certain that natural growth rates accelerated during the second half of the nineteenth century, how these rates compare with the earlier period remains uncertain.

---

54 Novosel'skii, "Statisticheskii material," 20; Jean-Noël Biraben, "Naissances et répartition par âge dans l'Empire russe et en Union Soviétique," *Population* 2 (1976): 454-56; David M. Heer, "The Demographic Transition in the Russian Empire and the Soviet Union," *Journal of Social History* 1, no. 3 (Spring 1968): 205; Ansley J. Coale, Barbara Anderson, and Erna Härm, *Human Fertility in Russia since the Nineteenth Century* (Princeton, 1979), 209. See also Robert R. Kuczynski (*The Balance of Births and Deaths [Eastern and Southern Europe]* [Washington, 1931], 2:100-1) for a quite similar assessment of registration data and the limited effects gaps had on the totals; and V. M. Kabuzan, "O dostovernosti ucheta naseleniia Rossii (1857-1917 gg.)," in *Istochnikovedenie otechestvennoi istorii: Sbornik statei, 1981* (Moscow, 1982), 100-17.

55 Novosel'skii, "Obzor glavneishikh dannykh po demografii i sanitarnoi statistike Rossii," in *Kalendar' dlia vrachei vsekh vedomstv na 1916 god* (Petrograd, 1916), 36- 37, and 73; Kuczynski, *Balance*, 14; A. G. Rashin, *Naselenie Rossii za 100 let* (Moscow, 1956), 215; and Heer, "Demographic Transition," 205.

56 Rashin, *Naselenie*, 41 and 215; and Shanin, *Russia*, I:188.

57 Steven L. Hoch and Wilson R. Augustine, "The Tax-Censuses and the Decline of the Serf Population in Imperial Russia, 1833-1858," *Slavic Review* 38, no. 3 (September 1979): 403-25.

High fertility has long been thought to be characteristic of European Russia, a finding confirmed at length by Coale, Anderson, and Hirm,[58] and has frequently been attributed to the repartitional land commune (the *mir*). Brutskus, Pavlovsky, Urlanis, Volin, Gerschenkron, Heer, and Chojnacka have all alleged such a connection. To Gerschenkron,

> the very system of distributing land in accordance with the manpower available to the households—the most frequent criterion of repartition—meant that the households in order to secure the relatively scarce factor—land—had to hoard the relatively abundant factor—labor. This prevented rational use of those factors and made for rural overpopulation.

Similarly, for Chojnacka, "the labour factor in land distribution not only made early and near-universal marriage possible but made it an economic necessity for both partners."[59] Even such a noted defender of the commune as A. I. Chuprov (although he tried to argue that the *mir* should not be held responsible for high rural birth rates) was forced to admit: "the repartitional land commune is little open to the malthusian homily of restraint" and is based on the principle "be fruitful and multiply."[60] Gerschenkron even alleged that "the very nature of the emancipation settlement, implying as it did agricultural over-population," intensified pre-reform fertility trends: freed from control of the serfowner, peasants were now able to pursue their familial interests unabated by seigneurial constraint.[61]

Atkinson and Gatrell have noted that a close correlation between the repartitional land commune and rural fertility has never been demonstrated, although Atkinson did attempt a crude comparison of

---

[58] Coale, Anderson, and Härm, *Human Fertility*.

[59] Gerschenkron, "Agrarian Policies," 755; Helena Chojnacka, "Nuptiality Patterns in an Agrarian Society," *Population Studies*, 30, no. 2 (1976):210-11; B. D. Brutskus, *Agrarnyi vopros i agrarnaia politika* (Petrograd, 1922), 61-62; Pavlovsky, *Agricultural Russia*, 83; Volin, *Century*, 92; Heer, "Demographic Transition," 228-29; B. Ts. Urlanis, *Rozhdaemost' i prodolzhitel'nost' zhizni v SSSR* (Moscow, 1963), 20.

[60] A. I. Chuprov, "Obshchinnoe zemlevladenie," in *Nuzhdy derevni po rabotam komitetov o nuzhdakh sel'skokhoziaistvennoi promyshlennosti: Sbornik statei* (St. Petersburg, 1904), 11:174-75.

[61] Gerschenkron, "Agrarian Policies," 771.

communal land tenure with net population growth.[62] But in introducing death rates into the equation, she complicated the analysis: she really measured how much of the high fertility was frustrated by the partially independent variable mortality.[63] Reservations were in order, however. Table 3 reveals only a weak correlation between overall rural fertility (and its components) and repartitional land tenure. With a coefficient of determination (R2) of 0.244, only one fourth of the variation in overall fertility might be explained by the system of land redistribution. The data, however, are not dispersed in a linear fashion, as the scattergram reveals (Figure 1), and therefore are not well suited to regression analysis. The poor relationship between the various components of fertility and communal land tenure is better illustrated in Table 4. Kiev and Poltava provinces are a case in point: with less than twenty percent of all their rural households living in repartitional land communes, both had overall rural fertility rates higher than Jaroslavl', Pskov, Kazan, and Kostroma provinces, each with virtually all peasant households living in repartitional communes. In each of the six provinces, rural marital fertility rates were above 0.75, which is usually taken to mean natural fertility was the rule.[64] In all, in the 47 provinces of European Russia (excluding the Baltic) fertility was high by European standards and bore only a weak relationship to the repartitional land commune or the labor principle of land distribution.

Gatrell attributes Russia's high fertility rates to "pro-natalist" policies of serfowners, a "cultural inheritance" which then endured

62 Atkinson, *End*, 30-32; Gatrell, *The Tsarist Economy*, 53.

63 That Atkinson does not appreciate the limitations of the demographic measures she uses is evidenced by her statement that "the death rate in Russia in the nineteenth century was often higher in the countryside than in urban areas" (Atkinson, *End*, 31). If by this she is implying that mortality conditions were worse in rural areas, she has made an elementary error. "Crude" death rates, which is what they are technically called, are so described because they are strongly affected by the age structure of the population. Death rates in Russia's cities were lower because the population was younger. Urban age-specific death rates were in fact higher and are a better indicator of overall mortality conditions (Henry S. Shryock et al., *The Methods and Material of Demography* [New York, 1976] 228 and 443; and S. A. Novosel'skii, "O razlichiiakh v smertnosti gorodskago i sel'skago naseleniia Evropeiskoi Rossii," *Obshchestvennyi vrach* 4 [April 1911]: 40-62).

64 Coale, Anderson, and Härm, *Human Fertility*, 20-21 and 41.

Table 3
Correlations Among Variables European Russia (excluding Baltic Provinces) (1897-1905)

	Population density	Percent communal	Rural I_g	Rural I_m	Rural I_f
Density	1.000				
Communal	-0.462	1.000			
Rural I_g	-0.159	0.502	1.000		
Rural I_m	-0.058	0.317	0.084	1.000	
Rural I_f	-0.018	0.494	0.501	0.900	1.000

Sources: Data on population density by province from A. G. Rashin, *Naselenie Rossii za 100 let* (Moscow, 1956), 77-78; on the percent of peasant households in repartitional land communes, from Tsentral'nyi statisticheskii komitet, *Statistika zemlevladeniia 1905 g.: svod dannykh po 50 guberniiam Evropeiskoi Rossii* (St. Petersburg, 1907), xxxii-xxxiii; and on rural marital fertility (rural I_g), on rural proportion married (rural I_m), and on overall rural fertility (rural I_f) for 1897, from Ansley J. Coale, Barbara Anderson, and Erna Härm, *Human Fertility in Russia since the Nineteenth Century* (Princeton, 1979), 20-21. For a discussion of these fertility measures, see Human Fertility, 9-14.

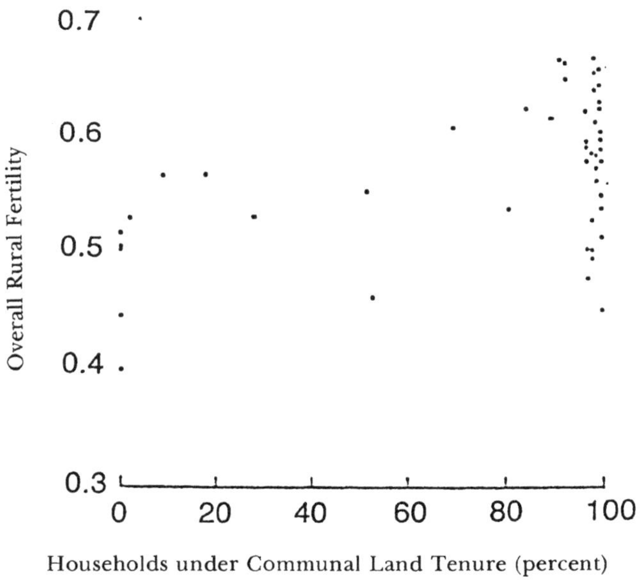

Sources: See Table 3.

Figure 1. Relation of Overall Rural Fertility to Percent of Households in a Province under Communal Land Tenure

Table 4
Descriptive Statistics for Rural Fertility by Percent of Households in a Province in Repartitional Communes

Rural fertility	Percentage of households under repartitional land tenure								
	≤33% n=9			34-66% (n=2)			≥67% (n=36)		
	I_g	I_m	I_f	I_g	I_m	I_f	I_g	I_m	I_f
Minimum	0.683	0.502	0.398	0.760	0.581	0.459	0.705	0.581	0.448
Maximum	0.776	0.763	0.565	0.768	0.703	0.550	0.840	0.828	0.665
Range	0.093	0.261	0.167	0.008	0.122	0.091	0.135	0.247	0.217
Mean	0.736	0.672	0.505	0.764	0.642	0.505	0.787	0.726	0.583
Median	0.739	0.710	0.515	0.764	0.642	0.505	0.795	0.746	0.589

Sources: See Table 3.

in post-emancipation rural society.[65] But there are drawbacks to this view as well. What is initially explained by functionalist economic considerations—serfowner pressures promoting early and universal marriage—then becomes a social norm, which in turn persists in spite of allegedly obvious economic dysfunction—overpopulation and impoverishment. On these grounds, one might equally assume that no relationship existed between serfdom and marriage patterns, and that emancipation would have had no effect on them. This would suggest that neither Gerschenkron nor Gatrell are correct. There is evidence to support this alternative view: first, state peasants, not subject to the manorial regulations of noble estates, had, as far as we know (which is not much), marriage and fertility patterns quite similar to privately owned serfs. Second, recent archival research by John Bushnell on the Orlov estates concludes that "as a set of social and cultural practices, peasant marriage actually suffered scarcely any manorial intrusion." This largely confirms my findings on the Gagarin estate of Petrovkoe in Tambov.[66] Gatrell, in contrast, suggests that this tradition of high fertility, forged as it was among serfs in earlier generations, "in turn can

65 Chojnacka, "Nuptiality Patterns," 212; and Gatrell, *The Tsarist Economy*, 53.

66 John Bushnell, "Did Serf Owners Control Serf Marriage? Orlov Serfs and their Neighbors," *Slavic Review* 52, no. 3 (Fall 1993): 419-45; and Steven L. Hoch, *Serfdom and Social Control in Russia: Petrovskoe, a Village in Tambov* (Chicago, 1986), 118-19.

be related to land:labour ratios."[67] He offers no figures to support this view, and there is no hint of a correlation between population density and fertility remaining in 1897 (see Table 3). In effect, he leaves us with the tautology of a possibly invented tradition persisting.

Coale, Anderson, and Hairm found stability in the average age at marriage in European Russia from the 1870s to the first decade of this century, and a flat index for marital fertility (with the exception of the Baltic provinces) from as far back as they measured (1881) to the early 1900s. Rural marital fertility was only weakly related to socio-economic variables during this time, and they hypothesized that age at marriage was powerfully influenced by local norms.[68] Stable fertility would in turn create a stable age structure, for fertility is the primary determinant of the age composition of a population. In fact, earlier research by Biraben directly on the age composition of the Russian population over the course of the nineteenth century noted precisely this stability.[69] The importance of these findings is twofold: they demonstrate that there was no malthusian response of moral restraint (reduced fertility) to presumed population pressures, and they make it possible to assess population trends as measured by otherwise problematic crude demographic rates, as the latter are strongly affected by the age structure of the population.

Figure 2 graphs trends in crude birth, death, marriage, and natural population growth rates. To produce a true locally weighted curve, the line has been calculated using distance weighted least squares. Note that the crude birth rate is flat almost until the turn of the century and conforms to the more sophisticated fertility measures of Coale and his colleagues. This result attests to the accuracy of the demographic trends as measured by the other crude rates. The contrary case would require evidence suggesting that the degree of accuracy in the registration in births and marriages remained relatively constant over time, while that

---

67 Gatrell, *The Tsarist Economy*, 54.

68 Coale, Anderson, and Härm, *Human Fertility*, 17, 47, 66 and 177-78.

69 Roland Pressant, *Demographic Analysis: Methods, Results, Applications* (New York, 1972), 344; A. J. Coale, P. Dememy, and Barbara Vaughan, *Regional Model Life Tables and Stable Populations* (Princeton, 1966), 33-35; and Jean-Noël Biraben, "Essai sur l'évolution démographique de I'U.R.S.S.," *Population*, special number (1958): 44.

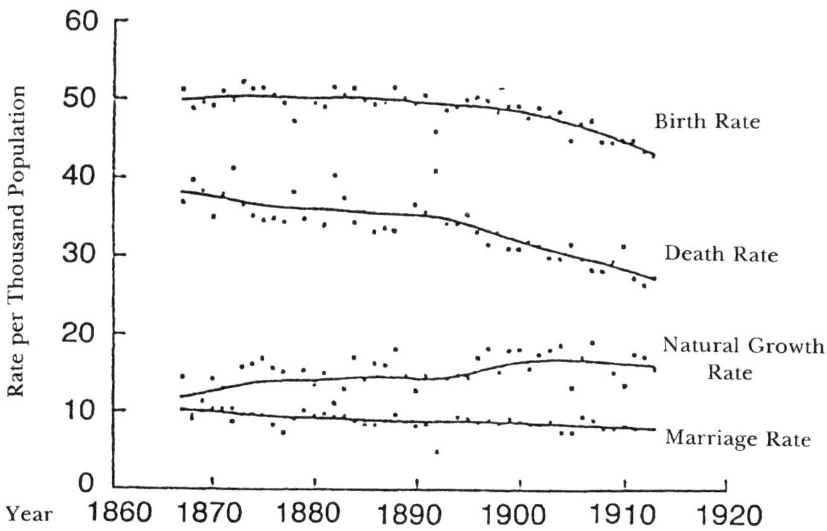

Sources: See footnote 55.

Figure 2. Crude Demographic Rates: European Russia

of deaths not only declined, but did so in a rather particular manner. There is little reason to doubt the trends themselves, though the actual levels may be somewhat elevated because of a presumed undercount in the population at risk especially prior to 1897. These results prove startling and go against much received opinion. Through the 1890s, acceleration in the natural growth rate is attributable solely to a downward trend in the death rate. The period is marked by a noticeable decline in the death rate from the earliest observation, 1867, until 1877, a relatively flat curve with only a slight negative slope through 1892, followed by a substantial and steady decline until 1913. As mentioned above, fertility began to decrease only in the late 1890s, leading to relatively flat, though high, natural growth rates in the very first years of the twentieth century.

Some of these findings are not entirely new. In 1908, drawing in part upon only recently available census data which afforded much greater accuracy, Novosel'skii published comprehensive results which demonstrated that mortality in Russia had been declining for more than ten years, a date which in later research he would push back almost another decade. Birth rates, he noted, began to decline later than mortality and initially at a much slower rate.[70] Clearly, if crisis were looming, it was not of a malthusian variety.

Novosel'skii estimated a rural life expectancy at birth for all of European Russia for 1896-1897 at 33.3 years (males = 32.44; females = 34.14). Urban life expectancy was lower and stood at 30.9 years.[71] Such a low expectation of life alarmed contemporary Russian scholars and officials at the turn of the century who were well aware of the very much more favorable mortality conditions prevailing in most of Europe. But if placed in the historical perspective of a pre- or early industrial society, the figure is not so shocking. In England and Wales, between 1781 and 1821, life expectancy at birth remained relatively stable at 31.5 years. In France at the end of the eighteenth century, the expectation of life was 28.8 years, and only 30 years at birth in mid- nineteenth century Italy, a level common in much of southern and eastern Europe.[72]

Unfortunately, given the methods and data available to Novosel'skii, he was unable to study the trend in life expectancy. Expectation of life, based as it is on age-specific death rates, is a considerably better measure than the crude death rate. But for one district, Borzenskii uezd, in Chernigov province, this is possible. From the outset it should be noted that what follows pretends to be nothing more than a case study and suffers from all the typical limitations. The advantages of a detailed case study are two-fold: it permits independent, even if partial, confirmation of the results obtained above; and the more sophisticated techniques employed allow for internal demographic checks on the data. The example is fortuitous, owing simply to the unusual statistical activity of the Chernigov provincial

---

70 Novosel'skii, "Statisticheskii material," 57; idem, "K voprosu o ponizhenii smertnosti i rozhdaemosti v Rossii," *Vestnik obshchestvennoi gigieny, sudebnoi i prakticheskoi meditsiny* (March 1914): 351; and *idem*, *Smertnost' i prodolzhitel'nost' zhizni*, 181. See also P. I. Kurkin, "Statistika dvizheniia naseleniia v Moskovskoi gubernii v 1883-1897 gg.," in *Sbornik statisticheskikh svedenii po Moskovskoi gubernii. Otdel sanitarnyi* (Moscow, 1902), VI, vypusk 6, 210; Osipov, "Statisticheskii ocherk," 37; and Kuczynski, *Balance*, 14.

71 Novosel'skii, *Smertnost' i prodolzhitel'nost' zhizni*, 120, 125 and 130; and M. Ptukha, *Smertnist' u Rosii i na Ukraïni* (Kharkov and Kiev, 1928), 115 and 120.

72 E. A. Wrigley, *Population and History* (New York, 1969), 131; T. H. Hollingsworth, *Historical Demography* (London, 1969), 5; Roger Schofield and David Reher, "The Decline of Mortality in Europe" in *The Decline of Mortality in Europe*, ed. R. Schofield, D. Reher and A. Bideau (Oxford, 1991), 4; and Graziella Caselli, "Health Transition and Cause-Specific Mortality" in ibid., 69.

zemstvo, the undertaking and subsequent publication of the results of a partial provincial household census conducted in November 1888.

Table 5 presents the age-specific death rates, mortality rates, and estimates of life expectancy for the rural population of Borzenskii uezd, essentially exclusive of the city of Borzna, for the three-year period 1887-1889. Average rural life expectancy for both sexes combined was 33.5 years; the median, 35.1 years. Table 6 compares hypothetical projected populations for Borzenskii uezd, assuming various levels of mortality between late 1888 and early 1897 (an intercensal period of 8.2 years), to that of the actual population as recorded in the census of 1897. This procedure is a standard method of estimation for statistically underdeveloped areas.[73] It is clear that the method employed entails some uncertainty; in particular, the distinction, or at least legal difference, between the urban and rural population is more sharply drawn in the January 1897 census than in the earlier enumeration. The results are given in Table 7.

It is important to note that this technique measures life expectancy across the period under consideration, 1888 to 1897, and not in 1897 alone. The results reveal an increase in average life expectancy at birth for both sexes combined of 4.3 years to 37.8; a median increase of 1.3 years to 36.4. These results in turn may be compared with those of Ptukha, who calculated rural life expectancy for the nine Ukrainian provinces for 1896-1897. Using the same method as Novosel'skii, Ptukha obtained the following: an expectation of life at birth of 36.31 years for males; 36.85 for females; or 36.58 for both sexes combined.[74] In sum, in all likelihood, the peasant population of Borzenskii uezd experienced a measurable improvement in mortality conditions between 1887-1889 and 1897, with a probable annual addition to life expectancy of at least 0.31 years, a rate of improvement wholly in line with that of many countries.[75]

---

73 In other words, the same cohort is compared at two points in time: the number of persons aged 10 and over in 1888 with those who survived to 1897 (8.2 years later) and are now aged 18.2 and over. The resulting survival rates (after making an adjustment for migration) can then be used to calculate the mortality level which prevailed over this period.

74 M. Ptukha, "Tablytsi smertnosti dlia Ukraïny. 1896-1897 gg.," in *Zapysky sotsiial'no-ekonomichnogo viddilu* (Kiev, 1923), 17-62; and *idem*, *Smertnist'*, 115 and 120.

75 T. Lynn Smith and Paul E. Zopf, Jr., *Demography: Principles and Methods* (Philadelphia, 1970), 433-34.

Table 5
Age-Specific Death Rates ($_{10}m_x$),
Age-Specific Mortality Rates ($_{10}q_x$),
and Expectation of Life at Birth (e_0^0)
Borzenskii uezd, Chernigov Province
(1887-1889)

Age	Average annual deaths	Total population (1888)	$_{10}m_x$	$_{10}q_x$	e_0^0
Males					
10-19	8.0	11,541	7.37	71.44	21.2
20-29	76.0	10,578	7.18	69.66	39.5
30-39	63.3	7,597	8.33	80.43	41.9
40-49	77.3	5,584	13.85	130.67	40.9
50-59	107.7	3,941	27.33	243.66	37.5
				Average	36.2
				Median	39.5
Females					
10-19	107.3	11,623	9.23	88.78	21.9
20-29	84.7	11,343	7.47	72.38	41.2
30-39	86.3	7,577	11.39	108.57	36.5
40-49	93.0	5,633	16.51	154.02	30.6
50-59	145.0	3,973	36.50	313.15	23.2
				Average	30.7
				Median	30.6
				Average (both sexes)	33.5
				Median (both sexes)	35.1

Note: Mortality rates calculated using the Reed-Merrell Table. See Roland Pressat, *Demographic Analysis: Methods, Results, Applications*, trans. Judah Matras (New York, 1972), 481-89. Life expectancy calculated using Ansley J. Coale, Paul Demeny, and Barbara Vaughan, *Regional Model Life Tables and Stable Populations*, second ed. (New York, 1983), "east" series.

Sources: E. Sviatlovskii, "K statistike naseleniia Chernigovskoi gubernii," *Zemskii sbornik Chernigovskoi gubernii*, nos. 11-12 (November-December 1889): 81-98; and A. G. Rozenel', "K statistike naseleniia Chernigovskoi gubernii: Borzenskii uezd," nos. 2-3 *Zemskii sbornik Chernigovskoi gubernii* (February-March, 1894): 122-73.

Table 6
Population of Borzenskii Uezd, Chernigov Province at Age x and over as Reported by the Census of 1897 and as Projected from the Zemstvo Household Census of 1888 Assuming Various Levels of Mortality in "East" Model Life Tables

Females

Age	1897 Census	Projected population assuming life expectancy at birth of 30.000	32.500	35.000	37.500	40.000	42.500	45.000
8.2+	53,328	51,770	52,349	52,897	53,405	53,884	54,325	54,751
18.2+	37,286	37,064	37,419	37,762	38,081	38,384	38,673	38,928
28.2+	26,250	26,164	26,460	26,746	27,014	27,267	27,508	27,723
38.2+	16,941	15,870	16,082	16,287	16,480	16,661	16,835	16,993
48.2+	9,798	9,137	9,284	9,427	9,563	9,689	9,812	9,922

Males

Age	1897 Census	Projected population assuming life expectancy at birth of 29.861	32.319	34.765	37.200	39.622	42.066	49.017	53.683
8.2+	51,294	51,289	51,800	52,274	52,722	53,140	53,540	54,560	55,205
18.2+	37,775	36,541	36,848	37,131	37,405	37,659	37,892	38,501	38,919
28.2+	26,217	25,623	25,881	26,122	26,354	26,568	26,768	27,280	27,638
38.2+	17,292	15,887	16,083	16,264	16,439	16,601	16,754	17,136	17,392
48.2+	10,079	9,100	9,236	9,361	9,483	9,594	9,702	9,963	10,142

Note: Calculated using 8.2 year survivorship ratios.

Sources: See Table 5 and Tsentral'nyi Statisticheskii Komitet, *Pervaia Vseobshchaia Perepis' Naseleniia Rossiiskoi Imperii, 1897 g.*, ed. N. A. Troinitskii (St. Petersburg: Tsentral'nyi Statisticheskii Komitet, 1905), XLVIII (Chernigovskaia guberniia): 16-17.

It is hard to square the image of deteriorating rural living standards with the observed demographic trends of declining mortality and stable fertility in the nineteenth century. To modern demographers working with Russian data from this period, an inverse relationship between mortality and standard of living is almost axiomatic and underlies the theory of the demographic transition.[76] But how good a surrogate for standard of living is mortality, and what specific evidence can be

[76] Coale, Anderson, and Härm, *Human Fertility*, 5 and 205-6; and Heer, "Demographic Transition," 194, 202, 218-21 and 238.

Table 7
Expectations of Life at Birth (e_0^0) Using Projections from Table 6

Age	Males	Females
8.2+	29.9	37.1
18.2+	40.8	31.6
28.2+	35.8	30.7
38.2+	51.8	44.2
Average	39.6	35.9
Median	38.3	34.4
Average	(both sexes)	37.8
Median	(both sexes)	36.4

Note: The estimates of expectation of life above exclude those estimates based solely upon the population aged 48.2+. It has been found that such cohorts often suffer from exaggerated reporting of age, which is in evidence here.

Sources: See Table 6.

mustered to support the view that this decline in mortality is attributable to improved nutritional standards?

In McKeown's classic view:

> the rise in population was due to the decline in mortality, which led to the increase of life expectancy. Mortality declined essentially because of a reduction of deaths from infectious diseases.... The earliest and most important reason for the decline in infectious diseases was an improvement in nutrition which resulted from advances in agriculture and transportation.[77]

A modern specialist on international health notes in reference to McKeown's views that "the profound effects of even subclinical malnutrition on morbidity and mortality from many of the common infectious diseases and, to a considerable extent, the mechanisms involved have been documented over the past two decades, and this information is a valuable tool for historians." Although this "synergism" between mortality and poorly nourished individuals has been described as

[77] Thomas McKeown, "Food, Infection, and Population," in *Hunger and History*, 46; and *idem*, *The Modern Rise of Population* (New York, 1976), 128-42.

"epidemiologically sound,"[78] it has been increasingly subjected to criticism. In McKeown's analysis, based upon British data, nutrition wins "on the principle enunciated by Sherlock Holmes: when we have eliminated the impossible, whatever remains, however improbable, must be the truth."[79] Thus, he comes to his conclusions after having rejected personal medical measures, fortuitous variation in the nature of infectious diseases, and increased exposure to these diseases attendant to industrialization as explanations for the mortality decline. McKeown has been criticized for this "reasoning by exclusion" and making "liberal use of reductive logic," for "there is no evidence of improved nutritional levels" in England between 1700 and 1850, and "indirect proof that living standards were in fact worsening during that period."[80] Moreover, Livi-Bacci has called into question the nutrition-mortality link on substantive grounds, while also noting that direct support for a nutrition-mortality link for much of Europe is lacking.[81]

The significance of this discussion is, first, that Gregory's findings, discussed above, are strong evidence of substantially improved rural nutritional levels dating from at least 1885; with increased amounts of grain *being retained in the village*, the likelihood is great that a considerable portion of rising per capita rural income was expended on food. And Gregory underestimated the potential extent of rural nutritional gain. Second, Novosel'skii held that a noticeable decline in deaths from infectious diseases took place in late Imperial Russia. In England and Italy, a reduction in deaths from infectious diseases was responsible for some forty percent of the increase in life expectancy (1871/1881-1951) and was most evident in the early stages of mortality decline.[82] Novosel'skii's evidence is not unequivocal, however. The collection of data on a national level on the causes of death began in Russia only in 1890 and was undertaken by priests, not physicians. Moreover, though Novosel'skii cites a

78 Carl E. Taylor, "Synergy among Mass Infections, Famines, and Poverty," in *Hunger and History*, 288; and Nevin S. Scrimshaw, "The Value of Contemporary Food and Nutrition Studies for Historians," in ibid, 332.

79 McKeown, "Food," 29.

80 Schofield and Reher, "The Decline of Mortality in Europe," 8-9.

81 Massimo Livi-Bacci, "The Nutrition-Mortality Link in Past Times: A Comment," in *Hunger and History*, 95-100; and his *Population and Nutrition: An Essay on European Demographic History* (New York, 1991), 41-62 and 79-110.

82 Novosel'skii, "Statisticheskii material," 47; *idem*, *Smertnost' i prodolzhitel'nost' zhizni*, 182-84; and *idem*, "Obzor," 70; Caselli, "Health and Cause-Specific Mortality," 79.

distinct decline in deaths from measles and whooping cough, for which mortality is definitely influenced by nutrition, and a significant reduction in deaths from typhus and diphtheria, for which nutrition's role is more variable or uncertain, he notes a decrease in mortality for a number of diseases, most notably smallpox, for which the nutritional state of the host is not a significant factor. Nevertheless, Novosel'skii's findings are consistent with the overall trends in disease-specific mortality for Europe, including those illnesses less influenced by nutritional factors.[83] Additional evidence, albeit limited and dated, suggests an increase in the mean height of Russian army recruits between 1890 and 1899, also a good indicator of improved nutrition. Although caution needs to be exercised, the existence of such data holds promise for future investigation.[84]

But there is an exception regarding synergism which is relevant here. Contemporary Russian demographers repeatedly found infant mortality rates (children aged 0-1) in the late Imperial period to be high and distressingly stable, with diarrhoeal diseases a significant factor. Increases in overall life expectancy had come largely as a result of decreased mortality among children, especially those aged 1-10, and to a lesser extent among adults, in large part a result of improved response to non-intestinal infectious diseases. This mirrors the pattern of mortality reduction for Europe in the eighteenth and nineteenth centuries and that of most developing countries in this century.[85] Most surprising, infant mortality rates were consistently highest among Great Russians of all the major ethnic groups,

---

83 H. O. Lancaster, *Expectations of Life: A Study in the Demography, Statistics, and History of World Mortality* (New York, 1990), 304-12 and 374-409.

84 G. I. Rostovtsev, "Dozhivaemost' muzhskago naseleniia do 20-21 g. i telesnoe razvitie prizyvnago naseleniia v Dmitrovskom uezde Moskovskoi gubernii," *Vestnik obshchestvennoi gigieny* (August 1902): 1187; Lars G. Sandberg and Richard H. Steckel, "Overpopulation and Malnutrition Rediscovered: Hard Times in 19th-Century Sweden," *Explorations in Economic History* 25, no. 1 (1988): 3-4; John Komlos, *Nutrition and Economic Development in the Eighteenth-Century Habsburg Monarchy: An Anthropometric History* (Princeton, 1989), 23-54; and Roderick C. Floud, Kenneth W. Wachter, and A. S. Gregory, *Height, Health, and History: Nutritional Status in Britain, 1750-1980* (New York, 1990).

85 McKeown, *The Modern Rise*, 138-39; Roberts Woods and P. R. Andrew Hinde, "Mortality in Victorian England: Models and Patterns," *Journal of Interdisciplinary History* 18, no. 1 (Summer 1987): 39; Jacques Vallin, "Mortality in Europe from 1720 to 1914: Long-Term Trends and Changes in Patterns by Age and Sex," in *The Decline of Mortality in Europe*, 38-67; and Livi-Bacci, *Population and Nutrition*, 70-71.

and contemporaries quite correctly blamed well known Great Russian child-rearing practices. The fact that Great Russian women breastfed their infants for only a short period before shifting them over to solid foods resulted in extraordinarily high rates of infant deaths from diarrhoeal diseases, often called "weanling diarrhoea."[86] Thus, as Livi-Bacci, Schofield and Reher, and even McKeown himself have pointed out, the relationship between infant mortality rates and nutrition may be broken by cultural factors quite distinct from income, output, food availability, or standard of living generally.[87] Nevertheless, for Imperial Russia, in spite of the above-noted exception, the evidence for a synergism between improved nutritional levels and the long-term secular decline in mortality from 1867 to 1913 appears stronger than elsewhere. Given our knowledge of the effects of immunization and therapy prior to the twentieth century in western Europe, and the lack of significant gains in Russia in the period under consideration in rural public hygiene affecting water, sewage, and food, these factors do not merit detailed consideration.[88]

---

86 Sokolov and Grebenshchikov (25, 37-38 and 45-55) and D. E. Gorokhov ("Obshchestvennoe znachenie izucheniia detskoi smertnosti i bor'by s neiu," *Vestnik obshchestvennoi gigieny* [October 1908]: 1633-36 and [November 1908]: 1734-43) provide a detailed survey of the literature on this subject. See also M. Ptukha, "Smertnost' 11 narodnostei Evropeiskoi Rossii v kontse XIX veka," *Pratsi demografichnogo instytutu* (Kiev, 1928), 6:25-26, and 31; Novosel'skii, "Statisticheskii material," 29-30; *idem*, "Obzor," 66-67; *idem*, *Smertnost' i prodolzhitel'nost' zhizni*, 181-82; Coale, Anderson, and Härm, *Human Fertility*, 75; and Stephen J. Kunitz, "Speculations on the European Mortality Decline," *The Economic History Review*, second series, 36, no. 3 (August 1983): 352 and 357.

87 Massimo Livi-Bacci, "The Nutrition-Mortality Link," 96; and Schofield and Reher, "The Decline of Mortality in Europe," 16. Thus the attempt by Gatrell to use infant mortality rates as a proxy for income are, for the Russian case, suspect (Gatrell, *The Tsarist Economy*, 30-7). In addition, Kahan's statement that the "mechanism of the increase in the size of population during this period [1860-1913] was the decline in the mortality rate (especially infant mortality)" is wanting (Kahan, *Russian Economic History*, 2-3).

88 McKeown, "Food," 28; *idem*, *The Modern Rise*, 152-54; *idem*, "Fertility, Mortality, and Causes of Death: An Examination of Issues Related to the Modern Rise of Population," *Population Studies* 31, no. 3 (November 1978): 541; W. R. Lee, "Introduction: Population Growth, Economic Development and Social Change in Europe, 1750- 1970," in his *European Demography and Economic Growth* (London, 1979), 15; and Alfred Perrenoud, "Mortality Decline in Its Secular Setting," in *Pre-Industrial Population Change: The Mortality Decline and Short-Term Population Movements*, ed. T. Bengtsson, G. Fridlizius, and R. Ohlsson (Stockholm, 1984), 43.

In all, the pervasive notion of an equilibrium between population and resources, first posited by Malthus, does not hold in this instance. Russia began as early as the 1860s "breaking out" of the high pressure demographic environment of high fertility and high mortality. It began in Russia, as in most European nations before it, with an "all-important decline in mortality," and the range of possible explanations must include "two main interacting areas-nutrition ... and the diminution of the incidence of infectious diseases."[89] Although a nutrition-mortality link seems clearer for Russia than elsewhere, how much of the mortality reduction can be tied to improved diet is uncertain. The mechanism for the mortality decline in Russia—especially age- and cause-specific mortality—has yet to be examined. In particular, the impact of such socio-biological and environmental factors as historically higher fertility and infant mortality, lower population densities, and greater climatic variability than in much of Europe needs to be assessed. Neither is it clear that the transmissibility of disease in Russia—both in terms of virulence and contagion—mirrored those in Europe. Ultimately, as with its pattern of economic development, Russia's mortality transition may prove distinctive. Some of the advantages along with the obvious disadvantages of being backward are relevant here. Parish registers, now readily available (national data exist only from the end of the last century), will prove essential to further research on this problem. But, given what is known at present, is it really plausible that an improvement in rural nutritional levels began as far back as the immediate post-emancipation period, considering the generally negative assessment among historians of all persuasions of the land reform legislation and the lack of significant investment in transport until later in the century? No one denies that peasant landholdings were reduced. And a recent essay by Evsey Domar raises the possibility that serfs were overcharged for their land far more than Lositskii's often cited figures would suggest: instead of a total overcharge of 34 percent (90% in non-black earth provinces, 20% in black earth provinces, and none in the western provinces), Domar estimates "on the average, the peasants were overcharged more than three times; in both black-earth and non-black-earth zones they overpaid more than four times, and only in the West were they

[89] Michael W. Flinn, *The European Demographic System, 1500-1820* (Baltimore, 1981), 101. See also Scrimshaw, "Nutrition Studies," 334.

lucky to escape with a modest double price!"[90] Domar, himself, wonders if these "fantastic ratios" could be true, and if the tsarist regime could "have perpetrated such a fraud?"[91]

But in assessing the impact of the 1861 land reform on rural living standards, one should consider whether serfs compensated landlords for all of their losses: land, labor, income, and serf property. Gerschenkron himself had some doubts:

> A point must be stressed here which, for whatever reasons, has not been made with sufficient clarity in the literature on the subject. Taken in isolation, the redemption provisions were highly advantageous to the peasantry as they did not involve much of an additional burden.... By and large, it is unlikely that the aggregate annual burden was higher than the previous quitrent. When all is said and done, it is clear that the procedure adopted made it very attractive to the peasants to enter into the redemption arrangements.[92]

Two recent archival case studies (based upon systematic analysis of all the available redemption agreements for two provinces) suggest not only that this concern was well founded, but that the post-reform redemption burden was in fact lower than pre-reform quitrents.[93] In Novgorod province, in the pre-reform period the average quitrent

---

[90] Evsey Domar, "Were Russian Serfs Overcharged for their Land by the 1861 Emancipation? The History of One Historical Table," in *Research in Economic History: Agrarian Organization in the Century of Industrialization: Europe, Russia, and North America*, supplement 5 (1989), part B, 434; A. E. Lositskii, *Vykupnaia operatsiia* (St. Petersburg, 1906), 38-39.

[91] Domar, "Were Russian Serfs Overcharged," 436.

[92] Gerschenkron, "Agrarian Policies," 740-41.

[93] A. Ia. Degtiarev, S. G. Kashchenko, and D. I. Raskin, *Novgorodskaia derevnia v reforme 1861 goda: Opyt izucheniia s ispol'zovaniem EVM* (Leningrad, 1989), 143-46; S. G. Kashchenko, *Reforma 19 fevralia 1861 goda v Sankt-Peterburgskoi gubernii* (Leningrad, 1990), 130-39; and Steven L. Hoch, "Introduction," *The Novgorod Countryside in the Reform of 1861: A Computer-Aided Experimental Study in Soviet Studies in History* 30, no. 4 (Spring 1992): 5. Peasants who reached voluntary agreements with their lords might have contracted to make supplemental payments. But only one third of all redemption agreements were voluntary (outside the western provinces where redemption was made mandatory in 1863), and in most of these instances no supplemental payments were involved (Hoch, "The Banking Crisis," 815).

(*obrok*) per desiatina (2.7 acres) of usable land was 1.20 rubles. For temporarily obligated peasants it rose 16.7 percent to 1.40 rubles. But when peasants shifted onto redemption, most payments were lowered, ranging from 1.05 to 1.12 rubles per desiatina. Similarly, in St. Petersburg province, the average pre-reform quitrent per desiatina of land was 1.43 rubles, 1.70 rubles for temporarily obligated peasants, and between 1.28 and 1.36 rubles for most ex-serfs on redemption. Thus, regardless of whether the peasants paid too high a price for the land, they were paying less per unit of land on redemption than as serfs, roughly seven to fourteen percent less in Novgorod province, and between five and twelve percent less in St. Petersburg. Though the peasants were worse off when temporarily obligated than as serfs, they were best off on redemption. In other words, serfowners were not fully compensated for all that they lost. Some benefit accrued to the peasants—clearly not what they would have liked and not determined by the value of the land they received. Nevertheless, reductions in the peasants' obligations were real and they help explain the observed mortality trends. The avowed intent of the Editing Commission which drafted emancipation legislation was to improve the peasants' lot, and perhaps it achieved its goal after all.

It is possible to assess accurately the pre-reform burden only for peasants on quitrent. Let me offer a more speculative example for serfs performing obligatory labor or corvee (*barshchina*). According to Gerschenkron, in the fertile black soil and steppe provinces, peasants lost 23 percent of their holdings attendant to land reform. Assume that the income, largely in kind, from all types of land in production in the pre-reform period was equally split between serf and serfowner. (This would be the logical corollary of a three-day-per-week labor obligation in a region where land was abundant and in an economy where labor was the primary determinant of output.) After reform, the peasants would have had direct use of only 38.5 percent of all productive land, while the ex-serfowners' percentage would have increased to 61.5 percent. But landlords would now have to pay for labor, while the peasants would have new redemption payments to the state. Sharecropping was one of the most widespread forms of tenure in the early decades following emancipation. If the share were half each (the most common arrangement), then the peasant would be deriving income from almost 70 percent of the land (38.5% from the allotment plus 30.8% from half a share). A split which gave the landlord a two-to-one advantage still would provide the peasant with 59 percent of the income (38.5 plus 20.5). This rather simplistic example illustrates that post-reform peasants were indeed likely to have substantial new income to meet their new financial obligations. It explains why ex-serfs could indeed make their redemption payments, and why gentry agriculture experienced a rather precipitous decline, at least in the early post-emancipation period. The fate of the newly emancipated peasant depended, therefore, to a large extent on the nature and dynamic of post-reform land tenure relations on privately owned and (at least initially) largely noble land. Of these relations remarkably little is known, but the trend in mortality would suggest the balance was distinctly in the peasants' favor.

Finally, two important historical benchmarks need rethinking. First, the reduction in redemption payments mandated by the autocracy in 1881, usually interpreted as evidence of peasant distress, was, at least in part if not entirely, due to other factors. The original 1861 emancipation legislation had required that the quitrents of temporarily obligated peasants be reassessed after twenty years. This, coupled with the stressed state of government finances following the Russo-Turkish War and the fact that the redemption operation was producing a surplus, precipitated a broad reconsideration of the financial aspects of emancipation.[94] Of primary concern to the government was tax reform, much needed and long avoided. What emerged was a fundamental and well known shift in fiscal policy, with increased reliance on indirect taxes. And a special government commission had concluded in early 1881 that "the first step in transforming the system of direct taxes had to be a lowering of redemption payments," since they averaged 3.5 to 4.4 times the level of the soul tax. Thus, abolition of the soul tax, a reduction in redemption payments, inclusion of the redemption operation in the state budget, and new indirect taxes were all part of a major reform of fiscal policy during the 1880s and largely directed at resolving budget problems.[95]

94 Linda Bowman, "Russia's First Income Taxes: The Effects of Modernized Taxes on Commerce and Industry, 1885-1914," *Slavic Review* 52, no. 2 (Summer 1993): 257.

95 *PSZ* II, vol. 36, no. 36,662, articles 185 and 186; no. 36,663, articles 191 and 192 (February 19, 1861); and vol. 54, no. 59,250 (January 23, 1879); Kovan'ko, *Reforma*, 201-29 and 481; Simms, "Crisis in Russian Agriculture," 384-85.

Second, the alleged malthusian positive check on population by famine, of the kind Russia experienced in the early 1890s, must be called into question. Grigg's analysis of overpopulation in Europe states: "Crisis mortality has not for the most part been related to population pressure," a finding subsequently confirmed by others. In the drought and crop failure in Russia of 1891-1892, it remains quite uncertain how much, if any, of the vulnerability to crisis can be ascribed to population pressure, "and how much was ... linked to modes of production that accumulated few surpluses, were not very diversified, and were not covered by systems of insurance and solidarity as have been developed by the modern state."[96] In fact, if Nifontov's figures are correct, an immediate consequence of the famine was a dramatic increase in potato cultivation in an attempt to expand the crop base.[97]

Russian economic and social historians need to consider modern critiques of Malthus, which look upon population growth positively.[98] In particular, the "natural indolence" of Malthus's "Siberian boor" and the drudgery avoidance of Chaianov's self-exploiting peasant—both victims of their unrestrained fertility—require re-examination.[99]

> A crucial point is that in the past farmers have produced only as much food as they could eat and market, and markets often were inaccessible. The amount produced, therefore, was not a clear-cut measure of capacity to produce; to suppose so has led many persons to worry unnecessarily that additional food could not be produced to feed additional mouths.[100]

---

96 Grigg, *Population Growth*, 47; Susan Cotts Watkins and Etienne van de Walle, "Nutrition, Mortality, and Population Size: Malthus' Court of Last Resort," in *Hunger and History*, 10-11 and 28.

97 Nifontov, *Zernovoe proizvodstvo*, 225.

98 Ester Boserup, *The Conditions of Agricultural Growth* (Chicago, 1965); idem, *Population and Technological Change: A Study of Long-term Trends* (Chicago, 1981).

99 T. R. Malthus, *The Works of Thomas Robert Malthus*, vol. 2, *An Essay on the Principle of Population*, ed. E. A. Wrigley and David Souden (London, 1986), 104, 108 and 188; and Chaianov, "On the Theory of Non-Capitalist Economic Systems," in *The Theory of Peasant Economy*, 1-28.

100 Julian L. Simon, "The Effects of Population on Nutrition and Economic Well-Being," in *Hunger and History*, 229.

Population growth does not necessarily lead to disastrous consequences; a reluctance, unwillingness, or hesitancy by historians to entertain such a view has not been helpful. In contrast to Malthus, population increases may induce positive changes in the demand for goods, the supply of labor, the level of agricultural technology, the development and profitability of rural industries and domestic craft production, the creation of credit markets, and the cost of investment in infrastructure. The fundamental realignment of agrarian class relations in Russia during the 1860s, an immediate result of autocratic policy, produced direct, measurable benefits to the formerly servile peasantry, in spite of the absence of other structural changes in the rural economy. Moreover, too much emphasis has been placed on the inadequacies of the peasant commune, without corresponding attention to the potential for increased efficiencies resulting from the new market forces in land tenure relations that emancipation implied. In addition, commercialization of the rural economy may well have fostered more intensive cultivation, especially in already settled areas close to urban centers; and these processes must be distinguished from the Leninist view of capitalization, class differentiation, and immiseration of agrarian society. It is becoming increasingly clear that rural Russia was far from the road of capitalist development and was not even headed in that direction.[101] Finally, even with a hostile state policy toward the agrarian sector—as is often claimed for Russia in the last decades of the nineteenth century—endogenous responses to rural population growth may well have outweighed, if not overwhelmed, government intent.

In sum, the established orthodoxy of an overpopulated Russia with a malthusian crisis threatening or having actually occurred is in need of revision. And, all that this "crisis" has meant for a broader understanding of developments in the late Imperial period is now seriously in doubt.

---

[101] Chaianov, "On the Theory," 28; Bideleux, "Agricultural Advance," 200-1; and Heinz-Dietrich Löwe, "Differentiation in Russian Peasant Society: Causes and Trends, 1880-1905," in *Land Commune*, 165-91.

3

Serfs in Imperial Russia Demographic Insights[1]

Early marriage and large, patriarchal families have long been thought to be characteristic of domestic groups in Imperial Russia, and the extremely limited recent research that has been conducted on this subject has confirmed the findings of nineteenth-century ethnographers. Yet, the broader demographic framework within which these two features existed provides a more fundamental understanding of the social history of the Russian peasant. This article provides new insights into this demographic structure and examines its relationship to the ecological, cultural, and seigneurial factors affecting the peasantry.

The documentary bases of this research are the private papers of the Gagarins, a noble family, and, more specifically, the records of the Votchina office for their Petrovskoe estate, which was located in Borisoglebskii uezd, Tambov guberniia. This highly profitable estate of approximately 3,500 peasants was organized around the production of grain, most of which was marketed. Therefore, virtually all serfs performed corvee (*barshchina*). *Dvorovye liudi*, serfs with special skills or, more rarely, those in domestic service, received a monthly food allowance and an annual salary for their maintenance. All others worked the estate fields and, in return, were allotted land in sufficient quantity to provide for most of their household needs.

Because the bailiffs of the Petrovskoe estate were periodically required to compile household inventories (*podvornye opisi*), it is possible to study the demographic characteristics of the estate population. These inventories specified the age, sex, marital status, and labor obligations, if any, of each household member. In addition, the livestock holdings, housing and storage facilities, and grain reserves were recorded for every household or *dvor* (pl. *dvory*). Thus, the main estate office of the

[1] This article was originally published in *The Journal of Interdisciplinary History* 13, no. 2 (Autumn 1982):221-246.

Gagarin family in Moscow could readily assess the productive capacity of the estate and judge the level of the serfs' well-being according to the unit of production and consumption-the serf household. With the podvornye opisi, the central administrators of the family holdings could check on the bailiff in the field, seeing that he assigned to the serfs adequate amounts of corvee without undermining the peasants' long-run capacity to perform *barshchina*.

The bailiffs, with their assistants and scribes, were capable of recording this information correctly, given their extensive experience in bookkeeping. Internal demographic tests on the data show them to be extremely accurate. Blending procedures reveal little heaping in the reporting of ages. The age distribution of the population suggests little or no under-enumeration of infants or children, a problem frequently encountered in historical demography. The results from the household lists conform to biological determinants affecting human populations and fall within anticipated demographic parameters for a premodern peasant society. Also, the data are consistent over the years, although they span the tenure of several different bailiffs.

The archives of the Petrovskoe estate contain nine nominative lists, seven of which were compiled between 1813 and 1827. The remaining two date from 1850 and i856. These lists did not include all of the inhabitants of the estate, but only the servile population. The one exception was that the wives of serfs recruited into the army (*soldatki*) and their illegitimate children, although free persons, were included in the first seven lists if they continued to reside on the estate with relatives who were serfs, as was usually the case. Only the last two lists were cross-referenced, making it possible to trace the fate of every serf between the years 1850 and I856. On the earlier lists, although immigration is obvious, it is impossible to distinguish between emigration and deaths taking place during the intervening years between compilations.[2]

Monthly summary data from the registration of all births, deaths, and migrations were also found in the archives for the years between 1854 and 1858. The figures, however, cannot be verified and must be taken at face value. Nevertheless, they are of considerable interest, as

[2] Tsentral'nyi Gosudarstvennyi Arkhiv Drevnikh Aktov (Central State Archive of Ancient Acts) (hereafter TsGADA), f. 1262, op. 1, ch. I, ed. khr. 1495; op. 4, ch. I, ed. khr. 41, 59, 121, 186, 344, 357; ch. II, ed. khr. 822.

they provide an independent confir-mation of the nominative lists, and in themselves are revealing.[3]

Because the nominative lists of 1850 and 1856 were cross-referenced, they permit the calculation by sex of age-specific death rates. These rates, in turn, can easily be converted into mortality rates from which an estimate of the expectation of life at birth can be determined. Table I gives age-specific death rates, mortality rates, and estimates for life expectancy at birth for the village of Petrovskoe, the largest of the eight settlements comprising the Petrovskoe estate. Because the time period is short and the sample small, ten-year age intervals have been used. A comparison of the observed mortality rates with model life tables, in this case the Princeton "West" tables, produces the estimates for life expectancy.[4]

The mean of the estimates for the expectation of life at birth during the six-year period under consideration is 24.8 for females and 29.8 for males, discounting the age interval 20-29 for males, which, if included, would push the estimate up an additional 3.1 years. It has been excluded because in all likelihood the data for males of this age group are distorted by the heavy recruitment levies that were raised as a result of the Crimean War. Between 1850 and 1856, twenty-two serfs from the village were drafted, eighteen of whom were in their twenties. One possible explanation for the high estimate of life expectancy for this age cohort is that the bailiff and the village commune, in filling draft quotas, rid the estate of serfs in ill health or of poorer households, who were likely to have experienced higher rates of mortality if they had remained in the village. This would have been a sensible policy. In fact, the reason that the estimates of life expectancy for males exceed those for females for all but the youngest age group is probably due in part to recruitment, although higher female mortality resulting from complications associated with childbirth is obviously a much more significant factor.

3 TsGADA, f. 1262, op. 4, ch. II, ed. khr. 652, 800, 823, 842.

4 The "West" tables have been chosen because they have been found to be more applicable at high levels of mortality and because they encompass a greater range of variants than do the other three models. Ansley J. Coale and Paul Demeny, *Regional Model Life Tables and Stable Populations* (Princeton, 1966), 1, 35, II, 4-7; Thomas H. Hollingsworth, *Historical Demography* (London, 1969), 342.

Table 1
Mortality Rates and Estimated Expectation of Life at Birth: Village of Petrovskoe, 1850-1856

			Females				
	Population						Estimated Expectation of Life at Birth (E_o^o)
Age	1850	1856	Mean	Total Deaths	Death Rate	Mortality ($_{10}q_X$)	
10-19	71	70	70.5	4	9.5	91.3	29.3
20-29	63	52	57.5	6	17.4	161.7	24.2
30-39	67	59	63.0	8	21.2	193.9	25.1
40-49	50	54	52.0	9	28.8	255.2	20.6
			Males				
10-19	83	78	80.5	4	8.3	80.1	27.2
20-29	56	69	62.5	3	8.0	77.4	42.5
30-39	56	42	49.0	5	17.0	158.3	30.7
40-49	35	49	42.0	6	23.8	215.4	31.4

Source: TsGADA, f. 1262, op. 4, ch. II, ed. khr. 822.

In spite of the problem posed by recruitment, the overall expectation of life at birth in the village, based upon all persons between the ages of ten and forty-nine (except for males aged twenty to twenty-nine) can be calculated and was found to be 27.3 years. Such a level was common throughout much of preindustrial Europe and was even encountered in developing countries until the 1970s. Although by 1850 many western Europeans and Scandinavians could anticipate living 41.6 years, this was a recent development. In England and Wales, between 1781 and 1821, life expectancy remained relatively stable at 31.5 years. In France at the end of the eighteenth century, the expectation of life was 28.8 years. In both instances, however, local and regional variations were substantial, and the figures cover all social classes.[5]

Expectation of life at birth is a useful measure because it summarizes mortality conditions, although a complex of factors affect mortality, diet

[5] For a discussion of life expectancy in the 1850s, see E. Anthony Wrigley, *Population and History* (New York, 1969), 131, 169-175. See Hollingsworth, *Historical Demography*, 346-348, for data on England and Wales.

and private and public hygiene being the most important. For Petrovskoe, all that can be said is that the observed level of mortality was neither high nor low by the standards of Europe before 1800. There is no evidence to suggest that serfdom had a markedly adverse effect on mortality. Nevertheless, as there are at present no comparable data for other estates in Russia, the question of the relationship between serfdom and mortality must remain open. It is clear, however, that the demographic changes which took place throughout many parts of Europe during the first half of the nineteenth century had not reached Petrovskoe by 1856.

Combining the observed level of mortality with data from the household lists showing the age distribution of the village population makes it possible to estimate crude birth rates and death rates, although the latter are subject to a wide margin of error. To estimate these vital rates, however, requires the application of stable population theory, which poses a number of problems, for the population of Petrovskoe did not grow at a constant rate and the age structure changed over the years. In particular, bad harvests in 1821 and I848 coincided with mortality rates that were considerably above the norm. These demographic crises clearly destabilized Petrovskoe's population, complicating the use of stable population models. Sudden jumps in mortality will lower the estimate of the birth rate for the age groups which were most affected. But under more stable conditions, fertility is the primary determinant of the age structure of a population and mortality has only a small effect: in such a case, estimates of the birth rate would be scarcely affected even if only an educated guess of mortality levels were used.[6]

To estimate the birth rate and level of fertility for Petrovskoe, it is necessary to assume that the mortality conditions in the village for the years between 1813 and 1827 approximated those which have been observed for the period 1850 to 1856. This assumption is necessary because the earlier lists, those up to 827, do not permit the calculation of mortality rates, and the age distribution of the population in the years 1850 and 1856 was affected too much by the crisis of 1848. Nevertheless, this assumption is not unreasonable. Data in the archives on per-capita livestock holdings, land allotments, and housing conditions reveal no major change in the standard of living of the Petrovskoe

6 Coale and Demeny, *Life Tables*, I, 33-35; Hollingsworth, *Historical Demography*, 341; Louis Henry, *Manuel de démographie historique* (Paris, 1970; 2nd ed.), 36-37.

serfs between 1813 and 1856. If life expectancy were lower earlier in the century, then the result would be an underestimation of the birth rate. But, as will be shown, this possibility is very unlikely. In any case, with a stable population, a variation by as much as 2.5 years in the expectation of life would change the estimates of the birth rate by only 2 per 1,000. Thus, in spite of obvious difficulties, using the mortality levels of the 1850s to approximate those of the earlier period should not introduce a substantial error.[7]

Table 2 shows the estimated birth rate for both sexes combined, based upon the cumulative age structure of the village population between 1813 and 1827. For females, mortality level three from the Princeton "West" stable population model was used; for males, mortality level six. These levels approximate the mean of the estimates for the expectation of life at birth determined previously.[8]

It is clear that the method employed entails uncertainty. The discrepancy between the sexes is sometimes very large, although on a village level such differences were not uncommon. Those estimates of the birth rate that rely upon data from the age groups that were most affected by the crisis of 1821 are necessarily low and, therefore, have been placed in brackets.[9]

The seven household lists compiled between 1813 and 1827 reveal an exceptionally high, but stable, birth rate. The median of all eighty-four estimates covering persons born between 1754 and 1827 is 52.9; the mean is 52.6. Because these rates are among the highest ever recorded, under-enumeration of the village population can be discounted, further

---

[7] For the data on livestock holdings, etc., see TsGADA, f. 1262, op. 1, ch. I, ed. khr. 256, 1495; op. 4, ch. I, ed. khr. 41, 59, 121, 186, 249, 344, 357, 515; ch. II, ed. khr. 822. See also I. D. Koval'chenko, *Krest'iane i krepostnoe khoziaistvo Riazanskoi i Tambovskoi gubernii v pervoi polovine XIX veka* (*Peasants and the Serf Economy of Riazan' and Tambov Provinces in the First Half of the Nineteenth Century*) (Moscow, 1959), 164. In spite of Koval'chenko's assertion that the standard of living of the Petrovskoe serfs declined during the course of the nineteenth century, his own data, when recomputed on a per-capita rather than a per-household basis, show this not to be the case.

[8] Coale and Demeny, *Life Tables*, II, 78, 180. The procedure employed to compute the birth rates is described in I, 35.

[9] Ronald D. Lee, "Methods and Models for Analyzing Historical Series of Births, Marriages, and Deaths," in his edited volume *Population Patterns in the Past* (New York, 1977), 343.

Table 2
Estimates of the Birth Rate from the Cumulative Age Distribution of the Village of Petrovskoe (Males e_0^0 = 29.8; Females e_0^0 = 24.8)

Age Group	1813	1814	1818	1821	1824	1826	1827
0-4	54.2	55.7	53.1	[45.9][a]	[36.4]	[45.7]	[45.6]
5-9	54.6	55.1	57.3	53.6	[44.0]	[45.7]	[42.8]
10-14	54.0	53.7	55.7	58.0	51.5	51.0	[47.4]
15-19	54.0	54.5	53.4	55.8	55.1	54.3	51.8
20-24	56.5	52.1	54.1	56.2	54.7	52.7	51.0
25-29	52.5	52.6	50.3	54.1	53.4	54.1	52.1
30-34	52.7	52.3	52.0	53.9	53.1	52.6	52.4
35-39	52.8	53.3	53.2	51.6	52.4	52.5	50.9
40-44	55.7	56.4	51.3	53.7	52.4	50.4	49.6
45-49	51.2	54.1	55.6	51.7	52.4	52.5	53.0
50-54	52.4	51.7	51.3	58.4	55.7	50.7	50.9
55-59	60.1	59.4	49.3	49.2	52.1	59.4	56.6
Median	54.0	53.9	53.1	53.8	52.4	52.5	50.9
Mean	54.2	54.2	53.1	53.5	51.1	51.8	50.3

Source: TsGADA, f. 1262, op.1, ch. I, ed. khr. 1495; op. 4, ch. I, ed. khr. 41, 59, 121, 186, 344, 357; ch. II, ed. khr. 822.

a. Figures in brackets represent estimates of the birth rate that rely on data taken from the age groups that were most affected by the crisis of 1821.

attesting to the accuracy of the original data. In addition, the likelihood that the expectation of life at birth underlying these estimates should be lower, forcing an upward revision of the figures, is very small.[10]

With a life expectancy at birth for females of 24.8 years, their age distribution between 1813 and 1827 reflects a gross reproduction rate (GRR) of 3.46, a very high level of fertility. In other words, the average woman living through her childbearing period would give birth to almost seven children. The net reproduction rate (NRR), however, was

[10] Wrigley, *Population*, 62. See David M. Heer, "The Demographic Transition in the Russian Empire and the Soviet Union," *Journal of Social History* I (1968): 205, for a similar comment on demographic data for the empire in the post-emancipation period.

only 1.36, implying a high death rate. On the basis of observed mortality levels, the overall death rate would be 38 per 1,000—34 for males and 41 for females. The rate for females may be closer to reality, however, because of the problems in estimating male life expectancy that result from recruitment. But estimating death rates and the NRR involves a substantial margin of error. Small changes in the expectation of life produce great differences in death rates, and the figures just given must be considered in this light.

The subsistence crisis of 1848-1849 had a significantly greater effect on Petrovskoe than did the crisis of 1821, destabilizing the population to such an extent that almost any attempt to estimate the birth rate based upon the age structure from the last two lists (1850 and 1856) would be fruitless. The age interval 0-4, from the 1856 list, however, was obviously not affected by the crisis, and may be used to estimate very roughly the birth rate for the years 1852 to 1856. Surprisingly, although a rise in the birth rate might be expected as part of the recovery process following such a crisis, the figures suggest a birth rate of only 40.6 per 1,000. In all likelihood, fertility was lower as a result of Crimean War recruitment levies. Also, neither the illegitimate children of *soldatki*, nor their legitimate children born within nine months of their husbands' recruitment, were included in the lists, and these omissions push the estimate downward.

This last estimate can be compared with the monthly summary data of all registered births found in the archives for the same time period. Again, illegitimate children were not mentioned, and it is doubtful if stillborn children or those who died prior to baptism were included. From October 15, 1850, to October 31, 1854, the bailiff recorded 121 births in Petrovskoe, an average annual birth rate of 40.2 per 1,000. During the following twelve months, the birth rate fell to 27.2, whereas between November 1, 1855, and October 31, 1857, the birth rate dropped to a very low 19.4. Allowing for a nine-month time lag, the decline in the birth rate coincides precisely with the pattern of recruitment. Of the twenty-two males who entered the military between 1850 and 1858, sixteen were drafted between 1854 and 1855. By 1858, however, two years after the last levy, the birth rate had recovered considerably and stood at 32.9 per 1,000.[11]

[11] TsGADA, f. 1262, op. 4, ch. II, ed. khr. 652, 800, 823, 842.

Any short-lived system of registration is likely to result in an underestimation of the true rate. The one-time effort required for the compilation of a nominative list, which has as its sole criterion who is alive and present in a village, is much simpler than an ongoing process of vital registration, which involves the more complex, but statistically important, problem of infant births and deaths. Nevertheless, the pattern revealed by the data is intriguing, and the results, if low, may be considered minimum estimates.

It is not surprising that the birth rate at Petrovskoe was stable for at least seventy years, from 1750 to 1820, and if more data were available they would probably indicate that the birth rate remained stable over a much longer period, because population stability was a feature of many preindustrial societies. What is surprising is that the birth rate was stable at an unusually high level, a fact that had serious social and economic implications. First, the population of the village was young. The average age of all persons (on the basis of all nine lists) was 23.4 years, with 51.2 percent of the total population being below age twenty. Consequently, the dependency ratio for both sexes (the number of persons younger than fifteen or older than sixty relative to those aged fifteen to fifty-nine) was high, averaging 0.84 between 1813 and 1827. In other words, there was a very large number of non-working-age persons relative to workers. Second, the mean age at first marriage for females must have been very low, and there can be no question of family limitation at Petrovskoe, although much of the very high fertility was frustrated by death. Finally, it is likely that an annual growth rate of 0.5 to 1. 5 percent persisted in the village for over 100 years, from at least as early as the mid-eighteenth century, interrupted, but not offset, by periodic demographic crises. The uncertainty in the natural growth rate is a reflection of the problems involved in ascertaining the death rate.

From the household lists it is clear that the serfs of Petrovskoe did not follow the so-called European marriage pattern of waiting until their mid-twenties to wed, which resulted in as many as 40 to 60 percent of the women of childbearing age being left unmarried. Rather, the mean age at first marriage in Petrovskoe was 18.9 for females and 19.3 for males (Table 3). Usually, 30 percent of all females between the ages of fifteen and nineteen, and well over 90 percent of women between twenty and twenty-four, were married. Even when the crisis of 1848-1849 forced

Table 3
Average Age at First Marriage

	Males		Females	
	N	Average	N	Average
1813-1827	68	18.8	67	18.4
1831	--	--	5	19.1
1850-1856	38	20.1	61	19.5

Note: It is possible that a few remarriages have been included in the data, as a serf listed as single on one list and married on the following could have married more than once during the interval. For the period 1813-1827, the maximum interval was 3.75 years; between 1850 and 1856, a six-year interval is involved as there are no intervening lists. The discrepancy between the number of marriages observed for males and females between 1850 and 1856 is a result of recruitment. Single women in 1850 who were *soldatki* in 1856 obviously married during the intervening years. However, recruited serfs who married after 1850, but prior to entering the army or navy, cannot be distinguished from single males who were conscripted.

Source: Besides the nine nominative lists, TsGADA, f. 1262, op. 4, ch. I, ed. khr. 754.

the postponement of many weddings, by 1850 only 29 percent of all females between the ages of twenty and twenty-four were still single.[12]

As one nineteenth-century ethnographer put it in discussing the high incidence of marriage among the peasants of Elatomskii uezd, Tambov guberniia, 300 kilometers directly north of Petrovskoe, "only freaks and the morally depraved do not marry." In fact, women between the ages of twenty and forty, the most fertile group, were rarely without husbands, and permanent celibacy was virtually unknown (Table 4). Thus, it is likely that family and social pressures favoring early and universal marriage were compelling. The data suggest few deviations from this pattern.[13]

---

[12] John Hanjal, "European Marriage Patterns in Perspective," in *Population in History*, ed. David V. Glass and David E.C. Eversley (London, 1965), 101-143; François Lebrun, *La vie conjugale sous l'ancien régime* (Paris, 1975), 31-33.

[13] A. P. Zvonkov, "Sovremennye brak i svad'ba sredi krest'ian Tambovskoi gub., Elatomskago uezda," *Izvestiia Imperatorskago Obshchestva Liubitelei Estestvoznaniia, Antropologii i Etnografii* ("Present-day Marriage and Wedding Rituals among the Peasants of Tambov Province, Elato District," *Proceedings of the Imperial Society of Lovers of Natural Science, Anthropology, and Ethnography*), LXI, *Trudy Etnograficheskago Otdela* (*Transactions of the Ethnographic Division*), IX (1889), 30-31.

Table 4
Percentages of Females of Childbearing Age;
Single, Widowed, or with Husbands in Military Service

	Single					Widowed				
Year	15-19	20-24	25-29	30-39	40-49	15-19	20-24	25-29	30-39	40-49
1813	68.0	5.0	0.0	2.9	0.0	0.0	0.0	0.0	11.4	35.7
1814	71.4	5.6	0.0	2.9	0.0	0.0	0.0	2.8	5.9	36.7
1818	77.8	4.2	0.0	2.0	0.0	0.0	0.0	0.0	0.0	31.0
1821	74.1	8.3	0.0	0.0	0.0	0.0	0.0	0.0	12.5	25.9
1824	55.3	3.7	0.0	0.0	0.0	0.0	0.0	0.0	14.6	24.1
1826	62.2	0.0	0.0	0.0	0.0	0.0	0.0	0.0	3.0	24.2
1827	77.8	3.4	3.7	0.0	0.0	0.0	6.9	0.0	0.0	14.7
1850	91.3	28.6	6.5	5.6	2.0	0.0	2.4	3.2	9.9	34.0
1856	57.1	12.0	10.3	8.5	0.0	0.0	4.0	0.1	8.5	14.8

Source: TsGADA, f. 1262, op. 1, ch. I, ed. khr. 1495; op. 4, ch. I, ed. khr. 41, 59, 121, 186, 344, 357; ch. II, ed. khr. 822.

High fertility made large, structurally complex, three-generation households possible; they existed in great part due to prohibitions against household fission and, to a lesser extent, because of patterns of child adoption and household or family mergers. The household (*dvor*) is taken here to mean all persons living under one roof, sharing a residential unit that combined production and consumption functions in which virtually all property was held in common. The household lists clearly distinguished between the members of a *dvor* and those within it who were related by blood, so there is no confusion of household and family in the sources to complicate the analysis. But, in actuality, extremely few households contained non-family members.

Tables 5 and 6 show households by structure and households by generational depth, respectively. For comparative purposes, the classification of households in Table 5 is a slightly modified version of Laslett's system in which a family (or, more properly, a conjugal family unit) "consists of a married couple, or a married couple with offspring, or of a widowed person with offspring."[14]

[14] Peter Laslett, "Introduction: The History of the Family," in his edited colume *Household and Family in Past Time* (Cambridge, 1972), 29-31.

Table 4 *Continued*

Soldatki					Totals				
15-19	20-24	25-29	30-39	40-49	15-19	20-24	25-29	30-39	40-49
0.0	10.0	29.0	8.6	0.0	68.0	15.0	29.0	22.9	35.7
0.0	5.6	27.8	5.9	3.3	71.4	11.2	30.6	14.7	40.0
0.0	0.0	10.5	18.4	6.9	77.8	4.2	10.5	20.4	37.9
0.0	0.0	0.0	15.0	11.1	74.1	8.3	0.0	27.5	37.0
0.0	0.0	5.6	9.8	13.8	55.3	3.7	5.6	24.4	37.9
0.0	0.0	4.0	9.1	9.1	62.2	0.0	4.0	12.1	33.3
0.0	0.0	3.7	8.8	8.8	77.8	10.3	7.4	8.8	23.5
—	—	—	—	—	91.3	31.0	9.7	15.5	36.0
—	—	—	—	—	57.1	16.0	10.4	17.0	14.8

Between 1813 and 1834, mean household size (MHS) at Petrovskoe varied from a high of 9.0 in 1818 to a low of 7.7 in 1824. Given the observed life expectancy, age at marriage, household structure, and GRR, a mean household size of eight to nine persons comes close to the biological maximum. In other words, the demographics of the village were the primary determinants of household size, and household fission was of secondary, although still critical, importance. Households could not have been considerably larger unless the predominant structure of blood relations within them was altered by allowing multiple family households to exist which had members more distantly related than first cousins. But such households were rare.[15] The fact that MHS approached the biological limit is supported by evidence of the relative infrequency of household fission. Between 1813 and 1827, there were

[15] With an e_0 of 40, a GRR of 4.0, and an age at marriage of 20, MHS in an extended family structure that included foster mothers would be 12.4 persons, whereas with an e_0 of 20, a GRR of 3.0, and the same household structure and age at marriage, the MHS would be 6.0. Petrovskoe comes very close to the midpoint of these parameters. Thomas K. Burch, "Some Demographic Determinants of Average Household Size: An Analytic Approach," in *Household and Family*, ed. Laslett, 94-96.

Table 5
Households by Structure

	1813		1814		1818		1821		1824		1826		1827		1850		1856	
	N	%	N	%	N	%	N	%	N	%	N	%	N	%	N	%	N	%
1. Solitaries																		
a. Widowed	2		1		0		3		2		2		1		5		8	
b. Single, or of unknown marital status	0		0		0		0		0		0		0		2		3	
Total	2	3%	1	2%	0	0%	3	4%	2	3%	2	3%	1	1%	7	7%	11	9%
2. No family																		
a. Coresident siblings	0		0		0		0		0		0		0		1		0	
b. Coresident relatives of other kinds	0		0		0		0		0		0		0		1		1	
c. Persons not evidently related	0		0		1		1		1		1		1		1		0	
Total	0	0%	0	0%	1	2%	1	1%	1	1%	1	1%	1	1%	3	3%	1	1%
3. Simple family households																		
a. Married couples alone	0		0		0		0		1		1		1		0		3	
b. Married couples with child(ren)	6		7		3		4		10		12		9		7		18	
c. Widowers with child (ren)	0		0		0		0		0		0		0		0		1	
d. Widows with child(ren)	2		2		1		3		2		2		2		10		8	
e. Soldatki with child(ren)	1		1		1		2		1		0		0		0		0	
Total	9	14%	10	15%	5	8%	9	13%	14	19%	15	20%	12	16%	17	16%	30	24%

4. Extended family households																		
a. Extended upwards	2		1		5		6		4		2		3		5		11	
b. Extended downwards	0		0		2		3		1		2		2		4		5	
c. Extended laterally	3		2		0		0		2		1		3		3		3	
d. Combinations of (a) through (c)	0		0		1		3		3		5		5		2		6	
e. Extension unknown	0		0		0		0		0		0		0		1		2	
Total	5	8%	3	5%	8	12%	12	17%	10	14%	10	13%	13	17%	15	14%	27	22%
5. Multiple family households																		
a. Secondary unit(s) up	15		14		13		6		11		9		12		11		13	
b. Secondary unit(s) down	9		13		14		13		3		5		5		4		12	
c. Units all on one level	2		2		5		6		10		9		9		6		7	
d. Frereches	5		6		5		5		6		4		4		9		6	
e. Other multiple families	17		16		13		14		17		20		19		32		18	
Total	48	75%	51	78%	50	78%	44	64%	47	64%	47	63%	49	64%	62	60%	56	45%
Totals	64	100%	65	100%	64	100%	69	99%	74	101%	75	100%	76	99%	104	100%	125	101%

Source: TsGADA, f. 1262, op. 1, ch. I, ed. khr. 1495; op. 4, ch. I, ed. khr. 41,

Table 6
Households by Generational Depth

Number of Generations	Number of Households																	
	1813		1814		1818		1821		1824		1826		1827		1850		1856	
	N	%	N	%	N	%	N	%	N	%	N	%	N	%	N	%	N	%
1	3	5	2	3	0	0	3	4	3	4	3	4	2	3	11	11	17	14
2	25	39	25	38	16	25	28	41	31	42	30	40	31	41	53	51	63	50
3	29	45	32	49	39	61	33	48	36	49	38	51	38	50	37	36	41	33
4	4	6	3	5	3	5	1	1	1	1	2	3	3	4	1	1	1	1
Unknown	3	5	3	5	6	9	4	6	3	4	2	3	2	3	2	2	3	2
Total Households	64	100	65	100	64	100	69	100	74	100	75	101	76	101	104	101	125	100

Source: TsGADA, f. 1262, op. 1, ch. I, ed. khr. 1495; op. 4, ch. I, ed. khr. 41, 59, 121, 186, 344, 357; ch. II, ed. khr. 822.

sixty-eight first marriages and fourteen remarriages in Petrovskoe, but the number of households increased from sixty-four to merely seventy-six, or just one new household for every 5.7 first marriages. All of these new couples, however, remained in the village, and in almost every case, the bride entered the household to which her husband belonged. Neither marriage, nor even the death of a head of a *dvor*, precipitated the formation of a new household.[16]

Of the twelve households which undertook division between 1813 and 1827, in only two instances did the original *dvor* then have a new head. In contrast, thirty-two heads of household died during these fourteen years. The mean age at which a male serf became the head of a household upon the death of the former head (assuming female ascendants could serve in this capacity) was 38.5 years. For those males becoming household heads due to the division of one household into two, the mean age was 40.8 years. Thus, a nineteen-year-old male serf, recently married, who had a life expectancy at this age of thirty to thirty-five more years, could anticipate becoming the absolute head of his own household only after waiting an average of twenty years.

In the life cycle of a peasant household, precisely the time when a male serf could first expect to become a grandfather (between age thirty-five and forty-five) was when he first established sole authority in his own household. Expressed in terms of probability, using the model life tables, fully 74 percent of all twenty-year-old males would survive to age forty to become heads of households. This fact suggests that the anxiety of never getting out from under an elder's authority would have been limited. If these same serfs were fortunate enough to live an additional twenty years, the cycle would repeat itself. The mean age of a male head of household undertaking the division of his own *dvor* was 58.7 years.

The rate at which households divided was a key factor regulating village life. Maintenance of the life cycle just described permitted the continuous realization of a three-generation, multiple family household

---

[16] See also F. Barykov, "Obychai nasledovaniia u gosudarstvennykh krest'ian," *Zhurnal Ministerstva gosudarstvennykh imushchestv* ("The Customs of Inheritance for State Peasants," *Journal of the Ministry of State Domains*) LXXXI (1862): 8-9.

Table 7
Pattern of Household Divisions

Old Head/New Head	1813-1827	1850-1865
Same generation:		
Brother/Brother	4	7
Brother-in-law/Sister-in-law	2	7
Cousin/Cousin	1	3
Total	7	17
Different Generations:		
Uncle/Nephew	2	5
Aunt/Nephew	-	3
Father-in-law/Daughter-in-law	2	1
Father/Son	-	1
Father/Stepson	-	1
Mother/Stepson	1	-
Total	5	11

Note: Between 1850 and 1856, 22 households divided, but they formed a total of 50 households, 22 old and 28 new; that is, some households split into 3 or 4 separate households.

Source: TsGADA, f. 1262, op. 1, ch. I, ed. khr. 1495; op. 4, ch. I, ed. khr. 41, 59, 121, 186, 344, 357; ch. II, ed. khr. 822.

ideal. An absolute prohibition on household fission, however, would have resulted in the development of inordinately large, agnatically structured households similar to certain variants of the south Slav *zadruga*. But, as Table 7 shows, the pattern of household division is evidence of a clear intent to prevent *dvory* from becoming extremely large and having persons more distantly related than first cousins living together.

Equally important, between 1813 and 1827, when the number of households kept pace with net population growth, there was no separation of fathers and sons as households divided. The same holds true for the later period, 1850 to 1856, even though the number of households grew much faster than the village population for a short time. In part, the absence of father-son divisions is attributable to the demographics of the village, for only a small percentage of forty-year-old serfs would have had fathers still alive. But these few sons clearly did not separate from their fathers.[17]

Thus, as the average age of a new head of household was forty and sons rarely lived apart from their fathers, fission consequently must have occurred between two more distantly related and competing foci of three-generational authority in the household, thereby avoiding tensions created by unfulfilled desires for patriarchal and matriarchal rights. For most male serfs, the years between the ages of thirty-five and forty-five involved becoming head of a household, a new patriarch, and a new grandfather. Their wives enjoyed a similar change in status. As Table 8 shows, there was little deviation in this mean age, except in instances involving the death of the previous head of household.

The most intriguing question which emerges from the study of household division relates not to the demographic factors favoring large agnatic households but to the pressures which prevented serfs from dividing before the potential head of household attained the age of forty. The evils of indiscriminate or unregulated household division in the regions where repartitional land communes existed were well known to landlords and bailiffs in prereform Russia. In Petrovskoe it was felt

[17] Between 1850 and 1856, households divided at a rate that was three times higher than it was between 1813 and 1827, when the number of households grew by 1% annually. Estate records indicate that this high frequency of household division was both unusual and short-lived, beginning in the early 1850s and ending by 1858. (See TsGADA, f. 1262, op. 4, ch. II, the nominative lists.) The essential characteristics of the households of Petrovskoe were only slightly affected by the crisis of 1848-1849, meaning that the household life cycle observed between 1813 and 1827 persisted until 1850. Nevertheless, the formation of many new *dvory* in the 1850s sharply reduced MHS and the number of multiple family households. The age at which a male became the sole head of his household, however, was only slightly lower than had been previously noted, thereby attesting to the recent nature of increased household fission. Had such fission existed for more than three or four years, the drop in the age of the head of household would have been dramatic. As to the cause, recruitment levies during the Crimean War are most suspect. Because larger households could more readily afford the loss of an adult male worker, in times of heavy recruitment members of these households were more susceptible to the draft. To avoid this situation, many larger households divided into smaller ones which, for some unclear reason, the bailiff permitted, and which eventually resulted in the termination of his services.

Table 8
Percentage of Males Never Having Been Heads of Household, by Age[a]

Age	1813	1814	1818	1821	1824	1826	1827	1850	1856	Average
25-29	91.7	100	93.8	100	81.8	88.5	91.7	84.6	87.5	91.1
30-34	66.7	73.3	91.7	80.0	68.4	70.0	73.9	92.6	75.5	76.9
35-39	56.3	52.6	61.1	100.0	66.7	53.3	71.4	77.4	45.5	64.9
40-49	33.3	29.4	33.3	31.8	42.7	35.0	29.2	40.0	32.7	34.2
50-59	21.7	11.1	10.0	8.3	7.1	0.0	6.7	9.5	16.7	10.0

Source: TsGADA, f. 1262, op. 1, ch. I, ed. khr. I495; op. 4, ch. I, ed. khr. 41, 59, 121, 186, 344, 357; ch. II, ed. khr. 822.

a: Female heads allowed.

necessary to force the serfs to live in "artificially" large and complex households. The failure to maintain the delicately balanced life cycle underlying the three-generation, patriarchal household would result, it was believed, in the economic ruin of the peasants and the rise of social disorder on the estate.[18]

[18] A. Dmitriukov, "Nravy, obychai i obraz zhizni v Sudzhenskom uezde, Kurskoi gubernii," *Moskovskii Telegraf* ("Manners, Customs, and the Way of Life in Sudzha District, Kursk Province," *Moscow Telegraph*) (May 1831), 267; A. Rudnev, "Sela Golun' i Novomikhailovskoe, Tul'skoi gubernii, Novosil'skago uezda," *Etnograficheskii sbornik* ("The Villages of Golun' and Novomikhailovskoe, Tula Province, Novosil'sk District," *Ethnographic Collection*) (St. Petersburg, 1854), II, 107-108 (hereafter cited as *ES*); *Zapiski Lebedianskago obshchestva sel'skago khoziaistva za 1853* (*Transactions of the Lebedian Agricultural Society for 1853*), n.v. (1854), 358-359 (hereafter *ZLOSKh za* and the appropriate year); Ia. P. Rudnev, "Zametki po raznym khoziaistvennym predmetam" ("Notes on Various Economic Topics"), *ZLOSKh za 1854*, n.v. (1855), 300-301; M. N. Kishkin, "Dannye i predpolozheniia po voprosu ob uluchshenii byta krest'ian v Kirsanovskom uezde, Tambovskoi gubernii," *Sel'skoe blagoustroistvo* ("Facts and Presuppositions on the Problem of Improving the Way of Life of the Peasants of Kirsanov District, Tambov Province," *Rural Improvement*), n.v. (I859), 227-228; A. N. Nasonov, "Iz istorii krepostnoi votchiny XIX veka v Rossii," *Izvestiia*, Akademiia Nauk SSSR ("From the History of a Serf Estate of the Nineteenth Century in Russia," *Proceedings*, The Academy of Science of the USSR), VI (1926), 506-507; N. K. Brzheskii, *Ocherki iuridicheskago byta krest'ian* (*Essays on the Juridical Way of Life of the Peasants*) (St. Petersburg, 1902), 62.

When a new bailiff took over the operation of Petrovskoe in 1834, he noted in a weekly report to his supervisors in Moscow:

> Division among the peasants was permitted by the previous management. Everyone fulfilled his whims, which were carried to excess; nephew divided from uncle, brother from brother. And, at the present time, the peasant who has a one-*tiaglo* family cannot carry out either his estate labor obligations or household field work, and such families will always be poverty-stricken. Because of this, it is strictly forbidden for the village elders to divide households at will without the permission of the estate management.[19]

Identical sentiments were expressed by another new steward when he arrived at Petrovskoe in 1858:

> From the lack of attention [given by the previous bailiff] to the way of life of the peasants, many of them have divided into the very smallest of families, with poverty the consequence of such division, and with poverty comes theft, drunkenness, and many other vices.... For the future, the division of peasants is prohibited.[20]

The fact that some adult males on the Petrovskoe estate were prevented from living in the smaller, less complex households which they preferred is supported by evidence from the manuals of discipline kept by the various bailiffs. In 1818, there were 418 households on the entire estate. Over the next twenty-five years, approximately 125 new households were established by division, or five per year, with an average annual increase of slightly over 1 percent. More households wanted to divide. Between 1821 and 1840, at least thirty-seven households split without appropriate approval, resulting in corporal punishment for the adult male attempting to set up his own *dvor* and the reestablishment of a single household. The punishment records are complete for only nine of these nineteen years, so it is probable that even more serfs divided their *dvory* without permission, seeking to accelerate the rate of household formation.[21]

---

19 TsGADA, f. 1262, op. 4, ch. I, ed. khr. 496 (April 21, 1834).

20 TsGADA, f. 1262, op. 4, ch. II, ed. khr. 866 (November 7, 1858).

21 TsGADA, f. 1262, op. 1, ch. I, ed. khr. 889, 1129, 2419; op. 4, ch. I, ed. khr. 212, 248, 269, 308, 345, 380, 408, 428, 447, 463, 479, 503, 523, 542, 561; op. 4, ch. II, ed. khr. 824, 843, 863.

What the bailiffs felt to be the optimum size and structure of serf households did not coincide with the desire of many adult serfs to avoid the authority of an uncle, aunt, elder brother, or cousin. Nevertheless, the dangers of permanent subordination were both appreciated and avoided. The pattern of household division reveals that the diligent steward carefully regulated peasant households so as to balance the demographic pressures which would quickly dilute kinship relations within the *dvor* with the desire for the independent, smaller, but feared poorer, units that many younger adult serfs plainly wanted. The bailiffs, therefore, believed that they were forcing on these serfs a way of life which sacrificed interpersonal relations among household members for a higher standard of living in the *dvor* and greater harmony in the village as a whole. The fact of being a serf in Petrovskoe stripped individuals of the right to resolve these matters for themselves, and so to decide their own appropriate equilibrium level. The peasant household in Petrovskoe thus stood between the stem family, common throughout much of central and western Europe, and the very large Serbian *zadruga* or Baltic *Gesind*, which usually had from ten to thirty members. With roughly three-quarters of all village residents living at any one time in households with two or more conjugal family units, and with two thirds of all inhabitants similarly in *dvory* of three or more generations, virtually every serf would have experienced these circumstances for a number of years. For many, all of their lives were spent in households of this type.[22]

A male serf rarely left the household of his father, as long as the latter was still alive. Even excessive division did not result in a son separating from his father, according to the bailiff's comment in 1834. Upon the death of the head of a household, the economic consequences were minimal. Although a brother or son might inherit the rights and privileges of the patriarch, nephews and other brothers were not dispossessed. Rather, they remained within the household until they could establish their own multiple-family, three-generation *dvor*, thereby maintaining the ideal. With household life cycles compressed into twenty years, the essential characteristics of any individual *dvor* varied only slightly over time. As a result, and of great importance, fluctuations in a household's productive strength were minimized, and vulnerability to cyclical extremes of poverty and wealth due to changes in household composition

[22] Edward Shorter, *The Making of the Modern Family* (New York, 1975), 35-37.

were reduced. *Dvory* as units of production and consumption persisted as if economically immune to the births, marriages, and deaths occurring within them. This stability was the real goal of the bailiff, for the smooth transition of every household through life's demographic rewards and traumas underlay the servile system of labor.

In summary, estimates of life expectancy at birth in Petrovskoe show that the overall standard of living must have been similar to that of many parts of preindustrial Europe. Yet life in Petrovskoe took place in a framework of stable and very high fertility; early and universal marriage; and large, closely related, structurally complex, three-generation households. These circumstances, although by no means unique to Petrovskoe, varied considerably from the pattern of much of central and western Europe, where later marriage and lower fertility made smaller, simpler households more common, if not the norm. Households in much of Europe were more fluid. They had more varied structures and longer life cycles, experienced comparatively high rates of extinction, and lacked continuity.[23]

Marriage patterns, household structures, and fertility levels were not simply mandated by the bailiff. It is difficult to distinguish among the ecological, cultural, and seigneurial influences affecting the development of the domestic groups formed by the serfs. Nevertheless, the functional advantages of the observed demographic patterns were numerous. In an agricultural society having a very low level of technology and more than adequate amounts of arable land, as in Petrovskoe and much of the central agricultural region of Imperial Russia, labor was of the utmost value and was the primary determinant of output. Capital inputs were extremely limited, other than draft animals. But in Russia, the climate uniquely affected the structure of field labor. As a consequence of the extremely short growing season (five-and-a-half to six months instead of the eight to nine months in western Europe), the harvesting of winter and spring cereals and the plowing and sowing of the winter field all came in quick succession within the span of six weeks. From mid-July to the end of August was the *stradnaia pora*—literally,

[23] Wrigley, *Population*, 131-134, 192; Lebrun, *La vie conjugale*, 57-63; Shorter, *Modern Family*, 29-39; William J. Goode, *World Revolution and Family Patterns* (New York, 1963), 7-17; Laslett, *Household and Family*; Louise Tilly and Joan Scott, *Women, Work, and Family* (New York, 1978), 24-27.

the time of suffering. It was an agonizing period of exertion demanding that numerous tasks be accomplished simultaneously. A work team or tiaglo, a husband and wife together, proved to be the best allocation of labor resources. A single male simply could not complete all of the necessary field work if he were to allow the cereals to mature fully yet avoid the danger of an early frost.[24]

There thus emerged in Russia a clear differentiation of field labor by sex. During the *stradnaia pora*, women used sickles to cut rye, winter wheat, and sometimes oats, while the men reaped the other spring cereals with a scythe. The women then tied the grain into sheaves for drying; the men began plowing the winter field. While the men then sowed the next year's rye crop, the women started to cart the sheaves from the fields and, if time permitted, were assisted by their husbands. In general, plowing, harrowing, sowing, cutting hay, and harvesting with a scythe were men's field work; tending the kitchen garden and hemp field, raking hay, cutting stalks with a sickle, tying them, and transporting them to the threshing floor were women's field work. A partnership was essential. Single or widowed females were never included in a *tiaglo*, and rarely did males carry a full *tiaglo* alone. Of all males aged fifteen to nineteen—the interval during which they first assumed some estate field labor obligations and in return received a land allotment—38 percent carried no *tiaglo*, and none of these men was married; 32 percent carried a half-*tiaglo*, and only 4 percent of this group was married; and 29 percent carried a full *tiaglo*, at least three quarters of whom were married.[25]

---

24 Nikolai Kalachov, "Iuridicheskie obychai krest'ian v nekotorykh mestnostiakh," in his edited work *Arkhiv istoricheskikh i prakticheskikh svedenii, otnosiashchikhsia do Rossii* ("The Juridical Customs of the Peasants in some Localities," *An Archive of Historical and Practical Knowledge, Related to Russia*) (St. Petersburg, 1859), II, 25; Kishkin, "Dannye i predpolozheniia," 226; A. Smirnov, *Ocherki semeinykh otnoshenii po obychnomu pravu russkago naroda* (*Sketches of Family Relations According to the Customary Law of the Russian Folk*) (Moscow, 1878), 76-81; Nasonov, "Iz istorii," 518. See also Olga Crisp, "The Pattern of Industrialization in Russia, 1700-1914," *Studies in the Russian Economy before 1914* (London, 1976), 21.

25 The weekly reports of the bailiff of Petrovskoe to Moscow usually noted the tasks assigned to men and women during the previous seven days, and these documents reveal this division of labor. See also Mashkin, "Byt krest'ian Kurskoi gubernii, Oboianskago uezda" ("The Way of Life of the Peasants of Kursk Province,

To maximize output on the Petrovskoe estate, the bailiff had to maximize the number of work teams. In practice, this meant that the distribution of corvee obligations had to be synchronized with internal changes in household composition so as to avoid the under-utilization of labor. When a young couple married, they immediately formed a new *tiaglo*, further increasing the productive capacity of the estate. The earlier the serfs married, the sooner this economic benefit to the estate would be realized.[26]

But if young couples had needed to establish their own households, early marriages would have necessarily entailed problems of capital accumulation and engendered parental concerns regarding the premature loss of an adult laborer. Had the serfs of Petrovskoe found it necessary to delay marriage seven to eight years, until their mid- or late twenties as in western Europe, then the productive capacity of the estate and of all of the serfs' households would have been reduced by anywhere from 17 percent (assuming all single males over nineteen carried a half-tiaglo) to 35 percent (if males had no corvee obligations until marriage).

Oboian District,"), ES, V, 95-96, 101; A. Preobrazhenskii, "Volost' Pokrovsko-Sitskaia, Iaroslavskoi gubernii, Molozhskago uezda" ("Volost' Pokrovsko-Sitskaia, Iaroslavl' Province, Molozh District"), ES, I, 79-80; D. I., "Zametki o krest'ianskoi sem'e v Novgorodskoi gubernii," in *Sbornik narodnykh iuridicheskikh obychaev* ("Notes on the Peasant Family in Novgorod Province," in *A Collection of Juridical Folk Customs*), II, in *Zapiski Imperatorskago Russkago Geograficheskago Obshchestva po Otdeleniiu Etnografii* (*Transactions of the Ethnographic Division of the Imperial Russian Geographic Society*, XVIII (1900), 266. The percentages of men in a *tiaglo* are based upon the data in TsGADA, f. 1262, op. 1, ch. I, ed. khr. 1495; op. 4, ch. I, ed. khr. 41, 59, 121, 186, 344, 357; ch. II, ed. khr. 822. In all likelihood, more than 75% of the men in the last group were married, as the nominative lists often failed to distinguish between single males and those who had been widowed shortly after their first marriage. A recently widowed male between the ages of fifteen and nineteen would have formed a full *tiaglo* upon marriage and was formally obligated to fulfill his responsibilities until the next redistribution of land and corvee duties. Nevertheless, young single men from families with no other working-age males did, on occasion, carry a full *tiaglo*, with a mother, sisters, or younger brothers assisting in the field work.

26 Alexander Gerschenkron, "Agrarian Policies and Industrialization: Russia 1861-1917," in *The Cambridge Economic History of Europe*, ed. H.J. Habakkuk and M. Postan (Cambridge, 1965), VI, 749; Peter Czap, "Marriage and the Peasant Joint Family in the Era of Serfdom," in *The Family in Imperial Russia*, ed. David L. Ransel (Urbana, 1978), 115.

Roughly speaking, a figure of 20 percent of gross grain production is reasonable to consider as the amount that would have been lost if marriages had followed the "European" pattern. Gross income would have suffered comparably.[27]

Overcoming these problems was accomplished first by tying the execution of estate labor obligations to the right of the peasant to use an allotment of arable land, a practice common throughout all of the central agricultural region of Russia. This arrangement provided a new couple with immediate access to land, the most crucial capital input. Second, virilocal postmarital residence not only obviated the need for much additional capital accumulation but constituted a windfall for the groom's household. Often, the addition of a daughter-in-law increased a household's total arable land by 50 to 100 percent. Parents thus had a strong economic incentive to see that their sons married young. Third, the payment of a substantial brideprice (*kladka*) given by the groom's father to the bride's, enticed households to part with mature, unmarried female laborers. *Kladka*, in effect, redistributed wealth among households without upsetting patriarchal authority within them.[28]

Investigations into social stratification within peasant communities have usually centered on the differentiation of households (or other appropriate units) by wealth and status. But a patriarchal society is also highly stratified, for inherent in it is a relationship which cuts across all households and provides the basis for generational control. At its fundament, a patriarchal society entails nothing more than the movement of

---

27 The figures predicting the consequences of later marriage are based upon the total number of working person-years lived for all males between the ages of nineteen and fifty-four, the latter being the mean age of retirement for surviving males, using the estimate of life expectancy at birth determined above. Coale and Demeny, *Life Tables*, II, 7.

28 The literature on *kladka* is extensive. See, in particular, Kalachov, "Iuridicheskie obychai," 24; Smirnov, *Ocherki semeinykh otnoshenii*, 174-177; Mashkin, "Byt krest'ian," 23; V. P. Mukhin, *Obychnyi poriadok nasledovaniia u krest'ian* (*The Customary Manner of Inheritance for Peasants*) (St. Petersburg, 1888), 17-19, 135-136; A. Efimenko, "Krest'ianskaia zhenshchina," *Delo* ("The Peasant Woman," *The Cause*), VII (1873), 196-199; D. K. Zelenin, *Opisanie rukopisei uchenago arkhiva Imperatorskago russkago geograficheskago obshchestva* (*Description of the Scholarly Manuscript Archive of the Imperial Russian Geographic Society*) (Petrograd, 1914-1916), 3v; S. V. Pakhman, *Obychnoe grazhdanskoe pravo v Rossii* (*Customary Civil Law in Russia*) (St. Petersburg, 1879), II, 60-67.

wealth and power away from the young and toward the old. Within the patriarchal structure of Petrovskoe, the household was more than anything else a unit of exploitation, used so not only by the noble landlord as a member of the political elite but also by peasant patriarchs.

The attempt by the bailiffs at Petrovskoe to regulate and uphold large patriarchal households certainly provides evidence of significant interference by seigneurial authorities in peasant family life. In addition, the mutual economic interests of the bailiff and the patriarchs in maintaining such household structures imply a collusion of authority in the institution of serfdom. Of course, the economic and demographic stability of the continuously realized three-generation, multiple family household, and the higher levels of agricultural production which resulted from early and universal marriage, benefited every serf in Petrovskoe. But the conjunction of interests between the bailiff and peasant patriarchs did not merely improve the overall standard of material well-being for the serfs. This structure could well have provided the basis for social control, with the estate and serf elders deriving the greatest share of wealth and power.

4

Serf Diet in Nineteenth-Century Russia[1]

Over forty years ago Marc Bloch wrote, "it is very naive to claim to understand men without knowing what sort of health they enjoyed. But in this field the state of the evidence, and still more the inadequacy of our methods of research, are inhibitive."[2] Since then, medical research on underdeveloped countries has tremendously increased the knowledge of subsistence food requirements and of the physiological and psychological effects of an insufficient caloric intake or an unbalanced diet. Historians have made valuable use of this work. It is now clear that improvements in diet along with better public sanitation were the primary factors affecting the steady decline in noninfant mortality throughout much of Europe during the nineteenth century.[3] But higher mortality is not the sole consequence of malnutrition or undernourishment. People may live for years on an inadequate diet, and the Food and Agriculture Organization of the United Nations has described such a community: "The whole manner of life is adapted to an insufficient supply of calories, with results that are socially undesirable: lack of drive and initiative; avoidance of physical and mental effort; excessive rest."[4] While starvation, it is now known, is rarely a direct cause of death, was the serf population in Imperial Russia malnourished or undernourished, thereby either falling prey to sickness and disease or necessarily behaving listlessly?

This study will examine the diets of the inhabitants of one serf estate during the first half of the nineteenth century. The estate of Petrovskoe, the property of the princely noble family, the Gagarins, consisted initially

---

1 This essay was published in *Agricultural History*, Vol. 56, No. 2 (Apr., 1982), pp. 391-414

2 Marc Bloch, *La Société féodale* (Paris, 1939); trans. L. A. Manyon (Chicago, 1961), 1:72.

3 Edward A. Wrigley, *Population and History* (New York, 1969), 164-80.

4 Cited in Colin Clark and Margaret Haswell, *The Economics of Subsistence Agriculture* (New York, 1967), 19.

of six and eventually of eight separate villages with a total population of 3,354 serfs in 1812, increasing to 3,890 by 1833, and declining to 3,681 by 1850. The estate was situated in the southern part of Tambov province (*guberniia*) in the fertile black earth zone of the central agricultural region. As will be shown, there is nothing to suggest that there was anything unique about the Petrovskoe estate for this region. In fact, an 1837 land survey of Borisoglebskii district (uezd), where the estate was located, stated that the level of peasant well-being at Petrovskoe was "average," below the 5 percent of the villages in the district listed as "good."[5] In part, this was because the soil at Petrovskoe was of a more sandy and somewhat inferior quality than elsewhere and had a high salt content in places. This was true of many settlements along the Vorona River, on which Petrovskoe bordered.

Most adult serfs in Petrovskoe were bound to the person of their lord and exchanged their labor for the right to work an allotment of plowland, to share communal pastures and meadows, to possess a home and an adjacent garden, and to have limited access to estate woodlands. The unusual, but well-known aspect of peasant life in Great Russia, which existed in Petrovskoe as well, was that husband-and-wife work teams (*tiagla*) or—more rarely—single or widowed male serfs enjoyed the use of peasant plowland only as long as they fulfilled labor obligations in estate grainfields.[6] Thus, plowlands were constantly being redistributed and held only temporarily on the basis of the number of working couples in a household (*dvor*). In contrast, the lands immediately surrounding a *dvor* and the structures themselves were held in perpetuity and never reapportioned. Everyone in the village had the right to common pastures, hayfields, and estate forests.

At Petrovskoe, as on most estates, there was a special category of serfs whose status was usually hereditary, the *dvorovye liudi*, frequently translated as household serfs. Yet these serfs were rarely in domestic service and worked rather as scribes, skilled masters, or various unskilled laborers carrying out some of the more specialized functions related to the

5 Tsentral'nyi Gosudarstvennyi Voenno-istoricheskii Arkhiv SSSR [Central State Military History Archive of the USSR, Moscow], f. Voenno-uchenyi arkhiv [Military Science Archive], ed. khr. 19079, Borisoglebskii uezd.

6 In many places, corvée was commuted to a quitrent, though this was not the case in Petrovskoe or the surrounding region.

needs of a large agricultural estate. Household serfs and their families were entirely supported by the estate. They did not work the demesne or an allotment of peasant plowland, but received instead a monthly grain ration. Most working dvorovye males were also given one and a half to two rubles per month for *kharchi* (nongrain food purchases), an annual salary, and a sheepskin coat and kaftan every three years. The diet of the household serfs was supplemented from their own household gardens, and housing and outbuildings were provided by the estate. These serfs were also permitted to raise livestock.

Though the household serfs were only 6 percent of the estate population, they are of considerable interest because much is known about their diet—the estate kept very detailed records of its grain and cash expenditures. These data both complement and confirm information about the lives of the field peasants (*krest'iane*), who were the overwhelming majority of the estate population.

Virtually all adult household serfs, including elderly persons and widows, received two *pudy* (72.2 pounds) of rye flour and one quarter *chetverik* (a volume measure approximately equal to 36 pounds) of either buckwheat groats or ground millet per month. Their children, including orphans between the ages of six and sixteen, got half that amount, but for those below age six no food was provided. Except for times of crisis, this was the standard food allotment which did not vary over the years for which estate records have been preserved.

These rations by the estate provided every household serf with 607 pounds of rye flour and 76 pounds of buckwheat groats or ground millet per year, after allowing for the young children and few adults who were not given any grain directly. It has been estimated that on a diet consisting solely of coarsely ground cereal, approximately 470 pounds of milled grain per person per year are the subsistence minimum providing not only adequate carbohydrates, but most essential proteins as well.[7] The household serfs of Petrovskoe with their allowance of 1.9 pounds of milled cereal per day were thus well above this minimum, consuming per capita at least 2,100 calories in grain alone.

---

[7] Clark and Haswell, *Economics*, 53-54. See also E. C. Albritton, ed., *Standard Values in Nutrition and Metabolism* (Washington, 1954), tables 27-32, 68, 72, and 80.

Unfortunately, there is no detailed information on the livestock holdings of the household serfs, but it is certain that they were able to supplement their diet either by purchasing meat and other food products or by investing their salaries in domestic animals. In the early part of the nineteenth century, only dvorovye widows and orphans were provided with monthly kharchi. But beginning in 1819 most adult male dvorovye received an allowance for nongrain food purchases, a policy which persisted on the estate for over forty years. In 1827, the estate paid out a total of 3,096 rubles in salaries and 1,608 rubles in kharchi to the household serfs, or a per capita average of 19.86 rubles. In 1854, their income (salaries and kharchi) per capita was 22.71 rubles.[8] As the household serfs did not pay any taxes themselves (their financial obligations were redistributed among the field peasants), the figures above are for disposable income, and with a mean household size of 7.9 persons, these serfs had over 150 rubles to spend annually per household.

The records of the estate give little indication as to what the household serfs did with their money, though clothes, bast for shoes, household implements, and church offerings were necessary expenses. Also, most of the household serfs raised livestock, a form of savings which provided them with eggs, milk, and meat.[9] Information on local commodity prices suggests that the household serfs with their ruble income would certainly have been able to balance their predominantly cereal diet with more than adequate amounts of fats and meat protein. In fact, meat and poultry prices were quite low, with beef, mutton, and whole slaughtered pigs per pud only two to four times the cost of rye flour.[10] With a per capita kharchi of 6.76 rubles in 1827, if every household serf used only half that amount to buy meat, approximately 40 to 50 pounds could have been purchased annually. Adult consumption of meat, therefore, could have easily been 60 pounds per year and was probably much

8 Tsentral'nyi Gosudarstvennyi Arkhiv Drevnikh Aktov [Central State Archives of Ancient Acts, Moscow, hereafter TsGADA], f. 1262, op. 4, ch. 1, ed. khr. 377 and 649.

9 TsGADA, f. 1262, op. 4, ch. 2, ed. khr. 862, 1. 6.

10 Ibid., ch. 1, ed. khr. 20, 29, 44, 61, 74, 94, 101, 123, 137, 190, 210, 233, 273, and Khr. Kozlov, "Tseny raznykh produktov v 1796-1856 godakh," *Ekonomicheskii Ukazatel'* ["Prices of various products between 1796-1856," *Economic Indicator*] no. 35 (1857): 805-12.

higher. Fats and oils were the most expensive nutrients required for a balanced diet, but as only small amounts are needed daily, these serfs should have suffered no deficiency. Finally, it should be kept in mind that the garden adjacent to every peasant household provided fruits, vegetables, and oils.

For the field peasants, 94 percent of the estate population, it is much more difficult to evaluate food intake, though there are generally good data on grain yields and livestock holdings. It was widely agreed that in the six provinces of the central agricultural region two desiatinas (one desiatina equals 2.7 acres) of plowland per work team or *tiaglo* in each of the three fields were the standard minimum peasant allotment.[11] The Lebedian Agricultural Society, which was established in 1847 and chartered to operate in Tambov, Voronezh, Tula, Orel, and Riazan provinces, took a great interest in the size per tiaglo of peasant allotments and demesne obligations. When the Society sent out a questionnaire to its members, one landlord living in the same district as Petrovskoe wrote back in 1848: "Under the local conditions of Tambov guberniia, Borisoglebskii uezd, one peasant work team cultivates in each field for itself and for the lord 4 desiatinas (30 measures) without any exhaustion."[12] Thus, a peasant tiaglo would have 10.8 acres, excluding the fallow fields, which to support itself, while tilling an equal amount for the lord. At the Society's annual meeting in 1850, the unanimous opinion of the persons present was that "2 desiatinas of thirty in a field per work team is customary"; "a two-desiatina proportion between peasant allotment and demesne is regular in our region and is accepted as the norm by all landlords"; "in our black earth gubernii, we find a two-desiatina proportion in each field correct"; and "in reality, with us two desiatinas are customary everywhere, but where there is much land, there lords give the peasants still somewhat more against the two

11 There were two land measures commonly used in the nineteenth century, *desiatiny kazennye* or *ukaznoi mery* (state or statutory measure), often called desiatinas of thirty measures, equal to 2.7 acres, and *desiatiny khoziaistvennye* (agricultural), which were a third larger. In this essay all land measures will be expressed in terms of statutory desiatinas.

12 Kh. Kozlov," Khoziaistvennye voprosy," *Zapiski Lebedianskago obshchestva sel'skago khoziaistva za 1848* ["Economic problems," *Transactions of the Lebedian Agricultural Society for 1848*] (1849), 89. Hereafter cited as *ZLOSKh za* and appropriate year.

estate desiatinas per field."[13] By 1857, these evaluations were slightly modified. On land that was easy to plow and required no manuring, it was now felt that one work team could easily work three desiatinas for the lord and three for itself per field. Only if the land needed manuring once every nine to twelve years would a reduction to two desiatinas per field be necessary.[14] Therefore, according to the Society, in any one year a tiaglo could be cultivating from 10.8 to 16.2 acres for its own use, excluding the field lying fallow.

Additional evidence supports the conclusion drawn by the Lebedian Agricultural Society on the size of peasant allotments. In 1858, one landlord living in a district bordering on that of the Petrovskoe estate noted: "Almost all the peasants of Tambov district on corvee receive from the lords 2.5 statutory desiatinas in each field, very rarely 2 and, with some lords, are given 3 desiatinas."[15] For the serfs of the neighboring Kirsanovskii district just a few miles from Petrovskoe, five desiatinas per work team in all three fields were considered insufficient to support a serf household. Six desiatinas were quite common, but on estates where land was not plentiful. Seven was thought adequate, eight comfortable, and more than eight was unknown.[16] Peasants in the village of Tarbeevka, Spaskii uezd, Tambov guberniia, received three desiatinas in each field per work team from their lord, while the parish priest of the villages of Golun' and Novomikhailovskoe, located 220 miles directly west of Petrovskoe, in Tula guberniia, wrote that serf tiagla there had

13 *ZLOSKh za 1850* (1851), 90-91.

14 *ZLOSKh za 1857* (1858), 247-48. See also *Obozrenie Deistvii Lebedianskago Obshchestva Sel'skago Khoziaistva za pervoe desiatiletie s 1847 po 1857god* [*A survey of the activities of the Lebedian Agricultural Society during the first decade from 1847 to 1857*] (Moscow, 1858), 21.

15 I. R. Gruzinov, "Byt krest'ianina Tambovskoi gubernii," *Zhurnal Zemlevladel'tsev* ["The way of life of a peasant of Tambov province," *Landowners' Journal*] 2:5 (1958): pt. 6, p. 7; see also I. R. Gruzinov, "Vozmozhnost' uluchsheniia byta pomeshchich'ikh krest'ian (Tambovskoi gubernii)," *Zhurnal Zemlevladel'tsev* ["The possibility of improving the way of life of the peasants (Tambov province)]," ibid. 4:13 (1858): p. 4, pp. 20-21.

16 M. N. Kishkin, "Dannye i predpolozheniia po voprosu ob uluchshenii byta krest'ian v Kirsanovskom uezde, Tambovskoi gubernii," *Sel'skoe Blagoustroistvo* (1859) ["Facts and presuppositions on the problem of improving the way of life of the peasants of Kirsanov district, Tambov province," *Rural Improvement*] no. 1 (1859): 234-35.

2.67 desiatinas in each field, or 14.4 acres for cultivation, with another 7.2 in the fallow field.[17]

In the early 1820s, on the estate of M. S. Lunin in Kirsanovskii district, just twenty-five miles from Petrovskoe, the peasants had access to 19.6 acres per work team in three fields from their lord. But an additional 4.6 acres of arable per work team were rented by the serfs from nearby landlords.[18] On the barshchina (corvee) estates of the Iusupov family in Kursk, Voronezh, Kharkov, and Poltava provinces the average serf holding per work team fluctuated from 16.8 to 22.7 acres between the years 1831 and 1846.[19]

However, all these statements on the size of peasant allotments, though reasonably accurate, mask the fundamental chaos in the fields which was the logical result of strip farming, the constant redistribution of both peasant plowlands and the demesne, and poorly surveyed estates. In Petrovskoe, at least, the bailiffs were never sure precisely how much land the peasants actually had. As late as 1837, the bailiff of Petrovskoe was pleading with his superiors in Moscow: "A surveyor is vitally needed on this estate for the estate fields are so mixed up with those of the peasants that even the very sowers of estate cereals scarcely

17 *ZLOSKh za 1851* (1852), 390-92; A. Rudnev, "Selo Golun' i Novomikhailovskoe, Tul'skoi gubernii, Novosil'skago uezda," *Ethnograficheskii Sbornik* (hereafter *ES*) ["The village of Golun' and Novomikhailovskoe, Tula province, Novosil'skii district," *Ethnographic collection*] 1-6 (St. Petersburg, 1853-1864), 2: 106.

18 B. D. Grekov, "Tambovskoe imenie M. S. Lunina v pervoi chetverti XIX v. (material k voprosu o razlozhenii krepostnoi sistemy khoziaistva)," *Izvestiia*, Akademiia Nauk SSSR, *Otdelenie obshchestrennykh nauk* ["The Tambov estate of M. S. Lunin in the first quarter of the nineteenth century (material on the problem of the breakdown of the serf system of agriculture)," *Proceedings*, Academy of Sciences of the USSR, *Social Sciences Division*], ser. 7 (1932), no. 6, pp. 489-90.

19 A. N. Nasonov, "Khoziaistvo krupnoi votchiny nakanune osvobozhdeniia krest'ian v Rossii," *Izvestiia*, Akademiia Nauk SSSR, *Otdelenie Gumanitarnykh Nauk* ["The economy of a large estate on the eve of the emancipation of the peasants in Russia,"] ser. 7 (1928), nos. 4-7: 346-47. See also A. N. Nasonov, "Iz istorii krepostnoi votchiny XIX veka v Rossii," ["From the history of a serf estate of the nineteenth century in Russia"], ibid., ser. 6 (1926): 505-6. Neither Grekov nor Nasonov specifies which desiatina was the basis of measurement, but because they were researching estate records and not government documents, it is more likely that the larger agricultural desiatina was being used.

know what's what."[20] Twenty years later, in 1857, another surveyor was requested for much the same reason.[21]

On a few occasions, documents summarizing land usage on the Petrovskoe estate simply noted that each work team was given eight desiatinas to cultivate for itself in all three fields.[22] But from materials providing more detailed information, it is clear that the serfs regularly had access to 8.3-8.8 desiatinas per tiaglo, including at least some long fallow lands, arable but not part of the three-field rotation. Thus, in 1810, the actual allotment was 8.8 desiatinas; in 1827, 8.4; in 1843, 8.4; in 1849, 8.3; and in 1859, 8.8.[23] Only once is there any evidence of serf holdings ever falling below eight desiatinas for each work team. In 1857, a surveyor hired by the estate was instructed to allot the peasants only 7.67 desiatinas, though within a few months each was given an additional third of a desiatina.[24] It does not seem unreasonable to conclude that between the years 1810 and 1859 the serfs of Petrovskoe annually cultivated no less than 14.4 acres of plowland per work team and no more than 15.8, not counting the fallow. Thus, the Petrovskoe serfs were adequately provided with land though their allotments were well in line with serf holdings elsewhere in the region.

The archives of the Petrovskoe estate provide no information on grain yields on peasant lands. However, for the demesne it is possible to determine not only seed/yield ratios, but yields in terms of quintals and hectoliters per hectare, these being better indicators of the level of agricultural intensification, though some error necessarily ensues given the inadequacies of land surveying. Table 1 presents the yields on estate grain fields for the period 1811-1860, using all three measures. Tables 2 and 3 compare these yields with published data for other serf manors or peasant villages in the southern districts of Tambov guberniia or the southern part of the central agricultural region The figures reveal both sharp annual fluctuations and marked

[20] TsGADA, f. 1262, op. 4, ch. 1, ed. khr. 558, June 14, 1837.

[21] Ibid., ch. 2, ed. khr. 846, October 15, 1857, and May 20, 1858.

[22] Ibid., ch. 1, ed. khr. 121, January 1, 1818, 11. 60-61; ed. khr. 161, July 19, 1820, ll. 1-2; ch 2, ed. khr. 906, 1848, 11. 44-48; ed. khr. 866, May 11, 1859.

[23] Ibid., op. 1, ch. 1, ed. khr. 256, May 1, 1810; op. 4, ch. 1, ed. khr. 369, 1827-1828; ed. khr. 615, December 1843-April 1844, 11. 5-11; op. 1, ch. 1, ed. khr. 2830a, 1849, 1. 2-3; op. 4, ch. 2, ed. khr. 866, May 22, 1859.

[24] Ibid., op. 4, ch. 2, ed. khr. 846, May 22, 1858.

Table 1
Estate Grain Yields, 1811-1860

	Rye			Oats			Buckwheat			Millet
	Seed/ yield	Quintals/ hectare	Hectoliters/ hectare	Seed/ yield	Quintals/ hectare	Hectoliters/ hectare	Seed/ yield	Quintals/ hectare	Hectoliters/ hectare	Seed/ yield
1811-1820	4.9	6.4	9.5	4.6	7.1	18.5	4.8	5.2	8.6	—
1821-1830	7.4	9.9	14.5	5.9	9.2	23.7	5.0	5.4	9.0	—
1831-1840	5.7	7.6	11.1	4.3	6.7	17.2	4.6	4.9	8.2	—
1840-1849	6.5	—	—	5.5	—	—	6.3	—	—	22.6
1851-52, 1855-60	6.5	8.7	12.8	4.4	6.9	17.9	3.1	3.4	5.7	—
Average	6.2	8.2	12.0	4.9	7.5	19.3	4.8	4.7	7.9	—

Note: Except for 1840-1849, seed/yield ratios assume that 1.36 chetverti of rye, 2.81 of oats, and 1.25 of buckwheat were sown per agricultural desiatina. These figures are the mean sown per agricultural desiatina for seven years between 1816-1858. Also, as grain was measured in chetverti (a volume measure equal to approximately six bushels), weight per chetvert' varied depending upon the cereal and seed size. Over the years, rye averaged 143 kilograms/chetvert', oats 81 kilograms, and buckwheat 126 kilograms.

Sources: Data for 1840-1849 from TsGADA f. 1262, op. 1, ch. 1, ed. khr. 2830a. For the other years, data is based upon the annual cereals records of the estate. See I. D. Koval'chenko, *Krest'iane i krepostnoe khoziaistvo Riazanskoi i Tambovskoi gubernii v pervoi polovine XIX veka* [The peasants and the serf economy of Riazan and Tambov provinces in the first half of the nineteenth century] (Moscow, 1959), 83.

Table 2
Average Grain Yields (hectoliters/hectare)

		Yields		
Locality	Years	Rye	Oats	Buckwheat
Petrovskoe, Borisoglebskii uezd, Tambov guberniia	1811-1860	12.0	19.3	7.9
Vataryno, Lebedianskii uezd, Tambov guberniia	1825-1850	10.3	20.7	9.0
Nizhedevitskii uezd, Voronezh guberniia	1843-1849	14.1	29.9	8.2
Mokhovoe, Novosil'skii uezd, Tula guberniia	1834-1849	23.6	49.0	19.5

Sources: Table 1 and *Zapiski Lebedianskago obshchestva sel'skago khoziaistva za 1850* [Transactions of the Lebedian Agricultural Society for 1850] (1851), 204-5; *za 1851* (1852), 26-29; *za 1852* (1853), 86.

Table 3
Seed/Yield Ratios (1:x) (nongovernmental published sources)

Locality	Rye			Oats			Buckwheat			Millet			Period of Observation
	Av.	Min.	Max.	Av.	Min.	Max.	Av.	Min.	Max.	Av.	Min.	Max.	
Tambov guberniia													
Petrovskoe, Boris, uezd[1]	6.2	—	—	4.9	—	—	4.8	—	—	—	—	—	1811-1860
Borisoglebskii uezd[2]	14.0	—	—	—	—	—	—	—	—	—	—	—	1853, 1855-56
Tambovskii uezd[3]	9.3	—	—	8.8	—	—	9.1	—	—	25.7	—	—	Not specified
Lunin estate, Kirsan. uezd[4]	8.6	7.2	9.6	5.2	2.7	8.0	5.8	0.3	12.0	24.9	13.9	40.6	1823-1825
Kirsanovskii uezd[5]	8.0	—	—	4.6	—	—	7.0	—	—	—	—	—	Not specified
Voronezh guberniia													
Nizhedevitskii uezd[6]	8.0	—	—	—	—	—	8.0	—	—	15.0	—	—	Not specified
Kursk guberniia													
Iusupov estates[7]	6.4	2.0	10.8	5.4	2.0	8.0	3.9	0.0	9.5	—	—	—	1831-1859
Oboianskii uezd[8]	—	—	15.0	—	—	13.0	—	—	12.0	—	—	60.0	Best years

Sources:

1 See table 2.

2 *Zapiski Lebedianskago obshchestva sel'skago khoziaistva za 1853* [Transactions of the Lebedian Agricultural Society for 1853] (1854), 196-97; *za 1855* (1856), 270-73; *za 1856* (1857), 81-83.

3 I. R. Gruzinov, "Byt krest'ianina Tambovskoi gubernii," *Zhurnal Zemlevladel'tsev* ["The way of life of a peasant of Tambov province," *Landowners' Journal*] 2:5, pt. 4, p. 8.

4 B. D. Grekov, "Tambovskoe imenie M. S. Lunina v pervoi chetverti XIX v.," *Izvestiia*, Akad. Nauk SSSR, *Otdelenie obshchestvennykh nauk* ["The Tambov estate of M. S. Lunin in the first quarter of the nineteenth century," *Proceedings*, Acad. of Sciences USSR, *Social Science Division*], ser. 7 (1932) no. 6, p. 493.

5 M. N. Kishkin, "Dannye i predpolozheniia po voprosu ob uluchshenii byta krest'ian v Kirsanovskom uezde, Tambovskoi gubernii," *Sel'skoe blagoustroistvo* ["Facts and presuppositions on the problem of improving the way of life of the peasants of Kirsanov district, Tambov province," *Rural Improvement*] no. 1 (1859): 229.

6 P. Malykhin, "Byt krest'ian Voronezhskoi gubernii, Nizhnedevitskago uezda," *Etnograficheskii sbornik* ["The way of life of the peasants of Voronezh province, Nizhnedevitskii district," *Ethnographic Collection*] 1-6 (St. Petersburg, 1853-1864), 1:229.

7 A. N. Nasonov, "Khoziaistvo krupnoi votchiny nakanune osvobozhdeniia krest'ian," *Izvestiia*, Akademiia Nauk SSSR, *Otdelenie gumanitarnykh nauk* ["The economy of a large estate on the eve of the emancipation of the peasants," *Proceedings*, Academy of Sciences USSR, *Humanities Division*, ser. 7 (1928), nos. 4-7, p. 350.

8 Mashkin, "Byt krest'ian Kurskoi gubernii, Oboianskago uezda," *Etnograficheskii sbornik* ["The way of life of the peasants of Kursk province, Oboianskii district," *Ethnographic Collection*] 5:95-96.

local differences within the region. For example, the yields reported for the village of Makhovoe in neighboring Tula guberniia were more than double those of Petrovskoe and Vataryno in Tambov. Nevertheless, the data from these eleven localities, including Petrovskoe, reflect a level of agricultural productivity common throughout much of contemporary Europe. A 1:6-7 return on rye or a harvest of 8-9 quintals per hectare was the average in Denmark and France in the eighteenth century and in Germany to the mid-nineteenth century. For oats, a seed/yield ratio of 1:5 was the norm during the 1700s in Germany and not unheard of in France, though by the 1820s yields had improved to over 1:7.[25] By way of further comparison, grain yields in the USSR as a whole during the years 1948-1952 were 7.6 quintals per hectare for rye, 8.1 for oats, and 4.5 for buckwheat, scarcely different from Petrovskoe and the surrounding area a century earlier. (See Table 1.) By 1970, however, the yields of these three cereals had increased by an average 74 percent.[26] Nevertheless, some of the most fertile lands in mid-nineteenth-century Imperial Russia had yields virtually identical to the average hectare of land under cultivation in the Soviet Union one hundred years later.

For those familiar with the history of Russian agriculture, the grain yields observed for Petrovskoe and elsewhere may seem surprisingly high. But, in fact, the belief that Russia suffered from a relatively low level of agricultural productivity with average yields for all grains of 1:3.5, "lower than those of any European nation," is quite simply incorrect.[27] Most such assessments, especially by Soviet historians eager, it seems, to minimize seed/yield ratios, have relied upon official data annually reported by the governor of each province.[28] But numerous

---

25 B. H. Slicher van Bath, *The Agrarian History of Western Europe A.D. 500-1800* (London, 1962), 280-81 and 331-33; Jerome Blum, *The End of the Old Order in Europe* (Princeton, 1978), 144-45.

26 Food and Agriculture Organization of the United Nations, *Production Yearbook, 1970* (Rome, 1970), 44, 52, and 79.

27 Jerome Blum, *Lord and Peasant in Russia* (Princeton, 1961), 330.

28 A. S. Nifontov, *Zernovoe proizvodstvo Rossii vo vtoroi polovine XIX veka* (Moscow, 1974), 61, 72-76, 121-23, and 275, in a detailed study of governors' reports and data of the Ministry of Internal Affairs and Ministry of State Domains for the 1850s, estimates a seed/yield ratio of 1:3.5 for all of European Russia. Between the years 1780-1796 (minus 1781 and 1784) the average yield in Russia was

government bureaucrats, landlords, and contemporary scholars were extremely critical of the governors' figures or other official data.[29] Many landlords, fearful of increased military demands for cereal and forage, purposefully underestimated the size of the harvest, a practice particularly widespread in the central agricultural region.[30] The district police, responsible for collecting official data from sample areas, viewed this as a duty of secondary importance[31] and, in all likelihood, were easily bribed. Equally, the governors' reports, which were due on January 1, failed to include grain threshed after the New Year, often a considerable portion of the harvest.[32]

There was, indeed, virtually universal agreement among contemporaries that government figures were too low. According to the results of the 1765 questionnaire of the Free Economic Society, the average yield in European Russia was 1:4.9.[33] Subsequent articles in the Society's *Transactions* (*Trudy*) suggest an average seed/yield ratio of 1:5.[34]

1:3.2, according to the governors' reports. See N. A. Rubinshtein, *Sel'skoe khoziaistvo Rossii vo vtoroi polovine XVIII v.* (Moscow, 1957), 355-56. For the intervening years, see I. D. Koval'chenko, *Russkoe krepostnoe krest'ianstvo v pervoi polovine XIX veka* (Moscow, 1967), which shows rather constant yields of 1:3-4 for over half a century. Similar results using the governors' reports can also be found in V. K. Iatsunskii, "Izmeneniia v razmeshchenii zemledeliia v Evropeiskoi Rossii s kontsa XVIII v. do pervoi mirovoi voiny," *Voprosy istorii sel'skago khoziaistva, krest'ianstva, i revoliutsionnogo dvizheniia v Rossii*; V. A. Fedorov, *Pomeshchich'i krest'iane tsentral'no-promyshlennogo raiona Rossii kontsa XVIII-pervoi poloviny XIX v.* (Moscow, 1974), 55-56; and I. D. Koval'chenko, *Krest'iane i krepostnoe khoziaistvo Riazanskoi i Tambovskoi gubernii v pervoi polovine XIX v.* (Moscow, 1959), 39. See also N. M. Druzhinin, *Gosudarstrennye krest'iane i reforma P. D. Kiseleva* (Moscow, 1959), 2: 350, and P. I. Liashchenko, *Istoriia narodnogo khoziaistva SSSR* (Moscow, 1974), 1: 522 for identical estimates of grain yields.

29 See Nifontov, *Zernovoe proizvodstvo*, 16-34, for an overview of nineteenth-century opinion on the validity of government agricultural statistics.

30 D. P. Zhuravskii, *Ob istochnikakh i upotreblenii statisticheskikh svedenii* (Kiev, 1846), passim; Rubinshtein, *Sel'skoe khoziaistvo*, 358.

31 N. S. Golitsyn, "O merakh k ustroistvu istochnikov i rabot v Rossii," *Zhurnal Ministerstva vnutrennikh del*, no. 3 (1860): 9-15.

32 General'nyi Shtab. Pervoe otdelenie, *Voenno-statisticheskoe obozrenie Rossiiskoi imperii*, vol. 13, pt. 1, Tambovskaia guberniia (St. Petersburg, 1851), 63.

33 Rubinshtein, *Sel'skoe khoziaistvo*, 355-56.

34 See Michael Confino, D*omaines et seigneurs en Russie vers la fin du XVIIIe siècle* (Paris, 1963), 124-25.

Similarly, the topographical descriptions compiled by the army during the 1780s show an average harvest of 1:5.[35] During the nineteenth century D. V. Bludov and P. A. Valuev, both ministers of internal affairs, as well as P. P. Semenov, director of the Central Statistical Committee, expressed serious doubts as to the accuracy of official agricultural data.[36] I. I. Vil'son, editor of a well-known agricultural-statistical atlas, felt that while the governors' reports might be used to determine general trends in grain yields, the reported absolute levels for cereals sown and harvested were dubious, with figures for the black earth region in particular much too low. In other words, the governors consistently underestimated yields by roughly the same proportion. In the fourth edition of his atlas, Vil'son assumed a 1:4.5 seed/yield ratio for winter cereals and 1:4 for spring crops as the average for European Russia during the 1850s and 1860s in attempting to calculate the size of the total harvest.[37] In studies of various provinces by the General Staff of the army, official figures were also repeatedly criticized for underestimating grain yields.[38] The statistician L. V. Tengoborskii claimed government estimates of the harvest should be increased by approximately 10 percent.[39] Nevertheless, for Tambov province the General Staff and the author of an article in the official *Journal of the Ministry of Internal Affairs* held that seed/yield ratios were in fact from 25 to 40 percent above the figures reported by the governors and the Ministry of State Domains, who claimed yields for all cereals of only

---

35 Rubinshtein, *Sel'skoe khoziaistvo*, 355-56.

36 See Nifontov, *Zernovoe proizvodstvo*, 17-21 and 25-26.

37 I. I. Vil'son, *Ob'iasneniia k khoziaistvenno-statisticheskomu atlasu Evropeiskoi Rossii*, 4th ed. (St. Petersburg, 1869), 75-113.

38 Glavnyi General'nyi Shtab, *Materialy dlia geografii i statistiki Rossii, sobrannye ofitserami general'nago shtaba*, 25 vols. (St. Petersburg, 1858-1868), vol. 2 (Bessarabskaia oblast'), 230 and 233-34; vol. 3 (Vilenskaia guberniia), 443 and 451; vol. 4 (Voronezhskaia guberniia), 77; vol. 15 (Minskaia guberniia), pt. 2, p. 14; vol. 20 (Simbirskaia guberniia), 336 and 400; vol. 21 (Smolenskaia guberniia), 193; and vol. 25 (Chernigovskaia guberniia), 183.

39 L. V. Tengoborskii, *O proizvoditel'nykh silakh Rossii* (Moscow, 1854), 1: 198-99. See also K. S. Veselovskii, "Neskol'ko dannykh dlia statistiki urozhaev i neurozhaev Rossii," *Zhurnal Ministerstva gosudarstrennykh imushchestv* 52 (1857): pt. 1, pp. 26-37, which contends that long-run analyses of various estate records would result in a more accurate idea of grain yields than would data supplied by the Ministry of State Domains.

1:3.7.[40] A ccording to the so-called Mende Land Survey of the early 1850s, jointly conducted by the Surveying Corps of the Ministry of Justice, the Russian Geographic Society, and the General Staff, the average yield on thirty-four estates and villages in Borisoglebskii district (where Petrovskoe was located) was 7.5 for winter crops and 8.4 for spring cereals, including millet.[41]

The bailiffs of Petrovskoe kept no records as to the amounts of peasant arable assigned to each of the various cereals cultivated by the serfs for their own maintenance. But household grain inventories, though crudely measured in stacks, are a fair indicator of land usage. Rye, a winter crop, was the peasants' main foodstuff and must have occupied most, if not all, of the winter field. Oats and millet, the predominant spring cereals, could serve as both food and feed. Buckwheat, consumed as porridge, in all likelihood occupied as much as one quarter of the spring field during the 1850s. This, however, remains uncertain. Peas and potatoes, which were raised in very small quantities on estate plowlands by midcentury, if cultivated by the serfs, were confined to the kitchen garden along with vegetables and possibly flax. Hemp was grown in special enclosures adjoining each *dvor*, these being considered part of the household plot (*usad'ba*) as distinct from the allotted arable.[42]

Wheat, as is well known, was not a significant item in the diet of the nineteenth-century Russian peasant. Nevertheless, in October 1813, almost one-third of all the households in the village of Petrovskoe had some wheat which was probably sown in the winter field.[43] In an inven-

---

[40] Koval'chenko, *Krest'iane*, 39; "Ocherki Tambovskoi gubernii v statisticheskom otnoshenii" ["Sketches of Tambov province in statistical respects"], *Zhurnal Ministerstva vnutrennikh del*, no. 7 (1858): otd. 3, p. 41; General'nyi Shtab. Department. Pervoe otdelenie, *Voenno-statisticheskoe obozrenie Rossiiskoi imperii*, vol. 13 (Tambovskaia guberniia), 59-62. Similarly, for Riazan' guberniia, northwest of Tambov, the governor's reports show an average seed-yield ratio of 1:3.3 for the years 1841-1859. But a landlord living in Ranenburgskii district, a fertile grain producing region, though not a part of the rich steppe, wrote that the very worst return was 1:3. See M. Semenov, "Khoziaistvennyia oshibki ot neurozhaia" ["Economic mistakes from a crop failure"], *Zemledel'cheskii Zhurnal*, no. 6 (1 840): 448.

[41] TsGADA, f. 1357, op. 4, ed. khr. 1/211, 11. 3-4.

[42] Ibid., f. 1262, op. 4, ch. 1, ed. khr. 41, 121, and op. 2, ed. khr. 822.

[43] Ibid., ed. khr. 41.

tory of January 1, 1818, only five of the sixty-four households in the village possessed any wheat, though most of the small amounts which were grown may have already been sold or eaten by this time of year.[44] But after 1818, there is no further evidence of wheat cultivation by the serfs on their allotted plowlands. A grain inventory form used in February 1834 failed to provide even a column for wheat, as had been done on the two previous inventory documents.[45] The November 1, 1856, grain inventory showed no wheat stored by any serf household on the entire estate.[46]

Though any conclusions must be tentative, for the evidence is far from conclusive, wheat, which was probably a cash crop early in the century, rather quickly disappeared from the serfs' fields for reasons which remain unclear. By the 1850s and 1860s, few observers make any mention of serf wheat cultivation in the central agricultural region, except that in Kursk guberniia some peasants were still growing very small amounts, mostly for sale.[47] This decline in the peasants' use of wheat, especially for cash income, is rather surprising, as beginning in the 1830s this cereal became a major source of revenue for the landlords of this region, largely due to the increased export of wheat from Black Sea ports.[48] In 1854-1855, wheat on the Petrovskoe estate was expected to account for 32 percent of all cereal revenues, second only to rye.[49]

This decline in wheat cultivation by the Petrovskoe serfs is difficult to evaluate. If the serfs consumed the wheat, the nutritional effects of its now being eliminated from their diet would have been slight. In any case, it is doubtful that the first decades of the nineteenth century were

---

44 Ibid., ed. khr. 121.

45 Ibid., ed. khr. 515.

46 Ibid., ch. 2, ed. khr. 822.

47 M. Semenov, "Khoziaistvennyia oshibki," 445-46; *Voenno-statisticheskoe obozrenie*, 61; P. Malykhin, "Byt krest'ian Voronezhskoi gubernii, Nizhedevitskago uezda, *ES* 1: 232-33; Gruzinov, "Byt,"8 ; Kishkin, "Dannye i predpolozheniia," 234-40; and Grekov, "Tambovskoe," 491. For Kursk guberniia, see Mashkin, "Byt krest'ian Kurskoi gubernii, Oboianskago uezda," *ES* 5: 94.

48 Nasonov, "Khoziaistvo," 352-57; D. I. Ablov, "Razsuzhdenie Vitse-Prezidenta Obshchestva Dmitriia Ivanovicha Ablova, o stoimosti ozimago khleba," *ZLOSKh za 1847* (1848), 95-99; Khr. Kozlov, "Khoziaistvennye voprosy," *ZLOSKh za 1852* (1853), 141-42.

49 TsGADA, f. 1262, op. 4, ch. 1, ed. khr. 649, l. 93.

witness to either a short-lived attempt to improve the quality of life by "whitening" bread or the ultimate conclusion of a long-run decline in wheat cultivation. It is more likely that the estate wished either to prevent serf competition in the wheat market[50] or to force the peasants to use their plowland for cultivating rye which, being a heartier cereal, guaranteed a more regular return. Finally, the serfs may have found livestock a safer and more rewarding investment, thereby expanding oat production at the expense of wheat. But all of these explanations are little more than speculation. Nevertheless, it is far from sure that the end of serf wheat cultivation signified a net decline in cash income, adversely affecting the standard of living of the Petrovskoe peasant.

To return to the peasants' use of their allotted arable, a study of the serfs of Kirsanovskii district, Tambov province, states that peasants with access to 7 or 8 desiatinas of plowland per work team would sow two of rye, two of oats, and one of buckwheat or millet. Similarly, in Nizhedevitskii district, Voronezh province, 240 miles west of Petrovskoe, serfs with smaller allotments of six desiatinas per work team would plant two of rye,1.5 of oats, and 0.5 of buckwheat or millet. Grain yields, it should be noted, in both of these districts were on the average slightly higher than those of Petrovskoe.[51] The household of Feodor Nepriakhin, a so-called typical serf living in Tambov district, cultivated per tiaglo 2.5 desiatinas of rye, 1.5 of buckwheat, 0.5 of oats, 0.3 of millet, and 0.2 of flax, though his yields were 50 to 90 percent above those observed on estate lands at Petrovskoe.[52]

Household inventories from the village of Petrovskoe for 1813 and 1818 suggest an allocation of arable not unlike that found in Kirsanovskii and Nizhedevitskii districts, though rather different from Nepriakhin's use of the spring field in Tambovskii district. With allotments of 8.0 to 8.8 desiatinas per work team on the Petrovskoe estate, it seems reasonable that each would have assigned at a minimum approximately 2.7 desiatinas to rye, designated an equal area fallow, and split the spring field two or three to one in favor of oats over both millet and buckwheat combined. For the earlier period, it is unclear whether wheat was raised as a spring or winter cereal.

---

50 Nasonov, "Khoziaistvo," 343.

51 Kishkin, "Dannye i predpolozheniia," 234-38; Malykhin, "Byt," 232-33.

52 Gruzinov, "Byt," 7-8.

If the Petrovskoe serfs, in sowing roughly 2.7 desiatinas of rye, 1.9 of oats, and 0.8 of buckwheat and millet together, had yields similar to those on estate lands, then on the average each work team would have produced 24.2 quintals of rye, 15.6 of oats, and at least 3.2 of buckwheat (or millet).[53] Subtracting the seed needed for the following year and allowing for a milling off of as much as 15 percent by weight of rye and buckwheat, the net yield would be 17.2 quintals of rye flour and 2.7 of buckwheat groats (or ground millet). If the serfs working the land consumed as much as the household serfs with their annual ration of 607 pounds of rye flour and 76 pounds of groats or millet per person, then with an average harvest the arable allotted each work team would have provided enough rye flour for 6.2 persons and buckwheat or millet for 7.8 persons. The millings along with 12.4 quintals of oats could be used to support livestock. Also, it should be noted that the above figures assume an allotment of only 8.1 desiatinas per work team, though frequently the serfs had access to as much as one-half desiatina more. In sum, a husband and wife work team cultivating a full unit of land could readily support itself and over four other nonworking persons, while maintaining sizable livestock holdings. At the bare subsistence level, 470 pounds of milled grain per person per year, one work team could, if necessary, feed 9.3 persons, without them having to consume oats.

Actually, between 1810 and 1856, one tiaglo maintained on the average from 4.6 to 5.5 serfs (based upon thirteen years of data) or two working adults and only 2.6 to 3.5 additional persons. Only one-fifth to one-third of the village population lived in households having tiaglo/person ratios which would have resulted in grain production falling below the per capita level consumed by the household serfs. Only 4.4 to 12.5 percent of the Petrovskoe serfs were members of households producing below the subsistence level, including all those with no working age couples: households of widows, soldatki, and elderly persons, all

[53] Because precise data were not available for the amounts of arable used for growing either buckwheat or millet, to calculate a minimum estimate of serf grain production per tiaglo, it will be assumed that buckwheat alone was planted. This cereal had a much lower return than millet, even though the latter, when ground, lost almost 40 percent in weight. See *Polnaia entsiklopediia russkago sel'skago khoziaistva i soprikasaiushchikhsia s nim nauk*, vols. 1-12 (St. Petersburg, 1900-1912), 3: 1035.

frequently with children.[54] Thus, only a very small number of persons would have needed assistance from the village commune or the estate. In fact, most Petrovskoe households apparently raised excess cereal, and that part over the ration established for the household serfs was presumably used to meet tax obligations and other money dues, to purchase farm implements, draft animals, and household goods, to provide a cushion against below average harvests, and to enjoy a standard of living higher than that experienced by the household serfs.

The extent of serf wealth on the Petrovskoe estate is best indicated by the size of peasant livestock holdings. After land, livestock was the most crucial element in serf life. Without a horse or ox, a serf could not work his fields; without sheep, he could not clothe himself and his family; without cows, pigs, and domestic poultry, he could not break the endless monotony of a cereal diet and have access to high protein foods. Land, however, was rarely a variable commodity in the serf economy, while livestock, especially that raised for personal consumption, necessarily responded quickly to changes in the serfs' fortunes.

Besides the allotted arable the serfs of Petrovskoe were provided with common pastures (*vygon*) and hayfields (*senokos* or *lug*) to support their livestock. The pastures and hayfields as a matter of convenience were apportioned among each of the eight villages separately, though used communally within each village. Over the years, substantial differences developed in the amounts of such lands per work team in the various villages. In 1857, for example, the village of Petrovskoe, one of the two oldest settlements of the estate with little room to expand, had only 160 desiatinas of common pasture for 156 tiagla (125 households). But the village of Viktorovna, established in 1848, had roughly the same amount of land for half the number of work teams and households.[55] A new land survey undertaken in 1858 corrected these inequities, allotting to each village 1.33 desiatina of both common pasture and hayfield per work team to be used communally.[56]

Hay, oats, chaff, and millings were all sources of feedstuff, which were supplemented by the grass and stubble of the common pasture fallow

[54] TsGADA, f. 1262, op. 1, ch. 1, ed. khr. 1495; op. 1, ch. 1, ed. khr. 41, 59, 121, 186, 344, 357, 515, and ch. 2, ed. khr. 822.

[55] Ibid., op. 4, ch. 2, ed. khr. 846, October 15, 1857.

[56] Ibid., May 20, 1858.

Table 4
Livestock Per Capita, Village of Petrovskoe

	Horses			Cows					
	Working	Colts	Total	Mature	Calves	Total	Sheep	Pigs	Beehives
May, 1810	.40	.17	.57	.24	.17	.41	1.56	.69	.81
October 1813	—	—	.43	.24	—	—	1.80	.55	.33
April-May, 1814	—	—	.41	.25	—	—	1.60	.48	.30
January, 1818	.37	.17	.54	—	—	.40	1.89	.65	.23
April, 1821	.40	.19	.59	.23	.21	.44	1.55	.38	.40
Fall, 1823	.37	.10	.47	.27	.16	.43	1.11	.47	.36
May, 1824	.38	.09	.47	.27	.14	.41	1.17	.47	.38
May, 1826	.35	.13	.48	.26	.16	.42	1.32	.52	.45
May, 1827	.35	.14	.49	.26	.16	.42	1.32	.52	.43
February, 1834	.33	.16	.49	.19	.10	.29	1.06	.28	.29
November, 1856	.38	.12	.50	.18	.11	.29	1.36	.43	.12

Sources: Tsentral'nyi Gosudarstvennyi Arkhiv Drevnikh Aktov [Central State Archives of Ancient Acts], f. 1262, op. 1, ch. 1, ed. khr. 256 and 1495; op. 4, ch. 1, ed. khr. 41, 59, 121, 186, 249, 344, 357, and 515; ch. 2, ed. khr. 822.

field, and forest. With these feedstuffs, the peasants of the village of Petrovskoe were able to maintain the per capita levels of livestock shown in Table 4. Domestic poultry, mostly chickens, some geese and ducks, and occasionally turkeys, were also raised. Data on these were available only for 1843, when there averaged more than two fowl per person.

Additional sources suggest that such livestock holdings were common in the region surrounding the Petrovskoe estate. Kh. Kozlov was the Marshal of the Nobility in Borisoglebskii district and the author of numerous articles on the economic life of this area. In 1848 in an essay intended for entry in a competition organized by the Scientific Commission of the Ministry of State Domains he wrote:

> The number of horses in the district is almost equal to the number of males because each tiaglo must have a working horse along with a colt, which pulls the harrow; but there are a lot of heads of households who have, for each male worker, besides colts, two working horses, which they sell off every third or fourth year.... It is not possible to calculate exactly the number of cattle, but it is possible to say that each family, consisting of five male souls, has from one to three cows plus young calves.... The number of sheep reaches as high as five head for each male soul.... The number of pigs reaches as high as two head per male soul.[57]

By these standards, the serfs of Petrovskoe, though substantially below the maxima observed by Kozlov for sheep and pigs, had almost exactly the average number of horses and were well provided with cows. Similarly, a topographical description of Tambov province published by the General Staff of the Army in 1851 noted that nearly all peasant households had from two to seven horses, one to five cows, and five to ten sheep, along with an unspecified number of pigs and domestic poultry.[58] In the village of Feodor Nepriakhin, the "typical" serf of Tambov district, the richest households had six horses and fifty sheep per male worker; the poorest, only two horses and five sheep per male worker. Nepriakhin himself, described as neither rich nor poor with two male and three female workers in his household of sixteen persons, had

[57] Kh. Kozlov, "Sel'sko-khoziaistvennaia statistika Borisoglebskago uezda," *Izvestiia Tambovskoi Uchenoi Arkhivnoi Komissii* ["Agricultural statistics of Borisoglebskii district," *Proceedings of the Tambov Scholarly Archival Commission*] (1 890), 29: 86-89.

[58] *Voenno-statisticheskoe obozrenie,* 67-78.

nine working horses, five colts, two milk cows, one heifer, forty sheep, nineteen pigs, forty chickens, ten geese, three turkeys, and twenty-five beehives.[59] Certainly, his family was much better off than the majority of households in the village of Petrovskoe. Finally, a work team in Nizhedevitskii district, Voronezh province, consisting of approximately five persons of both sexes, could usually support three horses, one colt, one cow, two heifers, seven sheep, and four pigs.[60] These figures are not much higher than those for Petrovskoe.

The abundance of livestock in the village of Petrovskoe and the persistently low prices at local markets for meat, poultry, and eggs throughout the first half of the nineteenth century make it quite unlikely that the serfs regularly suffered from a protein deficient diet, especially a lysine inadequacy. Though there are no data on the amount of meat annually consumed per capita by the peasants of Petrovskoe, with two chickens, almost one and a half sheep, and half a pig per capita, some form of meat was certainly available on a regular, if not weekly or daily basis. Contemporary observers of peasant life in southern Tambov province and the surrounding region agree that meat was found on most peasant tables on major religious holidays, parish festivals, wedding days, and funerals. Only the very poor were unable to have meat on these occasions. In Kirsanovskii district, prosperous peasants ate meat daily, purchasing fresh and salted beef in autumn and winter, slaughtering sheep in the summer, and never being without eggs, cream, or oil.[61] Nepriakhin's family of sixteen put a chicken in its cabbage soup every Sunday, while consuming 578 pounds of salted beef, twelve lambs, eighteen geese, three fattened pigs, and twenty piglets over the course of the year.[62]

Fruits, vegetables, and oils, the remaining essential nutrients for a balanced diet, came from the kitchen garden, of which as much as half was devoted to hemp, a source of oil and livestock feed. Unfortunately, estate records for Petrovskoe provide no information on the subdivision of household plots (*usad'by*) by the amount of land allocated to dwelling space, outbuildings, livestock stalls, a threshing floor, and the kitchen garden. It is clear, however, that peasant plots even within the same

---

59 Gruzinov, "Byt," 6-8.
60 Malykhin, "Byt," 232-33.
61 Kishkin, "Dannye i predpolozheniia," 231.
62 Gruzinov, "Byt," 10-11.

village of the Petrovskoe estate were not uniform in size, though those in older settlements tended to be larger.[63] In 1848, the 522 household plots on the estate occupied a total of 397 desiatinas, the average size being 2.1 acres, in the village of Petrovskoe, 2.4 acres.[64]

Kishkin reports that in Kirsanovskii district a household plot of 600 square sazheni (0.7 acres), equally divided among buildings, threshing floor, and garden, was considered sufficient. But the amount of land given to serfs in the district for household plots was far from equal. Plots of 1,200 square sazheni (1.4 acres) were not uncommon, all of the additional land being used to expand the size of the garden. With a small garden of 200 square sazheni, a household could produce 200 heads of cabbage, 27 pounds of hemp oil, seed for next year's hemp crop, and an undetermined amount of other vegetables.[65] Cabbage and cucumbers were the most important vegetables, sharing the kitchen garden with smaller quantities of onions, beets, Russian turnips, carrots, radishes, potatoes, and an occasional apple tree or gooseberry bush.[66] Per capita intake of such produce, however, is impossible to estimate.

To sum up the dietary regimen of the peasants of Petrovskoe, the daily per capita consumption of rye, buckwheat, and millet of the household serfs was1.9 pounds (860 grams), and the evidence suggests a comparable if not slightly higher level for the field peasants. Potato consumption, generally linked to a "certain relative pauperization" in western Europe during the eighteenth century, was a minor nutritional component in the diet of the Petrovskoe serfs.[67] When cultivated, the potato was confined to the kitchen garden, having made no inroad as an open field crop. In contrast, the absence of wheat from the serfs' diet is of no significance in terms of nutrition. Of much greater importance, both the mythical family pig of French peasant households and

---

63 TsGADA, f. 1262, op. 4, ch. 2, ed. khr. 846, l. 65.

64 Ibid., ed. khr. 902, ll. 44-45.

65 Kishkin, "Dannye i predpolozheniia," 230 and 235-36.

66 *Voenno-statisticheskoe obozrenie,* 65; Kishkin, "Dannye i predpolozheniia," 23 7; Mashkin, "Byt," 97; and P. Troitskii, " Selo Lipitsy i ego okrestnosti, Tul'skoi gubernii, Koshirskago uezda" ["The village of Lipitsa and its surroundings, Tula province, Koshirskii district"], *ES* 2:8 4-85.

67 Michel Morineau, "The Potato in the Eighteenth Century," in *Food and Drink in History* (Baltimore and London, 1979), 31-32. (Originally published in *Annales, ESC* 25 [November-December 1970].)

the "self-same chicken" that was "plucked for the last two centuries" of the Old Regime were quantifiable realities in Petrovskoe between 1810 and 1856.[68] And, with one mature milch cow for every four to five persons, even if average annual milk production per cow was as low as an unlikely 750 liters, milk and other dairy products must have been readily available.

Excluding for the moment years of agricultural crisis, the peasants of Petrovskoe were, therefore, better nourished than their French and Belgian counterparts at the turn of the nineteenth century and certainly had a better diet than most persons living in developing countries today.[69] Clearly, the serfs of Petrovskoe suffered less of an imbalance between proteins, especially those derived from animal products, and carbohydrates than many French or Belgian peasants, for whom meat was limited to special feasts, altogether no more than a few pounds per capita per year. And the effects of a more balanced diet on the part of the Petrovskoe serfs would necessarily be manifested in an increased biological resistance and lesser vulnerability to epidemic disease.[70] In essence, the serfs were a healthier lot. Furthermore, while quantifiable measures are useful for evaluating diet from a physiological standpoint, the pleasures of variety in food, though very real, cannot be so readily counted. Nevertheless, this more favorable nutritional standing is relative and should not be exaggerated. According to modern schemes of analysis, the dietary regime of the Petrovskoe peasants fits into the broad cereal-based category, in which approximately half of all proteins (42-66 percent) are derived from various cereals, a characteristic of virtually all of Western Europe from the Middle Ages into the nineteenth century and, in most parts, even later.[71] Yet, though within

---

68 Jean-Jacques Hemardinquer, "The Family Pig of the Ancien Regime: Myth or Fact," in *Food and Drink*, 58-59 and 66-72. (Originally published in *Annales, ESC* 25 [November-December, 1970].)

69 Marguerite Burk and Mordecai Ezekiel, "Food and Nutrition in Developing Economies," in *Agricultural Development and Economic Growth* (Ithaca, NY, 1967), 334-37.

70 Emanuel Le Roy Ladurie, *The Peasants of Languedoc*, trans. John Day (Urbana, 1974), 103.

71 Maurice Aymard, "Toward the History of Nutrition: Some Methodological Remarks," in *Food and Drink*, 5. (Originally published in *Annales, ESC* 30 [March-June, 1975].)

the confines of the same dietary structure the serfs of Petrovskoe were normally better off.

But in an "abnormal year," usually the result of a crop failure, these serfs suffered a miserable, pathetic existence. In Petrovskoe, throughout the period under consideration, subsistence crises and epidemic diseases repeatedly assumed catastrophic proportions. In 1850, on the basis of a household list compiled that year, only 20.1 percent of the village population was between the ages of 0-9, though this age cohort averaged over 29 percent between the years 1813-1827. In effect, approximately one-third of this age group was lost to the village as a result of the 1848-1849 famine and cholera epidemic by a combination of sharply increasedi nfant and child mortality, delayed marriages, and in all likelihood famine amenorrhea. Similar, though less severe, effects are visible on the age structure of the village population after the bad harvest in 1821. The age group 5-9 in 1827, which was 0-4 years old during the winter of 1822 when food was in short supply, represented only 10.7 percent of the total population, down from an average 14.6 percent between 1813 and 1824.[72]

Following the crop failure late in the summer of 1833, the weekly reports of the bailiff provide a detailed account of the deprivation that resulted. As early as mid-September, the bailiff prohibited the serfs from selling their own grain and requested the burmeister to make the rounds of neighboring bazaars to ensure that this order was not violated.[73] In mid-October, the bailiff wrote to his superiors in Moscow:

> With every passing day the peasants come more and more to the [estate] administration with requests for grain for food, which the administration somehow avoids giving out, but some millet mixed with rye is given to the very needy and the poorest.[74]

Beginning in November, the monthly rye ration for household serfs was reduced 25 percent, from 51 to 38 pounds per capita.[75] In mid-December estate grain reserves were opened to the neediest of households,

---

[72] TsGADA, f. 1262, op. 1, ch 1, ed. khr. 1495; op. 4, ch. 1, ed. khr. 41, 59, 121, 186, 344, 357; ch. 2, ed. khr. 822.

[73] Ibid., op. 4, ch. 1, ed. khr. 496, September 17, 1833.

[74] Ibid., October 17, 1833.

[75] Ibid., October 15, 1833 and November 2, 1833.

and on December 28 every serf on the estate began receiving a monthly ration. To cite, again, from the bailiff's weekly report:

> For the distribution to the peasants of grain for food, prominent elders from the estate administration [that is, respected peasant functionaries] have been selected and they have taken an oath in the church of God, because the bailiff and the burmeister cannot attend to all this. They [the elders] were directed to give each person from the eldest down to two years old one chetverik [of rye] each month.[76]

One chetverik of rye is the equivalent of 38 to 40 pounds of grain, which would permit a daily ration of slightly more than 1.2 pounds per capita, only 63 percent of the normal daily allowance for the household serfs. Estate reserves, however, were not the only source of grain at this time as the serfs had not yet exhausted their own supplies.

With the new year, however, the situation became more critical. In January, the parish priest buried serfs to whom, because of so many calls for his services, he had not been able to administer the final sacrament. That indicates a significant increase in mortality.[77] On February 8 the bailiff entered in his report, "The peasants are in extreme need of feed for their livestock, they even strip the thatch from the roofs of their houses; nowhere can they find any to buy."[78] To keep the Moscow office accurately informed of the dimensions of the crisis, the bailiff in late February inventoried peasant grain and livestock holdings. In the village of Petrovskoe, two-thirds of the households were found to be completely without grain; over three-fourths without any rye. The inventory revealed only 243 chetverti of milled and unmilled cereal, no more than 358 quintals of various grains. Over half were oats, but only one-third of the amount needed for seed in the spring. Supplies of buckwheat and millet were virtually exhausted, leaving nothing to sow in May. Livestock holdings per capita of sheep, pigs, and milk cows were at the lowest level ever observed in the village, though the number of horses had so far held up remarkably well.[79] (See Table 4.) Certainly, the normally abundant livestock resources of the peasants mitigated

[76] Ibid., December 14 and December 28, 1833.
[77] Ibid., ed. khr. 507.
[78] Ibid., ed. khr. 496, February 8, 1934.
[79] Ibid., ed. khr. 515, February 1834.

the effects of the crisis by providing high protein foods. But the serfs were consuming their savings by eating more meat and poultry, undermining the quality of their diet for years to come because they had no alternative.

By late March, the depletion of estate grain reserves forced a further reduction in food assistance to the serfs, and for the first time the lack of foodstuff had an effect on draft animals. The bailiff reported on March 22, 1834:

> As regards the supplying of food to the peasants, each family has been personally inspected and many of them were found to be in a most sorrowful state, not having the means to feed themselves, [and thus] for four and more days have been without food, from which compassion and the howling of children have required that all possible measures be taken for the benefit of Your Excellency.... Out of necessity the monthly ration was fixed at 30 funty [one funt equals 0.9 pound] per [adult] soul, 10 funty per child, and besides the taking of a household inventory was ordered for an accurate evaluation [of the situation], because it has been found that many[households]d o not have any horses.[80]

Regrettably, a copy of this inventory was not found in the archives of the estate, though the need for a second report within the span of a month to determine the level of peasant well-being can only suggest, in light of the comments above, a substantial worsening of the situation since February. The monthly ration for adults now stood at 27 pounds and for children under age sixteen only 9 pounds, overall roughly 22 pounds of cereal per capita. With very few households able to supplement this ration with their own grain stores, for most persons daily consumption of grain was limited to 0.7 pounds, just 37 percent of the normal daily per capita intake of grain by the household serfs. This is less than 800 calories per day, far below any subsistence minimum, and it is inconceivable that an increased consumption of meat or poultry could make up for the substantial deficiency in food energy. Presumably the remaining livestock was weak and emaciated, and continued to be adversely affected by the crisis until pasture or other grazing lands became available sometime in the early spring. Equally, either slaughter or starvation had reduced the number of work horses

[80] Ibid., ed. khr. 496, March 22, 1834.

on the estate, leaving numerous households without any means of cultivating their fields.

By April, insufficient caloric intake undermined the serfs' ability to work. Undernourishment, for some in its sixth month, hindered the preparation of the spring field. In April the bailiff noted, "many [serfs] do not worry about the future." To him, the peasants appeared irresponsible and "lazy," especially "when they give their own lands over to strangers [non-estate peasants] to sow."[81] The bailiff's concern was genuine given this negligent attitude on the part of the serfs toward their own well-being. The estate manager felt that the peasants were "more accustomed to take out loans [of food grain] than repay debts, being convinced that their Master would feed them, even if they were more lazy."[82] But such languid and listless behavior as occurred during the spring of 1834 should be understood as symptomatic of prolonged undernourishment, from which these serfs were undoubtedly suffering. The inability of Russian society to eliminate such "great crises" as those of 1821-1822, 1833-1834, and 1848-1849 as witnessed in Petrovskoe was one of the major features separating Eastern and Western Europe in the nineteenth century. Indeed, more than anything else, the lowering of "the peaks rather than the plateau of mortality" constituted the vital revolution of the eighteenth and early nineteenth centuries.

> In other words, it was not so much a reduction of mortality in normal years that produced the downward secular trend of the death rate, but an unmistakable abatement of the "great crises." The disappearance of the plague above all, but also a very sensible mitigation of subsistence crises seem to have been chiefly responsible for the increase in life expectancy.[83]

Outbreaks of the plague in Russia came to an end not long after their cessation in the rest of Europe. But the old demographic world was not dead on the Petrovskoe estate. Subsistence crises persisted. Thus, the

---

[81] Ibid., April 12, 1834.

[82] Ibid., ed. khr. 518, September 1834.

[83] K. F. Helleiner, "The Vital Revolution Reconsidered" in *Population in History*, ed. David V. Glass and D. E. C. Eversley (Chicago, 1965), 85. See also Wrigley, *Population*, 165, and Jonathan D. Chambers, *Population, Economy, and Society in Pre-Industrial England* (Oxford, 1972), 11-12.

comparative success of the Petrovskoe serfs in exploiting their agricultural resources, which normally yielded food in greater abundance and of higher protein quality than was available to their peasant neighbors in the West, nevertheless failed to break the cycle of dearth and famine, even though such crises may have been somewhat attenuated by the generally higher level of well-being. Still, these serfs were farmers with large amounts of land, even if used extensively, and large numbers of livestock when compared to their European contemporaries. Though the broader geographic implications of this study remain as yet unexamined, there is little evidence to suggest that the standard of dietary well-being at Petrovskoe was substantially different from that of other peasants of the central agricultural region. Contemporary sources, both archival and published, indicate nothing unique about the size of land allotments, household plots, grain yields, or livestock holdings of the Petrovskoe serfs. And, thus, it was on a base of relative prosperity that the institution of serfdom, the degradation of man into property, existed.

5

Famine, Disease, and Mortality Patterns in the Parish of Borshevka, Russia, 1830-1912

The impact of nutrition on mortality in the European demographic experience is a matter of much dispute among historical demographers, and results have proved contradictory. Over the last decade or so, research has tended to place greater emphasis on exogenous factors affecting mortality. The autonomous role of disease, the non-nutritional factors affecting infant mortality, and the social dislocation rather than the nutritional stress attendant on crop failure are now given considerable weight. It seems certain that the Malthusian positive check of famine and famine-related disease played only a modest role in regulating long-term population growth. In playing down the role of nutrition, biological factors have come to the fore. For Livi-Bacci it is primarily human biological adaptation—the ability of the human body to adapt to nutritional stress rather than succumb. For a number of Scandinavian scholars, "the beginning of mortality decline can be explained only in terms of immunological changes and the establishment of a new equilibrium between pathogenic agents and their human hosts."[1] What remains of the relationship between mortality and harvest size or grain price fluctuations has focused on the harvest-sensitive portion of the population as the most likely victims in a subsistence crisis—the landless, the cotter, and the wage labourer.[2]

This essay was originally published in *Population Studies* 52, no. 3 (Nov. 1998): 357-368.

1 Massimo Livi-Bacci, *Population and Nutrition: An Essay on European Demographic History* (Cambridge, 1991); Alfred Perrenoud, "The Attenuation of Mortality Crises and the Decline of Mortality," in *The Decline of Mortality in Europe*, ed. R. Schofield, D. Reher, and A. Bideau (Oxford, 1991), 22; Gunnar Fridlizius, "The Mortality Decline in the First Phases of the Demographic Transition: Swedish Experiences," in *Pre-Industrial Population Change: The Mortality Decline and Short-Term Population Movements*, ed. Tommy Bengtsson, Gunnar Fridlizius, and Rolf Ohlsson (Stockholm, 1984), 71-114.

2 Patrick Galloway, "Basic Patterns in Annual Variations in Fertility, Nuptiality, Mortality and Prices in Pre-Industrial Europe," *Population Studies* 42, no. 2 (1988): 277-278, 290.

Nineteenth-century European Russia (excluding the Baltic provinces), essentially lacked a landless peasantry. Perhaps more accurately, the regulations governing servile relations, the actual practice of serfdom, the emancipation legislation of 1861, and the status of free, state peasants throughout the nineteenth century meant that most peasants were provided with an allotment of land, at times one that was not easy to part with. The portion of the rural population without access to a sizeable plot of land was quite small in nineteenth-century Russia compared to Western Europe. In spite of this entitlement to land, historians of all persuasions have projected a dismal image of rural Russian society, one repeatedly punctuated by crop failures, high cereal prices, famine, starvation, and epidemics of famine-related diseases. The litany of supposed weaknesses of the rural economy in Russia is well- known: adverse climatic conditions marked by a short growing season and uneven levels of rainfall; an open-field, small-scale, peasant system of cultivation (even on large manorial estates); periodic redistribution of the arable lands in a peasant family's possession, thereby discouraging capital investment or long-term improvements; a weak credit market; an undeveloped system of transport; absentee land ownership; and little direct investment or even interest in agriculture by serf owners and landlords. In all, with Russia experiencing one year in five of significant deficiencies in the size of its grain harvest between 1801 and 1914, hunger, misery, and sudden, sharp increases in mortality allegedly reigned.[3] But there has been no rigorous attempt, using appropriate methods, to assess the nature of demographic crises in Russia and their overall contribution to mortality and population growth.

In fact, it is fair to say that remarkably little is known about the demographic history of Imperial Russia. Most research in Russian historical demography has been thwarted by animosity towards the social sciences as practised in the West during the Soviet period, outright hostility, deriving from Lenin himself, to Malthusian population

[3] Geroid Robinson, *Rural Russia under the Old Regime* (London, 1932), 94-116; Jerome Blum, *Lord and Peasant in Russia from the Ninth to the Nineteenth Century* (Princeton, 1961), 326-333; R.E.F. Smith and David Christian, *Bread and Salt: A Social and Economic History of Food and Drink in Russia* (Cambridge, 1984), 286-287, 327-360; Arcadius Kahan, "The Tsar 'Hunger' in the Land of the Tsars," in *Russian Economic History: The Nineteenth Century*, ed. Roger Weiss (Chicago, 1989), 108-144.

theory, and general antipathy on the part of Soviet scholars toward church-related sources such as parish registers and confessional lists. With few exceptions, Soviet historians were ignorant of the key historiographic issues, and their training precluded consideration of these materials. The inability of western scholars to conduct research in Soviet provincial archives made it impossible to apply most of the methods and techniques of historical demography.

The opening of Russian provincial archives to western scholars in 1989 and the much improved intellectual environment inside the Russian Federation, both of which can only be welcomed, have generated considerable interest in historical demography. These developments will allow specialists on Imperial Russia to enter into discussions and debates long of interest to scholars elsewhere. The situation is not entirely satisfactory, however. Most parish copies of register and confessional lists were lost in the 1920s and 1930s when churches were closed in large numbers. Of the duplicate consistorial copies, many were lost in World War II or discarded in the 1960s and 1970s owing to overcrowding in archival depositories. Those materials which remain are often poorly inventoried and inadequately preserved. In the Tula State Provincial Archive, for example, actually an old church, broken windows in the cupola allow rain and snow to fall on the registers, which are housed on the top floor.

In Borshevka, the parish to be examined here, as in much of nineteenth-century Europe, there was a weak association between mortality crises and crop failure or famine. This fact goes against much received opinion regarding rural life in this region of Russia. Nevertheless, the pattern of mortality evident in the parish is distinguished by an extremely high incidence of infant, diarrhoeal diseases and childhood, infectious diseases. This unfavourable disease environment and resulting high rates of infant and early childhood mortality, it will be suggested, were more closely related to fertility levels, household size, housing conditions, and weaning practices than to annual or seasonal food availability and the nutritional status of the population. In other words, in a disease-driven society, the susceptibility to infection and the force of infection can to a considerable extent be determined by demographic factors, familial norms, and climatic constraints.

The parish of Borshevka, located in Tambov district and province, was in the heart of the central black earth or agricultural region, often described as a much depressed part of the empire in the latter part of the nineteenth century. In the words of one economic historian, this region was destined "to become the equivalent of Bengal."[4] Cereal production was the primary pursuit of the peasants, though in the latter part of the nineteenth-century seasonal outmigration of men grew in importance. Before the emancipation in 1861, 62 percent of the parish population were serfs, belonging to six different owners; 24 percent were state peasants, and six percent were single homesteaders, both groups which, though legally free, owed an annual quitrent to the state and were subject to its loose administrative authority. Of the remaining eight percent, half were soldier's wives or retired soldiers. The parish was approximately 18 kilometres by road from the provincial capital, Tambov, and consisted of five separate settlements located in close proximity. In 1884, of 248 peasant households in the parish, only nine (3.6 percent) were described as landless. Lands allotted to the peasants exclusively for their use averaged five acres per male. In addition, peasants had income from lands rented or sharecropped and from local and migrant wage labour.[5]

Borshevka was selected because of the completeness of its registers and because the parish had a population of over 1,000 persons throughout most of the period to be examined, 1830-1912, thereby limiting the impact of random fluctuations. Analysis had to be confined to the period after 1830 since before this infant deaths suffered from a misreporting of age, with many simply listed as aged one, and from serious under-registration. It should be noted that some under-registration of infant deaths, especially neonatal deaths, is in evidence until the early 1880s. Registers are lacking for the years 1836 and 1872, and these years are not included in the analysis. Of some importance here, the registers provide the cause of death in all but three percent of the cases.

The only detailed information on the age structure and size of the parish population comes from an 1864 confessional list, which itself suffers from a substantial under-registration of children under age seven who, in accord with Orthodox practice, were not required to

4 Peter Gatrell, *The Tsarist Economy, 1850-1917* (London, 1986), 34.

5 Tambovskoe gubernskoe zemstvo, *Sbornik statisticheskikh svedenii po Tambovskoi gubernii. Tambovskii uezd* (Tambov, 1886), 10-21.

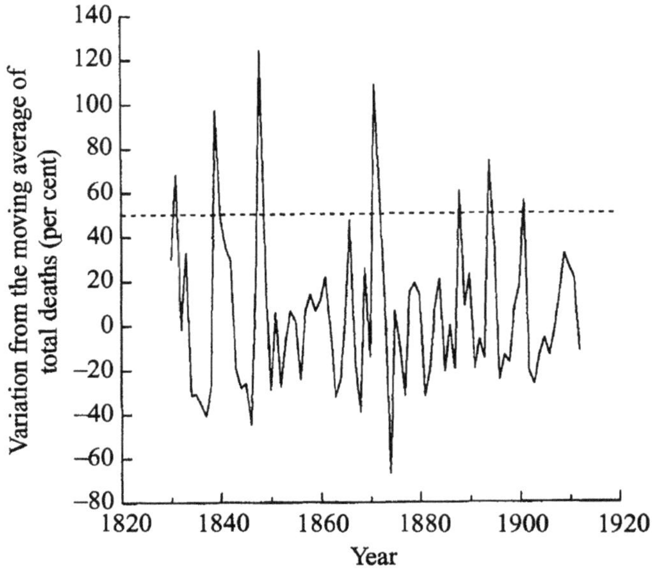

Figure 1. Annual fluctuations in mortality, Borshevka, 1830-1912.

receive the sacraments. Using parish registers to correct for this under-registration, I estimate a population of 1,470 in 1864. Applying the same correction factor to published summary data from a 1911 confessional list results in a population of 2,440 persons, reflecting a net growth rate of 1.1 percent per annum. Using the corrected data on the age structure of the population and the registration of deaths by age, I estimate a life expectancy in the early 1860s of 27 years at birth. Households in Borshevka tended to be large, averaging over eight persons, and usually consisted of multiple conjugal pairs and offspring, spread over three generations. Marriage was early and universal with over 77 percent of the population of women aged 15-49 married in 1864. To give a general indication of the high level of fertility, using Coale and Demeny's female, level 4, east model life table (e° = 27.5), the corrected cumulative age distribution of females for Borshevka for 1864 suggests a gross reproduction rate of approximately 3.5. The corrected age distribution for males produces a slightly lower result. All these characteristics are generally in accord with what little is known about the demographics of the rural population in the heart of

European Russia.[6] On the basis of Russian tax-census data, Blum and Troitskaya (1996) have recently concluded that there was little change in the overall level of mortality in Moscow province between 1750 and 1850, implying a well-established demographic regime.

As it was impossible to calculate death rates with any degree of reliability, mortality in this analysis was measured using the annual number of deaths, following a method developed by Livi-Bacci and Del Panta.[7] Thus, a normal series of deaths was created using a modified eleven-year moving average, excluding the two highest and two lowest values and then averaging the remaining seven years. This significantly reduced, but did not entirely eliminate, the effects of sharp peaks and troughs in the annual number of deaths. Defining a crisis as any year in which the actual number of deaths exceeded the moving average by more than 50 percent (the dashed horizontal line in Figure 1), it can be seen that Borshevka suffered elevated levels of mortality in seven of the 81 years under observation, 1830-1912, or 8.6 crises per 100 years. (As there was the potential for a crisis to span two calendar years, the same analysis was run using the agricultural year, from September to August, but the results were not different.) By way of comparison, central and southern Italy experienced 7.7 mortality crises per 100 years at the end of the seventeenth century.[8] By the early nineteenth century, the frequency had dropped to 5.1. On a rural parish level, Dupaquier,[9] though defining a crisis in a slightly different manner, found 13.3 crises per 100 years in the Bassin Parisien between 1681 and 1720, considerably higher than Borshevka. There is only slight evidence that would suggest any

---

[6] Ansley J. Coale, Barbara Anderson, and Erna Härm, *Human Fertility in Russia since the Nineteenth Century* (Princeton, 1979); Steven L. Hoch, *Serfdom and Social Control in Russia: Petrovskoe, A Village in Tambov* (Chicago, 1986), 65-90; Alain Blum and Irina Troitskaya, "La mortalité en Russie aux XVIIIe et XIXe siècles: Estimations locales à partir des Revizii," *Population* 1996, no. 2 (1996): 303-328.

[7] Massimo Livi-Bacci and Lorenzo Del Panta, "Chronology, Intensity, and Diffusion of Mortality in Italy, 1600-1850," in *The Great Mortalities: Methodological Studies of Demographic Crises in the Past*, ed. Hubert Charbonneau and Andre Larose (Liege, 1980), 69-81.

[8] Perrenoud, "The Attenuation of Mortality Crises," 29.

[9] Jacques Dupâquier, "L'analyse statistique des crises de mortalité," in *The Great Mortalities: Methodological Studies of Demographic Crises in the Past*, ed. Hubert Charbonneau and Andre Larose (Liege, 1980), 101-102.

stabilization of mortality in Borshevka throughout the period under consideration, in contrast to developments in much of northern and western Europe in the late eighteenth and early nineteenth centuries, if not before.[10]

But crises in Borshevka were marked by a low level of lethality, at least in comparison to the underlying trend or normal level of mortality. Only twice did deaths exceed the trend line by more than a factor of two. On average, a crisis resulted in an 84 percent increase over the normal series of deaths. Viewed in terms of excess deaths, total deaths in the seven crisis years averaged 94.4; in the 74 non-crisis years, there were 52.7 deaths.

Rye and oats were the principal foodstuffs of the Russian peasantry, and long-term price series are available for these crops for the nineteenth and early twentieth centuries.[11] Comparing annual rye and oat price fluctuations for Tambov (adjusted for changes in the general price level) with fluctuations in annual levels of mortality observed in Borshevka reveals little, if any, association between the two regardless of the lag employed—zero, one, or two years. In Figures 2-7, the x-axis denotes the percent fluctuation from the detrended rye or oat price with various lags; the y-axis, the percent fluctuation from the trend value of mortality as described above. In the seven years of crisis mortality in Borshevka (1831, 1839, 1848, 359, 1871, 1888, 1894, and 1901), rye prices the previous year, with which one would logically expect a strong relationship, were in six cases below the trend value, and in the seventh case only modestly above. For oats, again with a one-year lag, crisis mortality was not associated with high prices. For lag zero, for which the relationship between prices (or harvest size) and mortality is usually indirect, no association with rye or oat prices is in evidence.

The seasonality of the seven mortality crises, all but one (1901) occurring in the summer or autumn, further reduces the likelihood that they were subsistence-based. For nineteenth-century Russia, Smith and Christian[12] have described an annual dietary cycle in which the quantity and quality of food steadily worsened throughout the winter, spring

10 Perrenoud, "The Attenuation of Mortality Crises," 23-31.

11 B. N. Mironov, *Khlebnye tseny v Rossii za dva stoletiia (XVIII-XIX vv.)* (Leningrad, 1985).

12 Smith and Christian, 1984, pp. 335-338.

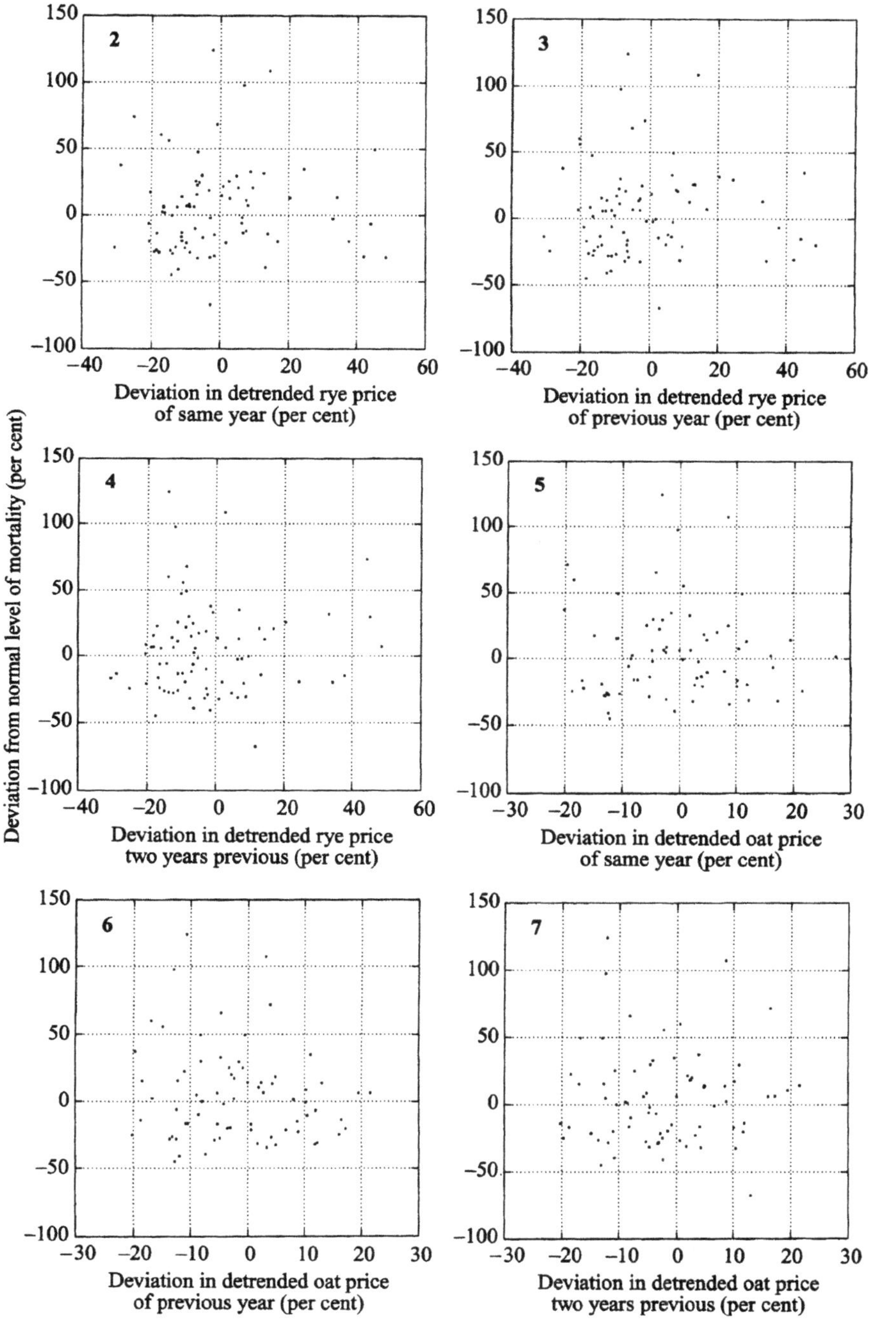

Figures 2-7. Mortality and rye/oat prices.

being the poorest part of the nutritional year. A subsistence crisis in seasonal terms would mean an earlier and more severe period of nutritional deficiency. In contrast, early summer saw rapid improvement and, though grain might still be in short supply, milk from pasturing cows, early vegetables, and wild plants were important dietary supplements. In eighteenth-century Sweden, mortality was highest in March and April, with the primary causes of death being nutrition-sensitive diseases—tuberculosis, influenza, the common cold, and other respiratory diseases.[13] Kaukiainen noted for nineteenth-century Finland that "'spring mortality' is exactly what can be expected during a dearth.... This is a well-known feature, and is generally seen as a mark of 'hunger mortality.'"[14]

In Tambov, rye prices fluctuated only modestly, rising 20 percent or more over their detrended value nine times between 1830-1912. But mortality in these years, regardless of the lag, was equally likely to go down as up, with no year reaching crisis levels as defined. In other words, price rises did not have uniform consequences. Tambov never witnessed a doubling of rye or oat prices in the years under consideration, as was often the case during subsistence crises *in ancien regime* France.[15] Lee has suggested that in England between 1548 and 1746 only extremely high prices (44 percent and higher over the trend) had any appreciable impact on mortality.[16] In Tambov, the maximum increase in the detrended rye price in any one year was just under 50 percent. Oat prices were more stable with a maximum increase of 27 per cent.

In all, the peaks of mortality in Borshevka appear to be wholly independent of food availability as measured by prices. High levels of

---

13 Tommy Bengtsson and Rolf Ohlsson, "Population and Economic Fluctuations in Sweden, 1749-1914," in Tommy Bengtsson, Gunnar Fridlizius, and Rolf Ohlsson (eds.), *Pre-Industrial Population Change. The Mortality Decline and Short-Term Population Movements*, ed. Tommy Bengtsson, Gunnar Fridlizius, and Rolf Ohlsson (Stockholm, 1984), 288-290.

14 Yrjö Kaukiainen, "Harvest Fluctuations and Mortality in Agrarian Finland, 1810-1870," in *Pre-Industrial Population Change. The Mortality Decline and Short-Term Population Movements*, ed. Tommy Bengtsson, Gunnar Fridlizius, and Rolf Ohlsson (Stockholm, 1984), 247.

15 Massimo Livi-Bacci, *Population and Nutrition: An Essay on European Demographic History* (Cambridge, 1991), 51.

16 Ibid., 58.

mortality at lag one usually suggest famine-based epidemic diseases or actual starvation. But crisis mortality in Borshevka was not related directly to food shortages (lag one). In this sense, Borshevka does not deviate as much from the European demographic experience as historians of Russia have been led to believe.[17] But an association at lag zero has been found for western and northern Europe, with adverse weather usually the cause behind both increased mortality and a bad harvest.[18] Excessive rain often increased the number of disease-carrying insect vectors; too little rain raised the bacterial count of the water supply; and excessively hot weather aided in the spread of food-borne diseases. All of these climatic fluctuations could have had a simultaneous, negative impact on the harvest. In addition, at lag zero, social dislocation attendant on crop failure, especially an increased level of human mobility as people searched for food, assistance, or employment, facilitated the spread of infectious diseases. But, for Borshevka, there is also no evidence to suggest that the weather adversely affected the harvest and mortality at the same time (lag zero). High cereal prices were not tied to weather conditions which aided in the spread of epidemic disease.

The age structure of crisis mortality can be used to assess its long-term and short-term impact. The age distribution of deaths in Borshevka reveals three distinct patterns of mortality: non-crisis mortality; non-cholera, crisis mortality; and cholera, crisis mortality (see Table 1). In non-crisis or normal years, 32.4 per cent of all deaths occurred to infants; 30.2 per cent to children aged 1-9; and 37.5 per cent to persons aged 10 and over. The five non-cholera, crisis years saw a major increase in the proportion of deaths of children (aged 1-9), who in these years comprised just under half (47.5 per cent) of all deaths, with the age group 2-4 most affected. In contrast, the two cholera epidemics in

17 Alfred Perrenoud, "The Mortality Decline in a Long-Term Perspective," in *Pre-Industrial Population Change: The Mortality Decline and Short-Term Population Movements*, ed. Tommy Bengtsson, Gunnar Fridlizius, and Rolf Ohlsson (Stockholm, 1984), 42-43; Galloway, "Basic Patterns," 290.

18 Gunnar Fridlizius and Rolf Ohlsson. "Mortality Patterns in Sweden 1751-1802: A Regional Analysis," in *Pre- Industrial Population Change: The Mortality Decline and Short-Term Population Movements*, ed. Tommy Bengtsson, Gunnar Fridlizius, and Rolf Ohlsson (Stockholm, 1984), 305; Alex D. Waal, "Famine Mortality: A Case Study of Darfur, Sudan 1984-5," *Population Studies* 43, no. 1 (1989) 20; Perrenoud, "The Attenuation of Mortality Crises," 36.

Table 1
Proportion of deaths by age and percent change, Parish of Borshevka, 1830-1912

Age	Non-crisis years	Crisis years (not cholera)	Crisis years (cholera)
<6 months	20.7	16.8 (-18.8)[a]	5.6 (-72.9)
6-11 months	11.7	10.8 (-7.7)	7.2 (-38.5)
1	12.1	16.1 (+33.1)	13.1 (+9.9)
2-4	12.2	23.0 (+88.5)	9.7 (-20.5)
5-9	5.9	8.4 (+42.4)	4.1 (-30.5)
10-19	3.4	3.0 (-11.8)	5.1 (+50.0)
20-59	17.4	10.3 (-40.8)	31.6 (81.6)
60+	16.7	11.6 (-30.5)	23.5 (+40.7)

[a] Percentage changes are given in parentheses.

Borshevka, 1848 and 1871—the most severe crises experienced between 1830 and 1912, with deaths more than doubling over the moving average—had unique effects on the age structure of the population. Cholera is particularly fatal to adults, and in Borshevka during these two years 60.2 percent of all deaths occurred in the population aged 10 and over.[19] The working-age portion of the population (aged 20-59) experienced a proportionate increase in deaths of over 80 percent.

As the mortality crises are rather evenly spread out over the period under consideration, it is possible to compare, albeit rather crudely, the distribution of deaths by age (Table 2). This is less exact than the proportionate shifts in the age distribution of deaths given above, but provides more detailed and useful information. In the 74 non-crisis years, total deaths per year averaged 53; in the five non-cholera, crisis years, the average was 93 deaths, or a 75.5 percent increase, which is quite close to the 71.4 percent average increase of these crises over the

[19] Louise Dêchene and Jean-Claude Robert, "Le cholerà de 1832 dans le Bas-Canada: mesure des inégalitiés devant la mort," in *The Great Mortalities: Methodological Studies of Demographic Crises in the Past*, ed. Hubert Charbonneau and Andre Larose (Liege, 1980), 240; Perrenoud, "The Mortality Decline in a Long-Term Perspective," 42; Patrice Bourdelais, "Cholera: A Victory for Medicine?," in *The Decline of Mortality in Europe*, ed. R. Schofield, D. Reher, and A. Bideau (Oxford, 1991), 128.

moving average. For the two cholera crises, because they come early in the period under consideration, the 85 percent increase in deaths (to 98 deaths per year), is lower than the average 118 percent increase over the moving average. The results are given in Table 2. Though they suffer from obvious distortions, they still give a good understanding of the three distinct patterns of mortality.

Crisis mortality, as is to be expected, meant an increase in the number of deaths at all ages. But, in non-cholera crises, the increase in deaths for adults (20-59) was negligible. Those aged 60 and over experienced a 21 percent increase; infant mortality rose by just under 50 percent. But the most dramatic effect was on children (aged 1-9), for whom the average annual number of deaths almost tripled. Thus, crisis mortality in non-cholera years essentially meant a shift in age-specific deaths from the very young (infants) to the young (children). Most of the excess deaths were children, not infants, adolescents, adults, or the elderly.

In the two cholera years, deaths in the population aged 20 and over tripled. Infants six months and older and children aged 1-9 had less dramatic increases of 14 percent and 63 percent respectively, while the number of deaths of infants under six months was cut in half. For 1871, part of the decline in infant deaths can be attributed to fewer births, presumably owing to the death of pregnant women and to a higher than normal

Table 2
Distribution of Deaths by Age, Parish of Borshevka, 1830-1912

Age	Non-crisis years	Crisis years (not cholera)	Crisis years (cholera)
<6 months	11.0	15.6	5.5
6-11 months	6.2	10.0	7.1
1	6.4	15.0	13.0
2-4	6.5	21.4	9.5
5-9	3.1	7.8	4.0
10-19	1.8	2.8	5.0
20-59	9.2	9.6	31.0
60+	8.9	10.8	23.0
Average deaths per year	53	93	98

level of spontaneous abortions among women suffering from cholera. But this was not the case in 1848, and there remains the likelihood that the recording of infant deaths was less accurate during these crisis years. Of greater import, cholera swept away a significant portion of the adult and elderly population. Assuming an age distribution in 1848 and 1871 similar to that of the corrected 1864 confessional list, just under five percent of the adult, working-age population and over a quarter of the elderly would have died in each of the two cholera epidemics.

Both patterns of crisis mortality in Borshevka, cholera and non-cholera, differ from the age distribution of deaths commonly thought to accompany famine. Perrenoud, Watkins and Menken, Walter and Schofield, Seaman, and Jannetta have noted that famine disproportionately affects both children and adults, with less impact on infants and the elderly.[20] Dyson, in his analysis of South Asian famines, described a normal pattern of mortality quite similar to that in Borshevka—high mortality in infancy, childhood, and at old ages[21]. But the proportional changes in the distribution of deaths by age during years of famine showed that children and adults suffered most, as other research has found.[22] In contrast, in Borshevka, non-cholera crises left the adult population intact, and neither the current reproductive nor productive capacity of the parish

[20] Perrenoud, "Tthe Mortality Decline in a Long-Term Perspective," 43; Susan Cott Watkins and Jane Menken, "Famines in Historical Perspectives," *Population and Development Review* 11, no. 4 (1985): 654-656; John Walter and Roger Schofield "Famine, Disease and Crisis Mortality in Early Modern Society," in *Famine, Disease, and the Social Order in Early Modern Society*, ed. John Walter and Roger Schofield (Cambridge, 1989), 26; John Seaman, "Famine Mortality in Ethiopia and Sudan," in *Mortality in Sub-Saharan Africa*, ed. Etienne van de Walle, Gilles Pison, and Mpembele Sala-Diakanda (Oxford, 1992), 363-364; and Ann Bowman Jannetta, "Famine Mortality in Nineteenth-Century Japan: The Evidence from a Temple Death Register," *Population Studies* 46, no. 3 (1992): 433.

[21] Tim Dyson, "On the Demography of South Asian Famines," *Population Studies* 45, nos. 1 and 2 (1991): 21-24, 289, 294-296.

[22] Hans-Oluf Hansen, "Some Age Structural Consequences of Mortality Variations in Pre-Transitional Iceland and Sweden," in Hubert Charbonneau and Andre Larose (eds.), *The Great Mortalities: Methodological Studies of Demographic Crises in the Past*, ed. Hubert Charbonneau and Andre Larose (Liege, 1980), 130-131; Sölvi Sogner, "Nature and Dynamics of Crisis (Including Recent Crises in Developing Countries)," in *The Great Mortalities: Methodological Studies of Demographic Crises in the Past*, ed. Hubert Charbonneau and Andre Larose (Liege, 1980), 319-320.

population was affected. Households remained unbroken, ties of kinship were maintained, and land allotments—generally allocated to adult males—did not require redistribution. In other words, a family's ability to work the land was essentially unchanged. The short-term effects of a non-cholera crisis would have been small, if not fleeting.[23]

In trying to assess the long-term impact of a crisis in a population with relatively high average fertility, Chagnon and Melancon found that an epidemic which saw the death of 57 percent of all children under age 10 (with the number of deaths at other ages much smaller) resulted in a total loss of 30 percent in expected future fertility.[24] In Borshevka, non-cholera crises (which also affected children most) resulted, on average, in the death of 16 percent of children under age 10. Thus, the total loss in expected fertility would be considerably less. Moreover, with married couples intact, the biological effect of a premature infant death (abbreviated postpartum lactational amenorrhea) could reduce the length of the successive birth interval.[25] However, it must be admitted that, given early and universal marriage in Borshevka, the ability of increased fertility to make up much of the population loss was limited. Over the long term there would be some impact on the future stock of reproducers. But with annual net population growth at 1.1 percent and a natural growth rate slightly higher over most of the period under consideration, the check on the population by these crises can hardly be described as Malthusian.[26] Assuming a quick return to previous fertility and mortal-

---

[23] Ajit Das Gupta, "Catastrophes and Their Population Symptoms," in *The Great Mortalities: Methodological Studies of Demographic Crises in the Past*, ed. Hubert Charbonneau and Andre Larose (Liege, 1980), 65; Watkins and Menken, "Famines in Historical Perspectives," 654.

[24] Napoleon A. Chagnon and Thomas F. Melancon, "Reproduction, Numbers of Kin and Epidemics in Tribal Populations: A Case Study," in *Population and Biology*, ed. Nathan Keyfitz (Liege, 1984), 152-156.

[25] A.K. Chowdhury, M. Alauddin, Atiqur Rahman Khan, and Lincoln C. Chen, "Experience in Pakistan and Bangladesh," in *The Effects of Infant and Child Mortality on Fertility*, ed. Samuel H. Preston (New York, 1978), 126; John C. Caldwell and Pat Caldwell, "Famine in Africa: A Global Perspective," in *Mortality in Sub- Saharan Africa*, ed. Etienne van de Walle, Gilles Pison, and Mpembele Sala-Diakanda (Oxford, 1992), 376; Jannetta, "Famine Mortality in Nineteenth-Century Japan," 441.

[26] Alain Bideau, "Autoregulating Mechanisms in Traditional Populations," in *Population and Biology*, ed. Nathan Keyfitz (Liege, 1984), 126-127.

ity levels, the population of Borshevka would have recovered its pre-crisis size within three to four years.

In the two cholera epidemics, the four to five percent reduction in the working-age population must have caused immediate hardship in a number of households, even though the high number of deaths among the elderly resulted in a slightly more favourable dependency ratio in the parish as a whole. But large, multiple family households, which were the norm in Borshevka, cushioned the loss of an adult worker in any individual household. Repartitioning the land, which often occurred in Russia soon after a demographic crisis, further facilitated economic recovery. By redistributing ploughlands in the light of changes in individual household composition, the land was used more efficiently. In other words, land was redivided according to the ability to work it. In spite of these limiting factors, increased losses among women who had yet to complete their childbearing period meant that the demographic effects would be permanent. Females of childbearing age (15-49) comprised 24.2 percent of all female deaths in cholera years against 14.9 percent in non-crisis years. Even if cholera crises resulted in increased nuptuality, with widows and widowers quickly remarrying, pre-crisis levels of reproductivity could not have been maintained as there was no reservoir of unmarried adults in Borshevka. Still, approximately half of the cholera deaths to women aged 15-49 occurred to those at the end of their reproductive cycle, to females aged 40 and over. Thus, although the impact of cholera in Borshevka could not be counteracted by marriage, that is, by tapping into a reservoir of unmarried adults, as was possible elsewhere in Europe, household structures, mechanisms of asset redistribution, and large numbers of deaths in age groups of limited or no reproductive capacity meant that both the short-term and long-term consequences were contained.[27] Cholera did not prove to be a threat to the social order.

In all, based upon cereal prices, the seasonality of deaths, and the age distribution of deaths, it appears that crisis mortality in Borshevka was not the result of famine or short-term climatic fluctuation, at least to the degree that these fluctuations affected the harvest. From as early as 1830, Borshevka was insulated from crop failure. Thus, decades before improved transport and even discussions of the need for better hygiene, the peasants in Borshevka were free of famine-based

[27] Ibid., 126-127.

mortality. Although there is evidence for improved diet in Russia as a whole from the 1860s onward, this is less likely to have been the case for Borshevka.[28] The dismal image of rural Russian society is not in evidence in Borshevka, although it was in the very heart of the country's most depressed region. Thus, it remains a distinct possibility that the social and economic relations which bound most peasants to a plot of land, even in the post-emancipation period, were, in Sen's terms, a mechanism allowing them to command an entitlement to food.[29] It is far more likely that these relations afforded this protection than any improvement in the level of economic well-being, for which there is little evidence until well into the second half of the nineteenth century. This emphasis on alternative socio-economic arrangements, in this instance household patterns and mechanisms of land distribution, is important because some scholars have been too ready to assume that only higher levels of urbanization, industrialization, and income could mute responses to grain price fluctuations.[30]

The pattern of crisis mortality in Borshevka is consistent with a society suffering not from harvest failure, but from repeated epidemics of acute infectious diseases. The exogenous nature of crisis or excess mortality can be confirmed by the causes of death recorded in the parish registers (Table 3). Mortality from smallpox is only minimally associated with the nutritional state of the population; for scarlet fever the relationship is equivocal or variable. There is increasing evidence that high measles mortality is more the result of crowding than poor nutritional status, the significance of which will be evident below.[31] In addition, the fact that crisis years saw a substantial decrease in the proportion of infant and child deaths from gastro-intestinal causes suggests that drinking

[28] Steven L. Hoch, "On Good Numbers and Bad: Malthus, Population Trends, and Peasant Standard of Living in Late Imperial Russia," *Slavic Review* 53, no. 1 (1994): 41-75.

[29] Amartya Sen, *Poverty and Famines: An Essay on Entitlement and Deprivation* (Oxford, 1981).

[30] Galloway, "Basic Patterns in Annual Variations," 291-298.

[31] Peter Aaby et al, "Determinants of Measles Mortality in a Rural Area of Guinea-Bissau: Crowding, Age, and Malnutrition," *Journal of Tropical Pediatrics* 30, no. 3 (1984): 167; Randall Reves, "Declining Fertility in England and Wales as a Major Cause of the Twentieth Century Decline in Mortality," *American Journal of Epidemiology* 122, no. 1 (1985): 112.

Table 3
Mortality Crises in Borshevka,
Parish of Borshevka, 1830-1912

Year	Cause	Percent of total deaths
1831	Smallpox	54.2
1839	Smallpox	57.5
1848	Cholera	33.7
1871	Cholera	57.9
1888	Scarlet Fever	38.5
	Measles	12.5
1894	Diarrhoea	30.8
	Measles	16.2
1901	Measles	25.0

unclean water or consuming adulterated foods, common during drought or famine, were unlikely to be behind the increase in deaths (Table 4).

A close examination reveals that crisis mortality was really nothing more than an exaggeration of the effects of normally recurrent epidemics. In Borshevka between 1830 and 1912 18.7 percent of all deaths were caused by five of the principal airborne childhood infectious diseases for which there can be some degree of reliability in the cause of death as listed in the parish registers (measles, smallpox, scarlet fever, whooping cough, and diphtheria). Such an overall incidence of death from these five diseases suggests that Borshevka was at the high end of the spectrum in terms of its vulnerability to infectious diseases.[32] Generally, "in traditional demographic regimes, the higher the level of mortality the greater the influence (on the overall level of mortality) of deaths resulting from infectious diseases.'"[33] Thus with a life expectancy of 27 years in Borshevka during the 1860s, the contribution of infectious disease to mortality would be expected to be quite high, as the data suggest.

Equally important here is the fact that deaths from these five diseases were marked by very young median and mean ages at death (Table 5).

[32] Samuel H. Preston, Nathan Keyfitz, and Robert Schoen, *Causes of Death: Life Tables for National Populations* (New York and London, 1972); Thomas McKeown, *The Modern Rise of Population* (New York, 1976), 54-55; Livi-Bacci, *Population and Nutrition*, 70-77.

[33] Livi-Bacci, *Population and Nutrition*, 69-70.

Table 4
Distribution of causes of infant and child death by age, Parish of Borshevka, 1830-1912

Cause of death	Non-crisis years	Crisis years (not cholera)
Aged 1-5		
Convulsions	7.4	3.8
Intestinal	69.1	69.8
Non-intestinal	21.7	24.5
Unknown	1.8	1.9
Aged 6-11 months		
Convulsions	10.1	1.8
Intestinal	53.8	14.7
Non-intestinal	34.5	80.9
Unknown	1.5	2.5
Aged 1		
Convulsions	11.9	1.3
Intestinal	41.0	24.0
Non-intestinal	45.4	73.3
Unknown	1.7	1.3
Aged 2-4		
Convulsions	9.9	3.7
Intestinal	32.9	16.8
Non-intestinal	55.8	77.6
Unknown	1.5	1.9
Aged 5-9		
Convulsions	5.7	0.0
Intestinal	19.7	7.7
Non-intestinal	71.2	84.6
Unknown	3.5	7.7

Over half of all deaths from smallpox, measles, and whooping cough were to children under age one. This suggests a disease environment in which infections were transmitted faster and case-fatality rates were higher, though this cannot be established from the data available.[34]

[34] Aaby et al, "Determinants of Measles Mortality," 165; Reves, "Declining Fertility in England and Wales," 122; A.J. Mercer, "Relative Trends in Morality from Related Respiratory and Airborne Infectious Diseases," *Population Studies* 40, no. 1 (1986): 129-145. ; Waal 1989, 24.

Table 5
Age at death (in years) from five principal infectious diseases and gastro-intestinal diseases, Parish of Borshevka, 1830-1912

Age at death	Measles	Smallpox	Scarlet Fever	Whooping Cough	Diphtheria	Gastro-intestinal Diseases
N	229	297	170	98	56	1371
Minimum	0.083	0.038	0.167	0.038	0.500	0.003
Maximum	10.000	28.000	24.000	6.000	14.000	83.000
Mean	1.901	2.285	3.177	1.135	4.671	3.877
Median	1.000	1.000	3.000	0.667	4.000	0.500

Figure 8 makes clear that Borshevka suffered from frequent epidemics of these five diseases. Far more often than not, however, the increase was not sufficient to raise the number of deaths over the moving average of deaths by 50 percent. In 22 years (out of a total of 81 years under observation), 15 or more persons died from one of these diseases; in 13 years, 20 or more persons. It would not be unreasonable to conclude that an epidemic of one or more of these five childhood infectious diseases struck Borshevka every four to six years, on average. The autonomous nature of these infectious diseases accords with the findings of numerous scholars. This is especially the case for Swedish and Finnish researchers who have examined Scandinavian mortality fluctuations in the eighteenth and nineteenth centuries.[35]

This unfavourable disease environment for airborne, childhood infectious diseases can be explained by the age structure of the population, the large mean household size in Borshevka, the size of the house, and the effects of the climate. John has found that the higher the fertility of a host population, and thus, the greater the proportion of children in the population, the higher the incidence of childhood infectious disease and the earlier the mean age at infection. High fertility, as experienced in Borshevka, maintained a high flow of susceptibles into the population.[36]

35 Kaukiainen 1984, 235-236; Livi-Bacci 1991, 18, 111-121.

36 Reves, "Declining Fertility in England and Wales," 116; Waal, "Famine Mortality," 25; A. Meredith John, "Transmission and Control of Childhood Infectious Disease: Does Demography Matter?" *Population Studies* 44, no. 2 (1990): 208-210.

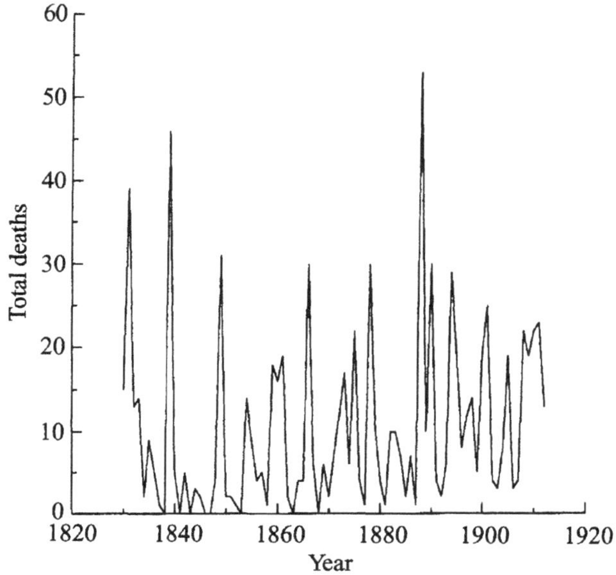

Figure 8. Frequency of deaths from five principal childhood infectious diseases, Borshevka, 1830-1912.

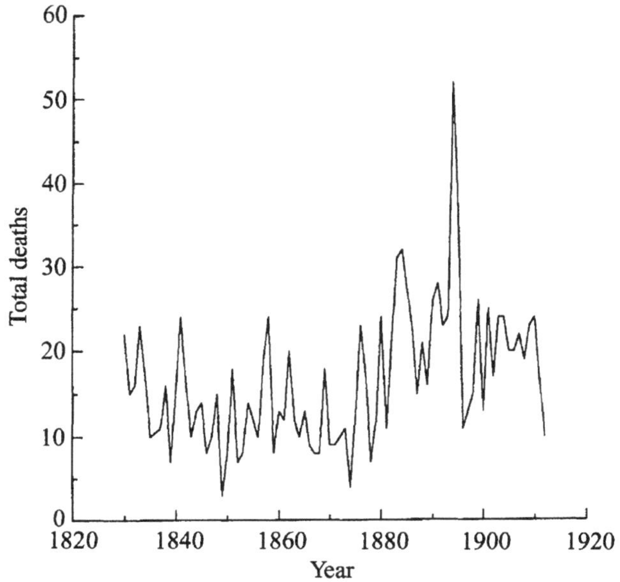

Figure 9. Frequency of deaths from gastro-intestinal diseases, Borshevka, 1830-1912.

Early mean rates of infection would result in higher case-fatality rates, thereby increasing the level of mortality. The incidence of airborne infections has also been shown to have a strong positive correlation with mean household size.[37] With households averaging slightly over eight persons in Borshevka, large by nineteenth-century European standards, and with all but three peasant huts in the parish occupying less than 350 square feet, these social conditions undoubtedly facilitated the spread of airborne disease. In addition, the long months of confinement beginning with the onset of colder weather in the autumn increased exposure to infection. The evidence from Borshevka makes clear the need to examine the structural vulnerability of a society to infectious disease. Here it is likely that demographic and social structures, fertility levels, and household and housing patterns, and not economic fluctuations or the biological consequences of social dislocation, directly stimulated the incidence of death from infectious disease.

In Borshevka, coupled to this high incidence of mortality from epidemics of childhood infectious diseases was an extraordinarily lethal level of endemic gastro-intestinal deaths, listed in the parish registers as colic, diarrhoea, and vomiting (Figure 9). These three causes accounted for 30.2 percent of all deaths in the parish and 61.6 percent of all post-neonatal deaths in Borshevka between 1830 and 1912, a rate which then steadily decreased with age. By age 5-9 years, just over 17 percent of all deaths were attributed to gastro-intestinal diseases. In addition, a number of deaths listed in the registers as convulsions, 5.5 percent of the total, were probably various gastro-enteric diseases. In no year was Borshevka free from deaths ascribed to gastro-intestinal causes, and there were a number of times when these endemic diseases reached epidemic levels, though only once or twice with the intensity of a major epidemic. Although comparisons are often problematic with nineteenth-century cause of death data, Borshevka appears to have experienced deaths from gastro-intestinal causes at three times the rate of late nineteenth-century Italy ($e^0 = 33.6$), and almost six times the rate of mid-nineteenth-century England ($e^0 = 41.8$). Indeed, it seems likely that most of the difference in life expectancy between Borshevka and Italy

[37] Reves, "Declining Fertility in England and Wales," 115; O.J. Benedictow, "Morbidity in Historical Plague Epidemics," *Population Studies* 41, no. 3 (1987): 426.

can be explained by this extremely high level of gastro-intestinal death. And, as with the childhood infectious diseases mentioned above, high fertility and large mean household size are associated with an increased risk of exposure to diarrhoeal diseases.[38]

The seasonality and age-specific nature of endemic gastro-intestinal death differs considerably from the pattern of infectious childhood epidemic disease. Half the deaths from gastro-intestinal causes were to infants under age six months, the extremely young, implying that some infants must have been weaned at a very early age indeed. The seasonality of deaths from gastro-intestinal causes is marked by a noticeable summer peak for post- neonatal deaths (July) and deaths to children aged one (July-August) (Figures 10 and 11). For children aged 2-9, the number of deaths is considerably reduced, and little can be deduced from the small numbers on seasonality. In contrast, the onset of cooler weather and growing hours of darkness in the autumn meant considerably more time indoors and increased vulnerability to airborne infections. Epidemic diseases for children aged 2-9 peaked in the autumn, October-December. For children aged one, the level of infectious disease was also higher in the autumn, though the peak is less distinct. Post-neonatal infectious-disease deaths were more evenly spread out over the year, though elevated in the late autumn and low in the period August- October. The explanation for the varied seasonality by age for deaths from infectious diseases relates to the seasonality of birth and the benefits of maternal antibodies. Births in Borshevka had a noticeable peak in June, July, and August, and thus during the autumn peak in airborne infectious diseases, many infants still had some degree of immunity. Thus, gastro-intestinal deaths swept away young infants in the summer, while infectious diseases were more likely to affect slightly older infants and young children in the autumn. To further distinguish these two patterns of mortality, summers of high gastro-intestinal disease deaths were not followed by autumns with high levels of death from infectious diseases.

In all, infant and child mortality in Borshevka was marked by an extremely high incidence of gastro-intestinal death and a high level of death from infectious disease, each primarily affecting different age cohorts at different times of the year in different years. Infant mortality

[38] Reves, "Declining Fertility in England and Wales," 114.

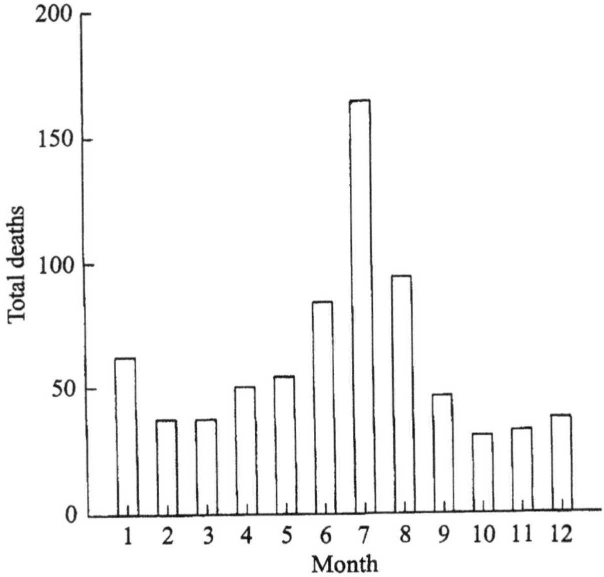

Figure 10. Seasonality of deaths from gastro-intestinal diseases: Children aged 1-11 months, Borshevka, 1830-1912.

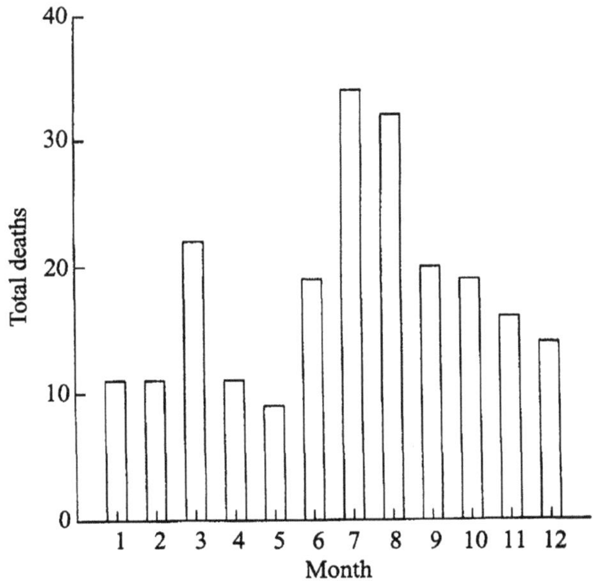

Figure 11. Seasonality of deaths from gasto-intestinal diseases: Children aged 1, Borshevka, 1830-1912.

and early childhood mortality did not move in tandem, though some of the social factors contributing to them—a large number of susceptibles, large mean household size, and crowded housing—were the same. With such a high incidence of mortality from gastro-intestinal disease, morbidity rates must also have been high, and the young in Borshevka are likely to have experienced repeated bouts of both acute and persistent diarrhoea. The long-term health consequences are likely to have been the same as those for a population exposed to acute and prolonged malnutrition, though in the case of Borshevka, it would be, in effect, age-specific malnutrition.

Nineteenth-century observers in much of Russia, and in Tambov province in particular, repeatedly claimed weaning practices were responsible for the extraordinary incidence of summer infantile diarrhoea in Russia.[39] Infants were weaned in August, a time of heavy women's field work, without much regard to age and often well under six months, a pattern which has been observed elsewhere in eastern Europe.[40] In Russia, as a consequence of the extremely short growing season, from mid-July to the end of August was the harvest season, the "time of suffering," as it was called. The harvesting of winter and spring cereals and the ploughing and sowing of the new winter field all came in quick succession within the span of six weeks. It was an agonizing period of exertion, demanding that numerous tasks be accomplished before the first frost.[41] Thus, infants were often weaned before harvest time and, as a consequence, were highly susceptible to gastro-intestinal diseases associated with unclean water supplies and contaminated foods, and were more vulnerable to infection as a result of the early loss of protection provided by breast milk. To be clear, it was not food shortages in crisis years that resulted in epidemics of diarrhoeal diseases. Rather, it was the habit of early weaning, aggravated by social conditions that heightened the risk of exposure, that brought about an environment of endemic gastro-intestinal disease. For very young infants, this meant

[39] Eduard Ikavitts, *Mediko-topograficheskoe opisanie Tambovskoi gubernii* (Moscow, 1865), 231; Nikol'skii 1885, 158-159, 335, 366-368.

[40] Robert Lee, "Mortality Levels and Agrarian Reforms in Early 19th Century Prussia: Some Regional Evidence," in *Pre-Industrial Population Change: The Mortality Decline and Short-Term Population Movements*, ed. Tommy Bengtsson, Gunnar Fridlizius, and Rolf Ohlsson (Stockholm, 1984), 170-171.

[41] Hoch, *Serfdom and Social Control in Russia*, 91-92.

susceptibility to diarrhoeal diseases; for those slightly older, increased susceptibility to airborne infectious diseases.

Estimates of infant ($_1q_0$) and early childhood mortality ($_4q_1$) for the 1860s in Borshevka result in rates of 271 0/00 and 230 0/00, respectively. The ratio of these rates suggest that Borshevka is more like Coale and Demeny's north, rather than east, model life table at early ages. Crises in Borshevka tended to be less lethal only because infant and early childhood mortality was relatively high even in normal times. It is this attribute that most distinguishes the underlying mortality in Borshevka. And this high level of underlying mortality can more readily be explained by the high levels of fertility, large household size, the small size of the house, and early weaning practices than by factors associated with food availability and nutrition, especially the frequency and impact of harvest failures.

6

The Banking Crisis, Peasant Reform, and Economic Development in Russia, 1857-1861

The mid-nineteenth century in Russia was a period of frenzied social engineering in which the autocracy sought to redesign society. Serfdom was abolished, the army overhauled, government finances and the banking system reformed, provincial and local administration revitalized, the judicial system restructured, censorship eased, the universities reorganized, and railroad development begun. Few historians would dispute the fact that the aptly named "Era of Great Reforms," the decade or so that followed Russia's humiliating defeat in the Crimean War (1854-1856), was the most important in the history of the empire between its establishment early in the eighteenth century and its demise early in the twentieth.

For rural Russia, reform meant a diminished role for the nobility as the managers of peasant life. The emancipated serfs were to become landowners by means of a vast credit, or "redemption," operation.[1] For economic development, reform signified a massive and sudden shift of capital out of monopolistic state credit institutions, which for years had provided long-term credit to serfowners and the state treasury, and into private joint-stock companies to finance railroads and steam navigation.

Researchers of the Great Reforms have been preoccupied with the motivation for emancipating the serfs and the subsequent impact of the legislation. But this has not helped explain why the legislation took the form it did. Notions that the causes of the emancipation of 1861 lay in humanitarian concerns, mounting peasant unrest, or an urgent desire on the part of the state to foster industrial development have been criticized

This essay was originally published in *The American Historical Review* 96, no. 3 (June 1991): 795-820.

[1] Where the land-equalizing commune existed, peasant lands were held in common rather than by individuals. In those areas of the Ukraine, Belorussia, and the Lithuanian provinces where the repartitional land commune did not exist, peasant households held their land individually.

as adding up "to nothing more than a list of motives which might reasonably appear to have influenced those making the decisions."[2] Seeking the origins of the emancipation in an agrarian crisis of the feudal-serf system—a view motivated more by ideology than history—has been attempted so often by Soviet scholars that even some Western historians now pay it deference, though with notes of caution.[3] Yet we have been duly warned of "the problem of establishing causal relationships between broad socioeconomic developments and specific historical events (such as revolutions) or deliberate human actions (such as reforms)."[4]

More recently, some answers have been sought in research on the political culture of Russia and on the dynamics of reform as played out among the monarch, enlightened bureaucrats, conservative elder statesmen, abolitionist squires, and self-interested serfowners. Such studies have done much to enhance our understanding of the politics of reform, but they have not elucidated how specific law came into being.[5] They are confined to the political context of emancipation. They especially disregard a banking failure that plagued reform, warped legislation, and weakened subsequent economic development. In 1859, at the moment government officials sat down to write the reform laws, they faced a crisis—mounting state debt, inflation, a negative balance of payments,

---

[2] Alfred J. Rieber, *The Politics of Autocracy* (Paris, 1966), 17. Nor has Rieber's own attempt to "identify the issue," serfdom as an obstacle to military reform, found wide acceptance. See Terence Emmons, "The Peasant and the Emancipation," in *The Peasant in Nineteenth-Century Russia*, ed. Wayne S. Vucinich (Stanford, CA, 1968), 44-45.

[3] M. N. Pokrovskii, *Russkaia istoriia s drevneishikh vremen*, 4 vols. (Leningrad, 1924), 4: 45-55; P. A. Khromov, *Ekonomicheskoe razvitie Rossii v XIX-XX vekakh, 1801-1971* (Moscow, 1950), 7-25; P. A. Zaionchkovskii, *Otmena krepostnogo prava v Rossii*, 3rd ed. (Moscow, 1968), 62; I. D. Koval'chenko, *Russkoe krepostnoe krest'ianstvo v pervoi polovine XIX v.* (Moscow, 1967), 378-86; Daniel Field, *The End of Serfdom: Nobility and Bureaucracy in Russia, 1855-1861* (Cambridge, MA, 1976), 29-33; R. E. F. Smith and David Christian, *Bread and Salt: A Social and Economic History of Food and Drink in Russia* (Cambridge, 1984), 340-41.

[4] Terence Emmons, ed., *Emancipation of the Russian Serfs* (New York, 1970), 4.

[5] Field, *End of Serfdom*; Terence Emmons, *The Russian Landed Gentry and the Peasant Emancipation of 1861* (Cambridge, 1968); W. Bruce Lincoln, *In the Vanguard of Reform: Russia's Enlightened Bureaucrats, 1825-1861* (DeKalb, IL, 1982); L. G. Zakharova, *Samoderzhavie i otmena krepostnogo prava v Rossii, 1856-1861* (Moscow, 1984).

an unfavorable climate for foreign loans, the inability to reestablish convertibility of the ruble, and, finally, the collapse of state credit institutions.[6] During reform, the autocracy did not simply move "in stages" toward the final, politically balanced version of the emancipation laws. Nor does the view that serfowners successfully defended their economic interests, while not opposing emancipation proper, tell the whole story.[7] Discussion needs to focus on the constraints that confronted policy makers.

The banking crisis of 1859 is central. In late 1858, the government adopted as the cornerstone of its peasant reform policy the principle of a landed emancipation with compensation for the nobility. But an unexpected banking crisis only a few months later, while not lessening the government's commitment to reform, greatly constrained reformers when they tried to turn policy into law. In fact, the terms of the 1861 land redemption law, as distinct from the political commitment to make the peasants property owners, cannot be understood without reference to the collapse of state credit institutions.

The banking crisis forced a sudden reordering of fiscal priorities. It prevented the government from subsidizing the serfs' acquisition of their lands as in Prussia and Austria. It burdened the peasants for years with high interest rates on their redemption debts, substantially increasing their annual payments. It abetted those who wished to minimize the size of the peasants' land allotments. It added weight to the view that redemption must be gradual, not immediate and mandatory. It necessitated the imposition of restrictions on the credit instruments issued to ex-serfowners to the disadvantage of the holders. All in all, the vast redemption operation and the harsh terms it imposed on the peasants were not simply the result of serfowners defending their interests. They were a response to fiscal constraints dictated by the collapse of state credit institutions.

In Russia, after defeat in the Crimean War, the pressure for reform forced a revolution in public and private finance. And recent financial

---

[6] Jacob W. Kipp, "M. Kh. Reutern on the Russian State and Economy: A Liberal Bureaucrat during the Crimean Era, 1854-1860," *Journal of Modern History* 47 (September 1975): 447-48.

[7] Field, *End of Serfdom*, 5, 359.

innovations in Western Europe did not go unnoticed. Overnight, a country that had never known securities trading created a stock and bond market. Domestically financed joint-stock companies, long prohibited, were suddenly permitted to organize. Chronic state budget deficits, for decades financed by borrowing from abroad or from monopolistic state banks, were now covered by floating internal treasury bonds. A century-old policy of liberal lending to serfowners for personal consumption was discarded. Transport development was made the investment priority, and the nobility was left without access to credit. All credit institutions of importance were abolished.

Throughout Europe, the 1850s saw intense financial innovation and expansion. Creation of the joint-stock bank Credit Mobilier in 1852 allowed France to overcome longstanding inadequacies in its capital markets that had hindered investment in public works and banking. Economic historians have hailed it "as a major innovation and discontinuity in the finance of not only France, but of Europe as a whole," for it soon had many imitators.[8] During this decade, the great German and Austrian investment banks were founded, providing capital for the boom in railroads as well as for mining and manufacturing. In Sweden, Italy, and Spain, several new banks were established. Even in England, with its sophisticated capital markets, this was a decade of considerable change. The Joint-Stock Companies Act of 1856 facilitated the formation of limited liability corporations and led to a spate of new finance companies. Of note to historians, it was these developments, especially the involvement of banks in the process of economic development, that underlay Alexander Gerschenkron's well-known theory of "relative backwardness."[9]

---

8 Charles P. Kindleberger, *A Financial History of Western Europe* (London, 1984), 109; Rondo Cameron, *France and the Economic Development of Europe (1800-1914)* (Princeton, NJ, 1961), 134, 147-71.

9 Kindleberger, *Financial History*, 12, 93, 112-24, 130-39, 148-49; Alexander Gerschenkron, *Economic Backwardness in Historical Perspective* (Cambridge, MA, 1962); Alexander Gerschenkron, *Continuity in History and Other Essays* (Cambridge, 1968); Rondo Cameron, et al., *Banking in the Early Stages of Industrialization* (Oxford, 1970), 107-09, 127, 162-63, 292; Rondo Cameron, *Banking and Economic Development: Some Lessons of History* (Oxford, 1972), 13-14, 38-39, 93-95, 104-05; Hugh Neuberger, *German Banks and German Economic Growth from Unification to World War I* (New York, 1977), 4, 64, 127;

Gerschenkron provided European economic historians with what still remains a useful framework for understanding state involvement in the early stages of industrialization under conditions of backwardness.[10] He pointed out the paradox of advantages in backwardness. The ability of late industrializers to borrow technological and institutional innovations at reduced cost from advanced countries was one such benefit. In emphasizing variability in the industrialization process, Gerschenkron described how backward nations mobilized capital differently from advanced ones. In Germany, investment banks took on the role previously played in England by the private entrepreneur. By contrast, "the scarcity of capital in Russia was such that no banking system could conceivably succeed in attracting sufficient funds to finance large-scale industrialization."[11] There, the state substituted its financial resources for the prerequisites the economy lacked.

Backward countries, however, are also apt to borrow policies, ideas, and institutions not well suited to their circumstances rather than to employ appropriate substitutes. In the late 1850s, Russia sought to create new financial institutions and credit instruments to address old problems it was finally willing to confront. But Russia at mid-century had only a primitive capital market. Borrowing ideas from Western finance capitalism was ill conceived, since the society lacked the capacity

---

Holger L. Engberd, *Mixed Banking and Economic Growth in Germany, 1850-1931* (New York, 1981), 23-25; Gabriel Tortella-Casares, *Banking, Railroads, and Industry in Spain, 1829-1874* (New York, 1977), 13-14, 109, 180; Richard L. Rudolph, *Banking and Industrialization in Austria-Hungary: The Role of Banking in the Industrialization of Czech Crown Lands* (Cambridge, 1976), 69, 95; Richard H. Tilly, *Financial Institutions and Industrialization in the Rhineland, 1815-1870* (Madison, WI, 1966).

10 Gerschenkron, *Economic Backwardness*, 5-50; Alexander Gerschenkron, "The Discipline and I," *Journal of Economic History* 27 (1967): 443-59; Cameron, *Banking and Economic Development*, 9-11; Paul Gregory, "Some Empirical Comments of the Theory of Relative Backwardness: The Russian Case," *Economic Development and Cultural Change* 22 (1974): 654; Henry Rosovsky, "Alexander Gerschenkron: A Personal and Fond Recollection," *Journal of Economic History* 39 (1979): 1012; Lars G. Sandberg, "Ignorance, Poverty, and Economic Backwardness in the Early Stages of European Industrialization: Variations on Alexander Gerschenkron's Grand Theme," *Journal of European Economic History* 11 (1982): 675.

11 Gerschenkron, *Economic Backwardness*, 19-20.

to use them effectively. Unlike the policy of state intervention adopted later in the century (which Gerschenkron describes), in the late 1850s the Russian autocracy, though hampered by the lack of national capital and developed financial markets, sought to rely on private, not state, resources. In doing so, the government precipitated a financial crisis, hitherto obscure, a consequence of a mania for private transport stocks.[12] In the end, the autocracy's attempt to provide for capital conflicted with its goal to create a free landed peasantry. Experimentation in Russia's immature capital markets at a crucial juncture in history had unfortunate consequences that persisted for decades. Two issues—the relationship of banks to economic development and the abolition of a servile system of labor—were linked in Russia.

State credit institutions were established in Russia in the second half of the eighteenth century to provide serfowners (*pomeshchiki*) with a cheap and reliable source of long-term credit. Essentially, the pre-1860 banking system consisted of four types of state credit institutions. Two were associated with welfare agencies, the Social Welfare Boards (*Prikazy Obshchestvennogo Prizreniia*) and the St. Petersburg and Moscow Savings Banks, which used their profits to support foundling homes and almshouses. In 1786, the State Loan Bank was restructured to increase the amount of long-term capital available to serfowners. Loans were not secured by the value of the land but by the number of serfs a landlord held. The term for these mortgage loans was frequently changed, although by the late 1850s most serfowner debt was for terms of twenty-eight or thirty-three years. A State Commercial Bank was set up in 1817 to provide short-term credit to merchants, although it remained an institution of little import. All state credit institutions were obligated to accept funds as demand deposits and pay interest on the accounts.

With long-term loans and demand deposits, the banking system was set up with a serious structural defect. In order to prevent a potential run on deposits, the government was forced to restrict the development

[12] For a definition of a financial crisis, see Charles F. Kindleberger, *Manias, Panics, and Crashes: A History of Financial Crises* (New York, 1978), 14-20; Julian Hoppit, "Financial Crises in Eighteenth-Century England," *Economic History Review,* 2nd ser., 39 (1986): 39-41.

of more profitable investment alternatives. Private commercial banks were prohibited, and the few joint-stock companies permitted to organize were required to raise their capital abroad.[13] This policy, coupled with regulations limiting the amount a serfowner could mortgage and prohibiting loans against small estates, often resulted in the state credit institutions holding surplus deposits on which they had to pay interest but for which they could find no borrowers. As a result, their profits were reduced considerably. In the 1820s, the state treasury solved the problem of accumulated idle capital by itself borrowing the money to cover budget deficits, thus eliminating the need to float internal public loans or to increase borrowing from abroad.[14]

In the wake of the Crimean War, the problem of surplus deposits resurfaced. To finance much of the war, the government resorted to printing money, over 400 million rubles, which more than doubled the

---

[13] Iu. Hagemeister, "O finansakh Rossii," *Tsentral'nyi Gosudarstvennyi Istoricheskii Arkhiv* (hereafter, TsGIA), f. 560, op. 43, d. 194, published in *Istoricheskii Arkhiv* 2 (1956): 114-15; M. Kh. Reutern: Report to the Council of Ministers (September 16, 1866); published in *M. Kh. Reitern: Biograficheskii ocherk*, ed. B. G. Reitern, et al. (St. Petersburg, 1910), 72-73; E. Lamanskii, "Vklady v bankakh ili bilety nepreryvnogo dokhoda," *Russkii Vestnik* 3 (1859): 223-38; E. Lamanskii, "Gosudartsvennye chetyrekhprotsentnye, nepreryvno-dokhodnye bilety," *Ukazatel' politiko-ekonomicheskii* 14 (April 4-6, 1859): 320; E. L. [E. Lamanskii?], "Sovremennoe polozhenie kreditnykh uchrezhdenii v Evrope i Amerike i otnosheniia ikh k promyshlennym predprinimateliam," *Russkii Vestnik* 2 (1857), book 1, 550-52; V. Sudeikin, *Gosudarstvennyi bank: Issledovanie ego ustroistva, ekonomicheskogo i finansovogo znacheniia* (St. Petersburg, 1891), vii-xii, 90, 114, 134, 493; *Birzhevye Vedomosti*, 255 (November 29, 1862); *Narodnoe Bogatstvo* 6 (November 7, 1862); E. Murav'ev, *Neskol'ko slov o novoi kreditnoi sisteme v sviazi s drugimi ekonomicheskimi voprosami* (Odessa, 1860), 14-15.

[14] *Ministerstvo finansov, 1802-1902* (St. Petersburg, 1902), part 1, 443; Hagemeister, "O finansakh Rossii," 114; S. Ia. Borovoi, *Kredit i banki Rossii (seredina XVIII v.-1861 g.)* (Moscow, 1958), 178-80; A. Pogrebinskii, "Finansovaia reforma nachala 60-kh godov XIX veka v Rossii," *Voprosy Istorii* 10 (1951): 78; [no author] "Finansovaia politika v period 1861-1880 gg.," *Otechestvennye Zapiski* 11 (1882), part 2, 11-12; *Pervoe izdanie materialov Redaktsionnykh Komissii, dlia sostavleniia "Polozhenii o krest'ianakh vykhodiashchikh iz krepostnoi zavisimosti,"* 18 vols. (St. Petersburg, 1859-1860), 11: vedomost' 3 (hereafter, PIM); E. I. Lamanskii, "Iz vospominanii Evgeniia Ivanovicha Lamanskogo (1840-1890 gg.)," *Russkaia Starina* 3 (1915): 580-81; E. L., "Sovremennoe polozhenie," 550-52; *Birzhevye Vedomosti*, 206 (August 4, 1867).

amount of paper in circulation.[15] With no investment options available, paper soon accumulated in the state credit institutions. By late 1857, they held over 180 million rubles of unused capital, far more than the 20 million rubles in cash they held on the eve of the war. Most disturbing, the government anticipated little treasury borrowing over the next two years. Serfowner demand was not expected to exceed 7 million rubles a year. The nobility had already pledged over 60 percent of its serfs, and many unencumbered estates were not eligible for mortgage.[16]

To reduce the losses that substantial idle capital would have caused the state credit institutions supporting welfare agencies and the small State Commercial Bank, the government permitted them to transfer funds to the State Loan Bank. In the 1856 annual report on the finances of the fifty-six Social Welfare Boards, the minister of interior

---

15 During the war, the government was not able to cover its budget deficits by borrowing. Foreign capital markets were limited. Only 12 percent of total military expenditures were borrowed from abroad. While the state credit institutions held deposits of over 850 million rubles, much of their money was tied up in long-term loans to the state treasury and serfowners. Between 1854 and 1857, 218 million rubles were lent to the government by the various state credit institutions. On January 1, 1858, the treasury owed 521 million rubles to state credit institutions. Serfowner debt stood at 426 million rubles. *Ministerstvo finansov, 1802-1902*, part 1, 443; Lamanskii, "Vklady v bankakh," 222-24; Lamanskii, "Iz vospominanii," 3: 582-83; *Birzhevye Vedomosti* (June 2, 1862); "Finansovaia Politika," 4-6; N. Kh. Bunge, "Zametki o nastoiashchem polozhenii nashei denezhnoi sistemy i sredstvakh k ee uluchsheniiu," in *Sbornik gosudarstvennykh znanii*, ed. V. P. Bezobrazov (St. Petersburg, 1880), 8: 106-08; Pogrebinskii, "Finansovaia reforma," 80; A. Pogrebinskii, *Ocherki istorii finansov dorevoliutsionnoi Rossii (XIX-XX v.)* (Moscow, 1954), 27-31.

16 *Polnoe sobranie zakonov Rossiiskoi Imperii*, Sobranie vtoroe, 55 vols. (St. Petersburg, 1830-94), vol. 34, no. 34,852 (September 1, 1859) (hereafter, *PSZ* II); *Otchet gosudarstvennykh kreditnykh ustanovlenii za 1859* (St. Petersburg, 1861), 4-5 (hereafter, *OGKU za* and the appropriate year); P. P. Migulin, *Nasha bankovaia politika (1729-1903)* (Kharkov, 1903), 61; I. S. Bliokh, *Finansy Rossii XIX stoletiia*, 2 vols. (St. Petersburg, 1882), 2: 49; V. Sudeikin, *Gosudarstvennyi bank*, 137-46; V. Sudeikin, "Aleksandr Maksimovich Kniazhevich," *Russkaia Starina* 11 (1892): 427-28; Hagemeister, TsGIA, f. 661, op. 1, d. 97, 1. 8. Cited in Pogrebinskii, *Ocherki istorii finansov*, 43; *PIM*, vol. 11, vedomost' 3; Iu. Hagemeister, "Vzgliad na promyshlennost' i torgovliu Rossii," *Russkii Vestnik* 1 (1857): 21-23; Lamanskii, "Vklady v bankakh," 223-24; Pogrebinskii, "Finansovaia reforma," 78-79.

noted: "Of the 126 million rubles which the boards have attracted, more than half remains unused, and a huge fund of 63 million rubles has been transferred to other [state] credit institutions, where it also has not been used.... During 1856, total deposits grew by 15.5 percent, while loans increased by only 2.5."[17] Similarly, on January 1, 1858, the State Loan Bank held over 229 million rubles in deposit from the State Commercial Bank, which required less than 30 million rubles a year for its own banking operations. The State Loan Bank thus bore the burden of paying the 4 percent interest, over 6 million rubles a year by 1857, on the unused deposits. But ultimate responsibility fell on the treasury, for it guaranteed all deposits. Slowly, the treasury was being forced to pay for some of the paper it had issued to finance the Crimean War.[18]

In 1857, the government addressed a major problem that had underlain military defeat: the inadequacy of the transport system. In January, it announced "the construction of the first railroad network in Russia" and the formation of the giant Russian Railroad Company with an authorized capitalization of 275 million rubles. Much of the capital, in the form of stocks and bonds, was to be raised internally on St. Petersburg and Warsaw credit markets.[19] Subsequently, the government made clear its desire to facilitate the formation of other similar joint-stock ventures. As a result, between 1857 and 1859, it approved the formation of seventy-five joint-stock companies, mostly railroad and steam navigation firms. Altogether, they were permitted to raise over 140 million rubles.[20]

Because of the financial crisis in much of Europe in 1857, initial stock offerings abroad went undersubscribed. To increase domestic incentive to invest in these firms, on July 20, 1857, the government announced a

---

[17] "Izvlechenie iz vsepoddanneishego otcheta g. ministra vnutrennikh del za 1856 god," *Zhurnal Ministerstva vnutrennikh del* 27 (1857): 48-49.

[18] N. Kh. Bunge, "O kreditnykh uchrezhdeniiakh v Rossii," *Zhurnal dlia Aktsionerov* 89 (September 18, 1858); Lamanskii, "Vklady v bankakh," 222-23, 225, 228-29; Lamanskii, "Iz vospominanii," 3: 580-81; Hagemeister, "O finansakh Rossii," 114; Reitern, *M. Kh. Reitern*, 76-78; Pogrebinskii, "Finansovaia reforma," 78-79. See also the *OGKU* for the appropriate year.

[19] *PSZ* II, vol. 32, no. 31,448 (January 26, 1857). See Alfred J. Rieber, "The Formation of La Grande Societe des Chemins de Fer Russes," *Jahrbucher für Geschichte Osteuropas* 2 (1973): 375-91.

[20] *Zhurnal dlia Aktsionerov*, 105 (January 8, 1859), and 194 (September 28, 1860).

lowering of interest rates on deposits in state credit institutions. Interest rates on loans were also reduced.[21] The government made part of its reasoning clear in the statute itself: "In recent years, very substantial capital has begun to accumulate in state credit institutions, and these institutions, by virtue of their operations, are not able to give it proper use. Desiring to avoid the losses foreseen from this for the banking institutions and to give idle capital a use more in accordance with state interests, We deem it proper to lower the interest rate on deposits."[22] The interest rate on deposits of private individuals was reduced from 4 to 3 percent, and the rate on all outstanding loans from 5 to 4 percent.

But other motives were behind this act as well. As a result of the war, debt service had become a considerable burden. In reducing the interest rate on loans to the state by 1 percent, the treasury would save over 5 million rubles a year. In addition, if the idle capital could be driven out of the banks, the government would save another 6 to 7 million rubles.[23] Thus the intent in lowering interest rates was to remove surplus capital from the state credit institutions, direct this money into joint-stock companies, and reduce government expenditures. In effect, the government manipulated interest rates to make up for an inefficient capital market, an act that was to cost it dearly for years to come. That this was made necessary by a financial crisis in Europe attests to the disadvantage of being dependent on foreign capital resources.

The initial response to the new interest rates was favorable.[24] At the first stockholders' meeting of the Russian Railroad Company on June 14, 1858, its president reported that "at present, the Russian public gives our undertaking its most eager support, offering its capital in amounts that exceed the expectations of the Company."[25] The same month, N. Kh. Bunge, then a professor of statistics and political economy in Kiev, wrote (in words he would later regret): "The lowering of bank interest

---

21 *PSZ* II, vol. 32, no. 32,082 (July 20, 1857). See also *Zhurnal dlia Aktsionerov*, 44 (October 29, 1857).

22 *PSZ* II, vol. 32, no. 32,082 (July 20, 1857).

23 Hagemeister, TsGIA, f. 661, op. 1, d. 97, l. 10. Cited in Pogrebinskii, "Finansovaia reforma," 79; Lamanskii, "Iz vospominanii," 3: 583-84. See also Borovoi, *Kredit*, 275-76; and Migulin, *Nasha bankovaia politika*, 62-63.

24 See Lamanskii, "Vklady v bankakh," 221-22, though Lamanskii himself did not hold such a view.

25 *Ukazatel' ekonomicheskii* (July 6, 1858): 610-11.

rates from 4 to 3 percent is beginning to bear fruit ... Fear concerning the withdrawal of deposits appears to be completely unfounded.... We dare to assert beforehand that the lowering of interest rates has had the most happy results, assisting on the one hand the establishment of a proper balance between deposits and loans and on the other hand the development of domestic industry."[26] In June 1858, the new minister of finance, A. M. Kniazhevich, in his first speech to the Council of State Credit Institutions, reported that "the new regulations on deposits and loans ... continue to be carried out without any difficulties."[27]

Since many stocks carried a 5 percent government guarantee compared to 3 percent paid on bank deposits, not only individuals but even the Social Welfare Boards withdrew substantial sums for investment in the stock market.[28] During 1858, withdrawals exceeded deposits by 50 million rubles.[29] The Stockholders' Journal reported in early 1858 that "on the St. Petersburg market, the prices of shares of all companies over the course of an entire year, and especially in recent months, have experienced an unparalleled increase. The main reason for this was the lowering of interest rates on capital in the state credit institutions, and as a result of this, the balance between the supply and demand for these shares has been destroyed."[30]

The only skeptic was Iu. A. Hagemeister, director of the Special Chancellery Credit Division. Hagemeister feared that "driving out deposits" from the state credit institutions would in fact lead to catastrophic withdrawals "ruinous for the treasury."[31] To meet demand, the

---

26 *Zhurnal dlia Aktsionerov* 77 (June 26, 1858).

27 *Ukazatel' ekonomicheskii* (September 7, 1858): 822; *Zhurnal dlia Aktsionerov* 85 (August 21, 1858); later published in the *OGKU za 1857* (St. Petersburg, 1859), 4.

28 Lamanskii, "Vklady v bankakh," 221-22, 234-35; Lamanskii, "Iz vospominanii," 3: 582-83 and 10: 58-59; Sudeikin, *Gosudarstvennyi bank*, 147-48; Bunge, "Zametki," 108-09; *Birzhevye Vedomosti* 187 (June 15, 1863) and 136 (May 26, 1868).

29 *OGKU za* 1858, 14.

30 *Zhurnal dlia Aktsionerov* 55 (January 16, 1858); see also 37 (September 10, 1857) and 75 (June 12, 1858).

31 TsGIA, f. 661, op. 1, d. 97, 1. 8, Report to the President of the Finance Committee of the State Council, cited in Pogrebinskii, "Finansovaia reforma," 79; A. Pogrebinskii, "Gosudarstvennye finansy Rossii nakanune reformy 1861 goda," *Istoricheskii Arkhiv* 2 (1956): 101.

government would be forced to print money or conclude a foreign loan on unfavorable terms.[32] As Hagemeister predicted, the situation deteriorated rapidly. By early 1859, it became clear to officials privy to the records of the state credit institutions that the banks would be unable to meet their obligations if the demand for withdrawals continued. Bunge wrote in late 1860 that "by the end of 1858, the crisis had become noticeable; by mid-1859, it was no longer a secret to anyone."[33] Similarly, E. I. Lamanskii, a key participant in resolving the banking crisis, recalled in his memoirs that "at the end of 1858 and the beginning of 1859, all the signs of a banking crisis had already appeared, which raised in turn the problem of a fundamental transformation of the then-existing banking system."[34] Eighteen months before, the banks had been drowning in money. Now insolvency threatened. Thus one of the first Great Reforms, the commitment of massive private resources to finance railroad construction and steam navigation, brought about the necessity for another: the liquidation of the state credit institutions, the restructuring of their deposits, and the establishment of a new banking system.

Kniazhevich, appointed minister of finance only in 1858, had not been involved in the decision the year before to lower interest rates, nor was he particularly experienced in financial affairs. One assessment of his four-year tenure at the ministry notes that, "while his name is not tied to one major piece of legislation," at least, in contrast to his predecessor, "he did not ruin matters." But Kniazhevich recognized the need to restructure existing bank deposits, and he appointed a number of men who were to dominate Russia's finances for the next three decades.[35] Bunge and M. Kh. Reutern, future ministers of finance, and Lamanskii, soon to be head of the new State Bank, all young men in their thirties, first rose to prominence through their involvement in resolving the banking crisis. Together with Hagemeister and N. A. Miliutin, former head of the economic department of the Ministry of Internal Affairs and

32 Report to the President, TsGIA, f. 661, op. 1, d. 97, 1. 10; Hagemeister, "O finansakh Rossii," 115.

33 *Zhurnal dlia Aktsionerov*, 194 (September 28, 1860).

34 Lamanskii, "Iz vospominanii," 3: 584-85.

35 V. Sudeikin, "Aleksandr Maksimovich Kniazhevich," 416. See also Lamanskii, "Iz vospominanii," 4: 68-69.

now its assistant minister, they constituted five of the eight members on the commission to reform the banks, which would liquidate the state credit institutions and establish the State Bank.

Although often described as enlightened bureaucrats, these were men of narrow vision who saw the solutions to Russia's problems largely in fiscal terms. All were believers in hired wage labor, private banks, and prudent banking practices, of which Russia had little or none. They were as enamored of railroads as they were hostile to serfowners, whose profligate spending they disparaged. All desired tax reform, and they staunchly opposed deficit spending. Most had traveled widely in Europe, knew financial experts there, and were impressed with recent innovations in commercial credit.[36]

The first recommendation of this group was enacted on March 13, 1859, when the government announced the issue of 4 percent termless bonds, or perpetuities. This was the first of two attempts to restructure bank debt, that is, to convert demand deposits into long-term bonds. The government was less than candid and assiduously avoided the words crisis or insolvency in order to keep the markets calm. It merely declared that the goals of the interest rate reduction in 1857 had been achieved. Now it wished to address another concern. "The income of depositors who had not withdrawn their capital from the credit institutions had been reduced by one quarter, as a result of which many were left in a difficult position. Desiring to give depositors the possibility for a more

[36] Lincoln, *In the Vanguard of Reform*; W. Bruce Lincoln, *Nikolai Miliutin: An Enlightened Russian Bureaucrat* (Newtonville, MA, 1977); Kipp, "M. Kh. Reutern," 437-59; George E. Snow, "Introduction," *The Years 1881-1894 in Russia: A Memorandum Found in the Papers of N. Kh. Bunge; A Translation and Commentary* (Philadelphia, 1981), 10; N. Kh. Bunge, "Preobrazovanie nashikh kreditnykh ustanovlenii i likvidatsiia vkladov," *Zhurnal dlia Aktsionerov* 164 (March 2, 1860); N. Kh. Bunge, "Ob izmenenii iuridicheskikh otnoshenii v Rossii, vsledstvie predstoiashchogo preobrazovaniia krepostnogo prava," *Otechestvennye Zapiski* 8 (1858): 64; N. Kh. Bunge, "Bankovye zakony i bankovaia politika," *Sbornik gosudarstvennykh znanii* (St. Petersburg, 1874), 1: 72-73; Lamanskii, "Iz vospominanii," 3: 575-77, 588, and 4: 63-69; Hagemeister,"O finansakh Rossii," 123-25; Hagemeister, "Vzgliad," 28; *Ukazatel' politiko-ekonomicheskii* (March 7, 1859), 231-32; Reitern, *M. Kh. Reitern*, 71-82, 100-02, 134-38; *Birzhevye Vedomosti* 264 (December 11, 1862); 136, 138, and 143 (May 26, 28, June 2, 1868); Migulin, *Nasha bankovaia politika* 93.

profitable and equally safe investment, We confirm ... the issuing of 4 percent state perpetuities."[37]

A more realistic but still official picture appeared in the financial press. In the two months that followed, Bunge and Lamanskii published a number of articles encouraging individuals to purchase the new bonds. Careful not to cite any alarming figures, they both spoke of the problem posed by demand deposits and long-term loans, referring to recent withdrawals attendant to the formation of joint-stock companies. Lamanskii in particular condemned the lowering of interest rates in 1857 as a mere palliative that completely ignored "the main problem," the structural defect in the banking system. Both explained that, although the new bonds did not involve government expenditures, the banks would have to forgo their profits. The 4 percent that serfowners paid on their loans would cover the 4 percent interest paid on the perpetuities. The benefit was that these bonds would conform better to the structure of existing long-term serfowner debt. The government pledged not even to raise the question of redeeming these perpetuities for twenty years.[38]

In spite of these efforts, the announcement of the 4 percent bonds resulted in panic and a run on deposits. Many people used their funds to purchase stocks, and the market soared higher. Others tried to send their money abroad. And the 4 percent perpetuities went undersubscribed.[39] In April, to reduce the amount of cash leaving the banks, the government suspended all new lending against serf estates and prohibited the rescheduling of any existing debt.[40] For the first time in over one hundred years, Russian serfowners were left without any source of institutional credit. The government explained that, with the impending emancipation and land settlement, future long-term loans would have to be based on land values, not the number of serfs.

---

37 *PSZ* II, vol. 34, no. 34,243 (March 13, 1859); published in *Zhurnal dlia Aktsionerov* 116 (March 26, 1859). See also Bunge, "O kreditnykh uchrezhdeniiakh."

38 Lamanskii, "Vklady v bankakh," 221-44; Lamanskii, "Gosudarstvennye chetyrekhprotsentnye," 317-24; N. Kh. Bunge, "Nepreryvno-dokhodnye chetyrekhprotsentnye bilety," *Zhurnal dlia Aktsionerov* 120 (April 30, 1859); N. Kh. Bunge, "Luchshe li dlia gosudarstva imet' protsentnyi dolg v 500 mil. rub. ili zhe na 500 mil. bumazhnykh deneg?" *Zhurnal dlia Aktsionerov* 121 (May 7, 1859).

39 "Finansovaia politika," 13-14; Pogrebinskii, *Ocherki istorii finansov*, 42-44; *OGKU za 1859*, 6.

40 *PSZ* II, vol. 34, no. 34,379 (April 16, 1859).

At best, this was a factor of slight import, since it was clear that not enough bonds were being purchased to save the banks. In fact, over the next six months, only 13 million rubles of deposits were converted into perpetuities.[41] Within days of suspending loans to serfowners, the government committed itself in secret to reforming the banking system and liquidating the state credit institutions. Hagemeister, Bunge, Lamanskii, Reutern, and Miliutin were appointed to a formal commission on banking reform to draw up legislative proposals restructuring the banks.

In June 1859, Kniazhevich felt compelled to inform the Council of State Credit Institutions that the banks were in "rather difficult circumstances at the present time." Reported in the financial press, this only increased withdrawals.[42] The deteriorating financial situation necessitated a number of interim measures. To cover the demand for withdrawals, the government authorized the issuing of 100 million rubles, of which 88 million were actually put in circulation, and a loan of 7 million pounds sterling was obtained.[43] Existing deposits in the banks were divided into four categories, with various treasury and other state funds no longer to receive interest.[44] The formation of new joint-stock companies was halted. In July 1859, the Social Welfare Boards and the St. Petersburg and Moscow Savings Banks ceased to be independent banking entities and were made subordinate to the Ministry of Finance. Thus, in another major reform, credit and banking policy were for the first time in modern Russian history separated from charitable agencies.[45]

On September 1, 1859, in a state of utter panic, the government announced the second and significantly more costly attempt to convert demand deposits into long-term notes. Five-percent bank notes, to be liquidated over a period of thirty-seven years, were to be issued.[46] The

---

41 *PSZ* II, vol. 34, no. 34,852 (September 1, 1859).

42 *Zhurnal dlia Aktsionerov* 29 (July 2, 1859); later published in *OGKU za 1858* (St. Petersburg, 1860), 14.

43 *OGKU za 1859*, 12; Reitern, *M. Kh. Reitern*, 10; Sudeikin, *Gosudarstvennyi bank*, 148-49; Sudeikin, "Aleksandr Maksimovich Kniazhevich," 427-28; "Finansovaia politika," 13-14; Pogrebinskii, *Ocherki istorii finansov*, 42-44, 65; Borovoi, *Kredit*, 278-79.

44 *PSZ* II, vol. 34, no. 34,692 (June 29, 1859).

45 *PSZ* II, vol. 34, no. 34,730 (July 10, 1859).

46 *PSZ* II, vol. 34, no. 34,852 (September 1, 1859).

government was now lending money for less than the cost of borrowing. In other words, serfowners were paying 4 percent on their loans to the banks, which in turn paid out 5 percent to bondholders. To entice, or perhaps force, depositors into conversion, the interest rate on bank deposits was lowered again, to 2 percent. It was now half of what it had been two years before. Appended to the statute was an unusually candid discussion of the need for banking reform.[47]

In his report, Minister Kniazhevich discussed the evolution of government banking policy:

> The structure of our main state banking institutions, the basis of which was established as far back as the previous century, no longer corresponds to present-day circumstances and requires fundamental reform.... This has been made especially noticeable of late, with the revival of industrial entrepreneurship, by the anticipated building of railroads and other improved systems of transport, and finally in light of the great economic reform, being prepared in accordance with the ideas and instructions of Your Imperial Highness, for a large part of the rural population.[48]

He described the problem of idle capital and the unfortunate consequences of lowering interest rates in 1857. The careful reader could see that as of July 1, 1859, the banks had on hand only 23 million rubles in cash. In contrast, excluding state deposits, private institutional endowments, and other restricted funds, 365 million rubles "could be demanded at any time." And these demand deposits "could create difficulties ... extremely burdensome for the government." There-fore, credit had to be placed "on a more rational basis."[49]

Kniazhevich revealed the full picture only a year later, after a number of reforms had been enacted. "From August 1857 over the course of the next twenty-two months, the withdrawal of deposits exceeded new deposits by 143 million rubles, and the cash on hand in the banks, which in June 1857 exceeded 150 million rubles, had fallen by June 1859 to 20 million rubles." Kniazhevich explained that he had foreseen for the

---

[47] Published in *Zhurnal dlia Aktsionerov*, 142 (September 17, 1859); *Ukazatel' politiko-ekonomicheskii*, 38 (September 18, 1859); *Zemledel'cheskaia Gazeta*, 77 (September 25, 1859). See also *Proizvoditel' i Promyshlennik*, 62-63 (September 19 and 22, 1859).

[48] *PSZ* II, vol. 34, no. 34,852 (September 1, 1859).

[49] *PSZ* II, vol. 34, no. 34,852 (September 1, 1859).

remainder of 1859 an immediate demand of up to "50 million rubles for corporate capital," with the threat of substantially greater withdrawals if existing joint-stock companies issued all the shares they were authorized to sell. He again spoke of the banks' "difficult situation." In reality, they had been insolvent, a word that could be used only after the fact.[50]

Upon Kniazhevich's retirement as minister of finance in 1862, *Stock Exchange News* (*Birzhevye Vedomosti*) described his efforts "to protect the banks from obvious insolvency."[51] His successor, Reutern, in documenting for the tsar and the Council of Ministers the reasons for the persistent problems in Russia's credit market, explained that, by lowering interest rates, "the credit institutions were made insolvent and could continue to make payments only by the issuing of new paper notes." In fact, he asserted, "not only did the credit institutions turn out to be insolvent but so, it could be said, did all of Russia."[52]

Fearful of failing a second time to get depositors to invest in long-term bonds and, consequently, having to print even more money or, worse, suspend the withdrawal of deposits, the Banking Commission sought to make the new 5 percent bank notes extremely attractive. Lamanskii ascribed the failure of the 4 percent perpetuities issued in March 1859 to the fact that no provision was made for their liquidation. Investors, not knowing when the capital would be returned, he believed, were not adequately compensated by the 1 percent interest above the rate on demand deposits.[53] Thus the new bonds not only carried a higher interest rate, 5 percent, but buyers could specify the term of bond they desired.

Also, the 5 percent bank notes were designed to be considerably more attractive than most stock investments. The bonds came with tear-off coupons to facilitate the receipt of interest payments, which could be

---

50 For the text of the speech to the Council of State Credit Institutions, see *OGKU za 1859* (St. Petersburg, 1861), 4-5; *Ukazatel' ekonomicheskii*, 40 (October 1, 1860); *Aktsioner* 38 (September 23, 1860); *Zhurnal dlia Aktsionerov* 192 (September 14, 1860).

51 *Birzhevye Vedomosti*, 255 (November 29, 1862).

52 Reitern, *M. Kh. Reitern*, 74, see also 134. Twenty years later, Bunge admitted that "after the mistake was made to lower interest rates on bank deposits," a "feverish activity in industry set in, which ended with the exhaustion of the banks' cash reserves"; Bunge, "Zametki," 108-09, 114.

53 Lamanskii, "Iz vospominanii," 3: 584-85.

obtained at any branch of the Commercial Bank and all 600 county treasury bureaus. In contrast, stock dividends were often difficult and costly to obtain for those living outside of St. Petersburg. Provisions were made for the bonds to circulate abroad, and they could be sold or transferred by simple endorsement much more readily than stock. In addition, they could be mortgaged at up to 90 percent of their value in the Commercial Bank or any office of the Social Welfare Boards, a privilege shared only with stockholders of the Russian Railroad Company. Other stocks could not be accepted as collateral. Later, the government ordered that these bonds be accepted at nominal value when used to pay off existing mortgage debt.[54] In sum, banking reform was now being given a higher priority than even railroad and steam navigation development, a shift in policy that the stock market was soon to recognize.

Only holders of unrestricted deposits in the state credit institutions were allowed to purchase the new bank notes. Restricted or institutional deposits could not be used, though these funds could still be invested in the 4 percent perpetuities issued in March. An early deadline of December 31, 1859, was set for the conclusion of the conversion, as there was considerable concern about a protracted crisis.[55] After that date, depositors choosing to leave their money in the banks as demand accounts would receive only 2 percent interest.

At first, response to the new 5 percent bonds was slow. Because this was a form of investment new to Russia, many feared the bonds would not be redeemed as promised. And, it seems, the administrators of the state credit institutions were not sympathetic to the reform. Lamanskii recounted in his memoirs that "Minister of Finance Kniazhevich was in complete despair." Members of the Banking Commission began to blame each other for the reform "not coming up to expectations."[56]

As they had during the previous spring, Bunge and Lamanskii launched a campaign in the press to encourage investment in the new bonds. They stressed that the restructuring of existing deposits was a necessary prelude to a complete reform of the banking system. The recent consolidation of all banking operations under the Ministry of Finance, they advised, would ensure accurate and proper accounting, not only

54 *PSZ* II, vol. 37, no. 38,490 (July 23, 1862).

55 Lamanskii, "Iz vospominanii," 4: 63.

56 Ibid., 66.

of the new bonds but of all state deposits and debts. Both Bunge and Lamanskii were straightforward about the costs. With the state credit institutions charging borrowers 4 percent and the new bonds paying 5 percent on the converted deposits, the annual loss, Bunge guessed, would run approximately 6.75 million rubles a year. Lamanskii was less specific, stating only that "initially this reform would be fairly costly; but, as can be seen from the minister's report, the treasury is prepared for these expenses."[57]

The deadline for purchasing the 5 percent bonds had to be extended, but the restructuring proved successful. By September 1860, 272.6 million rubles of deposits had been used to purchase the thirty-seven-year notes. The lowering of interest rates on demand deposits to 2 percent, which took effect on January 1, 1860, encouraged many institutions to buy 4 percent perpetuities. By late 1860, almost 148 million rubles of restricted and institutional deposits were converted into perpetuities or had been pledged to be converted. Thus over 43 percent of all deposits in the state credit institutions were exchanged for long-term bonds. Cash withdrawals were covered by the issuing of paper money and two foreign loans, including one on rather unfavorable terms. The first year's cost of the restructuring was 10.1 million rubles, considerably higher than Bunge's estimate.[58] Total costs over the life of the bonds were expected to approach 200 million rubles.

One neglected aspect of the Great Reforms is this massive shift of capital out of the state credit institutions. Because their records were not public and the state did not publish its budget, few persons outside the government's small circle of financial advisers were aware of the true dimensions of the crisis until late 1860, almost a year after it had

---

57 E. I. Lamanskii, "Neskol'ko slov ob"iasnenii po povodu piatiprotsentnykh bankovykh biletov," *Ukazatel' politiko-ekonomicheskii* 39 (September 26, 1859); N. Kh. Bunge, "Preobrazovanie russkikh bankov," *Zhurnal dlia Aktsionerov* 141 (September 24, 1859).

58 *OGKU za 1859*, 5-12; *Zhurnal dlia Aktsionerov*, 6, 92 (February 8 and September 14, 1860); *Aktsioner*, 38 (September 23, 1860); *Ukazatel' ekonomicheskii*, 4, 89 (October 1, 1860, and November 12, 1861); Reitern, *M. Kh. Reitern*, 148-49; *Birzhevye Vedomosti*, 10, 164, 255, 38 (January 13, 1861, August 3 and November 29, 1862, and May 28, 1868); "Finansovaia politika," 13-14; Sudeikin, *Gosudarstvennyi bank*, 148-49; Migulin, *Nasha bankovaia politika*, 78-87; Borovoi, *Kredit*, 278-79; Pogrebinskii, *Ocherki istorii finansov*, 30-31.

passed. The official explanation for the new banking legislation served to play down, if not cover up, the crisis. But in 1859, the government was not merely seizing an opportune moment for banking reform, it was confronted with the imminent collapse of the state credit institutions. Within six months, they were all abolished. A new State Bank assumed their assets and liabilities, including the heavy annual losses resulting from having to liquidate the 5 percent bank notes.[59]

The immediate crisis was thus resolved. But, during the spring and summer of 1859, debt conversion, transport development, peasant land reform, and agricultural credit became intertwined. It would be useful to review the sequence of events to see how the banking crisis constrained the government's handful of financial advisers. In December 1858, as the financial crisis was becoming evident, the government committed itself to a landed emancipation. In February 1859, the tsar ordered the formation of an Editing Commission (actually two, although only one was formed) to draft the legislation. This commission began its work in March. Simultaneously, the government's coterie of financial advisers struggled with the banking crisis, leading to the March issue of 4 percent perpetuities. By April, it was clear that the introduction of these termless bonds had only aggravated the problem. The state credit institutions were on the verge of collapse, and a formal Banking Commission was established. On April 27, a special Finance Commission was formed to write the peasant land redemption law, as this required expertise not possessed by members of the Editing Commission. The Banking Commission and the Finance Commission each consisted of eight persons. Bunge, Lamanskii, Hagemeister, Reutern, and N. A. Miliutin served on both. Out of necessity, banking reform took precedence. On July 10, the government announced yet another panel, the Commission on the Establishment of Land Banks, charged with drafting legislation to reestablish long-term agricultural credit. Landlords had been without access to credit since April. This fourteen-member commission included a number of legal experts. But, for financial matters, the government called upon the same five men and A. P. Zablotskii-Desiatovskii, former director of the agriculture department of the Ministry of State Domains and also a member of the Finance Commission. Hagemeister was appointed chair.

[59] *PSZ* II, vol. 34, no. 35,287 (December 26, 1859).

The Finance Commission spent much of the spring and summer preparing the first draft of the redemption law, which was completed on August 12. On August 25, the Commission on Land Banks began its work, which continued until December. By then, it seemed certain that the second attempt at debt conversion would succeed. The Banking Commission turned to writing the charter for the new State Bank. On July 1, 1860, with a figurehead as director and Lamanskii as vice-director, the State Bank opened. The government's financial experts continued their work on the redemption law throughout 1860. In late November, it was ready for approval.

The question was, could these men successfully develop a coherent policy to meet Russia's pressing transportation, agrarian reform, and banking needs? In September 1859, just after the first draft of the redemption law was completed and the second conversion of bank deposits had been announced, Bunge and Lamanskii addressed this issue in order to quell concern. To those who worried whether Russia possessed the financial resources both to convert the bank deposits and to fund peasant land reform, Bunge said it did. He expressed reservations, however, about whether sufficient capital would be available to provide the nobility with new forms of long-term credit to restructure their estates using hired wage labor.[60] Lamanskii was more optimistic. "There is no longer any reason to fear either the development of industrial enterprises, the issuing of obligations for the important social reform of peasant life, or justifiable borrowing by the government in periods of extraordinary need, in a word, all the things which we need and to which, until now, our credit institutions have continuously served as an obstacle."[61] As for rural land credit, he asserted, "Mortgage loans against immovable property will soon develop and in even greater amounts than before, but on other, more solid bases, safer for the banks, and under conditions just as advantageous for borrowers."[62] But Lamanskii was mistaken.

To many observers and officials, undertaking a massive redemption operation that required vast amounts of new credit so soon after the issue of 275 million rubles of easily circulating bonds was not possible. But the members of the Finance Commission expended considerable

60 Bunge, "Preobrazovanie russkikh bankov."

61 Lamanskii, "Neskol'ko ob"iasnenii," 875-76.

62 Ibid.

effort to tailor the redemption law to the banking crisis.[63] Initially, the government planned to extend substantial financial assistance to the redemption operation. In February 1859, Ia. I. Rostovtsev, chairman of the Editing Commission, suggested that as much as 15 million rubles a year might be available. In fact, prior to the formation of the Editing Commission, special legislation was passed, and then renewed in 1859 and 1860, that designated certain revenues from the Ministry of State Domains for emancipation purposes, though not necessarily for the redemption operation.[64] By the time the Finance Commission began its work in mid-1859, Rostovtsev had already lowered his figure of potential government assistance to 5 million rubles.[65] But the members of the Finance Commission were adamant that the redemption operation be a pure credit transaction, completely self-supporting. In the process of committing substantial government resources for thirty-seven years to restructure the deposits in the state credit institutions, the commission members opposed any new government expenditures except for railroad development.[66] The commission was firm on the question of government assistance. "The aim, which the government is able to take upon itself to guarantee ... consists strictly in expediting the peasants'

[63] Resolution of these matters was left almost solely to the Finance Commission. According to P. Kovan'ko, a nineteenth-century historian, "neither the Secret Committee nor its successor (in name only) the Main Committee [of Peasant Affairs] had the slightest idea of how to accomplish an emancipation of the peasants under the condition of allotting them land. Both to the Committee, and to Rostovtsev [its chairman], this financial operation represented something fearful, and scarcely practicable." The proposals of the Finance Commission were not reviewed by the Editing Commission, as was done with other emancipation legislation. They were little changed by higher government bodies. The Main Committee and the Ministry of Finance began their review of the draft law only in late November 1860. The draft statute reached the State Council just ten days before it was enacted in February 1861. P. Kovan'ko, *Reforma 19 fevralia 1861 goda i ee posledstviia s finansovoi tochki zreniia (Vykupnaia operatsiia 1861 g.-1907 g.)* (Kiev, 1914), 3-4, 156-58, 171-74.

[64] Ia. I. Rostovtsev, "Khod i iskhod krest'ianskogo voprosa," signed on February 14, 1859, and published in *PIM*, vol. 1, pp. 58-59; *PIM*, vol. 11, pp. 93-96. See also his comments to the full Editing Commission, Journal of the Editing Commission, *PIM*, vol. 1 (March 5, 1859): 5; (April 29, 1859): 36-37.

[65] *PIM*, vol. 1 (May 20, 1859): 48-50.

[66] Hagemeister, "O finansakh Rossii," 123-25; Hagemeister, "Vzgliad," 1: 28. See also *Birzhevye Vedomosti*, 264 (December 11, 1862).

purchase of land and in ensuring former serfowners the proper receipt of payments owed; it is impossible to go beyond this: obviously at the present time the government cannot take upon itself the obligation to provide financial resources, at any price, to make the [peasants] property owners; to do otherwise would mean subjecting the entire operation to an unaccountable risk."[67] As the commission's report succinctly stated, "By way of financial prudence, it should be taken as a principle that the redemption operation should, so to speak, sustain itself, and not burden the state treasury with new permanent expenditures."[68] Peasant payments were to cover all interest and principal, all administrative costs, and all contingencies. No funds were ever appropriated for the redemption operation itself.[69]

By comparison, in Prussia, the government paid a significant portion of the redemption loan principal, covered all administrative costs, and made it possible to liquidate the debt even faster, if certain funds became available. In Austria, government assistance was even greater. The Finance Commission discussed these redemption acts at length, since many expected the Russian redemption operation to be modeled on Prussian and Austrian precedents. But the commission found it necessary to limit the government's role to that of a mediator, not an underwriter.[70] The tsarist government did not spend a kopek in undertaking the Great Reform of making twenty million peasants property owners.

Such financial prudence cost the peasants dearly. The redemption law specified that once peasants became property owners (and no provision was made requiring this be done), a forty-nine-year credit operation would begin. The government would compensate serfowners for the land given to the peasants with 5 percent bank notes (bonds) and 5 percent redemption certificates. The bank notes, designated second series to distinguish them from the thirty-seven-year bonds issued to restructure bank deposits, were to be liquidated in series. The second series bank

67 *PIM*, vol. 11, p. 138.

68 *PIM*, vol. 11, p. 217.

69 Kovan'ko, *Reforma*, 27. Of the 23.5 million rubles appropriated for emancipation, most of it was spent by the government to purchase estates from serfowners whose lands did not qualify for redemption under the terms of the general statute.

70 Kovan'ko, *Reforma*, 105.

notes carried all the same privileges as the first. As for the certificates, every five years from the date of each redemption agreement, one-third were to be exchanged for bank notes (bonds), until, after fifteen years, a landlord no longer held any certificates. All obligations were to be liquidated within the forty-nine-year term.[71] In 1862, it was announced that 5.5 percent annuities were to be issued for lands initially not eligible for redemption. The government promised to announce the terms of their liquidation within ten years, although these annuities were also to be redeemed within forty-nine years of their date of issue.[72]

The peasants, in turn, were to pay the government 6 percent annually of the total redemption sum given their former owner. Of this, 5 or 5.5 percent was to cover the interest on the obligations issued and .5 percent to pay off the principal. The remaining .5 percent from the bank notes and redemption certificates was for administrative costs and defaults. In other words, on that portion of a redemption grant issued in 5 percent paper, 1 out of every 12 rubles the government received back from the peasants went not to pay interest or principal but to cover administrative expenses and contingencies. And most redemption grants paid 5 percent. Between 1862 and 1866, 62 percent of all redemption paper was in 5 percent obligations. After 1874, 5.5 percent paper was no longer issued. Through January 1, 1885, 78 percent of total redemption obligations paid 5 percent.[73] On over three-fourths of all peasant payments, the government was receiving 8.5 percent beyond what was needed to cover the interest and principal. This margin more than ensured that the treasury did not have to subsidize the redemption operation.[74] In other words, peasant redemption debt carried high interest

[71] *PSZ* II, vol. 36, no. 36,659, articles 114, 140-55 (February 19, 1861).

[72] *PSZ* II, vol. 37, no. 38,407 (June 27, 1862).

[73] *Otchet gosudarstvennogo banka po vykupnoi operatsii s otkrytiia vykupa po 1 ianvaria 1892 goda* (St. Petersburg, 1893), 48.

[74] Although the figures cannot be considered very reliable, various estimates place the surplus by 1877, after all administrative costs and accumulated arrears were deducted, between 20 and 65 million rubles. I. Vil'son, "Vykupnye za zemli platezhi krest'ian-sobstvennikov byvshikh pomeshchich'ikh, 1862-1876," *Zapiski Imperatorskogo Russkogo Geograficheskogo Obshchestva po otdeleniiu statistiki* (St. Petersburg, 1878), 5: 315-16; Kovan'ko, *Reforma*, 9, 11, 274-77, 434-35; P. P. Migulin, *Vykupnye platezhi: k voprosu o ikh ponizhenii* (Kharkov, 1904), 13; [no author] "Obshchii balans vykupnoi operatsii," *Vestnik Finansov* 23 (1903), prilozheniia, 12. See also *Birzhevye Vedomosti*, 218 (May 19, 1870).

rates and high reserve requirements. The impact of the banking crisis on market interest rates and on the government's ability to subsidize land redemption was the cause.

By way of ensuring even further that the redemption operation did not lose money, the Finance Commission imposed restrictions common to mortgage transactions. Under the terms of the redemption law, the compensation to landlords—and thus the size of peasant payments on this debt—was not to be determined by a valuation of the land to be redeemed. To do so would have necessitated compilation of a cadastre, delaying the reform for years. In this case, Prussian and Austrian models provided the solution. Quitrent (*obrok*), in effect, the peasants' ability to pay, became the basis for assessment. If peasants and landowners could not reach an agreement on the amount of quitrent, various regional norms were to be used. The quitrent was multiplied by a factor of 16.67 to obtain the proximate value of the land; that is, quitrents were capitalized at 6 percent.

A dilemma arose, however, because the actual land the peasants received, which served as collateral for their debt to the government, did not always correspond to its capitalized value. The Finance Commission recognized that, while there was a strong correlation between quitrent and land values, the relationship was not perfect. This gap could expose the government to unjustifiable risk. For example, the commission assumed that in regions where non-agricultural income was common, serf quitrent probably reflected these revenue sources.[75] The Finance Commission responded to the situation in the way any modern bank would; it refused to lend the peasants, or grant the landlord, the full valuation sum. Instead, a redemption grant was limited to 75 or 80 percent of the capitalized quitrent, depending on various circumstances. Thus, as the Finance Commission explained, "for greater prudence and by way of eliminating any risk to State credit," it was necessary to provide for a 20 or 25 percent margin on redemption collateral.[76]

---

[75] *Vtoroe izdanie materialov Redaktsionnykh Komissii, dlia sostavleniia "Polozhenii o krest'ianakh vykhodiashchikh iz krepostnoi zavisimosti"* (St. Petersburg, 1859-60), vol. 1, book 1, 160. See also Kovan'ko, *Reforma*, 137.

[76] *PIM*, vol. 11, pp. 157-61; *PSZ* II, vol. 36, no. 36,659 (February 19, 1861), article 66.

The most difficult problem for the Finance Commission became how to make the peasants property owners through a credit operation of 800 million rubles without endangering Russia's already strained credit markets. Fear was wide-spread in government circles that the redemption operation, even if it did not require government funds, was dangerous.[77] Lamanskii did not share these concerns. But, in his memoirs, he recorded that "the other members of the commission, including M. Kh. Reutern, feared that the appearance in circulation of such a mass of interest-bearing paper would destroy the money market, especially given the general unfamiliarity in Russia with large credit operations. These fears served, by the way, as a basis for all sorts of restrictions, at least at first, on redemption transactions."[78] In 1866, Reutern described his fears: "The Great Reforms ... found us with a system of credit institutions that was ruined, chaotic monetary circulation, and inadequate national capital."[79] The solution of the Finance Commission was to have redemption be a slow, gradual, and voluntary process. The amount of credit paper issued was limited and, once issued, hampered in its ability to enter the market.

Austrian and Prussian precedents of an immediate, mandatory redemption of peasant holdings were not followed in Russia. Rostovtsev, echoing the tsar's views, argued it would be "unjust" to force landowners to sell and peasants to buy land at fixed government prices.[80] But, in order to ensure that the tsar's views and those of his leading advisers did not change, as they did on many issues between 1857 and 1861, the Finance Commission added its weight to the principle of a voluntary or, at least, gradual redemption. Referring to Austria and Germany, the commission emphasized, "In general, *mandatory redemption was usually a consequence of political necessity* that demanded decisive measures for the quieting of the rural population."[81] This, the commission argued, was not the case in Russia. Of more direct financial concern, the commission warned the government, "Compulsory redemption would require the sudden issue of credit paper in huge amounts, which would

77 Kovan'ko, *Reforma*, 2-3; Migulin, *Vykupnye platezhi*, 1.
78 Lamanskii, "Iz vospominanii," 3: 586-87.
79 Reitern, *M. Kh. Reitern*, 135. See also *Birzhevye Vedomosti*, 274 (December 22, 1862).
80 *PIM*, vol. 1, p. 59; vol. 3, p. 13.
81 *PIM*, vol. 11, p. 133, emphasis in the original.

give rise to very ruinous consequences both for internal credit and for the landowners themselves."[82] Worried about flooding the market with redemption paper so soon after the issue of first series bonds, the commission asserted that "protecting internal credit from all sorts of fluctuations, even if only temporary, and from even the slightest risk, will necessitate certain measures for keeping redemption transactions within the bounds of strict, gradual development."[83] Finally, the commission noted that many serfs on corvee (*barshchina*) did not have the ability to earn sufficient cash income to meet redemption payments. In its view, this was yet another obstacle to immediate, universal, mandatory redemption.[84]

As a result of these concerns, the law did not extend redemption to peasants on corvee, and it limited the size of an allotment the government would take in mortgage. Article 30 of the redemption law stated: "Assistance from the government in the acquisition by the peasants of their allotment as property is extended only to peasants on quitrent." Many provincial committees, in reviewing the draft legislation, expressed their opposition to corvee estates being ineligible for redemption. The commission responded: "Indeed, the regulation cited gravely limits the application of the redemption operation, as at present scarcely a third of the serf population is on quitrent, and most probably the abolition of corvee will take place rather slowly, owing to inadequate cash resources of the peasants.... Meanwhile, the status of corvee estates under the new order will be particularly difficult for the owners, the residents, and the government."[85] Numerous serfowners suggested that measures be adopted to permit the redemption of corvee estates. But the commission was unmoved. "In spite of the importance of such arguments, the members of the Finance Commission do not see any possibility either to begin the redemption of corvee estates, or to facilitate, by some sort of artificial measures, the transfer of peasants onto quitrent."[86] The principle of a gradual redemption process to limit the flow of credit paper onto the market was enacted into law.[87]

82 *PIM*, vol. 11, p. 136.
83 *PIM*, vol. 3, pp. 15-16, 26.
84 *PIM*, vol. 3, p. 27; vol. 11, pp. 146-48; Kovan'ko, *Reforma*, 18-19.
85 *PIM*, vol. 11, p. 146.
86 *PIM*, vol. 1, p. 147.
87 Kovan'ko, *Reforma*, 116, 137-39, 147.

This same consideration gave rise to restrictions on the physical size of an allotment that the government would accept in mortgage. Prior to receiving the preliminary report of the Finance Commission, the Editing Commission, following the advice of the minister of the interior and his land department, came out strongly in favor of the peasants receiving their existing allotments. "It stands to reason that designated limits ought to be established within such wide boundaries so that cutting off surplus peasant land will not be a general phenomenon," the economic division of the Editing Commission wrote in its very first report.[88] But, as is well known, reductions in the size of peasant landholdings were common under the terms of the emancipation laws.[89] For this, the Finance Commission bore some responsibility, though other factors, especially the desire to maintain agriculture among the gentry, were of greater significance.

Redemption was to be largely a voluntary agreement, not mandatory or immediate, with landowners and peasants themselves determining when to proceed, the size of the allotment, and the value of the land. The government provided norms only if an agreement could not be reached and the landlord insisted on redemption.[90] In response to this policy of voluntary agreements, the Finance Commission cautioned, "It is necessary to establish regulations for determining the maximum size of the redemption sum allowed by the government."[91] The commission feared that a voluntary process with no limit on the amount of land both parties might subject to redemption could lead to a far larger redemption operation than the government desired and to the uncontrolled issue of credit paper. Moreover, the sheer size of the peasants' debt, even if adequately secured, might endanger both state finances and private credit.[92]

Thus, in contrast to the Editing Commission, which in its early deliberations desired that most peasants keep their existing allotments, the Finance Commission sought to limit the maximum allotment

---

88 *PIM*, vol. 2 (June 9, 1859), 9, 12-13, 27.

89 Zaionchkovskii, *Otmena krepostnogo prava*, 237-42.

90 *PSZ* II, vol. 36, no. 36,659, article 64; no. 36,662, article 159; no. 36,663, article 164; no. 36,664, article 138; *PIM*, vol. 1, no. 16 (May 20, 1859) (General Session of the Editing Commission); vol. 3, p. 16; and vol. 11, p. 136.

91 *PIM*, vol. 3, p. 19.

92 *PIM*, vol. 11, pp. 150-52; Kovan'ko, *Reforma*, 148.

out of fiscal considerations. Throughout 1859 and 1860, the Editing Commission was pressured by many groups, including the Finance Commission, to reduce the maximums, and eventually this was done. Under the redemption law, landlords and peasants were free to reach any agreement on the amount of land the peasants were to acquire and the price they were to pay. But the maximum amount of land that could be purchased through the government's credit operation was limited. Similarly, maximum quitrents were set for computing the capitalized value of the land. The allotment and quitrent norms used were the same ones the government established in the event that a voluntary agreement could not be reached and the landlord then forced redemption.[93]

The results proved devastating. After emancipation, many nobles, though willing to have their ex-serfs acquire land in excess of the maximum, refused to do so without a government guarantee for the proper receipt of payment. Landlords feared that, without seigneurial authority, it would be difficult to compel peasants to fulfill private obligations. To many peasants, the only difference between a voluntary agreement and one demanded by the landlord was that the voluntary agreement might cost more. Consequently, outside Russia's western provinces, only one in three redemption settlements was reached on the basis of voluntary agreement.[94] The government went further to minimize the amount of redemption paper that would have to be put in circulation and then to delay its issue. Beyond the restrictions limiting the size of a redemption grant and the exclusion of peasants on corvee from the redemption process, the law required that all outstanding mortgage debt to the state credit institutions be deducted from the total sum due the landlord (Article 69). Only the balance was to be issued in credit paper. The Finance Commission maintained that "this substantially facilitates the redemption operation.... All that is required from the government is a guarantee of the debt to the credit institutions without the issue of new credit paper, which is the greatest of all difficulties in the present

93 *PSZ* II, vol. 36, no. 36,659, article 65; *PIM*, vol. 11, p. 152.

94 *PSZ* II, vol. 36, no. 36,659, article 68. See P. Kovan'ko, "Osvobozhdenie krest'ian i obiazatel'nyi vykup: Na osnovanii arkhivnogo materiala," *Russkaia Mysl'* (June 1912): 27; Vil'son, "Vykupnye za zemli platezhi," 278-80. If a landlord demanded redemption, the law prohibited any supplemental peasant payments. If redemption was voluntary, beyond the maximum redemption grant, the landlord and peasants were free to reach any agreement on additional payments.

matter."[95] Serfowners were not given the option of receiving the full redemption valuation of their land and then continuing to pay off existing mortgage debt. Thus redemption was a massive, even if voluntary, foreclosure. To use official terminology, bank debts of nobles "were transferred" to the redemption operation. Peasant payments went directly to liquidate bank debt. Once redemption began, landlords lost the "right" to default on their loans, as was their habit on occasion, eliminating yet another risk to state finances. P. Kovan'ko argued that if it had not been possible to retire serfowner debt in this manner, the Finance Commission would have been inclined to propose an even more gradual redemption process. Instead, less credit paper had to be issued, landlords were freed of mortgage debt, state finances were more secure, and the peasants became property owners sooner.[96] This so-called transfer of bank debts to the redemption operation had yet another dimension of fiscal caution. In 1857, after interest rates on loans had been reduced, serfowners paid 4 percent interest. To amortize the debt, they paid an additional 2 percent for twenty-eight years or 1.5 percent for thirty-three years. When bank debts were transferred to the redemption operation, the government received from the peasants 6 percent (interest and principal) for forty-nine years. What did the Finance Commission propose to do with sixteen or twenty-one years of profit? "The difference ought to revert for the use of the redemption operation itself, increasing its reserve capital, and along with this guaranteeing and accelerating the proper conclusion of redemption."[97] No thought was given to reducing the size of peasant payments from the outset in anticipation of these revenues. Again, the Finance Commission exercised extreme, if not excessive, caution in ensuring the solvency of the redemption operation and in protecting the state treasury.[98]

Of the 948 million rubles of serfowner land to be allotted to the peasants, the commission estimated that the government would accept in mortgage a maximum of 758.5 million rubles, 80 percent of its total

---

95 *PIM*, vol. 3, p. 22. See also *PSZ* II, vol. 36, no. 36,659, article 143; Kovan'ko, *Reforma*, 299.

96 Kovan'ko, *Reforma*, 288. It should be noted that while the government was a lenient lender, on the whole serfowners did pay their bank debts, though not always on time and often only under threat of foreclosure.

97 *PIM*, vol. 11, p. 194.

98 Kovan'ko, *Reforma*, 9, 288-89, 299.

capitalized quitrent value. From this, 425 million rubles of landowner debt would be deducted, leaving 333.5 million rubles to be issued in credit paper.[99] Because redemption was limited to peasants on quitrent, the commission thought it unlikely that more than 2.5 million peasants would begin redeeming their land in the first five years, thereby requiring no more than 50 million rubles in credit paper to be issued during this period.[100] And the redemption paper issued was to be restricted in its circulation in order to protect the credit markets.

The law intended that, once redemption began on an estate, the noble landowner, though left with less land than before emancipation, would still possess substantial holdings, be free of debt, and hold two kinds of bonds, some readily convertible into cash and others yielding an annual income. The convertible bonds, coupled with new forms of long-term mortgage credit then being proposed, would give landlords the capital necessary to restructure their estates along commercial lines. If the redemption agreement was a voluntary one, the serfowner could also receive cash payments directly from the peasants.[101]

The intent of the Finance Commission was to keep much of the credit paper issued for redemption off the market. Under the law, most serfowners were to receive both 5 percent bank notes and redemption certificates. Only redemption grants of under 1,000 rubles were to be in bank notes alone. For progressively larger amounts, only one-fifth to one-twentieth was to be in bank notes, with the remainder in certificates (Article 70). Second series (redemption) bank notes or bonds were not to be issued in amounts of less than 50 rubles, to prevent them circulating like cash (Article 146).[102] But they could be freely traded on the bond market and, therefore, readily converted into cash.

In contrast, redemption certificates were not to be issued in denominations of less than 3,000 rubles when possible and under no circumstances in amounts of less than 300 rubles (Articles 144 and 145). Redemption certificates could not be traded on any exchange. Rather, they had to be issued in a person's name and could be transferred only

---

99 *PIM*, vol. 11, p. 172.

100 *PIM*, vol. 11, pp. 173-74.

101 Lamanskii, "Iz vospominanii," 3: 588; N. Kh. Bunge, "Kredit i krepostnoe pravo," *Russkii Vestnik* 4 (1859), part 2, pp. 336-39; Kovan'ko, *Reforma*, 150, 313; Migulin, *Vykupnye platezhi*, 3 -5.

102 *PIM*, vol. 11, p. 205.

in accordance with procedures governing immovable property, that is, by deed of purchase (Article 147). Large denominations and inconvenient exchange procedures, the commission reasoned, were necessary "for the soundness of internal credit, since the simultaneous issue of a huge number of new obligations could have an unfavorable influence on their rate of exchange and consequently [they] could circulate to the disadvantage of the holders themselves and interfere with the successful development of the entire operation."[103] As the Stock Exchange News explained to its readers, "Everybody understands that the basis of the redemption operation by means of 5 percent certificates, the exchange of which has to be undertaken by deed of purchase, all but coincided with the transformation of our credit institutions, most especially with the consolidation of bank debt by means of the issue of 5 percent [first series] bank notes. The fear of suddenly flooding the money market seemed at the time quite natural."[104]

The Finance Commission worried that 5 percent government-guaranteed redemption paper, flooding the market and selling substantially below nominal value, would compete with other investment options. Such a flow of free capital into redemption paper would hamper railroad development, adversely affect government borrowing, and push interest rates up even further. Thus, although the commission often spoke of the benefits of providing ex-serfowners with a long-term, guaranteed income, its intent was to keep redemption paper off the market.

In sum, peasant reform was not accorded a high financial priority. Unlike banking reform, the government was not to subsidize peasant acquisition of land. Nor were state or transport credit needs to be hampered by the redemption operation. The law was designed to keep total redemption debt within strict limits. The restriction of a redemption loan to 80 percent of the collateral's value and the transference of bank debts onto the peasants greatly limited the amount of credit paper that would have to be issued. Coupled with the high interest rates charged to the peasants, the transfer of debts provided for the accumulation of a

---

103 *PIM*, vol. 3, p. 23. See also Bunge, "Kredit i krepostnoe pravo," 367; Lamanskii, "Iz vospominanii," 3: 587-88; Kovan'ko, *Reforma*, 61; Migulin, Vykupnye platezhi, 2-3.

104 *Birzhevye Vedomosti*, 274 (December 22, 1862).

substantial capital reserve to cover all redemption costs and contingencies. To protect credit markets from the sudden issue of paper so soon after the banking crisis, redemption was to be voluntary; in order to be gradual, it was to exclude peasants on corvee. For the same reason, serfowners were not to be given liquid assets in compensation. Redemption was to stand alone and apart.[105]

Not all worked out as planned. On June 27, 1862, as a result of serfowner pressure and peasant discontent, corvee estates were made eligible for redemption.[106] Between March and November 1863, immediate mandatory redemption was ordered in the western provinces to prevent the spread of a revolt of the Polish nobility to the peasantry.[107] On June 24, 1863, the government rescinded the requirement that redemption certificates be exchanged by deed of purchase and permitted their transfer by notaries and stockbrokers. Although the certificates still carried more restrictions than bank notes (bonds), the market viewed them with more favor.[108] These sudden revampings of the redemption law reveal a lack of foresight among the autocracy's financial experts in regard to the broad social and political dilemmas in society.

In all, instead of a maximum of 2.5 million male peasants beginning to redeem their allotments in the first five years, as the Finance Commission expected, 3.6 million males concluded redemption transactions. The total value of these redemption grants was 329.5 million rubles, of which 48 percent was withheld for bank debts. By January 1, 1867, a total of 179 million rubles in redemption paper had been issued.[109]

Despite the law, the market won out over legal restrictions. Between 1862 and 1866, the easily exchanged bank notes kept their value, while restricted paper traded at a deep discount. As early as May 1863, bank notes could be realized for 97 to 98 percent of their value. By contrast, redemption certificates sold for only 80 percent of face value and the

105 Migulin, *Vykupnye platezhi*, 7-8.

106 *PSZ* II, vol. 37, no. 38,407.

107 *PSZ* II, vol. 38, no. 39,337 (March 1, 1863); no. 39,928 (July 30, 1863); no. 40,172 (November 2, 1863).

108 *PSZ* II, vol. 38, no. 39,779 (June 24, 1863). See also Birzhevye Vedomosti (July 13, 1863).

109 *Otchet gosudarstvennogo banka*, 67. See also N. Kh. Vessel', *Nasha novaia gosudarstvennaia finansovaia deiatel'nost' (1892-1894 gg.)* (St. Petersburg, 1894), 10.

5.5 percent annuities issued for the redemption of corvee estates only 78 percent, though they paid higher interest.[110] In order to ensure that redemption did not entail such large losses for serfowners that they would refuse to enter into any redemption agreements and to maintain the value of other credit paper, the government was forced to ease the restrictions on the exchange of certificates and annuities. This improved their value considerably. Even if certificates and annuities never traded as freely as bank notes, by mid-1864 the gap in market value closed roughly ten points, half of what it had been before.

But the overall picture remained bleak. The banking crisis had forced the issuance of more than 420 million rubles in long-term bonds and perpetuities. The *Stockholders' Journal* noted that many companies in their initial stock offerings of 1857 and 1858 had counted on capital in the state credit institutions being invested in their enterprises. "These hopes were not realized. Bank deposits were converted primarily into new 5 percent notes, and then our vital financial resources ran out."[111] Consequently, the stock market suffered a sharp reversal, and a period of tight money was ushered in. Bunge and Lamanskii continued to defend debt conversion as having restructured capital long since wasted by the government and serfowners. They attributed the continuation of the financial crisis to an excessive demand for capital. As early as September 1860, Bunge stated that "whereas at first the crisis was attributed to a surplus of paper, now, with tight money prevailing," many were blaming the conversion of bank deposits."[112] Lamanskii argued persuasively that the huge issue of paper money during the Crimean War had temporarily masked the true shortage of capital from which Russia suffered.[113] On the eve of emancipation, the *Economic Indicator* reported, "At present, with tight money common, with the decline of joint-stock companies and enterprises of various sorts, in a word, with a general financial-

110 *Birzhevye Vedomosti* began regularly quoting the market value of all redemption paper in May 1863. See also *Birzhevye Vedomosti* 274 (December 22, 1862); *Ezhegodnik ministerstva finansov za 1869* (St. Petersburg, 1869), 163-81; Kovan'ko, Reforma, 61-62, 311; Migulin, *Vykupnye platezhi*, 8-9; Bliokh, *Finansy Rossii*, 2: 52, 57, 77.

111 *Zhurnal dlia Aktsionerov* 172 (April 27, 1860).

112 N. Kh. Bunge, "Zametki o sovremennom ekonomicheskom krizise," *Zhurnal dlia Aktsionerov* 194 (September 28, 1860).

113 *Birzhevye Vedomosti* 43 (February 21, 1861).

commercial crisis, it is scarcely possible to meet two people who do not mention the word credit in the course of conversation."[114]

In England and France, only a small portion of capital was tied up in joint-stock ventures when the financial crisis hit in 1857. But in Russia's malnourished capital market, the adoption of a similar innovation proved disastrous. Wide application of new methods of finance in an unprepared environment put the entire modern sector of the economy at risk. Numerous transport firms went bankrupt, and others were forced to scale back. Faith in private ventures through joint-stock companies was shaken for years. By the end of the 1860s, this attempt at borrowing foreign methods of private finance was openly criticized.[115] The fact that the banking crisis in Russia came on the heels of a European financial crisis illustrates a disadvantage of being dependent on the savings rates of other countries. When Russia's traditional sources of foreign capital dried up, attempts to raise funds internally proved ruinous. But it is not surprising that the machinery of Western finance capital failed in Russia of the 1850s nor unusual for financial experimentation to precipitate crisis.[116]

Once the terms of redemption became known, and then were extended, the credit required for redemption deepened the crisis and prolonged the period of tight money. The promise of new forms of long-term mortgage credit for noble landowners could not be kept. The 1859 Commission on Land Banks, headed by Hagemeister, had recommended the establishment of private institutions financed by landowner capital. The commission, in a sharp reversal of longstanding government policy, opposed the expenditure of state funds to finance agricultural credit.[117] Given the tight market, it proved impossible to raise funds privately. Thus the agricultural system foreseen by the reformers—hired wage labor using modern landowner inventory—was not realized. Rather, it yielded to other forms of tenancy, especially small-scale sharecropping or land rental agreements, which required little

---

114 *Ukazatel' ekonomicheskii* 17 (February 26, 1861).

115 *Zhurnal dlia Aktsionerov* 196, 199, and 201 (October 12, November 2 and 16, 1860); *Narodnoe Bogatstvo* 6 (November 7, 1862); and *Birzhevye Vedomosti* 81, 138 (March 27 and May 28, 1868).

116 Hoppit, "Financial Crises," 50.

117 *Trudy komissii ustroistva zemskikh bankov*, 2 vols. (St. Petersburg, 1860), 1: vii-x; *Narodnoe Bogatstvo* 74 (April 7, 1863).

capital outlay by the landlord. Certainly, the financial crisis hampered noble landowners inclined toward agricultural improvement—few though they were.

All in all, the redemption operation and the harsh terms imposed on the peasants were to a considerable extent a response to fiscal constraints dictated by the collapse of state credit institutions. It was the autocracy's ill-fated decision to rely on undeveloped private capital markets to finance transport development that hindered growth, pushed interest rates up, lowered the value of redemption paper, and burdened the peasantry for decades. But the failure of the policy facilitated a return to Russian autocratic traditions of substantial state involvement in society. Still, state intervention in the economy in the early stages of industrialization under conditions of extreme backwardness, subsequently conceptualized by Gerschenkron, required the political will to be innovative and to search for alternatives. There was a need to formulate a distinctly Russian industrial policy rather than merely transplant foreign methods of finance, to recognize broader social and economic constraints rather than simply address fiscal limitations. Only then would politics be in concert with economic necessity. Yet it was precisely this vision that these reformers lacked.

7

The Tax Censuses and the Decline of the Serf Population in Imperial Russia, 1833-1858

Steven L. Hoch and Wilson R. Augustine

The demographic development of the serf population in Imperial Russia, particularly its rate of natural growth during the thirty years preceding the emancipation in 1861, has been the subject of considerable controversy. On the basis of data from the tax censuses (*revizii*), abolitionists contended that the serf population was dying out, implying that the death rate consistently exceeded the birth rate. Many Soviet historians and demographers have subsequently advanced this view, seeing a demographic crisis as one dimension of the collapse of the feudal serf system. The late Daniel Field lent his support to this interpretation.[1] But was serfdom so socially oppressive or economically stifling as to affect natural population growth adversely? Other contemporary statisticians and

---

This essay was originally published in *Slavic Review* 38, no. 3 (September 1979): 403-425.

[1] N. Khr. Bunge, "Izmeneniia soslovnago sostava naseleniia Rossii v promezhutkakh vremeni mezhdu 7 i 8, 8 i 9 reviziiami," *Ekonomicheskii ukazatel'* 44 (November 2-14, 1857): 1021-30; I. Gorlov, "Protektsionizm v Rossii i svoboda truda," *Biblioteka dlia chteniia* 148 (March-April 1858): 189-90; V. I. Lenin, *Ekonomicheskoe soderzhanie narodnichestva i kritika ego v knige g. Struve* (St. Petersburg, 1894) in V. I. Lenin, *Polnoe sobranie sochinenii*, 55 vols., 5th ed. (Moscow, 1958-65), 1:481-84; N. Oganovskii, *Zakonomernost' agrarnoi evoliutsii* (Saratov, 1911), part 2, 239-42; N. M. Druzhinin, *Gosudarstvennye krest'iane i reforma P. D. Kiseleva*, vol. 2 (Moscow, 1958), 294-95; A. G. Rashin, *Naselenie Rossii za 100 let (1811-1913 gg.)* (Moscow, 1956) 4, 34-35; N. M. Shepukhova, "Izmenenie udel'nogo vesa chastnovladel'cheskogo krest'ianstva v sostave naseleniia evropeiskoi Rossii (XVIII-pervaia polovina XIX v.)," *Voprosy istorii* 12 (1959): 130-34; I. D. Koval'chenko, *Krest'iane i krepostnoe khoziaistvo v Riazanskoi i Tambovskoi guberniiakh* (Moscow, 1959), 168-70; I. D. Koval'chenko, *Russkoe krepostnoe krest'ianstvo v pervoi polovine XIX veka* (Moscow, 1967), 306-7, 327; V. M. Kabuzan; *Izmneneniia v razmeshchenii naseleniia v Rossii v XVIII-pervoi polovine XIX v.* (Moscow, 1971), 8-9; Daniel Field, *The End of Serfdom* (Cambridge, MA, 1976), 29.

later historians—either less opposed to serfdom or more skeptical about the accuracy of population data—have avoided the issue. Nevertheless, it has repeatedly been suggested that, of all segments of the population, serfs had the lowest—though not necessarily a negative—rate of natural growth.[2] In contrast, some of the officers of the general staff of the army and one obscure lord in southern Tambov province argued that the decline in the serf population was the result of sizable movements of serfs into other legal categories and not a function of the natural growth rate.[3] Since the mid-1800s, only a few prerevolutionary scholars and one Soviet historian have supported this view.[4] The research on which this article is based, grounded in part on data provided by the tax censuses, essentially supports this alternative analysis.

---

2 V. V. Trubnikov, "Rezul'taty narodnykh perepisei v Ardatovskom uezde Simbirskoi gubernii," *Sbornik statisticheskikh svedenii o Rossii*, vol. 3 (St. Petersburg, 1858), 366; A. Troinitskii, *Krepostnoe naselenie v Rossii po 10-i narodnoi perepisi* (St. Petersburg, 1861), 55-56; P. N. Miliukov, "Krest'iane," *Entsiklopedicheskii slovar'*, vol. 16-A (St. Petersburg, 1895), 684; I. I. Ignatovich, *Pomeshchich'i krest'iane nakanune osvobozhdeniia*, 3rd ed. (Leningrad, 1925), 68-69; Geroid T. Robinson, *Rural Russia Under the Old Regime* (New York, 1932), 62-63; Jerome Blum, *Lord and Peasant in Russia* (Princeton, NJ, 1961), 420-22, 469; A. L. Perkovskii, "Krizis demograficheskogo vosproizvodstva krepostnogo krest'ianstva Rossii v pervoi polovine XIX stoletiia," *Brachnost', rozhdaemost', smertnost' v Rossii i v SSSR* (Moscow, 1977), 188-90.

3 Glavvnyi General'nyi Shtab, *Materialy dlia geografii i statistiki Rossii, sobrannye ofitserami general'nago shtaba*, 25 vols. (St. Petersburg, 1860-68). (Each volume in this series was prepared by a different author and contains geographical and statistical material for a specific province, the name of which appears as its subtitle. Hereafter, separate volumes will be cited as *Materialy*, giving the authors and subtitles.) See M. Baranovich, *Materialy: Riazanskaia guberniia*, 156; M. Domontovich, *Materialy: Chernigovskaia guberniia*, 160-62; A. Lipinskii, *Materialy: Simbirskaia guberniia*, 266; I. Zelenskii, *Materialy: Minskaia guberniia*, 514-15, 632-33; Kh. Kozlov, "O prichinakh ubyli pomeshchich'ikh krest'ian," *Ekonomicheskiia zapiski* 49 (1857): 387-90; Kh. Kozlov, "Neskol'ko slov o statisticheskikh dannykh otnositel'no uvelicheniia i umen'sheniia narodonaseleniia," *Zapiski Lebedianskago obshchestva sel'skago khoziaistva za 1858* (1859), part 2, 53- 61. See also A. Troinitskii, "O chisle krepostnykh v Rossii," *Zhurnal Ministerstva vnutrennikh del* 5-6 (1858): 30 (hereafter cited as *ZhMVD*).

4 V. I. Semevskii, *Krest'ianskii vopros v Rossii*, vol. 2 (St. Petersburg, 1888), 568-70; P. B. Struve, *Krepostnoe khoziaistvo* (Moscow, 1913), 145; A. Kornilov, *Kurs istorii Rossii XIX v.*, part 3 (Moscow, 1914), 23-25; P. G. Ryndziunskii, "Vymiralo li krepostnoe krest'ianstvo pered reformoi 1861 g. ?," *Voprosy istorii* 7 (1967): 54-70.

Given the absence of demographic studies using parish registers (*metricheskie knigi*), parish membership lists (*klirovye vedomosti*), governors' reports, or family records of individual serf estates, the tax censuses provide virtually all that is known about population movements in prereform Imperial Russia.[5] But the *revizii* are only summary totals of the population and therefore are of limited use to the historical demographer. In particular, it is not possible to compute birth rates, death rates, and thus rates of natural growth from the *revizii*. All previous analyses have relied not on these vital statistics, but on absolute and proportional changes in the legal composition of the total population.[6] However, such changes are the result not only of natural population movements, but of mechanical (migratory) and legal movements as well. To determine even the approximate weight of each of these factors in the net decline of the serf population requires cautious use of the tax censuses and other available materials.

When Peter the Great imposed a soul tax early in the eighteenth century, he ordered the registration of all males in those legal categories which were to be taxed under the new law. The first tax census was taken in every village and town, and it provided the basis for assessing the soul tax from 1724 until 1747. During this period, the lists of names on the tax registers were not revised to take into consideration population movements. Thus, a "revisional soul" was no more than a unit of account for taxation and recruitment purposes. A person recorded in the *reviziia* did not need to be physically present, nor, as Gogol reminds us, even alive to be taxed.

To reapportion the tax burden as a result of population changes, in 1742 the senate ordered a new tax census to be taken, and it was henceforth to be repeated at fifteen-year intervals.[7] The second *reviziia* took

[5] Rashin, *Naselenie Rossii*, 16-118.

[6] Trubnikov did attempt to calculate vital rates (Trubnikov, "Rezul'taty narodnykh perepisei," 365). His results, however, must be discounted because of the poor quality of the original data. For example, his figures show that the death rate for the population as a whole in Ardatovskii *uezd* was only slightly above that of modern Western Europe, but, undoubtedly, it was considerably higher.

[7] *Polnoe sobranie zakonov Rossiiskoi imperii s 1649 goda*, 1st series, 45 vols. (St. Petersburg, 1830-1916) (hereafter cited as *PSZ* I), vol. 11, no. 8,619 (September 17, 1742).

until 1747 to complete. Later *revizii* were conducted in 1761-67, 1781-82, 1794-96, and 1811, or roughly every fifteen years (the fourth [1781-82] was postponed five years because of administrative reforms and property disputes arising out of the General Land Survey).[8] Four more *revizii* were gathered in the nineteenth century, but the practice of taking one every fifteen years was abandoned, and the requirement set down by the 1742 law was no longer mentioned in the *revizii* legislation.[9] The seventh *reviziia* was taken in 1815-16, the eighth in 1833-36, the ninth in 1850-51, and the tenth in 1857-58. The soul tax itself was abolished during the years 1883-87. Unfortunately, it is impossible for the modern scholar to verify the results of the *revizii*. Most of the original lists upon which they were based (*revizskie skazki*) have been lost. More important, there is no way of knowing if the original compilers of the *skazki*—whether lord, bailiff, local government official, or peasant functionary—recorded the information accurately. There was certainly a good reason for underestimating the male population and, given the inadequacies of local government administration, it was quite likely that this would happen. The female population was included in the *skazki* for only seven of the ten *revizii*, but frequently the government did not even bother to total the data or verify them by checking parish registers and lists, the procedure followed for males.[10] Only two things can be learned from the ten tax censuses: (1) the approximate size of the male population for a particular administrative region at a given time, and (2) the approximate net growth of the male population between *revizii*. Even determining this information is difficult, however. Some of the *revizii* took a number of years to complete, not all areas of the empire nor all legal categories of the male population were included, local and provincial government reforms led to the redrawing of many administrative boundaries, and the empire itself expanded considerably. One Soviet scholar, V. M. Kabuzan, using the

---

8 Because some *revizii* took a number of years to complete, the so-called basic year of a *reviziia*, used by scholars for computation purposes, does not always conform to the fifteen-year interval. Also, on some occasions, the government calculated the fifteen years from the onset of the previous *reviziia*; on others, from its completion.

9 *PSZ* I, vol. 15, no. 11,364 (November 28, 1761); vol. 31, no. 24,635 (May 18, 1811).

10 V. M. Kabuzan, *Narodonaselenie Rossii v XVIII-pervoi polovine XIX v. (po materialam revizii)* (Moscow, 1963), 77.

summary lists (*perechnevye vedomosti*) and annual tax records (*okladnye knigi*) deposited in the archives of the Department of State Accounts of the senate and the Ministry of Finance, has done much to resolve many of the problems surrounding the *revizii*.[11] Using these documents, which take into account registered migration and some changes in legal status, along with periodically compiled verification lists which included many persons who had somehow escaped registration at the time of the *revizii*, Kabuzan has improved upon the figures that were published by the government and by scholars in the nineteenth century. A summary of his data for the total male population is given in Table 1.

Earlier works on the *revizii* do not contrast sharply with Kabuzan's results. In 1848, Peter Köppen, one of the founders of the Russian Geographic Society, published a brief article on the eighth *reviziia* (1833-36). Nine years later, he produced a very detailed study of the ninth *reviziia* (1850-51).[12] But Köppen was reluctant to move from statistical analysis to social analysis, preferring to present by guberniia the raw data for each of the over one hundred and ten legal categories included in the *reviziia*. Within a few months, N. Khr. Bunge, a professor of political economy and statistics at the University of Kiev and later the minister of finance, reorganized Köppen's data into ten social groups whose origins he traced back to the seventh *reviziia* of 1815-16. Bunge uncovered two striking but simple facts: the empire had experienced a sharp decline in the rate of population growth since the 1830s, accompanied by an even more startling decrease, both proportional and absolute, in the serf population.[13] In spite of discrepancies in the data, all subsequent studies, including the most recent figures, have borne this out. In fact, data from the tenth *reviziia*, unavailable to Bunge, show the trend continuing up to 1857-58 (see Tables 2 and 3).

---

11 Ibid., 99-104, 194-223. See also V. E. Den, *Naselenie Rossii po piatoi revizii*, vol. 1 (Moscow, 1902), 129-234 and appendix 3.

12 P. V. Köppen, "Über die Vertheilung der Bewohner Russlands nach Ständen, in der verschiedenen Provinzen," in *Mémoires de l'Academie Impériale des Sciences de St.-Petersbourg*, 6th series, vol. 7 (St. Petersburg, 1848), 401-29; P. Keppen [P. V. Köppen], *Deviataia reviziia: Izsledovanie o chisle zhitelei v Rossii v 1851 godu* (St. Petersburg, 1857). See also P. I. Keppen [P. V. Köppen], "O narodnykh perepisiakh v Rossii," *Zapiski Imperatorskago russkago geograficheskago obshchestva po otdeleniiu statistiki* 6 (1889): 1-94 (hereafter cited as *Zapiski IRGO*).

13 Bunge, "Izmeneniia soslovnago sostava," 1021-30.

Table 1
Total Male Population, Russia, 1719-1857

		Taxed						Temporarily Tax Exempt		Untaxed	
		Nonserf Peasant Population		Serf Population		Urban Population					
Reviziia (Basic Year)	Total Male Population[a]	Total	%	Total	%	Total	%	Total	%	Total	%
1 (1719)	7,788,000	2,209,000	28.4	4,342,000[b]	55.7	295,000	3.8			444,000	5.7
2 (1744)	9,095,000	2,546,000	28.0	5,247,000[b]	57.7	355,000	3.9			451,000	5.0
3 (1762)	11,617,000	4,366,000	37.6	5,611,000	48.3	321,000	2.8			293,000	2.5
4 (1782)	14,205,000	5,878,000	41.4	6,714,000	47.3	421,000	3.0			672,000	4.7
5 (1795)	18,617,000	6,534,000	35.1	9,787,000	52.6	771,000	4.1			1,075,000	7.6
6 (1811)	20,863,000	7,761,000	37.2	10,455,000	50.1	892,000	4.3			1,121,000	6.0
7 (1815)	21,538,000	7,861,000	36.5	9,987,000	46.4	1,208,000	5.6	77,000	.4	1,775,000	8.5
8 (1833)[c]	25,957,000	10,628,000	40.9	10,963,000	42.2	1,689,000	6.5	99,000	.4	2,111,000	8.1
9 (1850)[c]	28,555,000	12,490,000	43.7	10,859,000	38.0	1,909,000	6.7	145,000	.5	2,584,000	9.1
10 (1857)[c]	29,608,000	13,220,000	44.6	10,795,000	36.5	1,843,000	6.2	189,000	.6	2,886,000	9.7

[a] Figures include males in the regular army and navy. The Kingdom of Poland, the Grand Duchy of Finland, the Transcaucasus, and the territories of the Russian-American Company, though part of the Russian Empire, were not subject to the *revizii* and therefore are not included in the figures.

[b] Figures include serfs belonging to the church.

[c] After 1816-19, all serfs in the provinces of Kurliand, Lifliand, and Estliand became free peasants.

Source: V. M. Kabuzan, *Izmeneniia v razmeshchenii naseleniia v Rossii v XVIII-pervoi polovine XIX v.* (Moscow, 1971), pp. 59-181.

There are only three possible explanations for the decline in the serf population: (1) serfs had a lower rate of natural growth than the rest of the population, and in the worst case, a negative rate; (2) significant numbers of serfs were entering the nonserf population (in fact, using Kabuzan's figures, if legal movements alone were responsible for the decline, then approximately 1.7 million males registered as nonserfs in 1857-58 [tenth *reviziia*] were serfs in 1833-36 [eighth *reviziia*] or had male ancestors [fathers or paternal grandfathers] who were serfs); and (3) some combination of these two explanations.[14]

Bunge was the first to propose the idea of a negative rate of natural growth among the serf population, attributing this to the increasing demands lords made upon their serfs and to the effects of rural industrialization:

> This decrease of 473,719 [male and female serfs between the eighth and ninth *revizii*] is especially striking as it cannot be explained either by the transfer [of serfs] into the status of state peasants or by manumissions.... In the first period [between the seventh and eighth *revizii*, the population] grew by 1% annually; in the second [between the eighth and ninth] by a little more than ½%. This cannot be attributed to fortuitous events—war or epidemic illnesses; in both periods there were disasters of both kinds: in the first—war with Persia, Turkey, and the suppression of the Polish revolt; in the second—war with Hungary; in the first and second—a cholera epidemic. The sole reason, therefore, is the decline in the well-being of the rural population, in particular the serfs. This is not an unsubstantiated supposition but an unquestionable fact.... The fact which we have cited ought to attract attention. One segment of the population declines, and this loss is felt by the entire social organism as a decline in the rate of increase in the number of inhabitants.[15]

In the absence of reliable vital statistics, the problem of the decline in the serf population between the eighth *reviziia* (1833-36) and the tenth *reviziia* (1857-58) centers on the number of serfs manumitted or otherwise freed from servile status during this quarter-century. How many male serfs in 1833-36, along with their descendants, had been released

[14] There is no evidence to suggest that a massive emigration of serfs from Imperial Russia took place.

[15] Bunge, "Izmeneniia soslovnago sostava," 1025, 1027, 1029.

Table 2
Mean Annual Natural Growth Rate between Revizii, Total Male Population, by Sources (in percent)

Source	Seventh-Eighth *Revizii*	Eighth-Ninth *Revizii*	Ninth-Tenth *Revizii*
Ministry of Internal Affairs	....	0.54	0.63
Bunge	1.00[a]	0.50[a]	
Kabuzan	0.94	0.54	0.59
Hoch and Augustine[b]	0.89	0.57	0.56

[a] Approximate.

[b] Calculations are based on Kabuzan's data, but using different "basic years." We computed the intervals between *revizii* to be as follows: seventh-eighth *revizii*, nineteen years (Kabuzan, eighteen years); eighth-ninth *revizii*, sixteen years (Kabuzan, seventeen years); ninth-tenth *revizii*, seven and a half years (Kabuzan, seven years). Our intervals seem to be more in accordance with Kabuzan's own comments in V. M. Kabuzan, *Narodonaselenie Rossii v XVIII-pervoi polovine XIX v. (po materialam revizii)* (Moscow, 1963), 72-76.

Sources: "Svedeniia o narodonaselenii imperii v 1836 godu," *Zhurnal Ministerstva vnutrennikh del* 25 (1837): lxxviii-xcvi; "Vedomost' o narodonaselenii Rossii za 1851, po 9 narodnoi perepisi," ibid. no. 11-12 (1853): 61-76; "Vedomost' o narodonaselenii Rossii po 10 perepisi," ibid. no. 3-4 (1860): 1-14; N. Khr. Bunge, "Izmeneniia soslovnago sostava naseleniia Rossii v promezhutkakh vremeni mezhdu 7 i 8, 8 i 9 reviziiami," *Ekonomicheskii ukazatel'* no. 44 (November 2-14, 1857): 1027; V. M. Kabuzan, *Izmeneniia v razmeshchenii naseleniiia* (Moscow, 1971), 5, 56, 57.

from serfdom by 1857-58? Is it possible that as many as 1.7 million males were in this category? If so, then the serf population would have experienced a natural growth rate equal to that of the population as a whole.

Serfs were manumitted in a variety of ways. Table 4 presents a list of ways for which there are either exact figures or sufficient data to calculate reliable estimates. The many forms of manumission which, though important, cannot be included in the table because of the lack of adequate information will be discussed later in this essay. This essay will be concerned only with the manumission of serfs after the eighth *reviziia*. The figures in Table 4 are of two kinds: Those not derived from the *revizii* (column 3) give only the number of serfs freed at the time of their manumission. The subsequent natural growth of these ex-serfs up to the time of the tenth *reviziia* is not included, although we shall try to estimate

Table 3
Total Male Serf Population, Russia , 1833-1858

	Eighth *Reviziia*		Ninth *Reviziia*		Tenth *Reviziia*	
Source	Number of Serfs	Percent of Total Male Population	Number of Serfs	Percent of Total Male Population	Number of Serfs	Percent of Total Male Population
Ministry of Internal Affairs	10,914,000	42.9	10,805,000	38.2	10,772,000	36.2
Köppen	10,870,000	44.9	10,692,000	36.8		
Bunge	....	42.3	....	38.2		
Troinitskii					10,781,000	35.0
Kabuzan	10,963,000	43.0	10,859,000	38.8	10,795,000	37.3
Perkovskii	10,927,000	42.6	10,901,000	39.0		

Note: Percentages are based on total male population, excluding the regular army and navy. To be consistent with Kabuzan (*Izmeneniia v razmeshchenii naseleniia*, 180-81), serfs have been restricted to lords' peasants (*pomeshchich'i krest'iane*), household peasants (*dvorovye liudi*), and persons ascribed to privately owned factories (*pripisnye liudi*). Therefore, persons of special serf status (*na uslovnom prave*) or those who belonged to various private organizations are not included.

Sources: Ministry of Internal Affairs: as for Table 2; P. V. Köppen, "Über die Vertheilung der Bewohner Russlands nach Ständen, in der verschiedenen Provinzen," in *Mémoires de l'Academie Impériale des Sciences de St.-Petersbourg*, 6th series, vol. 7 (St. Petersburg, 1848), 420-21, and P. Keppen [P. V. Köppen], *Deviataia reviziia: Izsledovanie o chisle zhitelei v Rossii v 1851 godu* (St. Petersburg, 1857), 215 (except for *obiazannye* peasants); Bunge, "Izmeneniia soslovnago sostava," 1026; A. Troinitskii, *Krepostnoe naselenie v Rossii po 10-i narodnoi perepisi* (St. Petersburg, 1861), 40, 47, 49-50; Kabuzan, *Izmeneniia v razmeshchenii naseleniia*, 59-181, see also Table 1; and A. L. Perkovskii, "Krizis demograficheskogo vosproizvodstva krepostnogo krest'ianstva Rossii v pervoi polovine XIX stoletiia," in *Brachnost', rozhdaemost', smertnost' v Rossii i v SSSR* (Moscow, 1977), 176-77.

its effects later in the essay. In other words, if, in 1845, one thousand males were freed, to evaluate the full extent of the manumission it is necessary to know how many of these one thousand male serfs, along with their post-1845 male descendants, were registered in 1857-58 in the tenth *reviziia*. If these one thousand males had a natural growth rate of 5 percent annually, then by 1858 it would be as if one thousand sixty-seven males had been freed. The other figures (column 4) date from the time of the tenth *reviziia*, with only one exception.

Table 4
Number of Male Serfs Entering Other Legal Categories between the Eighth and Tenth *Revizii*, 1833-58

(1)	(2)	(3)	(4)
Type of Manumission	Years Manumitted	Number Changing Legal Status	Number Changing Legal Status with Nonserf Descendants
1. Law of 1803 (svobodnye khlebopashtsy)	1836-58	58,225	
2. Law of 1842 (*obiazannye krest'iane*)	1842-58	27,173	
3. Law of 1847 (*bezobrochnye krest'iane*)	1848-52	964	
4. Gifts of Serf Estates to Charitable and Educational Institutions	1835-45	8,987	
5. Manumission of Possessional Serfs	1840-51	19,309	
6. Registration as State Peasants of Males Illegally Counted as Possessional Serfs in Eighth *Reviziia*	1851	53,900	
7. State Confiscation of Estates of Nobles Convicted of Conspiracy	1839	4,794	
8. State Confiscation of Estates of Participants in Polish Revolt	1838-57	72,500[a]	
9. Purchase of Serf Estates by Ministry of State Domains	1838-58	58,275	
10. Purchase of *Odnodvorcheskie Krest'iane* by Ministry of State Domains	1842-58	7,886	
11. Purchase of Estate of Count Orlov by State Horse Breeding Administration	1845	6,562	
12. Purchase of Serf Estates by the Crown (*Udel*)	1836-58	25,000[a]	
13. Recruitment into Regular Army and Navy			433,750[a]
14. *Kantonisty*, under Authority of Military Orphan Department			122,500[a]
15. Criminal Exile to Siberia			60,000[a]
Total		343,575	616,250
Presumed Natural Growth between Manumission and Tenth *Reviziia*		22,800	
Total		366,375	
TOTAL (col. 3 + col. 4)		982,625	

[a] Estimated.

Sources: See pp. 201-208 and notes 16-44.

The laws of 1803, 1842, and 1847 provided for the emancipation, under various conditions, of entire serf villages.[16] Gifts of serf estates to charitable and educational institutions were another form of emancipation. In the twelve instances we have found, the serfs became state peasants, and the institutions received an annual compensation out of general government funds.[17] A number of possessional serfs ascribed to privately owned factories also obtained their freedom during the period under consideration. According to Köppen, in the 1840s about half of these factories ceased using possessional peasants, and the serfs attached to them were freed. However, Köppen's figure covers only the period 1840-50. We do not know if there were any additional cases between 1851 and 1858.[18]

At the time of the eighth *reviziia*, many privately owned mines had free workers (*nepremennye* or *urochnye rabotniki*) attached to them. In an attempt to deceive the government, some mine owners registered these workers as serfs. This fraud was only discovered many years later, and, in the legislation governing the ninth *reviziia*, mine owners were threatened with a fine of one hundred silver rubles for each soul thus misregistered. As a result, in Perm' guberniia,. 53,900 males registered as serfs in the eighth *reviziia* were reclassified as state peasants in 1851.[19]

---

16 *PSZ* I, vol. 27, no. 20,620 (February 20, 1803); *Polnoe sobranie zakonov Rossiiskoi imperii*, 2nd series, 55 vols. (St. Petersburg, 1830-84) (hereafter cited as *PSZ* II), vol. 17, no. 15,462 (April 2, 1842); vol. 22, no. 21,689 (November 8, 1847); V. Veshniakov, *Krest'iane-sobstvenniki v Rossii* (St. Petersburg, 1858), 59-61, 70-71, 81-134; "Vedomost'," *ZhMVD* no. 3-4 (1860): 4; N. I. Sergeeva, "Obiazannye krest'iane i reforma 19 fevralia 1861 g.," *Problemy obshchestvennoi mysli i ekoniomicheskaia politika Rossii XIX-XX vekov* (Leningrad, 1972), 82. Obligated peasants (*obiazannye krest'iane*) were serfs with fixed contractual obligations and therefore *na uslovnom prave*. They were not counted as *pomeshchich'i krest'iane* or *dvorovye liudi*, nor were they traditionally included in figures on the "serf percent." Therefore, they are part of the decline of serfs *na obshchem krepostnom prave*, to which our discussion is restricted.

17 Köppen, *Deviataia reviziia*, 218-19; *PSZ* II, vol. 16, no. 14,669 (June 19, 1841); N. Mel'nitskii, *Sbornik svedenii o voenno-uchebnykh zavedeniiakh v Rossii*, 4 vols. (St. Petersburg, 1857-60), vol. 2, part 3, pp. 187 and 217; vol. 2, part 4, pp. 52 and 119; vol. 3, part 5, p. 141.

18 Köppen, *Deviataia reviziia*, 62.

19 Ryndziunskii, "Vymiralo li krepostnoe krest'ianstvo," 66.

The estates of serf owners who were found guilty of crimes were subject to confiscation by the state, and a significant number of estates were seized for this reason. In 1839, for example, an undetermined number of nobles living in the western guberniias were convicted of conspiring against the state. Their estates, which included 4,794 souls, were seized, and the serfs became state peasants.[20] A much more significant instance of confiscation, however, occurred slightly earlier and requires some explanation.

On May 6, 1831, the government ordered the sequestration of the Belorussian and Little Russian estates of nobles who had participated in the Polish rebellion. Shortly thereafter, a special administrative body was set up to manage the estates, and the serfs living on the estates were declared state peasants. Confiscations were not limited to the immediate postrebellion period, however. In 1837, the government ruled that participants in the rebellion were to be dispossessed of any serfs later inherited, and restrictions designed to prevent disinheritance as a means of avoiding confiscation were placed on the ascendants of the would-be heirs. Only in 1859 did the government refuse to accept new cases of confiscation, and in 1862 all cases still pending were dropped.[21] Neither the total number of serfs so seized nor, more important for our purposes, the number taken between the eighth and tenth *revizii* are known. But it is possible to make a conservative estimate based on the available data. Between 1831 and 1836, in Kiev and Podol'ia guberniias 80,543 males were seized; from 1831 to 1838, in seven other western guberniias 110,870 peasants on 315 estates were confiscated.[22] For one guberniia, Minsk, it is known that of the total seizures between 1831 and 1857, 27.5 percent occurred after 1838.[23] Because legislation on this matter was uniform throughout the region involved, application of the same proportion to all nine guberniias would indicate that ap-

---

[20] *PSZ* II, vol. 13, no. 11,572 (September 30, 1838); vol. 14, no. 12,964 (December 11, 1839).

[21] *PSZ* II, vol. 6, no. 4,535 (May 6, 1831), no. 4,711 (July 17, 1831); vol. 12, no. 10,208 (May 4, 1837); vol. 34, no. 34,881 (September 8, 1859); vol. 37, no. 39,009 (December 6, 1862).

[22] *PSZ* II, vol. 11, no. 9,053 (April 4, 1836); *Istoricheskoe obozrenie piatidesiatiletnei deiatel'nosti Ministerstva gosudarstvennykh imushchestv, 1837-1887*, vol. 2 (St. Petersburg, 1888), part 2, p. 80.

[23] Zelenskii, *Materialy: Minskaia guberniia*, 632-33.

proximately 264,000 serfs were seized, roughly 72,500 of whom became state peasants after 1838. Although this procedure underestimates the total number of souls confiscated between the eighth and tenth *revizii* because it does not take into account those peasants taken by the state between 1836 and 1838, it does provide minimum approximation.

Purchase by the state of nobles' estates with serfs attached was another means of manumission. When the Ministry of State Domains was established in 1838, it was given the right to buy serf estates under special conditions. In 1847, a new law compelled the ministry to bid for all Great Russian estates which came up for public auction. Altogether, from 1838 to 1855, 178 estates were bought. In 1855, the statute was changed, and thereafter mostly small estates were acquired.[24] In 1842, the ministry also began to buy *odnodvorcheskie krest'iane* (serfs of single homesteaders), who were among the poorest peasants in the empire. Up to the time of the tenth *revisiia*, almost eight thousand serfs became state peasants in this way and were resettled on state lands.[25] Finally, in 1845, the State Horse Breeding Administration in Voronezh guberniia bought the estate of Count Orlov and converted its serfs into state peasants.[26]

Besides the state, the crown (*udel*) made some sizable purchases of serf estates, mainly to provide its own peasants with additional land. Between 1831 and 1860, the crown purchased fifty-two estates totaling more than four hundred thousand *desiatiny* (1.1 million acres) of settled land, about 95 percent of which was bought in the 1840s. Almost all of this land was in the provinces of Simbirsk or Orel. The number of serfs living on the estates is unknown, but in 1851, Simbirsk guberniia, which was less densely settled than Orel, had approximately one male per eight *desiatiny* of land. If it is assumed that the population density of the serf estates acquired by the crown was half of the norm—or sixteen *desiatiny* per male in the 1840s—then approximately twenty-five

---

24 "Obozrenie deiatel'nosti Ministerstva gosudarstvennykh imushchestv," *Sel'skoe khoziaistvo i lesovodstvo* 95, no. 4-6 (1867): 37; *Ocherk piatidesiatiletnei deiatel'nosti Ministerstva gosudarstvennykh imushchestv, 1837-1887* (St. Petersburg, 1887), 37 and 83.

25 *Ocherk piatidesiatiletnei deiatel'nlosti*, 36; "Vedomost'," *ZhMVD*, 1853, no. 3-4, p. 64; "Vedomost'," *ZhMVD*, 1860, no. 3-4, p. 4. See also the annual reports of the Ministry of State Domains, published in its *Zhurnal Ministerstva gosudarstvennykh imushchestv* (hereafter cited as *ZhMGI*).

26 V. Mikhalevich, *Materialy: Voronezhskaia guberniia*, 171.

thousand males were purchased.[27] This figure, of course, is little more than a guess, although local archives probably contain exact information

Thus, from sources not derived from the *revizii* (Table 4, column 3), between the eighth and tenth *revizii* 343,575 male serfs changed their legal status. Seventy-two percent of this figure (for ten of the twelve categories) is derived from exact data, and the remainder (for two categories) is based on estimations. But how many of these males and their male descendants were present at the time of the tenth *reviziia*? If we assume that manumissions were equally distributed throughout the period, and, more important, that these former serfs had a natural growth rate equal to that of the population as a whole, then an additional 22,800 males should be added to the total. This adjustment is not very significant, since it yields only 6.6 percent in the total figure for column 3. The validity of these assumptions will be discussed later.

The data in column 4 of Table 4, because they date from the time of the tenth *reviziia*, pose no problem as to the effects of natural growth after manumission. Other, more complex, problems are encountered, however.

If a serf had the misfortune of being recruited into the regular army or navy, it is doubtful that he was consoled by the fact that he was no longer a serf.[28] But recruitment was the prime factor responsible for the negative net growth rate of the serf population.

In 1858, at the time of the tenth *reviziia*, there were 979,113 men in the lower ranks of the regular army and navy.[29] But how many of these

---

27 *Istoriia udelov za stoletie ikh sushchestvovaniia, 1797-1897*, 3 vols. (St. Petersburg, 1901-2), 1:201-4, 2:119; Lipiniskii, *Materialy: Simbirskaia guberniia*, 307 and 339; Köppen, *Deviataia reviziia*, 126; P. Semenov, ed., *Geograficheskо-statisticheskii slovar' Rossiiskoi imperii*, 5 vols. (St. Petersburg, 1863-85), 3:693-97, 4:587-94.

28 *Svod zakonov Rossiiskoi imperii*, 15 vols. (St. Petersburg, 1832, 1842, 1857 [3 editions]). (Since we used three editions of the law code, hereafter we will cite this as *Svod zakonov* with the edition in which the articles referred to appear enclosed in parentheses following the article number.) The reference here is to *Svod zakonov*, vol. 9, *Zakony o sostoianiiakh*, article 706 (1833), article 1,087 (1842), article 1,200 (1857).

29 L. G. Beskrovnyi, *Russkaia armiia i flot v XIX veke* (Moscow, 1973), 546; *Vsepoddanneishie otchety o deistviiakh Voennago ministerstva za 1858-1914*, 57 vols. (St. Petersburg, 1861-1917). (This was an annual publication, with the year treated given in the title. Hereafter it will be cited as *Vsepoddanneishie otchety za* and the appropriate year.) The reference here is to *Vsepoddanneishie otchety za 1858*, p. 1.

soldiers and sailors were of serf origin postdating the eighth *reviziia*? The length of military service was twenty-two years for the guards regiments and twenty-five years for the army and navy. Thus the number of men present in active and reserve units in 1858 who were conscripted prior to the eighth *reviziia* can be considered negligible. But to determine the legal composition of the lower ranks requires some discussion.

How heavily did the recruitment process fall upon the serf population? Between 1836 and 1858, according to figures published by the general staff, 2,442,153 men entered the military, 81 percent of whom came as the result of general recruitment. The remainder came from groups subject to special recruit levies—kantonisty, Western *odnodvortsy*, military settlers, *Malorossiiskie* Cossacks, Jews, and Poles—and from volunteers.[30] We shall assume that none of these were serfs, although a very small proportion actually were. Within the rest of the population, many persons of free status were exempt from military service. In fact, the list of privileged legal categories is three pages long. No serfs enjoyed such exemptions, however. The pool from which general recruits were drawn was therefore considerably smaller than the total population, yet it included all the serfs.

One Soviet military historian, L. G. Beskrovnyi, has estimated that approximately 20 percent of the male population was exempt from military service.[31] Actually, data from the general staff suggest that this figure should be slightly higher. Of the number of males entering the military through the process of general recruitment in 1868-70, 49 percent was of serf origin.[32] Levies in these years were based upon the tenth *reviziia* of 1858, when serfs made up 37.3 percent of the total male population. By simple proportion, it would seem that almost 24 percent of the male population was exempt from the military. Assuming the same was true for the eighth *reviziia*, which governed recruitment levies for 1836-51, serfs would comprise 56.5 percent of the general recruits and 45.7 percent of all inducted men. For recruitments

[30] D. A. Skalon, ed., *Stoletie Voennago ministerstva, 1802-1902*, vol. 4, part 2, book 1, section 2 (St. Petersburg, 1907), 80-151; Bogdanovich et al., *Istoricheskii ocherk deiatel'nosti voennago upravleniia v Rossii*, vol. 1 (St. Petersburg, 1879), appendixes 11 and 14.

[31] Beskrovnyi, *Russkaia armiia i flot*, 70.

[32] *Vsepoddanneishie otchety za 1868*, 255; *Vsepoddanneishie otchety za 1869*, 218; *Vsepoddanneishie otchety za 1870*, 194.

in the years 1851-58, based on the ninth reviziia, serfs would constitute 51 percent of general recruits and 41.3 percent of the military. Thus, for the entire period 1836-58, 44.3 percent of the regular army and navy consisted of former serfs. This means that at the time of the tenth *reviziia*, there were 433,750 soldiers and sailors in the lower ranks of the army or navy who had received their freedom after 1836 as a result of general recruitment.

This figure is far from complete, however, because some men freed by recruitment were no longer in the army in 1858. Several thousand draftees were assigned to nonmilitary service—railway militia, gendarmerie, and customs guards. Each year between two thousand and five thousand men deserted, and undoubtedly many of them succeeded in finding their way into the free population. Finally, although the length of service assures that most retired soldiers present in 1858 had entered the lower ranks prior to the eighth *reviziia*, some men were prematurely retired because they were no longer fit for service. How many of the 487,924 retired soldiers[33] recorded in the tenth *reviziia* were prematurely retired is not known, but the number certainly must have been substantial owing to the injuries and illnesses sustained during the Crimean War. In 1856, the only year for which figures are available, 68,812 men retired, 10,239 of whom were released before fulfilling the obligatory term.[34]

After a man entered the lower ranks of the military, any male children he fathered—either legitimately or illegitimately—while in service or retirement became *kantonisty* and came under the authority of the Military Orphan Department.[35] If a *kantonist* was fit, he was obliged to enter the army at the age of twenty. *Kantonisty* born to fathers of serf origin would have been serfs if their fathers had not been drafted, and they were an important factor contributing to the decline in the serf population.

In August 1856, the tsar abolished military obligations for virtually all *kantonisty*. As a result, 378,000 were released, and a smaller

---

33 The figure includes their free sons.

34 Bogdanovich et al., *Istoricheskii ocherk*, appendix 15; see also Skalon, *Stoletie*, 80-151.

35 The children of legally settled retired soldiers were free. In 1851, only 13 percent of all retired soldiers were in this category ("Vedomost'," *ZhMVD*, 1853, no. 11-12, pp. 70 and 73).

number—11,350—were retained, and the latter eventually entered the army. In all, at least 389,350 *kantonisty* were present in 1856.[36]

Only active, reserve, or retired soldiers could father *kantonisty*. Assuming these men were equally fertile, regardless of legal origins, the legal composition of the *kantonisty* would be identical to that of the lower ranks as a whole. Therefore, 44.3 percent of the *kantonisty* was of serf origin. Of these, however, many had fathers who had been recruited prior to the eighth *reviziia*, and consequently they are not relevant to this study. At the end of 1835, 974,210 active, reserve, and retired men were included in the lower ranks of the military.[37] From 1836 to 1856, a total of 2,409,945 men became soldiers and sailors. Any of these 3,384,155 men could have produced a *kantonist* who was present in 1856. Since there are no data dividing *kantonisty* according to when their fathers were recruited, we shall proceed from the assumption that, since the 2.4 million post-1835 inductees comprised 71 percent of the potential fathers, they produced 71 percent of the *kantonisty*. Given the higher rate of fertility among younger males, the high rate of mortality in the army, and the high rate of infant and child mortality prevalent at the time, this procedure actually underestimates the number of *kantonisty* born to males recruited after 1835. Nevertheless, we estimate that 122,500 *kantonisty* whose serf fathers had been recruited after the eighth *reviziia* were present in 1856. Without recruitment, all of these *kantonisty* would have been serfs rather than part of the nonserf population.

This figure is incomplete, however. *Kantonisty* found unfit for military service had the right to register in the meshchanstvo, the legal estate which encompassed the lower groups of the urban population, and those who did so are lost from observation. Many peasants who did not want their sons to be registered as *kantonisty* practiced concealment and deception. An 1838 law describes how soldiers' wives, "before giving birth, frequently leave their place of residence and

36 *PSZ* II, vol. 31, no. 30,877 (August 26, 1856) Bogdanovich et al., *Istoricheskii ocherk*, 203-4 and appendix 14; Skalon, *Stoletie*, 300 and 327.

37 Beskrovnyi, *Russkaia armiia i flot*, 16; "Svedenie," *ZhMVD*, 1837, no. 25, pp. xcii, xciv; Skalon, *Stoletie*, 76. The figure for the military at the end of 1835 does not include the navy. But even if the navy were as large as one hundred thousand men, as it was on the eve of the Crimean War, this would have only a minimal effect on the results presented here.

return with newborn children, which they claim they have adopted or found abandoned ... sometimes ... they send their newborn sons to be brought up under other names in different villages or even different guberniias."[38] Fines of 25 rubles per month were levied for concealing a *kantonist*, and in five guberniias, over 340,000 rubles were owed as a result, although little was actually collected.[39] In 1833, on the estates of the Shepelev family alone, 404 concealed *kantonisty* were discovered.[40] In addition, in 1828, a retired soldier who had been wounded in service received the right to have one of his sons released from *kantonist* status and all its attendant military obligations. Later, this privilege was extended to sick and infirm retired soldiers, to soldiers' widows, and to retired soldiers who settled permanently in a city or farmed non-*pomeshchik* land.[41] By the 1850s, more than 500 *kantonisty* were being released in this way each year.[42] It should also be noted that the figure of 389,350 *kantonisty* present in August 1856 excludes all those born from that date to the time of the tenth *reviziia*, which was taken a year or two later depending on the locality. Assuming a traditional age structure, this could be a very significant number, although at present it is impossible to estimate.

Finally, a serf who was convicted of a crime and sentenced to exile in Siberia, despite his harsh sentence or penal servitude, became a free man, technically speaking, for upon arrival at his destination he was listed among the free population. Available data show that approximately six thousand males—43 percent of whom were serfs—were annually exiled to Siberia. This figure corresponds closely to their general proportion in the total population.[43] Because we have been unable to determine the number of male exiles present in Siberia in 1858, we shall use ninth *reviziia* data from 1851 even though these figures are low. In

38 *PSZ* II, vol. 13, no. 11,745 (November 14, 1838).

39 Skalon, *Stoletie*, 312-13.

40 *PSZ* II, vol. 8, no. 6,323 (July 15, 1833). See also the annual *Otchet Ministerstva iustitsii*, 35 vols. (St. Petersburg, 1834-68) (hereafter cited as *Otchet MIu*).

41 *PSZ* II, vol. 3, no. 2,489 (December 6, 1828); vol. 11, no. 9,761 (December 6, 1836); vol. 17, no. 15,492 (April 10, 1842).

42 Skalon, *Stoletie*, 295-302.

43 E. N. Anuchin, "Izsledovaniia o protsente soslannykh v Sibir' v period 1827-1846 g.," *Zapiski IRGO* 3 (1873): 71; N. M. Iadrintsev, "Statisticheskie materialy k istorii ssylki v Sibir'," *Zapiski IRGO* 6 (1889): 346-47.

1851, the five Siberian provinces held 140,000 male exiles, presumably 60,000 of whom were of serf origin.[44]

Thus, it is clear from Table 4 that almost one million males, either serfs or potential serfs, were released from servile status between the eighth and tenth *revizii*. Yet Table 4 is far from complete. Within the fifteen forms of manumission included in the table, a large but unascertainable number of male serfs have certainly escaped our purview. More important, however, Table 4 omits entirely many ways by which a serf could acquire the status of a nonserf. Because of the tax principles which governed the *revizii*, only scattered information was available for these other forms of manumission. Although a manumitted serf occasionally fell into a separate legal category based upon his tax privileges, more often he took up a legal or tax status which made him indistinguishable from the rest of the nonservile population. We shall now turn to these instances of manumission, for it is certain that very significant numbers of serfs were involved.

Although a lord could free his serfs with land only on the basis of the laws of 1803, 1842, and 1847, it was a very simple matter for him to emancipate a serf without giving him land. Until 1861, the law required only that acts of manumission which occurred during the lord's lifetime be registered with the appropriate civil authorities or that testamentary wills bequeathing freedom to the serfs be in proper legal order.[45] It is difficult to get an idea as to how frequently serfs were freed without land. Undoubtedly, the fact that the lord was responsible for the poll-tax obligations of the ex-serf until the next *revisiia* was a considerable drawback. But the law permitted the lord to set his own terms for freedom, and many private contracts of manumission required that the freed serf pay his own taxes.[46]

---

[44] Given the large sex imbalance in the exiled population, the fact that few families accompanied convicts to Siberia, and the assumption that life expectancy at the average age of exile was less than twenty-two years, it is safe to conclude that only a negligible number of exiles of serf origin present in Siberia in 1858 had been sent there prior to the eighth *reviziia*.

[45] *Svod zakonov*, vol. 9, arts. 674-80 (1833), arts. 1,148-84 (1857).

[46] *PSZ* I, vol. 20, no. 14,294 (April 6, 1775); V. I. Semevskii, *Krest'iante v tsarstvovanie Imperatritsy Ekateriny II*, vol. 1 (St. Petersburg, 1903), 389-90; Blum, *Lord and Peasant*, 474.

Regardless of the specific circumstances of manumission without land, many peasants were freed in this manner. Instances were frequent enough to cause errors in handling the necessary documents to come to the attention of the senate. In 1843, the minister of justice noted that guberniia-level civil courts "extremely often" handed over certificates of freedom to the lords, instead of to the former serfs as was required.[47]

In 1844, two new laws made it even more advantageous for a lord to free his household serfs (*dvorovye liudi*). One statute was not only flexible regarding the conditions upon which these serfs might receive freedom, but relieved the lord from further responsibility for the payment of the poll tax or other dues. The ex-serf himself was also exempt from taxation and military recruitment until the next *reviziia*, unless he inscribed in the *meshchanstvo* to become a tradesman, in which case his tax exemptions were limited to six years. The second law made it easier—and in some cases financially worthwhile—for a lord to free some of his *dvorovye liudi* if his estate were mortgaged to certain public credit institutions.[48]

Almost all serfs manumitted without land by their lords (*otpushchennye na voliu*) had the right to become *meshchane*. But those who were not freed on the basis of the 1844 *ukazy* were tax exempt only for two years.[49] According to Köppen, in 1851, almost eleven thousand *meshchane* in twelve guberniias were voluntarily manumitted serfs, enjoying temporary privileges.[50] But Köppen has no figures for other guberniias, for serfs who did not become *meshchane*, for those who had already exhausted their exemptions, or for the years after 1851.

From supplementary sources for other guberniias or for different years, it is clear that the data on voluntary manumission presented by Köppen are incomplete. In Ardatovskii uezd (in Simbirsk guberniia), 393 serfs were freed without land by their lords in the years between the eighth and ninth *revizii*.[51] In the guberniia as a whole, at the time of

47 *PSZ* II, vol. 18, no. 16,849 (May 13, 1843).

48 Ibid., vol. 19, no. 17,977 (June 12, 1844), no. 17,985 (June 12, 1844). See also vol. 9, no. 9,637 (October 23, 1836).

49 *Svod zakonov*, vol. 5: *Ustavy o podatiakh*, art. 485 (1857); *PSZ* II, vol. 7, no. 5,842 (December 22, 1832).

50 Köppen, *Deviataia reviziia*, 6, 7, 21, 62, 88, 95, 100, 127, 142, 144, 152, 159; see also 103 and Baranovich, *Materialy: Riazanskaia guberniia*, 144.

51 Trubnikov, "Rezul'taty," 360.

the ninth *reviziia*, 124 males under the age of twenty-five who had been born to manumitted women had inscribed in the *meshchanstvo*.[52] For Romanovo-Borisoglebskii uezd (in Iaroslavl' guberniia), 54 males and 178 females were emancipated during the last six months of 1852.[53] Voluntarily manumitted serfs were present in Kaluga and Minsk guberniias as well.[54] A study of the serfs of Riazan' guberniia (also not included in Köppen's figures) cites fifty-two cases of *dvorovye liudi* being granted freedom in the nineteenth century. This is not an exhaustive list, however, because the author was interested in examining the reasons for such voluntary manumissions, not the total number.[55] A similar study on Saratov guberniia reveals that during the 1850s almost seventy lords liberated serfs without land. However, many of these cases probably took place at the very end of the decade, after the tenth *reviziia*, because in the autumn of 1857 the government announced its intentions to emancipate all serfs in the near future.[56]

Aside from voluntary manumission, a serf could be released from servitude on legal grounds. The instances when this was possible are surprisingly many, although few figures are available in regard to the number of people emancipated in this manner.[57] The law was quite complex and extraordinarily detailed, but essentially a person was released if any of the following conditions were met:

1. If he could prove in court that he was of free origin or that he had been illegally bonded. Clergy, *odnodvortsy*, and retired soldiers

---

52 Lipinskii, *Materialy: Simbirskaia guberniia*, 264.

53 "Romanovo-Borisoglebskii uezd, Iaroslavskoi gubernii," *ZhMVD*, 1853, no. 7-8, p. 8.

54 In 1857, there were 1,961 male serfs in Kaluga guberniia who had been freely manumitted or ruled free by a court (M. Poprotskii, *Materialy: Kaluzhskaia guberniia*, part 1, p. 284). Between 1855 and 1859, 709 serfs in Minsk guberniia were similarly freed (Zelenskii, *Materialy: Minskaia guberniia*, 528-29); see also A. Korev, *Materialy: Vilenskaia guberniia*, 351.

55 A. Povalishin, *Riazanskie pomeshchiki i ikh krepostnye* (Riazan', 1903), 159-74.

56 N. F. Khovanskii, "Pomeshchiki i krest'iane Saratovskoi gubernii," *Materialy po krepostnomu pravu: Saratovskaia guberniia* (Saratov, 1911), 158; see also 60 and 75.

57 Recruitment, exile, purchase, and some confiscations—all belonging to this group—have already been discussed (see *Svod zakonov*, vol. 9, arts. 1,200, 1,202-4, 1,205[2] and [6] [1857]).

could not be enserfed, and their descendants frequently brought suit on this basis. Illegal bonding involved being registered to a person who did not have the right to own serfs, being improperly sold, especially apart from one's family, or being otherwise illegally inscribed.

2. If he or the estate to which he was registered reverted by escheat to the state or was seized for lack of eligible heirs.
3. If a serf, now married, had fled with his parents or grandparents when he was under the age of fourteen or if he was born after flight. If a widow or girl in flight married a free man. Or if a serf fled to Novorossiia, Bessarabia, the lands of the Don Cossacks, or the Transcaucasus, and temporary laws exempted serfs from being returned to their lords.
4. If the recovery of state debts involved an insolvent lord who had no other property besides *dvorovye liudi* and landless peasants.
5. If, after 1841, a landless noble bought, inherited, or otherwise acquired *dvorovye liudi* or landless peasants, or if a landed noble failed to inscribe such newly acquired serfs to an estate.
6. If a lord sold or mortgaged his land separately from his serfs, leaving them with less than 4.5 desiatiny (12.2 acres) per soul for more than one year.
7. If a serf, while still a minor, accompanied his father who, by the process of general recruitment in 1840, had been taken from Voronezh, Kharkov, or Stavropol' guberniias or the lands of the Don Cossacks to the Transcaucasus.
8. If a serf owner was found to be abroad illegally, or if a state official was convicted of stealing state property, exchanging counterfeit notes, embezzling state funds, or other similar crimes. The owner's property then was partially or wholly confiscated.
9. If the wife of a serf who was convicted of a crime did not wish to follow her husband into exile, or if her husband was taken into the army, and she did not want to follow.
10. If a serf had the right to commute his military obligations by a money payment to the state, after 1854, upon agreement with his lord, the same payment could be used to purchase freedom for himself and his family.
11. If a serf whose lord was a non-Christian converted to Orthodoxy.
12. If a serf was captured in war and taken abroad. Upon his return, he and his family were freed.

13. If a serf denounced his lord for treason or plotting against the life of the tsar, and the lord was found guilty.[58]

Of course, some of these laws had little or no effect on the negative net growth rate of the serf population. But, as regards the first three conditions, the few figures available suggest that these forms of emancipation were rather significant.

It should come as no surprise that lords were guilty of widespread abuses involving the registration and sale of serfs. What is unexpected is the number of serfs who demanded their freedom and brought court suits against such lords. Between 1835 and 1858, the senate heard no less than 15,153 cases involving unlawful enserfment or illegal bonding, and guberniia courts handled over 20,000 suits.[59] Unfortunately, there is no record of how many similar cases came before uezd courts, the judicial authority of first instance in this matter.

Serfs awarded their freedom by a court (otsuzhdennye) elnjoyed a five-year period of tax-exempt status.[60] According to Köppen, in 1851, 811 persons in twelve guberniias were in this position.[61] But, as usual, the figures are incomplete. For Tambov guberniia, not included in Köppen's data, a partial index of the guberniia archive published in 1906 shows that 123 cases of this type were appealed to the senate. Although virtually all the cases appealed date from the nineteenth century, it is not known how many serfs or serf families actually gained their freedom as a result of their suits.[62] The only indication of how successful serfs were in court is found for Saratov guberniia. Here again the list of cases is not exhaustive, but of 31 suits brought by serfs between

58 *Svod zakonov*, vol. 9, art. 957 V (1842), arts. 544, 1,040, 1,042(4), 1,078, 1,107, 1,185- 97, 1,199, 1,201, and 1,205 (1857); *PSZ* I, vol. 30, no. 23,806 (August 24, 1809); *PSZ* II, vol. 2, no. 906 (February 15, 1827), no. 1,444 (October 5, 1827); vol. 3, no. 1,696 (January 10, 1828), no. 2,052 (May 24, 1828), no. 2,245 (August 20, 1828), no. 2,378 (October 25, 1828); vol. 7, no. 5,425 (June 9, 1832); vol. 8, no. 6,163 (May 2, 1833); vol. 10, no. 7,982 (March 20, 1835); vol. 11, no. 9,203 (May 21, 1836); vol. 16, no. 14,152 (January 2, 1841); vol. 23, no. 21,929 (January 26, 1848); vol. 24, no. 23,508 (September 20, 1849); vol. 29, no. 28,846 (December 20, 1854).

59 See *Otchet MIu* for the years 1834-58.

60 *Svod zakonov*, vol. 9, art. 1,193 (1857).

61 Köppen, *Deviataia reviziia*, 7, 21, 62, 88, 95, 100, 103, 127, 142, 149, 152, 156.

62 *Izvestiia Tambovskoi uchenoi arkhivnoi komissii* 52 (1906): 1-76.

1800 and 1840, which claimed previous registration to persons who did not have the right to ownership, all but one were successful.[63] As a result, approximately a hundred and twenty persons were freed. And of the cases against nobles, 26 out of 39 suits were decided in favor of the serfs, liberating at least ninety persons.[64]

Finally, the state itself brought a number of lords to court for seizing state lands and illegally claiming the persons registered there as serfs. In the six-year period prior to the establishment of the Ministry of State Domains, 1,940 serfs were awarded to the state. But the new ministry pursued such abuses more vigorously than had the Ministry of Finanlce, its predecessor in this matter. As a result, from 1837 through 1842, 4,876 serfs were ruled to be state peasants.[65]

In a recent study based on archival materials, A. L. Perkovskii states that between the years 1826 and 1851 over 108,000 male serfs were either voluntarily manumitted by their lords or released from servitude by a court decision. Unfortunately, Perkovskii gives no details as to how he arrived at this number, but his figure at least suggests the dimensions of these two legal paths out of serfdom.[66]

Another important form of emancipation for which almost no information is available concerns serfs who reverted to the state because their deceased lord lacked any heirs. As there was no demesne on state lands, when an estate escheated, *dvorovye liudi* were allowed to enroll in the meshchanstvo with certain tax privileges.[67] All the serfs who worked the land, however, simply became state peasants, and they have left little trace. A similar situation arose when a lord left heirs who did not have the right to own serfs. Such estates were seized and the heirs compensated at a statutory rate per soul.[68] What is of great significance for our purposes is the probability that such seizures and escheats became more frequent during the last twenty years of serfdom. The law of 1841 prohibited landless nobles from inheriting landless serfs. As

63 Khovanskii, *Pomeshchiki i krest'iane*, 115-49.

64 Ibid., 77-115.

65 "Izvlechenie iz otcheta Ministerstva gosudarstvennykh imushchestv," *ZhMGI, 9* (1843), part 1, Vedomost' no. 8.

66 Perkovskii, "Krizis demograficheskogo vosproizvodstva," 189.

67 *Svod zakonov*, vol. 9, arts. 462-63 (1857).

68 *PSZ* II, vol. 11, no. 9,203 (May 21, 1836); vol. 14, no. 13,012 (December 20, 1839).

a result, by 1857-58 there were only 3,633 landless serf owners with 12,045 serfs, even though at the time of the eighth *reviziia* there had been 17,763 owners with over 62,000 souls. Undoubtedly, many of the serfs were sold to landed nobles, but some must have either been taken over by the state or manumitted without land.[69] Just as important in this regard was an 1845 statute which made it more difficult to become a hereditary noble. Since serf ownership was almost exclusively restricted to persons of this status, in all likelihood the new law reduced the number of nobles eligible to inherit serf estates.[70]

According to the Ministry of the Interior, at the time of the eighth *reviziia*, there were 1,242 male and 1,455 female serfs in the escheat process awaiting final disposition.[71] For the ninth *reviziia*, Köppen found 1,727 males in two guberniias in a similar position, but it seems unlikely that either of these figures is complete, unless the escheat was concluded very quickly.[72] Between 1835 and 1858, the senate heard 1,818 cases on escheated estates, and the guberniia courts heard 1,431 cases. How many of these cases involved estates with serfs is not known.[73]

In spite of all the legal paths out of serfdom, for the vast majority of serfs flight was the only recourse. At times they fled in extraordinary numbers, rarely to return.[74] Like deserters from the army, many simply evaded the authorities. Others, however, found it relatively easy to register as nonserfs in cities, towns, or state villages.[75] Moreover, serfs who fled to regions which the government was eager to settle were often permitted to remain there as free men. The government occasionally

---

69 Troinitskii, *Krepostnoe naselenie*, 67. See also A. Shebunin, "K istorii bor'by po voprosu o prodazhe krest'ian bez zemli," *Arkhiv istorii truda v Rossii*, 10 vols. (Petrograd, 1921-23), 6-7:110-29, 8:104-20.

70 *PSZ* II, vol. 20, no. 19,086 (June 11, 1845).

71 "Svedenie," *ZhMVD*, 1837, no. 25, p. 3.

72 Köppen, *Deviataia reviziia*, 113 and 138.

73 See *Otchet MIu* for the years 1834-58, except 1850.

74 E. Kots, "Pobegi pomeshchich'ikh krest'ian v Nikolaevskuiu epokhu," *Arkhiv istorii truda v Rossii*, 5:3-29; N. P. Semenov, *Osvobozhdenie krest'ian v tsarstvovanie Imperatora Alexandra II*, vol. 3 (St. Petersburg, 1892), part 2, 392-93; Povalishin, *Riazanskie pomeshchiki*, 292-300; Khovanskii, *Pomeshchiki i krest'iane*, 149-57. See also any of the 25 volumes produced by the Glavnyi General'nyi Shtab (*Materialy*) cited in note 3.

75 *PSZ* II, vol. 14, no. 12,362 (May 19, 1839).

compensated lords for these serfs, although the available figures account for only an insignificant portion of the total number.[76]

Of the remaining categories providing for the legal release of serfs, we were able to discover only a few isolated examples not worthy of note, but which may not at all reflect the number of serfs involved.[77]

Having discussed those instances of serf manumission known to us, three questions remain: Was there any movement in the opposite direction—enserfment—which must be taken into consideration? Is there any evidence to suggest that the serf population did experience a lower rate of natural growth than other social groups? And, finally, if the legal transfer of serfs into free categories accounted for virtually all of the proportional decline in the serf population, why did population growth for the empire as a whole slow down in the years following the eighth *reviziia*?

The first question is relatively easy to answer. During the reign of Catherine the Great, the legal means for enserfing free persons were severely restricted. An important exception in terms of numbers involved—the granting of settled state lands to private individuals—was discontinued by Alexander I in 1801.[78] By 1833, on the eve of the eighth *reviziia*, the law was explicit: "No person of free status, of whatever sex, race or religion, and on whatever lands he has settled, can be enserfed or bonded to someone, even if he himself agrees to it of his own free will; all such contracts, agreements, obligations or title deeds must be recognized null and void."[79] The only exception was for foundlings and vagabond children raised by persons having the right to own serfs.[80]

The other two questions are more difficult to resolve. What does seem clear, however, is that the cholera epidemic which swept Russia in 1847-48 caused a disproportionately large number of serf deaths, although the reasons for this were geographic, not economic. Official estimates,

76 Kots, "Pobegi," 23.

77 Many of the statutes first establishing these forms of manumission were actually extensions of specific rulings by the senate (see Blum, *Lord and Peasant*, 292).

78 Semevskii, *Krest'iane*, 10-15.

79 *Svod zakonov*, vol. 9, art. 546 (1833).

80 *Svod zakonov*, vol. 9, arts. 543, 560 (1833). See also arts. 550-59 (1833), and PSZ I, vol. 21, no. 15,198 (July 28, 1781).

for whatever they are worth, put the number of cholera deaths for the two-year period at almost seven hundred eighty-five thousand for both sexes.[81] But not all regions of the empire were equally affected by the epidemic. Although cholera deaths were reported in every province of European Russia, there were relatively few deaths in the thirteen guberniias which comprised the entire northern tier (with the exception of St. Petersburg). In these thirteen provinces, with a male population of over five and one-quarter million, serfs constituted only 18.7 percent of the population, less than half the national average. In Siberia, with approximately one million persons and virtually no serfs, the population escaped the epidemic almost entirely. But all the other thirty-seven provinces of European Russia had from five thousand to fifty thousand cholera deaths each, according to official figures.[82] Here serfs made up 45.5 percent of the total population at the time of the ninth *reviziia* just two years later. Unfortunately, the mathematical significance of the cholera epidemic in the proportional decline of the serf population is impossible to determine.[83]

The cholera epidemic raises an important question concerning the usefulness of the *revizii*. Whereas the first six *revizii* were conducted at more or less regular intervals and, more important, at random points in time, the last four *revizii*, usually considered the most reliable, were all taken immediately after sudden and sharp demographic changes which had adversely affected population growth.

The *ukazy* which ordered the seventh *reviziia* in 1815 and the tenth *reviziia* in 1856 explicitly stated that new tax censuses were required in order to take into consideration the demographic effects of the

81 "Obozrenie khoda i deistvii kholernoi epidemii v Rossii v 1847 godu," *ZhMVD*, no. 9 (1848): 476; and "Obozrenie khoda i deistvii kholernoi epidemii v Rossii v techenie 1848 goda," *ZhMVD*, no. 9 (1849): 319.

82 "Obozrenie ... 1847," 476-82; "Obozrenie ... 1848," 319-28.

83 Kabuzan, *Izmeneniia v razmeshchenii naseleniia*, 155-66. Our attempt to calculate this on the basis of the figures published by the Ministry of Internal Affairs revealed that serfs accounted for 43 percent of the cholera deaths, while on the eve of the epidemic they comprised roughly 39 percent of the total population. This would mean that disproportionately thirty thousand more serfs of both sexes died. There was no way, however, to test the validity of the original data, although urban deaths were probably reported better or more accurately than rural deaths.

Napoleonic and Crimean wars.[84] In regard to natural population growth, these wars had a dual effect: a rise in the death rate as a result of casualties and disease, and—probably of much greater significance—a decline in fertility caused by recruitment. During the period 1854-56, over six hundred seventy-five thousand males, the overwhelming majority of them in their early twenties, were recruited into the army. This is three times higher than the average annual recruitment levy for the years 1840-53.[85] Given a traditional age structure, the birth rate could have fallen by as much as half during the Crimean War years. If a boom then followed, most of it would have occurred after the tenth *reviziia*.

Both the eighth (1833-36) and the ninth (1850-51) *revizii* were preceded by cholera epidemics and crop failures. Little is known about the demographic dimensions of these disasters, although it seems the cholera pandemic of 1847-48 resulted in three or four times the number of deaths as that of 1830-32.[86] Whether the poor harvests of 1833-34 and 1848-49 gave rise to subsistence crises is unclear. Prices for cereals doubled or tripled almost everywhere, although it should be noted that most grain was produced for consumption, not sale. What is important is that the available evidence suggests that the years 1830-34 and 1847-49 witnessed the greatest demographic and economic crises in the first sixty years of nineteenth-century Russia. The government certainly recognized these years as such and enacted a whole series of extraordinary, often unprecedented, laws. Recruitment was interrupted, fines were cancelled for tax arrears and arrears themselves forgiven, customs duties were removed for imported cereals, the dates for filing *revizskie skazki* were changed, the salaries of government officials were temporarily increased because of the sharp rise in bread prices, peasants were permitted to hunt and sell wild fowl, payment of bank debts was postponed, and state-controlled salt prices were reduced.[87]

---

84 *PSZ* I, vol. 33, no. 25,882 (June 20, 1815); *PSZ* II, vol. 31, no. 30,877 (August 26, 1856).

85 Bogdanovich et al., *Istoricheskii ocherk*, appendices 11 and 14; Skalon, *Stoletie*, 209.

86 R. E. McGrew, *Russia and the Cholera, 1823-1832* (Madison and Milwaukee, 1965), 4-5.

87 *PSZ* II, vol. 5, no. 3,950 (September 24, 1830), no. 3,990 (October 10, 1830); vol. 6, no. 4,268 (January 17, 1831); vol. 24, no. 23,198 (April 25, 1849), no. 23,463 (August 19, 1849) (recruitment); vol. 6, no. 4,462 (March 30, 1831), no. 4,519

In sum, using the figures from the last four *revizii* to calculate mean rates of natural growth for the population as a whole necessarily induces errors which distort the results. Therefore, any assertion that the rate of natural population growth declined sharply after the eighth *reviziia* is based, in part, upon such distortions in the data. A post-Napoleonic War population boom would have pushed the figures upward for the period between the seventh and eighth *revizii*. The 1847-49 crisis would have lowered the growth figures for the years between the eighth and ninth *revizii*. And the Crimean War, with its high recruitmient levies, certainly reduced population growth between the ninth and tenth *revizii*. Such sudden changes in population movements are commonly found in traditional societies. What is unique to Imperial Russia is that population counts in the nineteenth century were taken immediately after these demographic slumps, and only then. Yet it was certainly a wise decision to undertake a *reviziia* immediately after a crisis. The new census redistributed the tax burden and provided relief to those regions which had suffered the greatest population losses. In addition, by conducting a *reviziia* at a time when the population was at a relative minimum, the government encountered less opposition from taxpayers or their lords.

The distortions inherent in the later *revizii* as a result of their timing mask actual changes in population movements, however. Unfortunately,

---

(April 28, 1831); vol. 9, no. 7,599 (December 1, 1834) (fines and arrears); vol. 8, no. 6,411 (September 1, 1833), vol. 9, no. 7,554 (November 19, 1834), no. 7,700 (December 28, 1834) (customs duties), vol. 8, no. 6,416 (September 10, 1833) (*revizskie skazki*). The *reviziia* legislation of June 1833 required that all *skazki* for European Russia be filed by May 1, 1834. After the crop failure in the autumn of 1833, the government delayed the beginning of the *reviziia* in eleven of the most affected provinces until September 1, 1834. But even in the provinces where the *reviziia* was not postponed, some of the effects of the poor harvest were undoubtedly felt prior to the registration of the population. See ibid., vol. 8, no. 6,563 (November 12, 1833) (salaries); vol. 9, no. 6,950 (April 3, 1834) (hunting fowl); vol. 5, no. 3,903 (September 9, 1830), no. 4,051 (October 28, 1830); vol. 6, no. 4,715 (July 21, 1831); vol. 23, no. 22,483 (August 3, 1848); vol. 24, no. 23,182 (April 15, 1849), no. 23,299 (June 7, 1849) (loans); vol. 23, no. 22,912 (January 11, 1849) (salt). See also Arcadius Kahan, "Natural Calamities and their Effect upon Food Supply in Russia (An Introduction to a Catalogue)," *Jahrbücher für Geschichte Osteuropas*, 16, no. 3 (September 1968): 358-73.

it is impossible to correct the data and to compute more accurate rates. Nevertheless, it is highly unlikely that the distortions alone account for the entire change in the rates cited in Table 2. The rate of natural growth for the population as a whole probably did decline during the first sixty years of the nineteenth century, although not nearly as dramatically as Bunge, Kabuzan, and others believed.

Clearly, this was not a result of the serf population dying out. With the exception of the effects of the cholera epidemic, virtually all the net decline in the serf population was due to changes in legal status. In light of all the paths to freedom which existed, it is certainly plausible that as many as 1.7 million male serfs (or would-be serfs) entered the nonservile population between 1836 and 1858. This would mean that changes in the rate of natural growth among serfs paralleled those for the population as a whole. In any case, the figures we have documented plainly show that the serfs had a positive rate of natural growth during the thirty years preceding the emancipation. In fact, should future archival research reveal that more than 1.7 million male serfs became nonserfs between the eighth and tenth *revizii*, this would indicate that the serfs had a rate of natural growth above the national average.

Because many ex-serfs became state peasants, the figures purporting to show that state peasants had a higher rate of natural growth are incorrect, since they include significant legal movements.[88] And, although much has been made of the fact that state peasants had larger land allotments and lower quitrents than serfs, the relationship between standard of living and the rate of natural population growth is far from clear.[89] At present, little can be said on this matter, because virtually nothing is known about age-specific fertility rates, marriage patterns, or mortality in Imperial Russia, and how they differed according to region and social class.

---

88 Bunge, "Izmeneniia soslovnago sostava," 1029; "Sravnenie chisla gosudarstvennykh krest'ian po 8 i 9 reviziiam, v guberniiakh evropeiskoi Rossii," *ZhMGI*, 54, no. 1 (1855): 17-27; "Dvizhenie narodonaseleniia gosudarstvennykh krest'ian i drugikh sel'skikh obyvatelei vedomstva Ministerstva gosudarstvennykh imushchestv s 9-i po 10-i revizii," *Materialy dlia statistiki Rossii*, vol. 4 (St. Petersburg, 1861), 124-37; Perkovskii, "Krizis demograficheskogo vosproizvodstva," 178-86.

89 D. E. C. Eversley, "Population, Economy and Society," in D. V. Glass and D. E. C. Eversley, eds., *Population in History* (London, 1965), 66-67.

The decline in the rate of natural growth for the population as a whole was probably attributable to a decline in fertility, though neither the dates nor the actual mechanisms of this change are clear. Because the *revizii* are only touchstones in time, it is impossible to determine precisely when such a downturn began. Certainly the contention of many Soviet scholars that this occurred during the 1830s remains unproven, for on the basis of the information provided by the *revizii*, a change could have begun as much as a decade earlier or later.

In regard to the reasons for a decline in fertility, there is evidence for at least two parishes that the mean age at first marriage rose slightly during the first sixty years of the nineteenth century.[90] Whether this was a widespread phenomenon, possibly tied to a series of statutes between 1830 and 1833 which raised the legal age for marriage, is unknown.[91] In addition, recruitment levies increased substantially during the reign of Nicholas I, and this undoubtedly had an adverse effect on fertility. In 1834, the army established a reserve system whereby soldiers who had served twenty years were given permanent leave and permitted to live with their families; and in 1851, active service was reduced to fifteen years.[92] To maintain the active army at a constant level, more young men were inducted—partially removing them from the reproductive process—while older men were released.

Thus, the last decades of serfdom were not accompanied by any long-run demographic crisis in the serf population. Rather, the government of Nicholas I, though often seen as rigidly preserving the status quo, in fact adlhered to policies which substantially reduced the serf population. While much of this stemmed from military or political considerations, the government was well aware of the effects of recruitment

---

90 Il. Mechnikov, "Vozrast vstupleniia v brak," *Vestnik Evropy*, no. 1 (1874): 257; Peter Czap, "Marriage and the Peasant Joint Family in the Era of Serfdom," in *The Family in Imperial Russia*, ed. David L. Ransel (Urbana, Chicago, and London, 1978), 111-12.

91 *PSZ* II, vol. 5, no. 3,807 (July 19, 1830), no. 3,981 (October 6, 1830); vol. 6, no. 4,277 (January 30, 1831); vol. 8, no. 6,668 (December 23, 1833).

92 Skalon, *Stoletie*, vol. 4, part 2, book 1, section 3 (St. Petersburg, 1912), 255 and 263. See also *PSZ* II, vol. 9, no. 7,374 (August 30, 1834); vol. 26, no. 25,352 (June 29, 1851); and Perkovskii, "Krizis demograficheskogo vosproizvodstva," 187-88.

and confiscation. Furthermore, no matter how undergoverned Imperial Russia may have been during these years, the bureaucracy acquired a greater hold on society and more vigorously enforced the rule of law, much to the benefit of persons who had been wrongfully enserfed.

In fact, it is possible to detect a concerted effort on the part of the government to constrict the institution of serfdom. Manumission, especially of household serfs or those ascribed to factories, was made easier. Under Alexander I, gifts of settled state lands were no longer made to private individuals, and under Nicholas I the government established a systematic—albeit limited—program of acquiring serf estates.

The net result was that serfdom was dying out, but that the serfs were not. It is obvious that the argument of a negative or depressed rate of natural growth among the serf population can no longer be used as evidence for the thesis that Russia underwent a profound crisis during the decades preceding the emancipation.

8

Tall Tales: Anthropometric Measures of Well-Being in Imperial Russia and the Soviet Union, 1821-1960

"From the soles of his feet to the roots of his hair, Paul Bunyan split the atmosphere exactly 12 feet 11 inches. His weight, he told me—and I don't doubt his word for a moment—was 888 pounds."[1] Together with precise measures of Paul Bunyan's hips, waist, shoulders, thighs, calves, and reach, subsequently detailed, we would, it seems, have a rather comprehensive anthropometric description of this legendary logger. But his companion, Babe the Blue Ox, "was seven axe handles wide between the eyes," quite a different anthropometric measure indeed. Moreover, "some persons give the measurement as forty-two axe handles and a plug of Star tobacco." And, we are told, "both figures are correct," all of which quickly brings us to the heart of the problem, species aside.[2]

Anthropometry, an important technique for the study of human auxology or growth, dates back to the eighteenth century, though it experienced long periods of scientific neglect. James M. Tanner revived this technique in the mid-1950s,[3] and over a decade later, a small but

---

This essay is a response to Boris N. Mironov, "New Approaches to Old Problems: The Well-Being of the Population of Russia from 1821 to 1910 as Measured By Physical Stature," and Stephen G. Wheatcroft, "The Great Leap Upwards: Anthropometric Data and Indicators of Crises and Secular Changes in Soviet Welfare Levels," both in *Slavic Review* (Spring 1999): 1-26 and 27-60 respectively. The essay was originally published in *Slavic Review* 58, no. 1 (Spring 1999): 61-70.

[1] Earl Clifton Beck, "Paul's Dinner," in *Legends of Paul Bunyan*, comp. and ed. Harold W. Felton (New York, 1947), 34.

[2] Ivan Benson, "The Big Blue Ox," in *Paul Bunyan and His Men* (Rutland, VT, 1955), 31.

[3] James M. Tanner, "A Concise History of Growth Studies from Buffon to Boas," in *Human Growth, vol. 3, Neurobiology and Nutrition*, ed. Frank Falkner and J. M. Tanner (New York, 1979), 515-93.

prominent group of historians, including Emmanuel Le Roy Ladurie and Robert Fogel, began to make use of available data on the stature or height and, on occasion, the weight of military recruits from the nineteenth and twentieth centuries to assess changes in well-being. In Fogel's research, "mean height at specific ages is used as a measure of standard of living" and is used to "supplement other evidence such as indexes of real wages, estimates of per-capita income, and measures of food consumption."[4] Others have used secular changes in stature to estimate national income; to study changes in the standard of living, as conventionally understood, or in a biological standard of living; to predict mortality; and to determine aggregate well-being, though all are clearly quite distinct measures.[5] It is this same method and its underlying premises that are taken up in the research here.

Boris Mironov and Stephen G. Wheatcroft both relate observed changes in height, and in the latter case sometimes weight, to shifts in biological status, clearly a different measure of well-being than standard of living. Both recognize that a complex of factors affect biological status, although these considerations are not always consistently applied in Mironov's analysis. They adhere, in principle, to the well-established medical view that "the most important exogenous factors [non-genetic]

---

4 Robert William Fogel, "Physical Growth as a Measure of Economic Well-Being of Populations: The Eighteenth and Nineteenth Centuries," in *Human Growth: A Comprehensive Treatise, 2d ed., vol. 3, Methodology, Ecological, Genetic, and Nutritional Effects on Growth*, ed. Frank Falkner and J. M. Tanner (New York, 1986), 263. See also John Komlos, *Nutrition and Economic Development in the Eighteenth-Century Habsburg Monarchy: An Anthropometric History* (Princeton, 1989), 23-54.

5 H. J. Brinkman, J. W. Drukker, and B. Slot, "Height and Income: A New Method for the Estimation of Historical National Income Series," *Explorations in Economic History* 25 (July 1988): 227- 64; John Komlos, ed., *The Biological Standard of Living on Three Continents: Further Explorations in Anthropometric History* (Boulder, CO, 1995); Jane Humphries, "Short Stature among Coal-Mining Children: A Comment," *Economic History Review* 50, no. 3 (1997): 531-37; Roderick Floud, Kenneth W. Wachter, and Annabel Gregory, *Height, Health, and History: Nutritional Status in the United Kingdom, 1750-1980* (Chicago, 1994). See also Robert W. Fogel, "Nutrition and the Decline of Mortality since 1700: Some Preliminary Findings," in *Long Term Factors in American Growth*, ed. Stanley L. Engerman and Robert E. Gallman (Chicago, 1986), 439 -555.

influencing growth are nutrition and disease."[6] As Phyllis Eveleth and James Tanner write: "There are many environmental factors which affect growth, and which combine in various proportions to constitute the environment of poverty; but in the final analysis most of them hinge upon the level of nutrition in conjunction with the prevalence of childhood infection."[7]

The use of anthropometric techniques to analyze time series shifts in the biological status of a population presents a number of problems. The issues relevant here include the validity of the actual measures used (do they measure what they say they measure), the accuracy of the recorded data, the periodization of the observed changes in the measures, and the causes of the observed changes, each of which will be discussed in turn. The importance of this discussion is to determine whether the application of anthropometric methods to available Russian and Soviet data can sustain the conclusions reached by Mironov and Wheatcroft.

Mironov relies solely on data on terminal height or stature (which is generally attained between the ages of 20-25) as an indicator of biological status, contending that "even the most insignificant increase or decrease in height can indicate a change in the biological status of a population." In contrast, Wheatcroft supplements his information on terminal stature whenever possible with available information on mortality, weight, weight-for-height or body mass indexes, height-for-age, and birth weights, reflecting many of the concerns medical professionals have regarding anthropometric measures, concerns that have more recently been directed to historians as well. Wheatcroft's approach is certainly more helpful because of the well-recognized problem of using a single variable, especially one that is widely regarded as imprecise, as we shall see.

Early practitioners of anthropometric history focused on terminal stature or height, as it was often the only anthropometric information available. In most of Europe, males eligible for military service were measured for height at ages close to their expected terminal height, as was the case in Imperial Russia and the Soviet Union. But the current

6 C. Van Wieringen, "Secular Growth Changes," in *Human Growth: A Comprehensive Treatise*, ed. Falkner and Tanner, 3:322; and James R. Hummert and Alan H. Goodman, "An Assessment of the Effects of Childhood Illness on Growth in Height and Weight," *Growth* 50 (1986): 371.

7 Phyllis B. Eveleth and James M. Tanner, *Worldwide Variation in Human Growth*, 2d ed. (Cambridge, 1990), 191.

state of anthropometric research will no longer support this approach. A 1991 study on the Anthropometric Assessment of Nutritional Status noted that "The most common anthropometric measures are weight and changes in weight, stature, segmental lengths, fat folds, and various body circumferences and diameters.... Their utility is that they provide rough estimates of body composition or changes in body composition if they are taken serially. They have the advantage of being inexpensive, easy to carry out, and reproducible with a modicum of training. Their main disadvantage is their lack of precision."[8] Because of this high level of uncertainty, current anthropometric standards for the evaluation of growth require twenty-five different measures including stature; weight; body mass index; sitting height; biochanteric breadth; elbow breadth; mid-upper arm circumference, area, and muscle area; mid-arm fat; triceps and subscapular skinfold thickness; and percent fat weight.[9]

Following earlier lines of research, Wheatcroft states: "Data on terminal height provide a history of 'net nutrition' up to the age at which growth ceases (normally between 20 and 24). Weight is an indicator of more recent net nutritional status.'"[10] Mironov holds that "an expert majority of anthropometricians at the present time endorse the paradigm that net consumption exerts a decisive influence on body height, and in this analysis, I rely on that paradigm." But it is unclear how useful or sensitive final stature alone is as a measurement of well-being, however defined. "The major increase in the prevalence of stunting ... occurs in the first two years of life. After that period the curve flattens." Height-for-age, weight-for-age, and weight-for-height as anthropometric measures are perhaps better applied to children only through the age of 7, "because from then on genetic factors start playing a greater role in the determination of a child's height and weight."[11] To quote Eveleth and Tanner again:

---

8 Johanno T. Dwyer, "Concept of Nutritional Status and Its Measurement," in *Anthropometric Assessment of Nutritional Status*, ed. John H. Himes (New York, 1991), 16 (emphasis added).

9 A. Roberto Frisancho, *Anthropometric Standards for the Assessment of Growth and Nutritional Status* (Ann Arbor, MI, 1990).

10 See also Komlos, *Nutrition and Economic Development*, 27.

11 Kees Kostermans, *Assessing the Quality of Anthropometric Data* (Washington, DC, 1994), 5-6; WHO Working Group, "Use and Interpretation of Anthropometric Indicators of Nutritional Status," *Bulletin of the World Health Organization* 64, no. 6 (1986): 931.

"The average values of children's heights and weights reflect accurately the state of a nation's public health and the average nutritional status of the population of its citizens, when appropriate allowance is made for differences, if any, in genetic potential. This is especially so in developing or disintegrating countries."[12] For these same reasons, comparisons with populations of differing genetic background are impossible, though Mironov attempts to make them. Even current research admits the difficulty of establishing nonpopulation-specific anthropometric reference standards that can permit such comparisons.[13] Equally, the methods employed require the assumption that the genetic composition of the population measured across the period under observation remain relatively stable, proportionally speaking. This is true for only some of the populations or subgroups analyzed by Wheatcroft and Mironov.

Although data concerning final stature are unfortunately often the only data available to historians, the dependability of this measure as an indicator of well-being is low.[14] Given the problems of relying exclusively on stature or height, the World Health Organization noted as early as 1986: "It is generally desirable to use more than one method of presenting and analyzing anthropometric data."[15] Heeding this caution, John Riley, using data on height and weight to compute a body mass index for adult males in Britain in the 1860s rather than relying on height alone, demonstrated, as suggested by the World Health Organization, that "weight matters. The addition of information about weight, which allows calculation of body mass, calls into question the use of height as a gauge of quality of life, nutritional status, and mortality risk."[16] Similarly, recent research on men of Amherst College between 1834-1949 found that "no relationship between height and mortality could be detected," while at the same time a "bulk-mortality relationship received strong confirmation."[17] Examination of the height and health of the army of

---

12 Eveleth and Tanner, *Worldwide Variation*, 1 (emphasis added).

13 Frisancho, *Anthropometric Standards*, 3.

14 Kostermans, *Assessing the Quality*, 3.

15 WHO Working Group, "Use and Interpretation," 938.

16 John C. Riley, "Height, Nutrition, and Mortality Risk Reconsidered," *Journal of Interdisciplinary History* 24, no. 3 (Winter 1994): 492.

17 John E. Murray, "Standards of the Present for People of the Past: Height, Weight, and Mortality among Men of Amherst College, 1834 -1949," *Journal of Economic History* 57, no. 3 (September 1997): 585.

the East India Company has led to the conclusion that "it may be time to tone down some of the overly hopeful claims made for the application of anthropometric data to economic history made in the earlier stages of the literature."[18] In all, it would seem that height without weight cannot bear the burden of anthropometric analysis.

Another factor confounding the use of anthropometric measures, and especially of height as a measure of well-being, is the autonomous role of infectious disease. During the period under consideration, Imperial Russia and the Soviet Union experienced major changes in the infectious disease environment. Smallpox was brought under control in many parts of the empire by the end of the nineteenth century and eradicated, in all likelihood, just prior to World War II. Cholera first became epidemic in the 1830s; poliomyelitis in the 1950s. Tuberculosis became endemic toward the end of the last century. Measles and whooping cough may well have become more prevalent, and scarlet fever less virulent.[19] In addition, a shift in breast-feeding practices and the increased availability of unadulterated milk supplies may well have reduced the biggest killer of all, infant and childhood diarrheal diseases, which are often implicated in stunting. All these diseases affect quite different age groups and have differential consequences for human growth.[20] Although some of these changes in the disease environ-

---

18 Joel Mokyr and Cormac O' Gràda, "Height and Health in the United Kingdom 1815-1860: Evidence from the East India Company Army," *Explorations in Economic History* 33 (April 1996): 163.

19 Kenneth F. Kiple, ed., *The Cambridge World History of Human* Disease (New York, 1993), 1063; Joseph H. Bates and William W. Stead, "Tuberculosis as a Global Epidemic," *Medical Clinics of North America* 77, no. 6 (November 1993): 1208-10; Steven L. Hoch, "Famine, Disease, and Mortality Patterns in the Parish of Borshevka, Russia, 1830-1912," *Population Studies* 52, no. 3 (October 1998); K. G. Vasil'ev and A. E. Segal, *Istoriia epidemii v Rossii (Materialy i ocherki)* (Moscow, 1960), 214-353; O. V. Baroian, *Results of Half a Century of Combating Infections in the USSR and Certain Urgent Problems of Modern Epidemiology* (Moscow, 1968); E. I. Chazov, ed., *70 let sovetskogo zdravookhraneniia*, 1917-1987 (Moscow, 1987).

20 Hans-Joachim Voth and Timothy Leunig, "Did Smallpox Reduce Height? Stature and Standard of Living in London, 1770-1873," *Economic History Review* 49 (1996): 541-60; Ida Johnston et al., "Reading Attainment and Physical Development after Whooping Cough," *Journal of Epidemiology and Community Health* 39 (1985): 314-19; R. C. Hauspie and H. Pagezy, "Longitudinal Study

ment can be attributed to direct medical or public health interventions, others are due to random variation in the nature of disease or shifts in the seasonal demand for women's labor, all of which complicate any analysis of changes in well-being.

Finally, even to the degree that anthropometric measures are correlated to the net nutritional status or well-being of a population, it needs to be noted that an entitlement to food, especially on the part of the young, reflects social values, and not simple availability.[21] This is especially the case in patriarchal societies in which wealth and status are stratified by generation. Changes in entitlement practices resulting from fundamental shifts in attitudes toward children can be a significant factor affecting nutritional status and well-being, quite apart from net gain or loss in availability.

The raw data used by Mironov and Wheatcroft present formidable problems for analysis, especially given that the 100-year secular increase in stature under discussion is less than 10 cm, or just under 4 inches (see Wheatcroft, figure 3). First, it is important to understand that Mironov, exclusively, and Wheatcroft, frequently, use summary data, grouped variously in anywhere from five to seventeen height intervals. Such an inconsistent grouping of the raw data across time can seriously distort serial estimates of mean stature. Second, they are often using truncated data, that is, only for recruits who met the minimal height requirements, a level that changed over time. Third, problems such as age-heaping, frequently encountered in historical demography, and difficulties in obtaining accurate height measurements, cited in many anthropometric studies, could skew their height-for-age results. Fourth, no serial data appear to be available on changes in the proportion of men who fell below the minimum height requirement. This will distort any calculation of mean height in a population. Fifth, it is unclear that

of Growth of African Babies: An Analysis of Seasonal Variations in the Average Growth Rate and the Effects of Infectious Diseases on Individual and Average Growth Patterns," *Acta Paediatrica Scandinavia*, Supplement 350 (1989): 37-43; A. Prader, J. M. Tanner, and G. A. Von Harnack, "Catch-up Growth Following Illness or Starvation," *Journal of Pediatrics* 62 (1963): 646-69; and Hummert and Goodman, "An Assessment," 371-77.

[21] Richard H. Steckel, "Stature and Standard of Living," *Journal of Economic Literature* 33 (December 1995): 1904.

recruits, especially prior to 1874, are representative of the population as a whole. Landlords and peasant communes with good reason often selected recruits from the poorest households.[22] Finally, in much of the nineteenth century, annual recruitment levies were regional, and Mironov admits to regional differences in stature.

Though both authors admit to some of these problems, they do not appear able to correct them. They express serious reservations about the data, but proceed anyway. Neither Wheatcroft nor Mironov appears to have undertaken any internal tests on the data to see if they conform to the known distributions of stature in human populations. It is widely recognized that height reflects a Gaussian distribution, and it would have been useful to know if the summary data employed conform to this anticipated distribution.[23] This would have permitted Mironov to test for accuracy over time and to correct for shifts in the minimal height requirements for recruitment. Finally, no evidence is presented in Wheatcroft's essay that will allow me to agree with his claim that "Soviet statistical data are generally far more reliable than are normally presumed." Wheatcroft candidly admits to problems of "censorship," "purposefully misleading data," "demonstrably false" claims, and "selectively reproduced figures." But no analysis of the data on stature, either statistical or substantive, is presented to demonstrate its reliability and justify its use. At present, I remain unconvinced.

For all these reasons, it is not surprising that Wheatcroft and Mironov come up with contradictory results for the years in which their research overlaps. Wheatcroft identifies "two fairly steady periods in which there was a distinct upward trend: 1) from the 1850s birth cohort to the late 1880s, and 2) from the mid-1930s birth cohort to the late 1950s."[24] In contrast, Mironov holds, "for 1821 to 1910, we can discern three periods: in the first period, 1821-1850, or roughly thirty years, physical stature increased; in the second, the fifteen years between 1851 and

22 Steven L. Hoch, *Serfdom and Social Control in Russia: Petrovskoe, a Village in Tambov* (Chicago, 1986), 155; Rodney D. Bohac, "The Mir and the Military Draft," *Slavic Review* 47, no. 4 (Winter 1988): 652-66.

23 Eveleth and Tanner, *Worldwide Variation*, 5; Frisancho, *Anthropometric Standards*, 31.

24 Wheatcroft, "The Great Leap Upward," 44.

1865, stature decreased; and in the third, between 1866 and 1910, or forty-five years, stature again increased."[25] Wheatcroft also identifies two major periods of decline "1) for birth cohorts 1899-1909, and 2) for birth cohorts 1923- 1934, and possibly one minor decline for birth cohorts 1913-1918." In other words, between 1851 and 1865, Mironov has stature decreasing and Wheatcroft has it increasing; Wheatcroft sees this increase continuing to the late 1880s, followed by a major decline in the first decade of the twentieth century. Mironov sees an increase from 1866-1910.

These discrepancies highlight the problems of trying to periodize observed changes in final stature with shifts in either biological well-being or standard of living. In organizing height data of 20-year-old recruits by birth cohort, Mironov is of the view that "the difference in the height of recruits between 1877 and 1876—that is, 1 mm—can essentially be explained by that one year, 1856." Consequently, Mironov contends that "the annual change in body height permits one to determine when the tendency toward increased height is replaced by the tendency toward decreased height, and correspondingly, when the tendency toward improved biological status is replaced by a tendency toward declining biological status, and vice versa." This is a serious statistical flaw that undermines the entire discussion that follows. In essence, Mironov uses cohort analysis to draw conclusions that can only be drawn from period analysis. Cohort (or longitudinal) analysis traces the fate of a specific group of individuals from the time the cohort is exposed to the risk being studied, in this instance the risk of being short in stature which begins at age 0 and lasts until age 20-25. In contrast, period (or cross-sectional) analysis involves "a quantitative description and analysis of the data for many cohorts observed during a specified time interval, such as a year, with respect to some variable."[26]

In other words, the final stature of a birth cohort can be affected by factors across a considerable period of time and, thus, observed changes in height cannot readily be periodized or fixed in time. First, Tanner has noted that a "contributory cause of the shortness [persisting into

[25] Mironov, "New Approaches to Old Problems," 17-18.

[26] Henry S. Shryock and Jacob S. Siegel, *The Methods and Materials of Demography* (New York, 1976), 550 -51.

adult life] might have been the undernutrition of mothers much earlier, when they themselves were children, causing stunting of size and in consequence the production of small babies."[27] Thus, we are presented with the possibility that a cohort of short mothers born in 1820, giving birth to children largely between 1840-1860, had male sons who, when measured between 1860-1880, were found to be of short stature.

Second, the impact of childhood infectious diseases on final stature is quite age-specific. In Russia, diarrheal diseases predominated in the very early months of life, as early weaning was common. Measles, smallpox, and whooping cough occurred slightly later. Diphtheria and scarlet fever primarily affected children aged 3-4. The age-specific nature of various infectious disease insults results in quite different impacts on successive birth cohorts. Thus, Mironov is incorrect in his assumption that the cause of stature differences in successive birth cohorts is limited to events occurring in the first year of life in the older cohort.

Third, and of greater import, as Wheatcroft recognizes, periodization is greatly confounded by the quite varied nature of catch-up growth. Some birth cohorts stunted at a younger age may well have had both the time and the food energy to recover. Other birth cohorts may simply have lacked the time; others may have lacked sufficient nutrition to recover all of the growth lost. At any age, "it is difficult to determine if complete catch-up has occurred."[28] Moreover, there have been instances which "demonstrate that the fluctuations in the share of undersized conscripts generally coincided with the food situation in the years immediately preceding the examination."[29] Finally, tuberculosis, which first entered the disease environment during this period, inhibits catch-up growth far more than most other diseases, and thus would be a new random factor affecting final stature.[30]

---

27 Tanner, "A Concise History of Growth Studies," 3: 546.

28 Jere D. Haas and Jean-Pierre Habicht, "Growth and Growth Charts in the Assessment of Pre-School Nutritional Status," in *Diet and Disease in Traditional and Developing Societies*, ed. C.A. Harrison and J.C. Waterlow (Cambridge, 1990), 175.

29 C.A. Mandemakers and J.L. Van Zanden, "The Height of Conscripts and National Income: Apparent Relations and Misconceptions," *Explorations in Economic History* 30 (January 1993): 83.

30 Haas and Habicht, "Growth and Growth Charts," 161.

These problems make period analysis of all but very long-term secular changes impossible and call into question Mironov's detailed but unsupportable periodization of shifts in biological status and all the conclusions that follow. For any one birth cohort, a complex of factors across a sixty-year period needs to be taken into consideration. Wheatcroft's basic argument does not rest on a detailed periodization of changes in final stature, though at times he does imply one. But, in fact, the factors influencing the final stature of a birth cohort are hard to determine and impossible to date with any degree of accuracy. Consequently, shifts in biological well-being cannot be determined with the chronological precision Wheatcroft and especially Mironov suggest. As Joel Mokyr and Cormac O'Gráda have cautioned: "Time-series inferences from height data therefore remain, in our view, hazardous."[31]

In reference to observed changes in stature, Mironov states: "The task of the historian is to explain which components of this [biological] status have produced these changes; these components would include the quality of nutrition, intensity of work or training, illness, environment, massive and prolonged stress, and physical overexertion." In contrast, Wheatcroft is much more cautious, generally eschewing any discussion of causality. He is content to observe the improved stature in the population in the long run, which, he holds, serves as a counterweight to well-known periods of demographic and economic crisis and biological stress. Again, Wheatcroft's approach is more prudent.

To Massimo Livi-Bacci: "Variations in height reflect not only variations in nutrition but also differences in the frequency of contagious diseases, independently of prevailing nutritional habits. The state of the art does not yet enable us to unravel the causal tangle of food-hygiene-infection- height, even in current studies."[32] Similarly, attempts to weigh "the relative individual importance of such variables on growth is further complicated by the complexity of their synergistic relationship.... Dietary deficits and disease cannot be completely disassociated

---

31 Mokyr and O' Gràda,, "Height and Health," 163.

32 Massimo Livi-Bacci, *Population and Nutrition: An Essay on European Demographic History*, trans. Tania Croft-Murray, with the assistance of Carl Ipsen (Cambridge, 1990), 108.

when evaluating their effects on growth and development. This is undoubtedly true in underdeveloped countries in which diseases are potentially life threatening, generally show a profoundly negative effect on growth, and are frequently found in consort with various forms of malnutrition."[33] In the end, Mironov discovers, as have many others, that shifts in stature do not correlate well with other indicators of well-being. Mironov blames the other variables. Given all the problems of anthropometric history, this does not appear to be justified.

Wheatcroft's research into stature highlights the fact that short-term crises do not preclude important secular improvements in well-being. In fact, recovery is often swift. This accords with the findings of Susan Cott Watkins and Jane Menken and of Ajit Das Gupta, as well as with my own findings.[34] His suggestion that this secular gain in well-being occurred without an improvement in food availability implies that future lines of research should focus more intently on public health policies and campaigns as well as changes in the infectious disease environment. Equally significant, his description of a long-term increase in height provides additional support for established views. In a well-known collection of essays published in 1960 by some of America's best cold warriors, a long-term increase in life expectancy was recognized as the result of "in good part a genuine improvement in conditions affecting mortality, as may be seen in data on life expectancy at birth: 32 years in 1896-97, 44 years in 1926-27, 48 years in 1938-1940 and 67 years in 1955-1956," much attributable to a significant decline in infant mortality, as is to be expected.[35] This view has not changed in the last forty years. A 1999 edition of a textbook on Russian and Soviet history, in discussing the period up to 1960, states that "the USSR was in the forefront of improving public health, raising

33 Hummert and Goodman, "An Assessment," 371.

34 Susan Cott Watkins and Jane Menken, "Famines in Historical Perspectives," *Population and Development Review* 11, no. 4 (1985): 654; Ajit Das Gupta, "Catastrophes and Their Population Symptoms," in *The Great Mortalities: Methodological Studies of Demographic Crises in the Past*, ed. Hubert Charbonneau and André LaRose (Liege, 1980), 65; Hoch, "Famine, Disease, and Mortality Patterns," 363.

35 Warren W. Eason, "Population Changes," in *The Transformation of Russian Society: Aspects of Social Change since 1861*, ed. Cyril E. Black (Cambridge, MA, 1960), 79-80.

life expectancy, and reducing infant mortality."[36] To quote Wheatcroft, "there were remarkable changes and improvements in welfare, mortality, and height."

On this basis, Wheatcroft urges us to reassess "what the Soviet experience meant to the mass of the Soviet population." He concludes, "it 'probably' was the best time for most of its citizens." Rebuking Richard Pipes, Zbigniew Brzezinski, and Robert Conquest, Wheatcroft prefers to stand in the camp of our legendary logger. "Paul Bunyan was the one historian of the useful and the beautiful; other writers of history tell only of terrible and dramatic events."[37] To Wheatcroft, as to many before him, the Soviet experience is to be subjected to cost-benefit analysis. We need "to gain a more balanced view" as we debate "the achievements of Soviet communism, and how these should be weighed against the costs." In particular, he argues that short-term crises, however emotionally or morally charged, must be viewed in the perspective of significant secular improvement.

Social scientists and historians should indeed pay attention to what the Soviet regime accomplished. Markers of ordinary people's lives are useful and help illuminate the views and opinions of those who lived through this period. These achievements help us understand the social bases of support for the regime. But good and evil, certainly familiar terrain for the historian, cannot always be the subject of cost-benefit analysis. Even those regimes most would recognize as evil had social welfare goals for society, and clearly Soviet ideology demanded that. For the vast majority of Germans living between 1914 and 1950, the early years of Nazi rule were the best of times. But none of the accomplishments of the Nazi regime will permit me to view it in a more beneficial light.

Although it might be possible to use stature as an indicator of economic or biological well-being, we need to be cautious of rhetorical slips suggesting that we can measure intellectual and ethical health similarly. They cannot be placed in the same ledger book. The new information provided by Wheatcroft leads him to make moral claims.

---

[36] David MacKenzie and Michael W. Curran, *A History of Russia, the Soviet Union and Beyond*, 5th ed. (New York, 1999), 573.

[37] James Stevens, "The Winter of the Blue Snow," in *Paul Bunyan* (New York, 1925), 11.

But improvements in stature or life expectancy must not be allowed to place the Soviet experience "into some form of perspective," rebalancing the moral ledger. Pipes, Brzezinski, and Conquest are not simply discussing mortality data as a measure of well-being, for which other indicators indeed might be more useful, they are describing state policies of extermination, and we must not confuse these two distinct aspects of life. It may be ironic that at a time of great human brutality there was a significant gain in economic or biological well-being. But such improvements cannot serve as a counterweight to the repressive policies of the Soviet state. Rather, we need to be reminded of Charles Dickens: "It was the best of times, it was the worst of times," an age of wisdom, foolishness; belief, incredulity; Light, Darkness; hope, despair; everything before us, nothing before us. All these were surely part of the Soviet experience.

9

Bridewealth, Dowry, and Socioeconomic Differentiation in Rural Russia

In an agricultural society with a very low level of technology and more than adequate amounts of arable lands—as in Petrovskoe (the serf estate under examination in this study) and in much of the central agricultural region in Imperial Russia—labor was of the utmost value and the primary determinant of output. Other than draft animals, additional capital inputs were extremely limited. But in Russia, the climate uniquely affected the structure of field labor organization. As a consequence of the extremely short growing season, five-and-a-half to six months instead of the eight to nine months in western Europe, the harvesting of winter and spring cereals and the plowing and sowing of the winter field all came in quick succession within the span of six weeks. From mid-July to the end of August was the harvest season, the *stradnaia pora* as the Russians called it; literally the time of suffering. It was an agonizing period of exertion demanding that numerous tasks be accomplished simultaneously. A work team, a *tiaglo* (a husband and wife together), proved to be the best allocation of labor resources. A single male simply could not complete all the necessary field work if he were to allow the cereals to mature fully while avoiding the danger of an early frost.[1]

There thus emerged in Russia a clear differentiation of field labor by sex. During the harvest season, women used sickles to cut rye, winter wheat, if any, and sometimes oats, whereas the men reaped the other

---

This essay was originally published in *Agrarian Organization in the Century of Industrialization: Europe, Russia and North America, Research In Economic History*, suppl. 5, 1989, 389-410.

[1] N. Kalachov, "Iuridicheskie obychai krest'ian v nekotorykh mestnostiakh," *Arkhiv istoricheskikh i prakticheskikh svedenii, otnosiashchikhsia do Rossii*, vol. 2 (St. Petersburg, 1859), 25; M.N. Kishkin, "Dannye i predpolozheniia," 226; A. Smirnov, *Ocherki semeinykh otnoshenii po obychnomu pravu russkogo naroda* (Moscow, 1878), 76-81; and A.N. Nasonov, "Iz istorii," 518. See also Olga Crisp, "The Pattern of Industrialization in Russia, 1700-1914," *Studies in the Russian Economy before* 1914 (London, 1976), 21.

spring cereals with scythes. The women then tied the grain into sheaves for drying; the men began plowing the winter field. While they sowed next year's crop, the women started to cart the sheaves from the fields and, if time permitted, were assisted by their husbands. In general, plowing, harrowing, sowing, cutting hay, and harvesting with a scythe were men's field work; tending to the kitchen garden and hemp field, raking hay, cutting stalks with a sickle, tying them, and transporting them to the threshing floor were women's field work.[2]

A partnership was essential. Single or widowed females were never part of a work team, and rarely did males carry a full tiaglo alone. Of all males aged 15-19, the interval during which they first assumed some estate field labor obligations receiving in return a land allotment, 38% carried no tiaglo, none of whom were married; 32 carried a half-tiaglo, of whom only 4% were married; and 29% carried a full-tiaglo, of whom at least three-quarters were married.[3]

To maximize output on the Petrovskoe estate the bailiff had to maximize the number of work teams. In practice, this meant the distribution of corvee obligations had to be synchronized with internal changes in household composition resulting from marriage and death so as to avoid the underutilization of labor. When a young couple married it immediately formed a new tiaglo which further increased the productive

---

[2] The weekly reports of the bailiff of Petrovskoe to Moscow usually noted the tasks assigned to men and women during the previous seven days, and these documents reveal this division of labor. See also Mashkin, "Byt," 95-96 and 101; A. Preobrazhenskii, "Volost' Pokrovsko-Sitskaia," 79-80; and D.I., "Zametki o krest'ianskoi sem'e v Novgorodskoi gubernii," in *Sbornik narodnykh iuridicheskikh obychaev,* vol. 2, in *Zapiski Imperatorskago russkago geograficheskago obshchestva po otdeleniiu etnografi,* vol. 18 (St. Petersburg, 1900), 166.

[3] TsGADA, f. 1262, op. 1, ch. 1, ed. khr. 1495; op. 4, ed. khr. 41, 59, 121, 186, 344, 357; ch. 2, ed. khr. 822. Of this last group, in all likelihood, more than 75% were married because the nominative lists often failed to distinguish between single males and those who had been widowed shortly after their first marriage. A recently widowed male age 15-19 would have formed a full tiaglo upon marriage and was formally obligated to fulfill his responsibilities until the next redistribution of land and corvee duties. Nevertheless, young, single males from families with no other working-age males did on occasion carry a full tiaglo, with a mother, sisters, or younger brothers assisting in the field work. See also I. Tiutriumov, "Krest'ianskaia sem'ia. Ocherk obychnogo prava," *Russkaia Rech'* 7 (1879): 135-37.

capacity of the estate. The earlier serfs married, the sooner this economic benefit to the estate would be realized.[4]

But if the young couples would have had to establish their own households, early marriage would then have necessarily confronted both the problem of capital accumulation and parental concerns regarding the premature loss of an adult laborer. In contrast, had the serfs of Petrovskoe found it necessary to delay marriage seven to eight years, until the mid- or late-twenties as in western Europe, then the productive capacity of the estate and all serf households would have been reduced by anywhere from 17% (assuming all single males over age 19 carried a half-tiaglo) to 35% (if males had no corvee obligations until marriage).[5] Roughly speaking, a figure of 20% seems reasonable as the amount of gross grain production that would have been lost if marriages had followed the "European" pattern. Gross income would have suffered comparably.

Overcoming thcse problems was accomplished, first, by tying the execution of estate labor obligations to the right to use an allotment of peasant arable land, a practice common throughout all of the central agricultura1 region and much of Great Russia as well. This provided a new couple with immediate access to a plot of land, the most crucial capital input for its maintenance. Arable land was thus constantly being redistributed to reflect marriages, retirements, and deaths. Second, virilocal postmarital residence not only obviated the need for much additional capital accumulation, but constituted a windfall for the bridegroom's household. Often, the mere addition of a daughter-in-law increased the number of tiaglo in a household from one to two or two to three, thereby increasing a *dvor's* total arable land by 50 to 100%. Parents thus had a strong economic incentive to see that their sons married young.

---

4 D.I., "Zametki," 262-263; Kalachov, "Iuridicheskie obychai," 25; Kishkin, "Dannye i predpolozheniia," 226; Nasonov, "Iz istorii," 518; A. Gerschenkron, "Agrarian Policies and Industrialization: Russia 1861-1917," in *The Cambridge Economic History of Europe*, vol. 6, part 2 (Cambridge, 1965), 749; and P. Czap, "Marriage and the Peasant Joint Family in the Face of Serfdom" in *The Family in Imperial Russia*, ed. David I. Ransel (Urbana, IL, 1978), 115.

5 These figures are based on the total number of working person-years lived for all males between 19 and 54, the latter being the mean age of retirement for surviving males, assuming the estimate of expectation of life at birth determined above. Coale and Demeny, *Regional Mode Life Tables*, part 2, p. 7.

"Get married at eighteen in order to settle on a tiaglo" *(V vosemnadtstat' let zhenit'sia, chtob na tiaglo sadit'sia)* was common advice given to young males.[6] Third, the payment of a substantial brideprice (or bridewealth) known as *kladka,* given by the groom's head of household to the bride's, enticed dvors to part with their unmarried, mature female laborers. *Kladka,* in effect, redistrubuted wealth among households without upsetting patriarchal authority within them.

Kladka had both characteristics of a bridewealth, the permanent movement of resources from the groom's household in exchange for rights to the bride, and indirect dowry, gifts of "money indirectly contributed by the groom to the endowment of the bride."[7] The distinction is important, even if blurred within the custom of kladka itself, for bridewealth was a "circulating societal fund," a redistribution of resources limiting socioeconomic differentiation among households, whereas an indirect dowry did not necessarily entail the permanent alienation of any property from either household. Indirect dowry with virilocal postmarital residence resulted in all wealth remaining in place.[8]

Marriage almost everywhere involves the transmission of property, but in most of Great Russia supplying a newly married couple with a conjugal fund by direct or indirect dowry was not important. At Petrovskoe,

---

[6] P. Efimenko, "Sem'ia Arkhangel'skogo krest'ianina po obychnomu pravu," *Sudebnyi zhurnal* (July-August, 1873): 97-98. Efimenko is referring here to customary practices in central Russia, not in the far north. V. Dal', *Polovitsy russkogo naroda*, 362. *Tiaglo* in this case means the unit of allotted land associated with the formation of work team and the assumption of corvee. On the benefits of early marriage for peasant elders, see Brzheskii, *Ocherki iuridicheskogo byta*, 180-81; Zvonkov, "Sovremennyi brak," 30-31; Efimenko "Sem'ia," 97; P. Efimenko, *Pridanoe po obychnomu pravu krest'ian Archangel'skoi gubernii* (St. Petersburg, 1872), 39-41; A. Zaloskin, "Khoziaistvennye statisticheskie zamechaniia po selu Abakumovo, Riazanskoi gubernii, Pronskogo uezda, Pomeshchika G ... na," *Zhurnal zemlevladel'tsev* 2., no. 6 (1858): 41; N. Lebedev. "Byt krest'ian Tverskoi gubernii, Tverskogo uezda," *ES* I, p. 186; K. Myl'nikova and V. Tsintsius, "Severno-velikorusskaia svad'ba," *Materialy po svad'be i semeino-rodovomu stroiu narodov SSSR,* vol. 1 (Leningrad, 1926), 24-27; N. Otto, "Iz narodnogo byta: Novgorodskaia svad'ba," *Severnaia Pchela,* no. 137 (1862): 545; and Pr V. E-iu, "Opisanie sel'skoi svad'by v Sengileevskom uezde, Simbirskoi gubernii," *Etnograficheskoe obozrenie* 42, no. 3 (1899): 108-109.

[7] J. Goody, "Bridewealth and Dowry in Africa and Eurasia," in *Bridewealth and Dowry* (Cambridge, 1973), 1-5.

[8] Ibid., 2, 46.

the estate provided arable land through the repartitional land structure, and the groom's family, an established household. Little else was needed except clothing. In fact, the custom of direct dowry *(pridanoe,* which also means trousseau), "a type of pre-mortem inheritance to the bride"[9]) from her family was of little or no consequence where the repartitional land commune existed.

Between 1871 and 1874 a special government commission concerned with the reorganization of the township courts *(volostnye sudy)* investigated peasant customary practices in 15 provinces of European Russia, including all 12 districts *(uezdy)* of Tambov guberniia. In Borisoglebskii district where Petrovskoe was located, 10 of the 29 townships were studied, although the Petrovskoe estate, a *volost'* by itself, was not one of them. Nevertheless, in two of the townships adjacent to Petrovskoe the commission noted that "a dowry (*pridanoe*) is not given, but the bridegroom pays a *kladka* for the bride (*zhenikh platit za nevestu kladku*)." In seven of the eight remaining townships, dowries were "never given," and in the eighth, closest to the district seat of Borisogleb, they were given "very rarely."[10]

Many nineteenth-century ethnographers were quite surprised to discover that peasants did not give their daughters direct dowries, but the evidence is overwhelming. Observers for the Imperial Russian Geographic Society found the practice of *kladka* widespread in regions where the repartitional commune existed.[11] Direct dowries were common only in the far north and in Little Russia where lands were held in perpetuity. In fact, after the introduction of the repartitional commune in Arkangel'sk guberniia, direct dowries declined in importance.[12] To

---

9 Ibid., 1.

10 *Trudy komissi po preobrazovaniiu volostnykh sudov,* vols. 1-7 (St. Petersburg, 1873-1874), I, 389-486.

11 D.K. Zelenin, *Opisanie rukopisei uchenogo arkhiva Imperatorskogo russkogo geograficheskogo obshchestva,* 3 vols. (Petrograd, 1914-1916), *passim;* V.P. Muhkin, *Obychnyi poriadok nasledovaniia u krest'ian* (St. Petersburg, 1881), 88-90, 132-136; Tiutriumov, "Krest'ianskaia sem'ia," 155-156; A. Efimenko, "Narodnye iuridicheskie vozzreniia na brak," *Znanie,* no. 1 (1874): 15; Smirnov, "Ocherki semeinykh otnoshenii," 182-183; [no author], "Sloboda Trekhizbianskaia," *ES* II., 7.

12 P. Chubinskii, "Ocherk narodnykh iuridicheskikh obychaev i poniatii v Malorossii," *Zapiski Imperatorskogo russkogo geograficheskogo obshchestva po otdeleniiu etnografii* 2 (1969): 690-691; Efimenko, *Pridanoe,* 8-17.

Table 1
Customary Amount of *Kladka*

Province	Uezd	Year	Amount of *Kladka* (rubles assignats)
Arkhangel'sk	Shenkurskii	1854	20-35
Vladimir	Muromskii	1849	17-35
Voronezh	Pavlovskii		Not more than 20
	Korotoianskii	1850	50-100
Viatka	Elabuzhskii	1850	35-105
Kazan'	Zakamskii krai	1850	25-45
Kaluga	Medzynskii	1856	40-140
	Zhizdrinskii	1849	9
Kursk[a]	Oboianskii	1862	3-24 and more
Nizhegorod	Sergachskii	1850s	Up to 50
	Sergachskii	1850s	7-14
	Not specified	1849	15-50
	Vasil'skii	1849	40-100
	Kniagininskii	1849	20-40
	Kniagininskii	1849	10-60
	Arzamaskii	1850	15-30
	Alizhegorodskii	1848	Up to 100
	Likoianovskii	1850	5-80
Novgorod	Cherepovskii	1850	Up to 50
Penza	Not specified	1850	15-20
	Kerenskii	1857	Up to 50
	Saranskii	1843-54	35-85
Perm	Verkhoturskii	1848	20-30
	Shadrinskii	1849	10-210
Riazan'	Zaraiskii	1867	20-35
	Mikhailovskii	1876	5-50
	Spasskii	1854	7-50
Iaroslavl'[b]	Molozhskii	1853	20-40
Simbirsk[c]		1840	Rarely more than 150
Simbirsk		1862	3-105
Vladimir and Nizhegorod[e]		1853	50-100
Iaroslavl'[e]		1853	20-40
Kaluga, Kursk, Tambov[e]		1853	70-245
Great Russia[f]		Second half of the eighteenth century	15-150

Table 1 notes:

[a] Mashkin, "Byt krest'ian Kurskoi gubernii, Oboianskogo uzda," *Etnograficheskii sbornik* 5 (1862): 23.

[b] A. Preobrazhenskii, "Prikhod Stanilovskii na Siti, Iaroslavskoi gubernii, Molozhskogo uezda," *Etnograficheskii sbornik* 1 (1853):141-45.

[c] V. B., "Simbirskie obychai pokupat' nevest," *Otechestvennye zapiski* 9 no. 7 (1840): 28-29.

[d] N. Aristov, "Ocherk krest'ianskoi svadby," *Volga,* no. 13 (1862): 49-50.

[e] A. Afanes'ev, "Kritika: Etnograficheskii sbornik," *Otechestvennye zapiski,* nos. 9-10, part 4 (1853): 25.

[f] V.I. Semevskii, "Domashnii byt i nravy krest'ian vo vtoroi polovine XVIII v." *Ustoi,* no. 2 (1882): 76.

Source: Unless noted, D.K. Zelenin, *Opisanie rukopisei uchenago arkhiva Imperatorskago russkago geograficheskago obshchestva,* 3 vols. (Petrograd, 1914-1916), passim.

quote the ethnographer V. P. Mukhin; "the custom of giving a *kladka* for the bride is very strictly observed in those areas where it is not usual to give a dowry; thus *kladka* in this case is like a surrogate dowry, coming from the side of the groom."[13] In 1874, Aleksandra Efimenko, another student of peasant life, noted that where *kladka* was part of the marriage contract, no conditions were set for a bride's dowry.[14] There was nothing, however, that prohibited the bride's household from giving their daughter or new in-laws small gifts or from contributing directly to the wedding feast, and this was sometimes done.

Kladka was essentially a payment of money from the groom's household to the bride's, the amount being set at the time of betrothal. Often a fur coat or other clothes for the bride were also specified in the marriage agreement. Neither livestock nor, of course, land was ever exchanged as *kladka,* although these were common endowments where direct dowries existed. Some, and occasionally all, of the *kladka* money went to cover the costs of the bride's trousseau, wedding expenses (*stolovye den'gi*), and gifts, usually clothes, to the future husband and in-laws. This is what is meant by the indirect dowry aspect or portion of *kladka,* for

[13] Mukhin, *Obychnyi poriadok,* 135-136.

[14] Efimenko, "Narodnye iuridicheskie vozzreniia," 15. See also S.V. Pakhman, *Obychnoe grazhdanskoe pravo v Rossii,* 2 vols. (St. Petersburg, 1877), II, p. 68; and A. Afanas'ev, "Kritika: Ethnograficheskii sbornik," *Otechestvennye zapiski* 90, nos. 9-10 (1853): part IV, p. 25.

no redistribution of wealth was involved; it all returned to the groom's household with the bride, minus, of course, the expenses of the actual festivities.[15]

But *kladka* payments were usually very substantial, frequently far exceeding the expenditures required of the bride's family. Table 1 presents information on the customary amount of *kladka* paid in the middle of the nineteenth century for regions where it was common. Most of the figures come from responses to a questionnaire sent out by the Imperial Russia Geographic Society in 1848 on the investigation of the "ordinary Russian person." Contributions were primarily village priests, local landlords, doctors, statisticians, teachers, and seminary students—"the wide mass of the rural intelligentsia," as one archivist describes them.[16] Abstracts of many of the responses from 36 guberniias, Arkhangel'sk through Saratov, were published.[17] For 14 guberniias of European Russia, this was not done. In addition, from some of the 36 provinces came only a few responses, and frequently authors did not specify the amount of *kladka*. Not many figures were available from other sources. Thus, the absence of a guberniia from Table 2 should not necessarily be interpreted as signifying absence of the custom of *kladka*.

It is not clear how much of the *kladka* the bride's family was required to spend on gifts, but her household generally kept a sizeable portion of the *kladka* for itself, this being the bridewealth or wealth equalizing aspect of the exchange. Simply put, because the repartitional land commune immediately provided the bridegroom's household with a unit of peasant arable land upon the formation of a new work team, the bride's household required compensation for the loss of its female laborer and

[15] Zelenin, *Opisanie,* passim; Muhkin, *Obychnyi poriadok,* 113-116, 123-134; Rudnev, "Selo Golun'," 107-108; Efimenko, "Narodnye iuridicheskie vozzreniia," 14; Efimenko, *Pridanoe,* 7; Semenova, *Zhizn' Ivana* " 3; Troitskii, "Selo Lipitsy," 89; Tiutriumov, "Krest'ianskaia sem'ia," 155; M.E. Mikheev, "Opisanie svadebnykh obychaev i obriadov v Buzulukskom uezde, Samarskoi gubernii," *Etnograficheskoe obozrenie* 3 (1899): 146-147; N. Aristov, "Ocherk krest'ianskoi svad'by," *Volga* 13 (1862): 49-50; N. Vinogradov, "Narodnaia svad'ba v Kostromskom uezde," vol. 8 (1917): 74-79; and N. Kostrov, "Svadebnye obriady Minusinskikh krest'ian," *Illiustratsiia* 176 (1861), 10.

[16] Akademiia nauk SSSR. Geograficheskoe obschestvo, *Russkie geografy i puteshestvenniki.* Fondy arkhiva Geograficheskogo obshchestva (Leningrad, 1971), 9.

[17] Zelenin, *Opisanie,* I-III, passim.

Table 2
Dynamic Study of Peasant Mobility, Village of Petrovskoe (1813-27)

Number of Tiaglos	*Number of Households in 1813*	Number of Households in 1827		
		Fewer Tiaglos	Same No. of Tiaglos	More Tiaglos
0.0	2	—	—	2
1.0	22	3	9	10
1.5	2	—	—	2
2.0	10	5	2	3
2.5	4	3	1	—
Total	40	11	12	17

Number of Horses	*Number of Households in 1813*	Number of Households in 1827		
		Fewer Horses	Same No. of Horses	More Horses
0	1	—	—	1
1	2	—	—	2
2	11	1	3	7
3	9	3	2	4
4	9	3	1	5
5	7	2	1	4
6	1	1	—	—
Total	40	10	7	23

Source: TsGADA, f. 1262, op. 1, ed. khr. 1495: op. 4, ch. I, ed. khr. 41, 59, 121, 186, 344, 357.

any decline in its economic and social status resulting from her departure. Kalachov noted that a girl's parents, concerned about the loss of a female worker, would stipulate in the marriage agreement that either she spend the stradnaia pora at home or "that the family of the bridegroom pay a redemption for her, known as *kladka*."[18] Pakhman saw the dual nature of *kladka*, both a payment to reduce wedding costs and to compensate for the person of "the bride herself, as a laborer the family

[18] Kalachov, "Iuridicheskie obychai," 24. See also Tiutriumov, "Krest'ianskaia sem'ia," 137, for a virtually identical statement.

is losing by the girl marrying out."[19] According to Efimenko, "in some southwestern steppe guberniias the payment for the bride is determined by simple competition," with the highest bidder getting the girl, and the price reflecting true market demand.[20] Muhkin found that the amount of *kladka* was greater in regions where a female's labor was more highly valued. In Nizhegorod guberniia, women involved in bast production could do exactly the same work as men, and thus a bride's family could demand a high bridewealth for her.[21] Bridewealth also had its counterpart: "groomwealth." On the rare occasion when the male became part of the bride's household, usually because it had no other working-age males, his parents required compensation for the loss of his labor.[22] In sum, to quote another nineteenth-century ethnographer: "Dowries do not play a large role in peasant life; frequently the bridegroom not only does not receive a dowry, but even further he has to compensate the parents of the bride for their loss of her free labor."[23]

The acquisition of a daughter-in-law was a major expenditure, and the bridegroom's household had to be sure it acquired a good worker in order to recoup its investment. A bad choice could ruin a household for the additional allotment of peasant arable land and the extra worker had to offset not only the costs of the *kladka*, but an extra mouth to feed, higher taxes, and increased obligations. Marriage was too important for the household seeking either to minimize its losses or recoup its investment, the commune having to pay taxes, and the estate trying to maximize production to permit the young persons involved to play any significant role in mate selection. Marriage rituals included the mutual inspection of households by the parents (*smotrina* or *osmotr*) and differed little from the transaction of property. The matchmaker, often a relative, having been sent by the boy's parents, would usually greet the father of the potential bride saying, "we have a buyer, and you have the goods" *(U nas est' kupets, a u vas tovarets)* to signify the reason for the visit. Love was not a factor in marriage and was even thought to be harmful. The groom's family was concerned solely with the bride's health, skills, and

19 Pakhman, *Obychnoe grazhdanskoe pravo,* vol. 2, 60-62.
20 Efimenko, "Krest'ianskaia zhenshchina," 194-198.
21 Muhkin, *Obychnyi poriadok*, 17-19.
22 Semevskii, "Domashnii byt," 77.
23 Tiutriumov, "Krest'ianskaia sem'ia," 155-156. See also Afanas'ev, "Kritika," 25, and Smirnov, "Ocherki semeinykh otnoshenii," 122.

ability to work; the girl's, with being sure it would receive a fair *kladka*. Terms were set orally by a marital agreement (*brachnyi sgovor*), made binding by a *rukobit'e*, a ritual clapping of hands by the two fathers or heads of household, occasionally sanctified by a priest, and celebrated by a bout of heavy drinking (*zapoi* or *propoi*).[24]

Young, unmarried females were in a very ambiguous position in their natal households. Whereas their labor was valued, they were viewed as temporary members of the *dvor*. They had no claim to land where agriculture was the primary pursuit, although their departure would bring in a *kladka*, which should allow a brother or male cousin to marry. Marriageable daughters, granddaughters, and nieces were both consumers and laborers yielding small, short-run benefits, but having no prospects for substantial long-run benefits, but having no prospects for substantial long-run gains for their elders like unmarried males. Thus peasants were constantly balancing the mean age at marriage with the customary size of *kladka*, an equilibrium that would vary with changing economic circumstances.

Economic motives were clearly in the minds of the Petrovskoe serfs when they arranged marriages. Household serfs required the permission of the central estate office in Moscow to marry, and the archives of the estate hold many of the parents' petitions. The language was formal, undoubtedly having been composed by a scribe, but the reasons were plain. Karneia Abramova, a widow with four daughters, sought to marry

[24] Descriptions of marriage and wedding rituals are numerous. See A. Efimenko, "Krest'ianskaia zhenshchina," 77, 197-198; Smirnov, "Ocherki semeinykh otnoshenii," 228-242; P. Efimenko, *Pridanoe*, 39-41; A. Efimenko, "Narodnye iuridicheskie vozzreniia," 1-22; P. Efimenko, "Sem'ia," 32; Aristov, "Ocherk," 49; Pr. V.E.-iu, "Opisanie sel'skoi svad'by," 110-111; Tiutriumov, "Krest'ianskaia sem'ia," 123-129; Otto, "Iz narodnogo byta," 545; Mikheev, "Opisanie svadebnykh obychaev," 144-146; Vinogradov, "Narodnai svad'ba," 74-79; Myl'nikova, "Severno-velikorusskaia svad'ba," 35-36; A. Nikolaev, "Krest'ianskaia svad'ba v Zvenigorodskom uezde, Moskovskoi gubernii," *Severnaia Pchela* 209-210 (1863): 921-925; N.F. Sumtsov, *O svadebnykh obriadakh, preimushchestvenno russkikh* (Kharkov, 1881), 22-34; E.G. Kagarov, "Sostav i proiskhozhdenie svadebnoi obriadnosti," in *Sbornik Muzeia antropologii i etnografii AN SSSR* 42 (1899): 160-163; V.A. Aleksandrov, "Vologodskaia svad'ba," *Biblioteka dlia chteniia*, no. 5 (1863): 6-13; N.R., "Svadebyne obychai v Ostashkovskom uezde v pervoi polovine XIX veka," *Tverskaia starina* (1913): 39; and V.P., "Simbirskie obychai pokupat' nevest," *Otechestvennye zapiski* (1840): 28-29.

off her eldest, Praskov'ia, 18 years old, "in order to avoid my having to support [her].[25] Arkhip Aglovin, the father of six children, including a 22-year-old daughter, Elena, with an illegitimate infant, requested permission for her to marry a free man for exactly the same reason.[26]

Parents were also often desperate for their sons to marry and bring a daughter-in-law into the household, as the following petition reveals:

> Having two sons, of whom Savelii is in Moscow on a passport, and Fedot lives with me, and both have come of age, [but] are not married. And as my wife and I have gotten old and fallen into decrepitude, and with all this moreover, I have at home a daughter who is constantly afflicted by illness, because of this I suffer a great need of bedclothes and other domestic items, so I dare to trouble the Main Office with my most humble request to be favorably disposed to pay merciful attention to our extreme situation to allow our son Fedot to enter into marriage. For this we should pray to God for the health of Your Excellency and the director of the Main Office.
>
> Ivan Smetanin[27]

Economic concerns even affected the seasonal pattern of marriages. The limited evidence available suggests that most first marriages took place in the fall, between September and November, somewhat less often in January and February following the prohibition of Advent, much less frequently in the spring, and almost never in the summer. Peasant sentiments were summed up by the sayings: "A betrothed girl in the household—a corpse at the table" (*Nevesta na dvore-mertvets na stole*), or, the reverse, "All winter I fed her, so let her work for me this summer" (*Zimu, ia ee prokormil, tak pust' mne eta letom zarabotaet*)."[28] Thus, the very timing of a wedding itself was a mechanism for the redistributrion of wealth.

---

[25] TsGADA, f. 1262, op. 4, ch. I, ed. khr. 649, 1.255 (December 22, 1854).

[26] Ibid., 1.150 (October 18, 1954).

[27] TsGADA, f. 1262, op. 4, ch. II, ed. khr. 866, 1.24 (January 12, 1959).

[28] Czap, "Marriage," 107-108; Mashkin, "Byt," 23; Mukhin, *Obychnyi poriadok*, 121-122; N. Lebedev, "Byt krest'ian Tverskoi gubernii, Tverskogo uezda," *ES* 1, p. 186; N. Gagentorn, "Svad'ba v Saltykovskoi volosti, Morshanskogo uezda, Tambovskoi gubernii," in *Materialy po svad'be i semeino-rodovomu stroiu narodov SSSR*, vol. 1 (Leningrad, 1926), 171-173; and N. Shternberg, "Novye materialy po svad'be," in ibid., 10.

But it was primarily the abundance of land, its constant redistribution, and the bridewealth aspect of *kladka* that prevented socioeconomic differentiation from developing in much of Great Russian peasant society, as in Petrovskoe. Bridewealth provided for "a double dispersal of property." Money passed in one direction; the bride and land in the other. Moreover, the bride's new household was where the children would be, and they would further dissipate the wealth resulting from the added unit of arable land.[29] *Kladka* was a "circulating pool of resources" in the sense that "what goes out for a bride has to come in for a sister." Thus, it served essentially "as a regulator of marriage and not as a means of increasing the father's wealth."[30] In contrast, the intent behind a bride's dowry is to endow a woman "with property to attract a husband of the same rank." Dowries exist in societies with substantial socioeconomic differentiation for their purpose is to preserve the status of the family into the next generation. A daughter with a dowry would not have to marry down, and this reinforces stratification in the society. "Dowry differentiates, just as bridewealth tends to homogenize."[31]

In Russia, bride wealth had no concern with the future status of the household. Rather, it merely facilitated marriage, greatly easing economic constraints. "The distribution of wives" was "very closely related to the distribution of sisters." In effect, *kladka* constantly moved toward creating an economic equilibrium. As long as villages had adequate amounts of arable "to satisfy the needs of *net* additional numbers of married couples" or other ready means of earning a living, wealth would flow in both directions.[32] In addition, these land reserves served to overcome any sex imbalance in the offspring of individual households. Furthermore, because of the high bridewealth payments, children were very dependent upon the head of the household or father to arrange marriages and to negotiate properly regarding the *kladka*. A bad deal, accepting too low a *kladka*, for example, might leave the household with too little money to find a bride for its own unmarried males. Bridewealth, therefore, directly affected the social and material well-being of the pres-

---

29 Goody, "Bridewealth," 13.

30 Ibid., 5.

31 Ibid., 17-25, 47.

32 Ibid., 18, and Gerschenkron, "Agrarian Policies," 749. Emphasis in Gershenkron's original.

ent generation, whereas necessity for correct patriarchal management of marriage enhanced the authority of the elders in the household.[33]

Boserup has argued that bridewealth is common in rural societies where very primitive systems of field cultivation are used and where "the major part of agricultural work is done by women." In contrast, "where plough cultivation predominates and where women do less agricultural work than men ... a dowry is usually paid by the girl's family."[34] Goody has suggested that bridewealth and dowry were "related less directly to women's contribution to agriculture and more to the problem of 'status placement' in societies with varying degrees of socioeconomic differentiation." Goody does note, however, that more advanced plow cultivation allows for much greater stratification to develop than primitive slash/burn, digging stick, and hoe techniques which were practiced where population densities were low and land was not usually scarce.[35]

According to these interpretations, the presence of bridewealth in much of Great Russia would be rather difficult to explain. Whereas population density was lower than in the rest of Europe, the three-field system of plow agriculture was well in place in Great Russia by the early nineteenth century, more primitive tillage systems existing only on the periphery.[36] Nevertheless, the theses of Boserup and Goody have something to contribute to the understanding of life in Petrovskoe and much of Great Russia.

But first, what was the extent of socioeconomic differentiation at Petrovskoe? Certainly some serfs' households were better off than others. "The majority of the field peasants are in good economic condition; among them there is a part middling and poor," the bailiff noted in the spring of 1844.[37] Soviet historians have seen stratification almost evervwhere in serf society in Russia throughout the first half of the nineteenth century, the process quickening in the 1830's and sharpening the crisis of the feudal system until its collapse in 1861. This viewpoint is virtually a cliche in Soviet historical literature. Koval'chenko, in examining data from Petrovskoe, concluded that between 1813 and

33 Goody, "Bridewealth," 5.

34 Boserup, *Women's Role in Economic Development* (London, 1970), 50.

35 Goody, "Bridewealth," 23, 46.

36 M. Confino, *Systemes agraires et progres agricole* (Paris, 1969), 26-55.

37 TsGADA, f. 1262, op. 4, ch. I, ed. khr. 615, 1.11 (December 1843-April 1844).

1856 "the characteristic feature of the stratification of the peasantry at the Petrovskoe estate was the rapid growth of the stratum of the poorest peasants," that is, households having less than three horses.[38] To examine stratification in a peasant society requires a dynamic analysis of household mobility. Socioeconomic stratification is not the uneven distribution of wealth at a single point in time, but is differentiation over time giving rise to separate strata with distinct members, each stratum having its own economic interests, social orientation, strategies for survival, and means for maintaining or improving its status. An analysis of stratification, however, cannot be done solely on the level of the household, ignoring possible changes in its size and structure. Often per capita measures are more useful and accurate.[39]

At Petrovskoe, until 1825 partial redistributions of peasant allotments, demesne obligations, and tax burdens, all of which were apportioned by tiagla, took place annually in the spring; thereafter, once every two years. There was never a need for a general repartition as the on-going process of readjustment took care of all serf marriages, recruitment levies, flight, migration, retirements, and deaths. With the repartitional system, the total area of a household's arable depended on the number of tiagla, which was essentially a function of household size (see Figure 1). Larger households thus had more land; however, as Figure 2 shows, land holdings per capita were quite equal regardless of the number of tiagla or members in a *dvor*. Eighty-two percent of the population in the village of Petrovskoe lived in households of 6 to 14 persons. In these dvory, the average holding by household size fluctuated from 1.46 to 1.70 desiatinas per capita, a range of only 16%. Very large households, those with more than 14 members and with 8% of the village population, had slightly lower average per capita holdings, varying from 1.22. to 1.70 desiatinas. Finally, households of less than six persons were subject to wide statistical variance, but they were neither uniformly richer nor poorer than larger households. The communal process of annual or biennial partial repartitions was, therefore,

---

[38] Koval'chenko, *Krest'iane*, 205-208. For other scholarship echoeing the same interpretation regarding stratification, see Koval'chenko, *Russkoe krepostnoe krest'ianstvo, passim*; Fedorov, *Pomeshchich'i krest'iane*, 251-253; Grekov, "Tambovskoe imenie," 489-491; and P.A. Zaionchkovskii, *Otmena krepostnogo prava v Rossii* (Moscow, 1968), 21-24.

[39] T. Shanin, *The Awkward Class* (Oxford, 1972), 45-80.

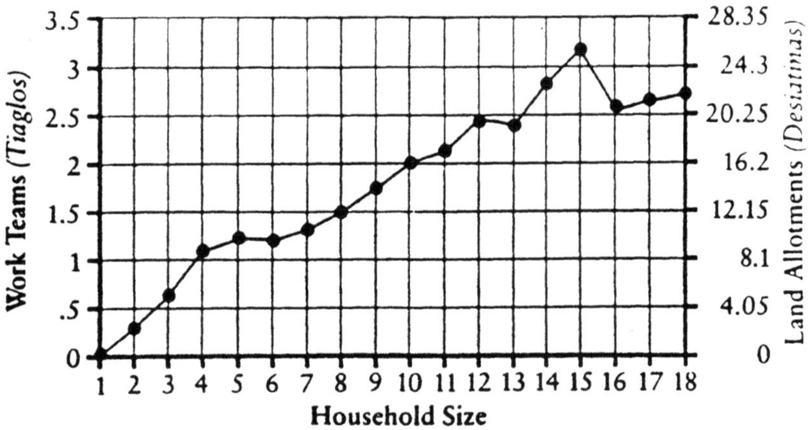

Source: TsGADA, f. 1262, op. 1, ed. khr. 1495; op. 4, ch. 1, ed. khr. 41, 59, 121, 186, 344, 357.

Figure 1. Work Teams (Tiaglos) and Land Allotments (Statutory Desiatinas) by Household Size, Village of Petrovskoe (1813-27)

extremely effective in providing an equal access to arable land based on labor capabilities and consumption needs.

There were few additional sources of revenue at Petrovskoe that could have given rise to substantial economic differentiation. Cereal cultivation was the primary pursuit of the peasants, whereas wealth in livestock was derived from the land. The serfs had very limited access to extra land, the estate renting out only 243 acres of reserve arable land to both its own and non-estate peasants, the bailiffs preferred letting the reserves lie fallow. Handicrafts and cottage industries were poorly developed in this region, and the Petrovskoe peasants did not engage in such pursuits. During the winter, the peasants spent much of their time threshing grain and transporting it to market, although they were able to undertake some private carting. Distribution of this work, however, depended in large part on the distribution of horses, which was rather equitable. Estate records do indicate that four serfs rented the fishing rights to the lake on estate property, presumably providing them with some additional income, but there are no references to other similar arrangements.[40]

[40] TsGADA, f. 1262, op. 4, ch. I, ed. khr. 615, 1.10-11; ed. khr. 649, 1.93; and ch. II, ed. khr. 862, 1.6,7.

Studies of many preindustrial societies have found a positive correlation between household size and wealth per capita. According to a number of empirical investigations, larger households tend to have higher capital/workers ratios and seem to benefit "from more efficient use of productive factors as a result of the larger scale of production."[41] Nevertheless, the data from Petrovskoe shows that if there were any accumulation of advantages by larger households that might have functioned collectively as a societal centrifuge separating the peasants into distinct economic layers, these advantages were confronted with strong egalitarian and leveling mechanisms.[42] In fact, Figure 2 suggests that in Petrovskoe, as households increased in size they were slightly poorer per capita. Actually, because larger households were those that had recently experienced higher fertility and consequently had a greater proportion of children, their consumption requirements per capita were somewhat lower, reducing, if not offsetting, the apparent advantages in wealth for smaller households.

This does not imply that there were not substantial differences among individual households in wealth per capita. Compare the following two households in the village of Petrovskoe in 1813. The first, *dvor* number twenty, was headed by Fedor Ivanov, age 45m and his wife Afim'ia Egorove. They had three children: Ivan, whose wife Afim'ia Nazarova lived with them; Andrei, age 12 and retarded; and Alena, age 3. In all, there were 6 persons with 2 tiagla, 3 horses, 2 cows, 15 sheep, and 5 pigs. The second, *dvor* number twenty-five, headed by Peter Nazarov and his wife Arina Federova, was much worse off. Peter had three daughters of his own, a widowed sister-in-law, and her three unmarried children all living with him. Peter and his wife comprised the only tiaglo in the *dvor* and had to support 12 persons with half the land and virtually the same livestock holdings as Fedor Ivanov.[43]

But such differences were not the result of customary, legal, or institutional factors favoring socioeconomic differentiation. At Petrovskoe, wealth did not depend on inheritance, family status, or the ability to command a disproportionate amount of productive resources. The biological life cycle of households and luck determined much of the

41 Shanin, *The Awkward Class*, 63-68.

42 Ibid., 63-121.

43 TsGADA, f. 1262, op. 4, ch. I, ed. khr. 41.

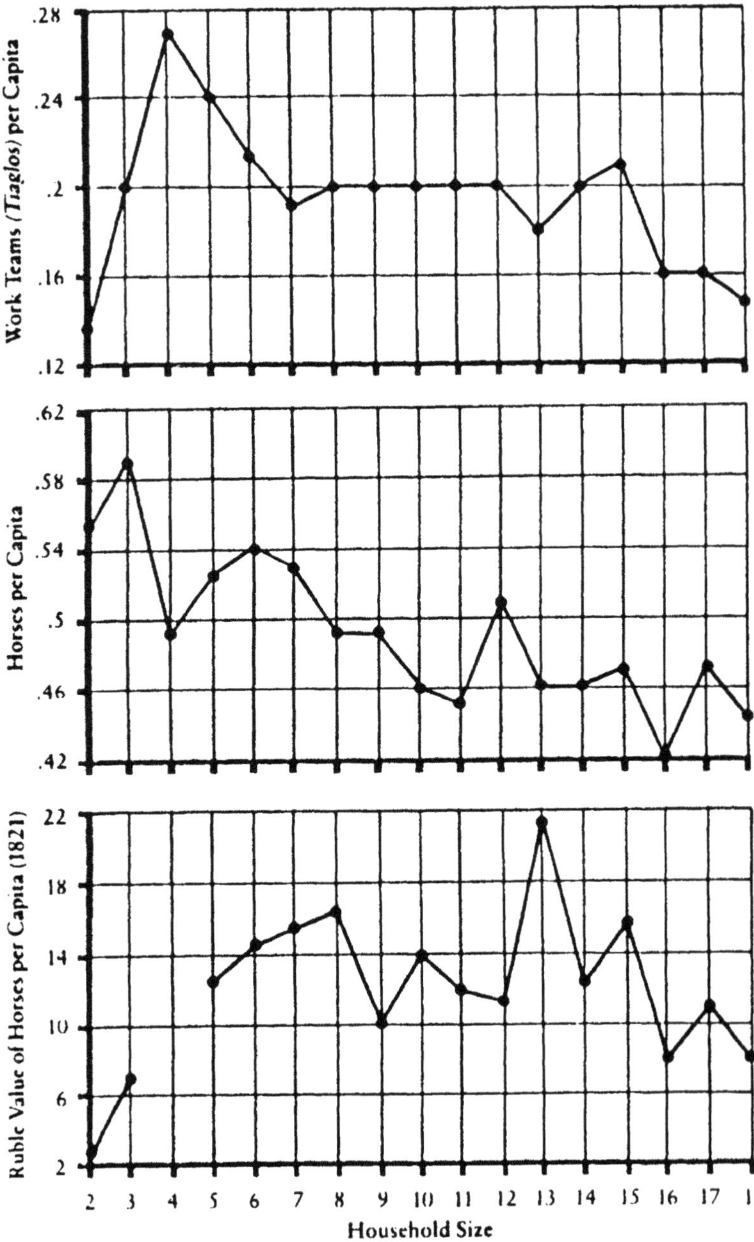

Source: TsGADA, f. 1262, op. 1, ed. khr. 1495; op. 4, ch. 1, ed. khr. 41, 59, 121, 186, 344, 357

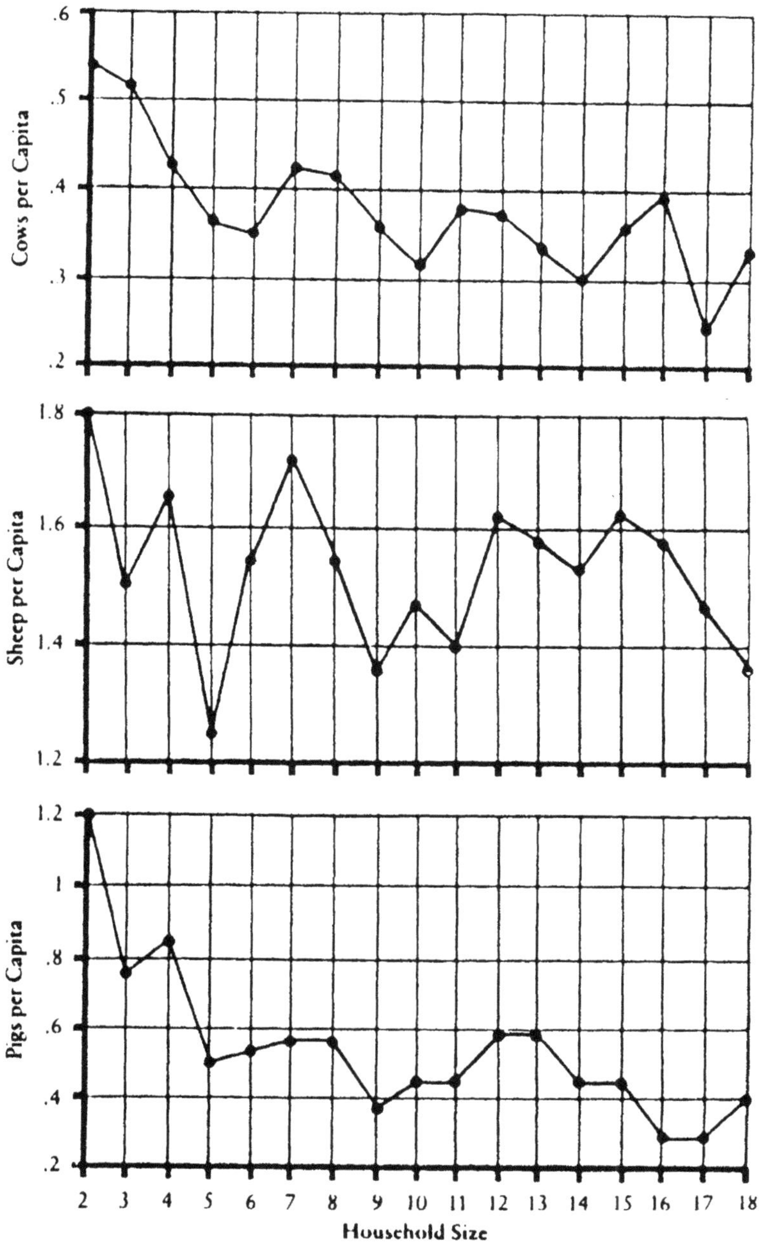

Figure 2. Per Capita Distribution of Land and Livestock by Household Size, Village of Petrovskoe (1813-27)

differentiation. For Peter Nazarov, it was unfortunate that his parents died leaving him with three unmarried sisters, that his brother died leaving him with four dependents, and that all of his own children were as yet unmarried. In contrast, fate was generous to Fedor Ivanov by giving him four adult workers in his household of six persons. "Far from being extraordinary occurences, crises and strokes of luck formed an integral part of peasant life," and they "must, therefore, have caused market socioeconomic mobility among peasant households."[44]

Fate could indeed be generous, but only temporarily. At Petrovskoe, whether due to biological or random factors, the rich got poorer, and the poor, richer. A dynamic analysis of peasant households, excluding those that underwent partitioning, merger, or extinction (these substantive changes being inherently levelling mechanisms)[45] reveals the presence of very strong equalizing tendencies in the village. Table 2 traces the fate of the 40 households in Petrovskoe that did not experience any substantive changes between 1813 and 1827. They comprise 63% of all households. The table shows that the more tiagla (and allotted arable land) a household had in 1813, the greater the likelihood that it had less in 1827. Of the 14 households that had two or more tiagla in 1813, 8 (57%) had fewer work teams by 1827, 3 (21%) had the same number, and 3 had more. Conversely, of the 26 households with less than two tiagla, 14 (54%) had more, 9 (35%) the same, and only 3 (12%) fewer in 1827.

The distribution of horses is the measure most frequently used by Soviet historians. The results for Petrovskoe are somewhat masked by an aggregate shift upward, an increase of 40 in the total number of horses owned by the households, the consequence of an estate program assisting the peasants in the purchase of horses. Nevertheless, the pattern was the same. Households with fewer horses (0-2) in 1813 were on the whole in a better position in 1827. Those dvory with many horses (5-6) in 1813 were poorer, relatively speaking, fourteen years later. Finally, it should be noted that mobility for households not undergoing substantive changes has a built-in upward bias caused by population growth.

At Petrovskoe, all indices indicate that wealth was distributed on an extremely equitable basis, limited only by biological and random

44 Shanin, *The Awkward Class*, 115.
45 Ibid., 81-94.

fluctuations over which the serfs, the commune, and the estate had little or no control. Moreover, there was no permanent or definitive socioeconomic differentiation, no kulaks or *bedniaks* (poor peasants) only households that were in a constant state of flux. Household mobility was endemic, stratification nonexistent. Social status, if it were to exist at Petrovskoe, could not have been defined by land, the most valuable asset in the society, because it was not in the serfs' hands, regularly redistributed, and allotted according to the ability to work it. Livestock, although a potential source of status, depended on cereal cultivation and communal pastures, and consequently mirrored their distribution. Beyond land and livestock, there was little of value.

Thus, Goody's argument that bridewealth reinforces economic equality and is practiced in societies "relatively homogeneous" with little socioeconomic differentiation and little concern for status placement holds true for Petrovskoe. Bridewealth, however, does not require a primitive level of agricultural technology for elaborate mechanisms as the repartitional commune, biological life cycles, the pattern of household division and extinction, and random multidirectional mobility may provide the same egalitarian socioeconomic structure. Further, Boserup's suggestion that bridewealth is common in rural societies where women make a substantial contribution to field labor is also valid, although ecological and not just technological reasons may explain the high value priced on female agricultural labor.

Kladka complemented other levelling practices and tendencies at Petrovskoe by limiting the economic differentiation that would necessarily have resulted from marriage and the addition of a new work team to the bridegroom's household. Bridewealth favored universal marriage by evenly distributing daughters and daughters-in-law, by exchanging one for the other. The economic costs of not participating in the process, of having an unmarried daughter instead of a *kladka* to attract a daughter-in-law or to keep for oneself were extremely high. "In Russia, the organization of the repartitional commune is such that there are always more married male peasants, than unmarried, that it is seldom possible to meet an unmarried man there. And this striving to marry for economic motives has led in some places to monstrous consequences."[46] According

[46] Cited in A. Efimenko. "Sem'ia." 107-113. See also Semevskii, "Domashnii byt," 74.

to the author of this statement, there were ludicrously early ages for boys at marriage, sometimes as young as six or seven years old, and *snokhachestvo*, sexual relations between the father-in-law and daughter-in-law. Neither of these seem to have been problems at Petrovskoe. But given the availability of arable land, *kladka* and the repartitional system are linked with early marriage because they facilitated the creation of new wealth, increased productive capacity, broadened the commune's tax base, and most importantly, implied the sharing of this new wealth between the bride and bridegroom's households. These benefits were obviously desired as soon as possible, as soon as the young couple could assume the necessary responsibilities.

The egalitarian distribution of wealth among households according to their size or number of tiagla, the balance of land, labor, and livestock, was also the optimal use of resources. Any imbalance would have lowered total production for too many horses in one *dvor* given its land and labor and too few in another meant the estate and both households would have suffered. Consequently, bailiffs and landlords were very conscious of the need for the equitable distribution of wealth. Sir Donald Mackenzie Wallace, on his travels through Russia in the 1870s, noted that serfowners, "for evident reasons of self-interest, as well as from benevolent motives" prevented the development of socioeconomic differentiation. With the emancipation in 186 I, however, "the Communal equality thus artificially maintained" by serfowners was wcakened as enterprising individuals sought to better their status.[47]

During the course of the nineteenth century, estate managers came to realize that merely increasing the number of tiagla or the size of the demesne did not necessarily increase revenues. In fact, such policies could ruin an estate by undermining the peasants' well-being and exhausting their livestock. High revenues rested on the ability of an estate administration to make each tiaglo equally capable of cultivating the land.[48] Nasonov found that on the estates of the Iusupov family, poor management resulted in economic differentiation among the serfs. In other words, the bailiff had to intervene directly in peasant affairs to

[47] Sir Donald Mackensie Wallace, *Russia on the Eve of War and Revolution*, ed. C. F. Black (New York, 1961), 342.

[48] A. N. Shishkov, "Mysli o khoziaistve i otchetnosti," *ZLOSKh za 1855*, part 2 (1856): 142-146; Nasonov, "Khoziaistvo krupnoi votchiny," 345.

prevent stratification, even that caused by luck or the biological life cycle of households. Enforcement of the constant redistribution of plowlands and the assurance of equal access to communal pastures and meadows for all dvory were of the utmost importance. But the bailiff also had to prevent the serfs from renting out their allotments to one another, to restrict their sale of grain and livestock, and to assist poorer households in acquiring draft animals.[49] Of course, maximizing the number of tiagla and the size of the demesne were still important, but they could be carried to excess. The vigorous pursuit of the equalization of wealth had no inherent economic dangers.

Many anthropologists and sociologists have noted that the constant fear of subsistence crises has, in most recapitalist peasant societies, given rise to what might be appropriately termed a subsistence ethic. This moral outlook, it has been suggested, was shared by the French, Russian, and Italian peasants in the nineteenth century and is present in many developing countries today.[50] The subsistence ethic meant that, economically, peasants were risk-avoiders, whereas socially they sought relationships that would provide assistance in times of crisis. But more importantly, it entailed "the right of all to a subsistence niche," and "in normal times it assured the 'survival of the weakest.'"[51] Communal lands, open fields divided into strips, and even periodic redistributions of arable land were all techniques of the subsistence ethic. Essentially, a community shared the risks of an uncertain environment, and there is no reason to suspect that this attitude was not present at Petrovskoe. But this moral outlook required only a limited reallocation of wealth to provide "a minimal subsistence insurance," not the limitation of socioeconomic differentiation as much as possible.[52]

---

49 A.N. Nasonov, "Iusupovskie votchiny v XIX-om veke," *Doklady AN SSSR,* series 5 (1926): 1-3.

50 James C. Scott, *The Moral Economy of the Peasant* (New Haven, CT, 1976), 2.

51 Ibid., 3, 41, 43. See also Jere R. Behrman, "Supply Responses and the Modernization of Peasant Agriculture: A Study of Major Annual Crops in Thailand," in *Subsistence Agriculture and Economic Development,* ed. C.R. Wharton, Jr. (Chicago, 1969), 236; J.W. Mellor, "The Subsistence Farmer in Traditional Economies," in ibid., 214; H. Myiant, "The Peasant Economies of Today's Underdeveloped Areas," in ibid., 103; and K. Polanyi, *The Great Transformation* (Boston, 1957), 163-164.

52 Scott, *The Moral Economy*, 5.

At Petrovskoe, more than simply a subsistence ethic was involved. The remarkable egalitarian distribution of wealth was a vital part of the social and political order on the estate. The forces levelling economic differences along with early marriage and stable forms of domestic groupings served to structure and distribute power among the serfs and to uphold the central purpose of the institution of serfdom, income for the landlord. All these characteristics of serf life were fundamental supports in a system of control that rested on the collusion and cooperation of the bailiff and patriarchs, the heads of household.

Investigations into social stratification within peasant communities have usually centered on the differentiation of households by wealth and status. Small landholders, tenant farmers, and landless laborers are generally contrasted, or peasants with a similar relationship to the productive process, are distinguished on the basis of land and livestock holdings per capita. Certainly, this method of analysis would be fruitless for Petrovskoe, for there were no such differences. But a patriarchal society is also highly stratified. There exists a sharp, intergenerational division that cuts across all households, limiting their role as symbols of self-identification and providing a foundation for interhousehold control.

A partriarchal society at its foundation entails nothing more than the movement of wealth and power from the young and toward the old. With the patriarchal structure in Petrovskoe, the household was more than anything else the unit of exploitation used not only by the noble landlord as a member of the political elite, but by serf patriarchs as well. A patriarch sought to better himself not by claiming a disproportionate share of wealth or productive resources in the village, not by competing with other households, but by exploiting more effectively the members of his own household. Status was defined by position with the *dvor*, the ability to control economic and fertility decisions, and the power to maintain advantages over other household members.

The egalitarian distribution of land, labor, and livestock not only maximized estate and peasant production of cereal at Petrovskoe, raising the standard of living for all, it minimized conflicts between households, limiting disputes over wealth and power within the political leadership of the village. What emerged was a ruling stratum of peasants in which membership was primarily a function of age. This ruling elite, the heads of households, shared with the estate management a number of concerns, and together they functioned in a social system that advanced and protected their common interests. By upholding the large patriarchal family either by directly controlling household fission or by granting village elders the right to regulate household size, the bailiffs supported the very foundation of patriarchal authority. And, this authority assured the estate of a strong ally in the battle to get the remainder of the serf population to work productively and behave properly.

The immediate economic advantages of early and universal marriage to both patriarchs and the estate have already been discussed. In essence, for the male's household, a marriage never worsened and almost always improved its consumer/labor ratio and its allotment size/capita, to the benefit of all family members but the new couple. Equally important, the high fertility that resulted from this marriage pattern was the only means by which a patriarch and his wife could avoid destitution in their old age, given the high level of mortality. Moreover, high fertility made it possible for serf elders to be freed from their field work responsibilities by their mid-fifties, thereby avoiding some of the drudgery of peasant life. After age 55, most patriarchs were simply managers, while others in the household worked. But even before this, it is likely that heads of household enjoyed a privileged position in the nature and amount of work they performed. Stable high fertility and large households considerably enhanced the managerial functions of the patriarchs. They were called the *bol'shak,* the big one, the boss, the one who gives orders; their wives, the *bol'shitsa* or *bol'shukha.*

Nineteenth-century Russian ethnographers frequently commented on the strict, almost despotic control that patriarchs exercised in their household.[53] At Petrovskoe, households worked an average of 42 acres of arable, including the demesne, all in scattered strips. The bol'shak was responsible for allocating and overseeing his labor and livestock to get the most out of the land. Larger households also permitted some degree of specialization of labor. This was especially true for women, some cooking year-round, others tending the livestock and watching the children, and in the spring and summer working the fields and taking care of the kitchen garden. It was for the bol'shutsa to see that the household benefitted as much as possible from the proper division of these tasks.

In other peasant societies with stable high fertility, the advantages of patriarchs have included not only the choice of work, but better food

53 Zvonkov, "Sovremennyi brak," 24-27; Tiutriumov, "Krest'ianskaia sem'ia."

and clothing, precedence in feeding, and privileged use of house space and facilities.[54] In Russia, the bol'shak clearly had preferential use of space in the *izba*. In the winter, the bol'shak and his wife slept on the *polati* (sleeping platforms) directly over the stove, the warmest place in the hut. In the summer, it was the other married couples who had to move out and into various outbuildings and storerooms. The so-called beautiful, holy icon corner (*krasnyi, sviatoi, obraznnoi ugol*) was also the elder's (*starshii*) corner. In this corner was a table where the family ate its meals with the place beneath the icon reserved for the head of household. He relinquished his place only on the wedding day of a son, when the newly married couple sat under the icon during the celebration feast.[55]

The spiritual owner of a peasant *dvor* and a symbolic idealization of the patriarch was the *dedushka-domovoi,* the grandfather house-spirit, thought by peasants throughout Great Russia to share a similar economic fate with the household in which he lived. Every household had its own domovoi, who lived behind the hearth beneath the bed of the bol'shak and was often addressed as "khoziain," head of household. If the domovoi looked favorably upon the family, its horses were strong and healthy; if he became angry, the animals became thin and died. The domovoi saw to all trifles in the *dvor*. He liked fertile domestic fowl and livestock and was intolerant of needless expenditures. In a word, the domovoi was laborious, thrifty, economical, and painstaking, and the peasants took great care not to offend him in any way.

The domovoi was thought to be a good-natured, elderly being with a grey beard and stooped posture. He would only communicate with the eldest member of the *dvor* if he wished to inform the family of some good or evil to come. If a family moved into a new izba, the patriarch would ask the domovoi to accompany them and bring his favor to the new hut. As an invitation, a few hot cinders were taken from the stove of the old hut and were buried in the elder's or another beautiful corner of the new izba under the icon, where the head of household normally sat. The domovoi always accepted. Fights between different households were seen as one house-spirit trying to better his *dvor* at the expense

---

54 J.C. Caldwell, "A Theory of Fertility: From High Plateau to Destabilization," *Population and Development Review* 4 (1978): 555-557, 560-561.

55 Sumtsov, *O svadebnykh obriadakh,* 186-187; Malykhin, "Byt," 210-211; Semevskii, "Domashnii byt," part I, 110-112; and Troitskii, "Selo Lipitsy," 83-84.

of the other. A domovoi could not live with another house-spirit, and if two households merged there was fighting between the domovoi as they clashed for control of the house. Such was the great power of the domovoi that families often found it impossible to stay together.[56]

Whether peasant patriarchs were better fed and clothed than other members of their *dvor* is unknown. But stable high fertility clearly brought considerable power and benefits to the heads of household. Lower fertility and smaller households would have undermined quite substantially the position of the patriarchs. In essence, a reproductive pattern was "needed to support the economic one and to maintain the existing gradations of material advantage within the family."[57] Stable high fertility at Petrovskoe was also one of the key factors that stabilized household structures, greatly compressing the duration of household life cycles and providing for the constancy of the three-generation, multiple family *dvor*. This, coupled with the egalitarian distribution of wealth, meant that patriarchal power within a household varied little over time as the bol'shak did not have to adapt to greatly different familial patterns, labor and livestock resources, and levels of well-being.[58] In sum, the power of the patriarchs, supported by the entire economic and social structure of life, was unequaled and unchanging.

The stability of households and the maximization of production benefited not only the estate and the heads of household, but every serf at Petrovskoe. Nevertheless, the estate and the patriarchs derived the greatest share of wealth and power based on a conjuction of interests. As a result, intergenerational antagonism was structurally endemic at Petrovskoe, with the patriarch and his wife on one side and the exploited members of the *dvor* on the other. This structure of authority helped maintain the social and economic order.

---

56 Bondarenko, "Pover'ia krest'ian Tambovskoi gubernii," 116-120; A. Afans'ev, "Dedushka-domovoi," *Arkhiv istoriko-iuridicheskikh svedenii otnosiashchikhsia do Rossii*, vol. I (Moscow, 1850), 16-22; and M. Dobrozrakov, "Selo Ul'ianovka, Nizhegorodskoi gubernii, Lukianovskogo uezda," *ES*, I, 57-59.

57 Caldwell, "A Theory of Fertility," 566.

58 Ibid., 565.

10

The Serf Economy, the Peasant Family, and the Social Order

The crucial problem in examining a rural society is to understand the parameters that determine the success or failure of a population to keep in balance with the economic space it inhabits.[1] How did serfdom in Russia affect this balance? Were agrarian class relations the determining factor, or was serfdom overlain over an ecology, demographic regime, or social order, a thin, translucent cover sufficient only to distort our view of the inner workings of Russian peasant society? How important for Russia was the political power structure governing the ownership of property in the process of accommodation between economic and demographic processes? How much were value systems affecting interpersonal relations within the family (or household) and the wider collectivity key to this process of accommodation? To what extent did serfdom determine the intensity of peasant labor?

Robert Brenner, in a controversial article in *Past and Present,* opened a major debate among European agrarian historians when he attacked "what he considered to be a form of demographic determinism in the interpretation of the development of the preindustrial European agrarian economies."[2] He rejected the idea that long-term development might be explained either by changing market conditions, especially the supply and demand for land and labor (the demographic model), or by growing market development (the commercialization model). To Brenner, "serfdom involved the landlord's ability to control his tenant's

---

This essay was originally published in *Imperial Russia: New Histories for the Empire,* ed. Jane Burbank and David L. Ransel (Bloomington: Indiana University Press, 1998).

1 Roger Schofield, "Family Structure, Demographic Behavior, and Economic Growth," in *Famine, Disease, and the Social Order in Early Modern Society* (Cambridge, MA, 1989), 279.

2 R. H. Hilton, "Introduction," in *The Brenner Debate: Agrarian Class Structure and Economic Development in Pre-Industrial Europe* (Cambridge, MA, 1985), 1-2.

person, in particular his movements, so as to be able to determine the *level* of the rent in excess of custom or what might be dictated by the simple play of forces of supply and demand."[3]

In this very late addition to the Brenner debate, let me begin by asserting that in Russia peasant unfreedom, especially restrictions on peasant movements, and landlord rights to arbitrary exactions,[4] were of lesser significance than peasant self-exploitation (A. V Chayanov), patriarchal familism (Steven L. Hoch), and the repartitional land commune.[5] That is to say, in the question of exchange entitlements, the privileged position given by Brenner (along with most Soviet scholars) to class relations ignores key components in a highly integrated agrarian social system in which many forms of expropriation existed. Rural social relations fit much less readily than those created by industrial capitalism into the categories of class analysis, and dynamics of the Russian peasant family farm is an excellent example.[6] Familism, peasant self-exploitation, and mechanisms of land redistribution (where the latter existed) imposed strict limits on the manorial economy and determined the nature of class-based expropriation. Specifically, the redistribution of wealth in a patriarchal, household-centered, peasant society involves not merely master and serf, but serf over serf (or "free" peasant over peasant). This greatly complicates the problem of class relations.

It is surprising how much of the discussion of serfdom east of the Elbe, and especially for Russia, is phrased in terms of the key issues for Western Europe, especially what constitutes freedom. But Brenner's definition of freedom (or unfreedom), one often employed by historians, is but one kind and fails to address the relative freedom from destitution and the lesser vulnerability to Malthusian crises that Russian peasants enjoyed. In fact, being tied to the land is a much underrated notion; in Russia, from the mid-seventeenth century being a peasant (with few exceptions) implied an entitlement to land, which is not a

3 Robert Brenner, "Agrarian Class Structure and Economic Development in Pre-Industrial Europe," in *The Brenner Debate,* 26. Originally published in *Past and Present* in 1976.

4 Brenner's definition of unfreedom. Brenner, "Agrarian Class Structure," 26.

5 A. V. Chayanov, *The Theory of Peasant Economy*; and Steven L. Hoch, *Serfdom and Social Control in Russia, Petrovskoe, a Village in Tambov* (Chicago, 1986).

6 Robert G. Moeller, "Introduction," *Peasants and Lords in Modern Germany* (Boston, 1986), 5.

bad deal, if you are subsistence-oriented. And, as we shall see, this was perceived by the state as such a good idea that the emancipation legislation of 1861, the so-called liberation of the serfs, would carry this even one step further.

The familistic practices of Russian peasant society were vibrant enough in the late Imperial period (1861-1917) to lead "to the destruction of [rural] capitalism." In order to meet consumption needs, peasants "paid more for the land than the capitalized rent in capitalist agriculture."[7], Under serfdom, familistic and communal structures—whether they predated, coincided with, or arose as a response to the imposition of restrictions on the peasantry—proved to be major obstacles to manorial control. Lords by no means had complete control over the servile peasantry, especially regarding the intensity of serf labor, the disposition of productive resources, and peasant consumption norms and levels.

Manorial farming throughout the pre-emancipation period was small-scale peasant production, even where the primary intent of the lord was commercial cereal production.[8] The absence of large-scale estate production, the peasants' entitlement to land, and the lack of an essentially feudal infrastructure (coupled with the obvious lack of free wage labor) gave a very distinctive nature to servile relations in Russia. There was no struggle over commons, no conflict over traditional tenurial rights. Under the conditions of peasant family farming, decisions on employment and how to dispose of the land were not concentrated in a few hands. Peasants worked with their own inventory (implements, draft animals, and knowledge), and lords' fields were hardly distinguishable from those of the peasants. A consolidated demesne was less common than intermingled fields. Thus, the manorial factor in rural economic development (as opposed to commercialization of the manorial economy) was not significant. In other words, lords had little power to effect change in the structure of agricultural production, and they expressed little interest in agriculture itself, in spite of state-sponsored

[7] A. V. Chayanov, "On the Theory of Non-Capitalist Economic Systems," in his *The Theory of Peasant Economy* (Madison, WI, 1986), 28. Originally published in 1924.

[8] Michael Confino, *Systèmes agraires et progrès agricole: L' assolement triennal en Russie aux XVIIIe-XIXe siècles* (Paris, 1969).

efforts to do so. For the lord employing compulsory labor, the result was what might best be described as high transaction (managerial) costs-benefits which ultimately accrued to serf patriarchs. Landlords needed a large number of intermediaries to compel the remaining servile population to work. The widespread practice of quitrent (*obrok*)—family farms resorting to the market to obtain money rents—further attests to the relatively competitive nature of the peasant household as the unit of production. Presumably, if quitrent were uncompetitive, no lord would have had recourse to this form of expropriation. Simply put, restrictions on movement in Russia did not have the same consequences of dependency as elsewhere. The peasant family farm survived largely intact.

Peasant goals in Russia were less to establish freehold control over the land (France) than to establish distributive mechanisms which reduced risk in an uncertain environment and limited the group most vulnerable to crisis by providing more equal access to productive assets. Nor were lords primarily interested in consolidation, creating large farms, and leasing them to capitalist tenants (England). Both Russian peasant and intramanorial society were remarkably free of those land disputes which seem at the heart of so many Western European rural communities. Perhaps rural Russia had come up with a solution to a problem which had plagued Western Europe, one phrased in terms of land access or use and not in terms of rights. West of the Elbe, it was primarily land rights and disputes that fostered the development of mechanisms to address conflict. Resistance to seigneurial action and intrusion served to enhance peasant class power and heightened the political consciousness of the rural inhabitant, attributes barely visible among the servile population in Russia.

In much of servile Russia what was unique was that the land was mobile, not the population. Instead of family members moving in and out of the household through wage labor, sharecropping, tenancy, apprenticeship, or service in an attempt to adjust to changes in household composition and status, it was the land that moved around. This is in concert with the often noted weak sense of property in Russian peasant society. But rather than lamenting this development as inhibiting the rise of freedom, capitalism, and bourgeois values, it might equally be used as evidence that a vast legal system to ensure control of productive assets was not required.

The periodic redistribution of land among households according to some unit of consumption or production (adult males, married couples, or eaters—in the aggregate it does not matter, demographically speaking: they are all the same) was more than a radical risk-reduction technique in a system of open field cultivation. The egalitarian distribution of the key productive asset—the balance of labor and land implied by the repartitional land commune—was the optimal use of productive resources and necessarily maximized output irrespective of the structure of compulsion. Egalitarianism enlarged the total pie, while leaving unaffected the conflict over the class distribution of goods. In addition, constant adjustment of a peasant family farm's access to land lessened the pressure for migratory movements. Thus, one might reasonably argue, the repartitional land commune facilitated fixing the peasant population in place, a key goal of landlords in Eastern Europe, and especially in Russia with its low population densities and the premium it placed on labor.

But the repartitional land commune came with high costs for lords. It was even more resistant to rationalization and improvement than the simple open field. With long-term capital improvements (manuring or drainage) unlikely to accrue to the sufficient benefit of the peasant investor, the short-term intensity of labor (proper and timely plowing, sowing, reseeding, weeding, harvesting) became an even more significant factor in determining output than elsewhere. This turned out to be a substantial constraint on the lord's ability to command the fruits of servile labor. Equally, the movement of land, not people, created greater familial stability—both structurally and in terms of membership. This prevented Russian lords from taking much advantage of cyclical household dynamics for arbitrary exaction (entry fines, exit fines) common in much of the West.

Describing rural Russia as familistic implies not merely a peasant family economy (Chayanov), but more importantly a social structure through which authority was maintained, power distributed, and reward and punishment dispensed. A patriarchal society at its foundation entails nothing more than the movement of wealth and power away from the young and toward the old. With the patriarchal structure which predominated in rural Russia, the household (family) was more than anything else the unit of exploitation used not only by the lord as a member of the political elite, but by serf patriarchs as well.

A patriarch sought to better his status not by claiming a disproportionate share of wealth or productive resources in the village, not by competing with other households, but by exploiting more efficiently the members of his own household. Status was defined by placement within the household, the ability to control economic and fertility decisions, and the power to maintain advantage over other household members.[9]

A high-pressure demographic regime upheld this familistic society. Peasant marriage in Russia was generally not dependent upon access to a relatively fixed number of units of physical capital, such as a farmstead. Population densities throughout European Russia were low. In any case, for peasants living in repartitional land communes (the vast majority), no such obstacle would have existed. Increasing evidence suggests there was remarkably little intrusion of the lord in serf marriage.[10] Thus, age at marriage and proportions married were more closely linked to the dynamics of the family farm than serfdom. Households were large. Three generations and multiple conjugal pairs lived under one roof and ate out of a common pot. An unusually high premium was placed on the reproduction of children not primarily to ensure elders adequate economic support in later years, but to provide them with a labor supply to exploit throughout their tenure as head of household. In turn, early and universal marriage and high fertility levels disabled the Malthusian preventive check (reduced fertility or a greater incidence of celibacy). With fertility being the primary determinant of the age structure of a population, the resultant high dependency ratios (the number of persons under 15 and 60 and over to the number 15 to 59) put yet another substantial constraint on the ability of the lord to extract wealth. Overall, therefore, the peasant family farm is best regarded as being the primary determinant of the rural economy, modified, to a greater or lesser extent, by serfdom.

The practice of land redistribution and the egalitarian distribution of wealth that resulted limited the accumulation of reserves and provided a substantial disincentive for capital investment. Coupled

---

9 Hoch, *Serfdom and Social Control*, 128.

10 John Bushnell, "Did Serf Owners Control Serf Marriage? Orlov Serfs and their Neighbors, 1773-1861," *Slavic Review* 52 (Fall 1993): 419-45; Hoch, *Serfdom and Social Control*, 91-132.

with the demographic patterns and social structures described above, they would, it seems, enhance the possibilities for increased poverty by creating a society highly vulnerable to economically positive checks (sudden sharp increases in mortality due to food shortages) and likely in the long term to overreproduce itself in relation to available resources.[11] But the evidence for rural increased poverty in Russia, in spite of all that has been alleged to the contrary, is quite weak. First, Russia had the largest output of cereals per capita in all of Europe, and contemporaries repeatedly complained of the constant overproduction of cereals.[12] Second, Russian cereal prices as measured by B. N. Mironov were chronically low when compared to Western Europe, even in spite of their rapid increase in the eighteenth and nineteenth centuries. It was only early Soviet scholarship which challenged this widely held view, when P. I. Popov argued Russia did not produce enough grain to feed the population. Subsequent historians of all persuasions have been ready to accept this dismal portrayal of Russian peasant society for reasons all too apparent. Both "Western and Marxist literatures explain that the Russian revolution was caused, in no small part, by the agrarian crises that plagued Russian agriculture."[13] But, in fact, pre-reform Russian agriculture was remarkably productive by European standards. Its productivity may have been low per unit of land, but too often we are fixed on this measure. Per capita output and availability were high; markets were distant and inaccessible. The late Jerome Blum, a leading scholar on the Russian peasantry, felt that these high levels

11 R. H. Hilton, "A Crisis of Feudalism," in *The Brenner Debate*, 123.

12 Jerome Blum, *Lord and Peasant in Russia from the Ninth to the Nineteenth Century* (Princeton, 1961), 332-33. In contrast, Paul R. Gregory, *Russian National Income* (Cambridge, MA, 1982), 154, estimates per capita grain output in Russia in 1861, at the very end of serfdom, to be 79 percent of the level in France, 70 percent of the level in Germany, and 95 percent of the level in Austria-Hungary. It should be noted that Russia at this time, unlike Germany or France, exported relatively small amounts of grain. In addition, official published figures for Russia and subsequent attempts to correct them remain in all likelihood underestimations of actual levels, especially for the period before 1885. See Hoch, *Serfdom and Social Control*, 30-36. Finally, Gregory's actual figure for Russia of 0.561 metric tons of per capita grain output, even after allowing for seed and feed, would still support a favorable cereal-based dietary regime.

13 Paul R. Gregory, *Before Command: An Economic History of Russia from Emancipation to the First Five-Year Plan* (Princeton, 1994), 36.

of production were "needed to meet the deficiencies of bad years, and were carefully stored away for that purpose," a view shared by Kahan[14] Subsequent assessments of Russian peasant diet have been even more favorable. To R. E. F. Smith and David Christian, "the dietary regime of nineteenth-century Russia was remarkably well-balanced.... It is the sort of diet to which some modern nutritionists are inclined to look with renewed respect." This broader statement confirms my earlier conclusions regarding the dietary regime of the serfs of Petrovskoe.[15]

The image of Russia suffering famine once in three years is surely incorrect, based as it is upon simplistic methodologies and inadequate sources.[16] Elsewhere in Europe even in the years of the worst national crises rarely were more than one-third of all parishes affected.[17] Work I am presently undertaking, which makes use of recently available Russian parish registers, suggests that in the eighteenth and nineteenth century an individual parish was likely to experience mortality levels 50 percent above the norm only once in eleven years. Of these crises, the majority appear wholly independent of harvest or grain price fluctuations. A doubling of mortality was an event visited on any parish only once or twice a century and more likely to be linked to those epidemic diseases where the nutritional state of the population was not a significant factor. As evidence, most mortality crises came in the late summer, suggesting that diseases spread by contaminated food and water rather than food shortage played the major role. Thus, subsistence crises were not only much less frequent than we have been led to believe, but were less severe.

Of much greater importance, it needs to be borne in mind that the Russian path to economic entitlement was structural, not institutional; social, not statist; and more peasant than manorial. Neither the state nor the manor invested much effort in survival mechanisms to respond

---

14 Blum, *Lord and Peasant,* 333; Arcadius Kahan, "The Tsar 'Hunger' in the Land of the Tsars," in *Russian Economic History: The Nineteenth Century* (Chicago, 1989), 116.

15 R. E. F. Smith and David Christian, *Bread and Salt: A Social and Economic History of Food and Drink in Russia* (Cambridge, 1984), 287; and my "Serf Diet in Nineteenth Century Russia," *Agricultural History* (April 1982): 391-414.

16 See, in particular, Kahan, "The Tsar 'Hunger'," in *Russian Economic History*, 138.

17 John Walter and Roger Schofield, "Famine, Disease and Crisis Mortality in Early Modern Society," in *Famine, Disease, and the Social Order*, 59.

to economic distress. For those who were left out, emergency grain reserves, almshouses, hospitals, dispensaries, and the like could rarely be found. Neither did the parish church play any significant role in poor relief. The basic response of Russian peasant society was to control access to productive resources. Institutional forms of assistance were not used. Though lords did distribute grain in times of dearth, the social order as embodied in the large, patriarchal family farm and the repartitional land commune rendered society structurally less vulnerable to subsistence crises.

All this did not impart to rural Russian society a strong sense of peasant community or class solidarity. Rather quite the opposite. Manorial intervention into Russian peasant society went through the intermediary of the patriarch, not the commune, in the vital day-to-day aspects of labor management and supervision. From the lords' perspective, patriarchy broke serf society into manageable units of control. To patriarchs, that is, the heads of peasant households, the fact that serfdom did not encroach upon their familial prerogatives and even enhanced their authority made them more amenable to collusion. Together they functioned in a "low maintenance" social system that by its fundamental structure advanced and protected their mutual interests. Each patriarch used familial structures to ensure he had a labor supply to exploit. Simply put, relations between serf patriarchs and lords were collusive, hedonistic, and cooptative. In Russia, cooperative exploitation was the result.

This image stands in sharp contrast to the prevailing view of a "traditionally antagonistic relationship" between lord and peasant.[18] It also helps to explain relative absence of peasant disturbances throughout the servile period.[19] Though Russian peasants may have evinced greater communal solidarity than American Negro slaves, as Kolchin argues, surely a better comparison would be with Western Europe, where peasant cooperation and self-government were generally more highly developed. Again, we have a very distorted picture here, largely the result of generations of Soviet scholars working on the so-called peasant movement. In this view, virtually any expression of unrest was assumed to be

---

[18] Brenner, "Agrarian Class Structure," 51.

[19] Peter Kolchin, *Unfree Labor: American Slavery and Russian Serfdom* (Cambridge, MA, 1987), 241-301.

evidence of class conflict. But rarely was a distinction made between anti-autocratic protest and resistance to servitude. The ethnic dimensions or nonclass dimensions of many popular uprisings (so evident today) were simply discounted.[20] In the end, historians really ought to admit, with over 110,000 manors, twenty million serfs, and over 200 years of serfdom, we really have not found much.

The peasant social order not only survived serfdom, it outlived the state as well. Understanding the Russian autocracy as a strong/weak state helps explain the peasants' ability to resist manorial intrusion and prevent the restructuring of agrarian society. The autocracy may have monopolized political processes as understood in the traditional sense, but its ability to effect change, that is, the actual amount of power at its disposal, was small. The role of the state in the rural social and economic order was almost negligible. Throughout the servile period the state was forced to use landlords as its agents for the extraction of taxes, recruits, and government labor obligations. By the middle of the eighteenth century, the state no longer even sought to intrude in the regulation of lord/ serf relations. The terms of servitude were negotiated between the two principal parties, and the state barely perceived itself as having independent interest or a separate role. At no point did the state ever seek to regulate the size of quitrent in order to ensure the viability of the peasant economy to pay state obligations. The manifesto of April 5, 1797, limiting labor obligations *(barshchina)* to three days per week, was, in fact, not a law but a suggestion and was taken seriously in only a few places.[21] Lords could have recourse to the state to control extreme deviance, but they lacked the force of the state behind them to compel a specific level of expropriation. In the vast world of servile relations (dues, obligations, commons rights, peasant inheritance rights, and forms of punishment) the state had little or no sense of what serfdom ought to be.

Indeed, I would argue that it was only in the middle of the nineteenth century that the autocracy decided to refashion rural society with state interests in mind, governed in part by a sense of what peasants should pay. The nobility were removed as agents of authority, and

---

20 Marc Raeff, "Pugachev's Rebellion," in *Preconditions of Revolution in Early Modern Europe*, ed. Robert Forster and Jack Greene (Baltimore, 1970), 161-202.

21 Blum, *Lord and Peasant*, 445.

the autocracy regulated the terms of the peasants' financial and labor obligations. It attached the peasants to the land even more firmly than serfdom had done to ensure them a way of life, which it hoped would improve. The state divided power between itself and the peasantry, believing it had removed the nobility as a political authority in the countryside.

The serfdom that developed in Russia was particular and local, the function of a vast array of negotiations between lords and peasants. Serfdom was not a system, but a widely varying set of practices. There appears little uniformity among serf estates in the obligations owed masters. Within the same uezd (the smallest administrative unit) per capita quitrent could vary by factors of twenty or more.[22] Much less is known about labor obligations, but what we do know from actual manorial records reveals that the situation was substantially more variable and complex than is suggested by the widely accepted notion of three-day barshchina. We need to consider if such a wide spread is more likely explained by flexibility and negotiability than unbridled manorial power.

Studies on postemancipation levels of labor intensity have revealed that peasant "farm families possess considerable stocks of unutilized time. Accordingly, labor intensity rates, not being fully utilized, can fluctuate one way or another."[23] In Tver', in the early twentieth century, in only two months of the year, June and July, did the average working day exceed eight hours (9.3 and 9.1 hours respectively) and in eight months of the year averaged less than 6.5 hours. Research on peasants from Tambov, Iaroslavl', and Moscow provinces reached similar conclusions. *"In the [peasant] labor farm, rates of labor intensity are considerably lower than if labor were fully utilized."*[24] Therefore, there is no necessary reason to assume that increases in the level of expropriation (under serfdom or capitalism), especially by elites interested primarily in income, necessitated fundamental structural changes in the peasant family mode of production.

---

[22] A. Ia. Degtiarev, S. G. Kashchenko, and D. I. Raskin, *Novgorodskaia derevnia v reforme* 1861 *goda: Opyt izucheniia s ispol'zovaniem EVM* (Leningrad, 1989), 147-98; and S. G. Kashchenko, *Reforma 19 fevraliia 1861 goda v Sankt-Peterburgskoi gubernii* (Leningrad, 1990), 159-94.

[23] Chayanov, *The Theory of Peasant Economy*, 75-76.

[24] Ibid. Italics in the original.

Russian peasants were not merely premodern and precapitalist, they were prefeudal. This is what distinguished the second serfdom. Peasants lived a viable moral economy that proved resistant to feudal and capitalist attempts at restructuring its modes of production. Resistance was not political, in the usual sense of institutional and legal, and rarely communal. The fundamental moral principle was not fair prices or fair exaction, but fair access. Familism is a dependency which does not readily relate to traditional notions of freedom. At times, it was a dependency of great emotional and economic benefit; at times, a tyranny far worse than any class-based expropriation or repression.

If the implicit assumption in historical analysis is to be development, especially capitalist development, then rural Russian society will not measure up under any circumstances. But to favor interpretations of capitalist development is to ignore the vibrancy of the peasant family farm and the significance of the practice of land redistribution. The peasant family farm controlled the intensity of its labor and its allocation of labor resources. Periodic redistributions of land kept the key productive asset in balance with a family's labor capability. These familistic policies and land-use practices coupled with the observed demographic regime constricted class-based expropriation. It cannot be denied that the rise of serfdom meant the extraction of substantial wealth from the peasantry by the nobility. But it was not "the structure of class relations, of class power" that determined "the manner and degree to which particular demographic and commercial changes" affected "the distribution of income and economic growth."[25] Neither was it a neo-Malthusian homeostatic mechanism that was the motive force in Russian rural development-a population expanding beyond the means of subsistence and brought in check by war, famine, and disease. Brenner is clearly right that it does not all come down to population densities, the supply and demand for land and labor.

Russia did not follow the path of France (complete property rights and underdevelopment) or England (the obverse), nor Prussia or America for that matter. Russia took the path of class collusion, weak village solidarity, structural constraints on access to productive forms of wealth, and, most importantly, the peasant family farm. This did not lead to capitalist development, but neither did this lead to the development of

---

25 Brenner, "Agrarian Class Structure," 11.

underdevelopment. Russian history cannot be conceptualized in terms of the debate on the transition from feudalism to capitalism. Nor did Russian peasant society, resilient as it was to the imposition of external exploitative constraints, preclude agrarian development. In those parts of Chayanov's book few historians read are detailed "the family farm as a component of the national economy and its possible forms of development."[26] Vertical cooperative concentration, as Chayanov hoped, never came about. But, regardless of what came, the most thoughtful observers of Russian rural society—those members of the Organization and Production School—firmly believed something very different could have occurred. In the end, peasant self-exploitation, familism, and land redistribution practices fashioned the conditions of rural society until the early 1930s. The social order did indeed matter.

[26] Chayanov, *The Theory of Peasant Economy*, 224-69.

11

The Great Reformers and the World They Did Not Know: Drafting the Emancipation Legislation in Russia, 1858-61

On its first work day, the Editing Commission, the body appointed to draft much of the emancipation legislation, summarized the previously-established principles that were to govern peasant reform.[1] An emancipated serf was "to feel immediately that his way of life had improved, and a lord immediately reassured that his interests had been protected." And this was to be accomplished while creating as little tension as possible between the two. Along with being granted personal freedom, an ex-serf was to have the possibility to acquire from his lord "an adequate amount of land to secure his agrarian way of life and to guarantee his daily existence." Redemption would allow the peasants to buy, through negotiation with their lords, a household plot, arable fields, and other useful land, together and at one time. This would greatly reduce the likelihood that a newly freed serf would end up possessing only a small household plot, that is, a hut, attendant outbuildings, and a kitchen garden, but no fields, pastures, or meadows. Lords were to receive compensation for the lands the peasants were buying, but the peasants' annual mortgage payments (interest and principle) were not to exceed their existing quitrents or cash dues. For all parties it was recognized that the sooner redemption began, the better. With the proceeds from the sale of land to the peasants, lords would have the financial resources to restructure and modernize their estates on the basis of free labor,

---

This essay was originally published in *Everyday Life in Russian History: Quotidian Studies in Honor* of *Daniel Kaiser*, ed. Gary Marker, Joan Neuberger, Marshall Poe, and Susan Rupp (Bloomington, IN: Slavica Publishers, 2010), 247-75.

1 Russia. Redaktsionnye Kommissii dlia sostavleniia Polozhenii o krest'ianakh, vykhodiashchikh iz krepostnoi zavisimosti, *Pervoe izdanie materialov,* 18 vols. (St. Petersburg, 1859-60) (hereafter, *PIM*), 1: 1 (March 4, 1859).

which it was assumed would be more costly and could be offset only by considerable capital investment. The government pledged to serve as a mediator during the implementation of the reform settlement and to use its financial resources to facilitate the peasants' redemption of noble land. Whether the land the peasants bought was to be held by individuals or jointly by the commune was to be decided in accord with local practice. Finally, obligatory labor services (*barshchina*) were recognized as a form of servitude. Therefore, if there were any provisional status between serfdom and freedom, as was being contemplated, labor services were to be subject to state regulation, with the intent of moderating the peasants' burden. The commission was also instructed to try to make this transitional period as brief as possible. The continued existence of mandatory labor services, it was thought, did not comport with the intent of the government to abolish serfdom and would be the cause of ceaseless problems.

But when the members of the Editing Commission sat down in the winter of 1859 to write the emancipation legislation, following the guidelines of the Main Committee on Peasant Affairs, what they did *not* know about serfdom, agriculture, and peasant life in Russia would soon fill volumes. Oddly enough, they had much to say about what they did not know.[2] The members of the Editing Commission in the words of its chair, A. I. Rostovtsev, "either had been diverted from agricultural pursuits by State service, or owned sizeable serf estates, and therefore are familiar with peasants' practices [only] in general outline or on a large-scale."[3] Indeed, most members of the Editing Commission were quite ignorant of peasant life and the practice of serfdom. Moreover, many were downright hostile to serf owners. Rostovtsev toyed with the idea of creating an Advisory Commission of serf owners who had directly managed their estates to assist the Editing Commission. He also flirted with the notion of summoning peasants and estate managers to comment on the legislation as it was being drafted. Neither was ever done.

2 *PIM* and Russia. Redaktsionnye Komissii dlia sostavleniia Polozhenii o krest'ianakh, vykhodiashchikh iz krepostnoi zavisimosti, *Prilozheniia k trudam Redaktsionnykh Kommissii dlia sostavleniia polozhenii o krest'ianakh vykhodiashchikh iz krepostnoi zavisimosti*, 14 vols. (St. Petersburg, 1860).

3 *PIM*, 1: 23-26 (April 15, 1859).

In writing the history of emancipation and land reform, scholars have placed too much emphasis on the political context of reform, with little or no appreciation of the administrative, financial, social, agricultural, and economic factors and constraints that plagued reform, warped legislation, and obstructed desirable goals. A number of interrelated factors determined the specific conditions of emancipation and freedom in Russian peasant society. Politics was but one, and far from the most important. In the end, the Editing Commission would operate under three major constraints: the policies and goals laid down by the tsar and the Main Committee which, even if they could not be fully implemented, could not be entirely ignored; limited information on manorial farming, the peasant economy, and the practices of servitude; and an unanticipated and rapidly developing financial crisis.[4] All these marked the final emancipation legislation.

Russian reformers were at a serious disadvantage when they tried to construct reform legislation following the guidelines of the Main Committee. The autocracy had never compiled a cadastre for the empire, although this had been done in much of Europe, including virtually all of the German and Austrian states, on which the Editing Commission would seek to model its reform. Thus, in 1859, the Russian government was unable to determine the financial value of any individual serf estate. It did not possess information for individual serf estates on peasant dues and obligations, harvest size, acreage sown, livestock holdings, physical assets, commodity prices, soil quality and productivity, and revenues from crafts and trade, such that it could even begin to assess the value of a specific estate.[5] All this would have normally been recorded in a cadastre for each estate or landholding. The General Land Survey, undertaken during the reign of Catherine II in the late eighteenth century, had measured, and only crudely at that, the total population of an estate and the amount of land under arable, pasture, meadow, and forest. There were no data on the size of the demesne, if one existed, and no valuation of the land and other assets on the estate. The General Land Survey did not describe how the lands were used, the amount or nature of revenues the lords received from them, or the dues

[4] Steven L. Hoch, "The Banking Crisis, Peasant Reform, and Economic Development in Russia," *The American Historical Review* 96, no. 3 (June 1991): 795-820.

[5] *PIM*, 13: 2 (September 6-7, 1860).

and obligations owed by the serf population settled on them. In fact, the Editing Commission had only a general sense of how serf labor was actually utilized, and virtually no basis to assess its value or productivity.

Although it is often thought otherwise, it is something of a misnomer to say that the value of an estate in pre-reform Russia was best measured in serfs. One of the disadvantages of being undergoverned is institutionalizing administrative practices that were obsolete elsewhere. In effect, this is what Peter I had done by enacting a soul tax and undertaking the first tax-census in Russia in the early 18th century. From 1719 to the end of the servile period in 1861, serfs were the sole asset which had been adequately counted, and thus were the only basis for assessing wealth. It was by default that male serfs were the accounting unit of collateral for state mortgage loans. But the number of serfs was a poor indicator of the revenues generated by an estate. For example, as was stated previously, within the same uezd, the smallest administrative unit, it was not uncommon for quitrent payments per male to vary by a factor of 20 or more among serf estates. By employing such a poor indicator of wealth, throughout the pre-reform period the state misallocated both taxes and credit, and behaved more conservatively in its fiscal and monetary policies than was necessarily warranted. In other words, the autocracy collected taxes and allocated credit on the basis of the distribution of labor, and not land, capital, gross revenues, output, or net income. Taxation based on land and other income-producing assets would have required a cadastre, the compilation of which proved to be beyond the administrative capacity of the autocracy, though many reformers wished it were not so.[6]

For decades, the Russian autocracy lacked the means to administer the society effectively, best evidenced by its inability to gather the most basic data about itself. This administrative weakness, trying to solve complex problems with imprecise information, is a key dimension of Russian underdevelopment. Most of the emancipation legislation cannot be understood without recognizing the vacuum in which reformers operated. In its first months of work the Editing Commission

---

[6] N. Kh. Bunge, "Ob izmenenii iuridicheskikh otnoshenii v Rossii, vsledstvie predstoiashchego preobrazovaniia krepostnogo prava," *Otechestvennyia zapiski* 119, no. 8 (1858): 64; E. I. Lamanskii, "Iz vospominanii Evgeniia Ivanovicha Lamanskago (1840-1890 gg.)," *Russkaia starina*, no. 3 (1915): 589.

inventoried what it did not know and made sincere efforts to obtain and analyze the information it required. Some data collection efforts had been undertaken slightly earlier at the request of the Main Committee of Peasant Affairs and the Ministry of Internal Affairs. However, the tasks of analyzing these data and using them as a basis for reform policy resided with the Editing Commission. Fleetingly, the commission even contemplated compiling a cadastre until it recognized that this would delay emancipation for decades.[7]

Although the members of the Editing Commission had hoped to follow Austrian and German precedents in agrarian reform, they quickly came to realize this would not be possible. In Austria, by the Patent of September 7, 1848, and the law of March 4, 1849, peasants were to indemnify their lords based upon the cadastral evaluation of their dues and obligations and the value of free labor. This cadastre, however, which had just been completed, had taken 25 years to compile.[8] While the Editing Commission gathered and analyzed much information on Russia, nothing comparable to a cadastre was undertaken. Some of the information the commission collected did impact reform. Much the Editing Commission rejected out of hand because of its unreliability. Unfortunately, later critics of the emancipation as well as historians used these data to assess the success of agrarian reform. This has lead to considerable misunderstanding and confusion.

The Editing Commission was remarkably candid about what it was doing and fully aware of the inconsistencies and limitations in the policies that it developed. In the end, although the commission was charged with protecting the income of the lords, it had no idea what any lord actually received. It did not know how much land the peasants on an estate had as provision plots for their subsistence needs, although it was to allot all of them land. It did not know the price of this land, though it was to be purchased by the peasants from the lord. It did not know how to convert obligatory labor obligations into cash equivalents so that peasant payments post-reform would not exceed their existing dues as serfs, although it was to ensure that after emancipation ex-serfs would feel that their well-being had been improved. It had only a general

[7] *PIM*, 13: 14 (September 6-7, 1860).

[8] Jerome Blum, *Noble Landowners and Agriculture in Austria, 1815-1848* (Baltimore, 1948), 212 and 236.

sense of the quitrent serfs paid. In essence, the work of the Editing Commission "given," in its own words, "the complete absence of precise statistical data for each locality," consisted primarily in overcoming the problems presented by the lack of the most basic information about manorial farming and the peasant economy, that is, the society it was reforming.[9]

Whatever visions for Russian social and economic development the reformers had, the opportunities that were open to them were constrained by the practices of serfdom and the limited information they possessed about them. Moreover, what little the reformers did know placed them in an even more unfortunate situation. It was clear to the commission that serf owners were of very different wealth and status, holding lands of widely divergent natural endowment in regions subject to different climatic constraints. In some places, off-farm earnings were considerable; elsewhere, negligible. On some estates, potential sources of income were fully utilized; on others, they were barely tapped. Some estates were land rich and labor poor; others, just the opposite.[10] Similarly, serfs paid their dues in kind, in cash, in labor, or in some combination, but the amount of these dues and intensity of serf labor required to fulfill them varied considerably by estate and even by household. As subsistence peasants, serfs had different abilities to absorb risk and to earn cash. Some serfs had more than enough land to subsist as peasant farmers; for others, no amount of land would have made this possible. Estates had diverse histories of labor practices and relations. All in all, the administrative weakness of the state made it impossible to draft an emancipation that could take into consideration the complex of servile relations in Russia.

In the end, the Editing Commission would have three principal sources of information to assist it in the formulation of policy. Two came from the serf owners themselves. The first and most comprehensive was a survey of every serf estate undertaken in 1858-59 with the assistance of provincial committees that were established to aid in the drafting of the emancipation legislation.[11] Serf owners were required

9 *PIM*, vol. 2, Report of the Economic Division no. 3, 20.

10 *PIM*, vol. 3, Report of the Economic Division no. 5, 8-10; Report of the Economic Division no. 15, 16-20.

11 *PIM*, 2: 3-4 (July 3, 1859).

to respond to a series of questions regarding the number of serfs they owned, the size and composition of the serfs' land allotments, the amount and nature of their dues, their access to woodland, pasture, and commons, and their income from crafts and trade. Serf owners were also required to provide information on local rental and sale prices for all kinds of farmland; on day, seasonal, and annual wage and piecework rates; and on estate earnings and profits.[12] Partial data for estates with over 100 male serfs, approximately 20,000 of the roughly 130,000 serf estates in the empire, were published for 38 provinces. The commission itself had access to all the information including the data related to smaller estates.[13]

The second source of information from serf owners came from the provincial committees directly. Many such committees had prepared comprehensive draft land reform projects. In explaining their proposals most committees provided considerable, though unsystematic, information to the Editing Commission. However, little use was made of this information. In fact, the Editing Commission had resolved a number of major issues before it even received many provincial committee reports. Eventually, the Editing Commission did respond to the provincial committee proposals and in doing so referred to the information they provided. Nevertheless, these data were not used to formulate reform policies.[14]

The commission spent almost 18 months analyzing the data provided by serf owners and some of the provincial committees. Of the information received, the commission felt it had little reason to doubt the accuracy of the data on the number of souls, households, and work teams (*tiagla*) on an estate, or the total amount of land an estate possessed.[15] Moreover, the commission noted, these data could be readily verified by the government from its own sources. On peas-

---

[12] Tsentral'nyi gosudarstvennyi arkhiv drevnikh aktov (hereafter, TsGADA), f. 1262, op. 4, ch. 2, ed. khr. 862 (1858).

[13] *Prilozheniia k trudam Redaktsionnykh Kommissii dlia sostavleniia polozhenii o krest'ianakh vykhodiashchikh iz krepostnoi zavisimosti: Svedeniia o pomeshchich'ikh imeniiakh,* 6 vols. (St. Petersburg, 1860).

[14] *Prilozheniia k trudam Redaktsionnykh Kommissii dlia sostavleniia polozhenii o krest'ianakh vykhodiashchikh iz krepostnoi zavisimosti,* vols. 3-5, 7-10 (St. Petersburg, 1860).

[15] *PIM,* vol. 3, Report of the Economic Division no. 15, 5-6.

ant land use, many problems arose. Often landlords failed to include common lands—forests, meadows, and pasture—in the peasant allotment. Some did not include household plots. In addition, there was confusion in the terminology. Some estates and districts reported the average allotment, others the most common or modal allotment, and still others the minimum allotment a serf required.[16] Often allotment size was specified not by male soul, but by *tiaglo* (husband and wife work team). But depending on local practice and estate labor needs, the number of male souls per *tiaglo* varied.[17] On many serf estates, the demesne and the peasants' fields were not clearly demarcated, and the intermingling of strips was common. Even if a lord knew which land had been allocated to the serfs, rarely had it been surveyed with any degree of accuracy. Lords reported that the area had been "estimated by eye" *(glazomerno),* using local instruments, and the like.[18] Even more unfortunate, lords were asked to report their data to the state in *desiatiny kazennye* or *ukaznoi mery* (state or statutory measure), while land was often measured in *desiatiny khoziaistvennye,* which were one-third larger. Frequently, contemporaries confused the two or failed to distinguish between them.

The commission also suspected that many lords and bailiffs had intentionally misreported information and, in an early report, tactfully concluded: "Of course, the amount of land in the peasants' use was sufficiently well-known to the owners and their bailiffs, but various considerations could induce a reduction in the figures reported."[19] These fears were subsequently confirmed. During the second convocation of deputies from the provincial committees in 1860, a number of members openly admitted to the Editing Commission that the data which they reported on the size of peasant allotments were not to be believed. The commission ultimately concluded that "in a great number of cases, the amount of land used by the peasants was reported as

[16] Ibid., 3-5.

[17] *PIM,* vol. 3, Report of the Economic Division no. 5, 13.

[18] I. Polosin, "Shuvalovshchina v 1858-1878 gg.," *Moskovskii krai v ego proshlom,* in *Trudy Obshchestva dlia Izucheniia Moskovskoi Oblasti* (Moscow, 1930), 6: 13; A. Ia. Degtiarev, S. G. Kashchenko, and D. I. Raskin, *Novgorodskaia derevnia v reforme 1861 goda: Opyt izucheniia s ispol'zovaniem EVM* (Leningrad, 1989), 24.

[19] *PIM,* vol. 16, "Vyvody o denezhnykh povinnostiakh," 14.

being much lower than reality."[20] Generally, the Editing Commission had somewhat more confidence in the data on household plots and arable land. But as regards hayfields and meadows, it noted, "there is much inaccuracy."[21]

The commission did not even bother to analyze the data gathered on serf labor obligations.[22] In accord with the policy set down by the Main Committee on Peasant Affairs, the Editing Commission intended a considerable reduction in what it thought was a widespread practice of serfs working three days per week for their lord, and a significant decrease was, in fact, enacted into law. In so doing, both the Main Committee and the Editing Commission hoped that lords would be enticed to shift their peasants onto quitrent, and then eventually onto redemption.

The commission recognized that lords had an incentive to exaggerate the amount of quitrent the serfs paid, and it was highly skeptical of the information for any specific estate. The commission noted wide discrepancies in the information reported for neighboring or similar estates which could not be explained by local or regional differences.[23] Of greater import, there were whole sections of the empire where quitrent was uncommon, if not unknown, especially in the black soil region. In fact, almost two-thirds of all serfs performed some form of labor services, and the commission admitted it knew of no rational way to convert the value of compulsory labor into comparable money dues.[24] Nevertheless, it did feel that it had a reasonably accurate sense of the range of quitrents, and that it would not be difficult to obtain more accurate information, if that were subsequently required. "Every lord knows how much quitrent he receives from the peasants, and every peasant knows how much he pays."[25]

Finally, the data on land prices submitted by landlords were summarily rejected as they appeared to be greatly inflated. "There are those

---

[20] *PIM,* vol. 13, "Doklady po otzyvam chlenov gubernskikh komitetov. Khoziaistvennoe Otdelenie" (July 21, 1860), 44-45.

[21] *PIM,* vol. 16, "Vyvody o denezhnykh povinnostiakh," 14.

[22] See *Prilozheniia k trudam Redaktsionnykh Kommissii. Svedeniia o pomeshchich'ikh imeniiakh,* vol. 5, *Vyvody iz opisaniia imenii vo* 100 *dush, po* 28 *velikorossiiskim guberniiam* and vol. 6, *Vyvody iz opisaniia imenii po guberniiam, pomianutym v 6-m t.*

[23] *PIM,* vol. 3, Report of the Economic Division no. 17, 80.

[24] Ibid., 85-97.

[25] *PIM,* vol. 16, "Vyvody o denezhnykh povinnostiakh," 13.

figures," the Editing Commission wrote, "in the original data on serf owner estates which will not withstand the slightest critique, that is, the data on land prices." The commission described these prices as "arbitrary numbers ... completely useless for deriving averages."[26] Many provincial governors informed the Editing Commission that the land prices reported were greatly inflated.[27] On these data one commentator graciously concluded: "It is apparent that many landlords did not know how to appraise their lands, which they had never sold separately," that is, apart from the serf population and other assets on it.[28]

In anticipation of this problem, the *Zemskii Otdel* of the Ministry of Internal Affairs compiled information on land prices for the Editing Commission. This was the third source available to the commission for policy formation. It provided: 1) data on land sold between January 1, 1854, and January 1, 1859, which was transferred by deed of purchase, including both settled and unsettled land, although the vast majority was serf estates. The sale price included the serf population, the land, and all other assets on it; 2) data on the price of land sold at public auction for the non-payment of states taxes and debts for the same period, including both settled and unsettled land, but again primarily serf estates; and 3) general information on prices reported by local officials and serf owners on unpopulated land sold without restriction, that is, to all persons of all legal status, between 1856 and 1859; and 4) data for similar lands that had been collected by the Ministry's Department of Agriculture for various administrative purposes. The results were published by the Editing Commission in 1859 and 1860.[29] A small portion of these data was republished in 1897 by D. I. Rikhter and used by A. Lositskii in his well-known essay of 1906, in which he sought to show that the serfs were considerably overcharged for the land they acquired under the terms of the government-regulated redemption operation, which I have discussed

26 Ibid., 14. See also *PIM,* vol. 11 [Finance Commission], 158-59.

27 *PIM,* vol. 11 [Finance Commission], 161.

28 S. Ianovskii, "Statisticheskoe obozrenie pomeshchich'ikh imenii Kaluzhskogo uezda," *Zemledel'cheskaia gazeta,* no. 84 (October 20, 1859).

29 *Prilozheniia k trudam Redaktsionnykh Komissii dlia sostavleniia polozhenii o krest'ianakh vykhodiashchikh iz krepostnoi zavisimosti,* vol. 14, *Svedeniia o tsenakh na zemli naselennyia i nenaselennyia;* and *Svedeniia o tsenakh na zemli prodannyia* s *publichnago torga* s *1 ianvaria 1854.*

elsewhere.[30] Of import here is what the Editing Commission thought of these data and how they were used in drafting reform legislation. All in all, on the key problem of determining the value of the land the lords were to sell and their ex-serfs were to buy, the Editing Commission felt it had information either grossly inflated or significantly undervalued. Of great import, it rejected all the data on land prices that it had at its disposal.[31] As a result, the often expressed desire of the commission that "only household plots and field and useful lands were to be subject to redemption, and under no circumstances the person of the peasants and their labor" was impossible to realize.[32] Without accurate land price data, how could the peasants possibly redeem their lands?

In failing to obtain reliable data on the serf economy, the Editing Commission was forced to depart from those European precedents it sought to copy. In particular, it proved impossible to draft legislation for the Russian empire similar to the successful land reforms of the Hapsburg monarchy and the German states. Without a cadastre the Editing Commission could not draft a law that would accord with the economic reality of each individual estate. For example, "all real property in the German-Slav lands was entered in a series of registers which were maintained in every province. These registers were known as *Grundbiicher.*

30 D. I. Rikhter, "Zabytyi material po statistike prodazhnykh tsen na zemliu," *Trudy Imperatorskogo Vol'nogo Ekonomicheskogo Obshchestva,* vol. 2, bk. 4 (September 1897): 1-23; A. Lositskii, *Vykupnaia operatsiia* (St. Petersburg, 1906), 16; N. Druzhinin, "Likvidatsiia feodal'noi sistemy v russkoi pomeshchich'ei derevne (1862-1882 gg.)," *Voprosy istorii,* no. 12 (December 1968): 6; Alexander Gerschenkron, "Agrarian Policies and Industrialization, Russia 1861-1917," in *The Cambridge Economic History of Europe* (Cambridge, 1965), vol. 6, pt. 2, 738; Geroid T. Robinson, *Rural Russia under the Old Regime* (New York, 1932), 88; Lazar Volin, *A Century of Russian Agriculture from Alexander II to Khrushchev* (Cambridge, MA, 1970), 51; Jerome Blum, *The End of the Old Order in Rural Europe* (Princeton, NJ, 1978), 390; Evsey Domar, "Were Russian Serfs Overcharged for Their Land by the 1861 Emancipation? The History of One Historical Table," *Research in Economic History,* Supplement 5 (1989): 429-39. See also Steven L. Hoch, "Did Russia's Emancipated Serfs Really Pay Too Much for Too Little Land? Statistical Anomalies and Long-Tailed Distributions," *Slavic Review* 63, no. 2 (2004): 247-74.

31 *PIM,* vol. 3, Report of the Economic Division no. 17, 98.

32 *PIM,* vol. 1, Journal of the Main Committee (May 4, 1858); and P. Kovan'ko, "Osvobozhdenie krest'ian i obiazatel'nyi vykup," *Russkaia mysl',* no. 6 (1912): 10.

Their purpose was, first, to give an exact and reliable description of the realty with all the components, rights, and obligations adhering to it; second, to record the proprietor as the legal possessor; and third, to record the rights that other persons might have in the realty."[33] Consequently, in 1848-49, attendant to agrarian reform, with land accurately surveyed and assessed, land ownership and usage firmly established, and peasant dues carefully recorded, simple capitalization formulas based upon the cadastral records of the peasants' obligations determined the current monetary value of the landlords' right to these dues.

Generally, emancipations throughout all of Europe had the goal of making the peasants land owners, while providing the lords with some level of compensation. Neither in Russia nor elsewhere were emancipations social revolutions, dispossessing the landowning elite entirely of its property. Similarly, no thought was ever given to compensating the peasants for their many years of labor. In Austria, "the dues and services the peasant had paid were recognized as the property rights of the landlord."[34] In both Austria and Germany, peasant dues as recorded in the cadastre for each estate were capitalized at the prevailing interest rate or at the rate of return of capital in agriculture. Capitalization was simply a means to determine the present or market value of an estate. In other words, capitalization made it possible to convert peasant annual dues into a capital sum, which the peasants could then redeem. In Austria and Germany, although not in Hungary, the capitalized sum as calculated was then reduced, often by as much as one-third. This was justified by the claim that lords would no longer bear the administrative costs of hereditary subjugation. In addition, to ensure an improvement in peasant well-being, the compensation due the lords was subsidized by the state or province, with only a portion coming from the emancipated peasants themselves.

In most of central Europe, the capitalized sum the peasants owed was not paid off in full at the time of emancipation, but was amortized over terms running from 5 to 54 years.[35] Lengthy periods of amortiza-

---

33 Blum, *Noble Landowners and Agriculture*, 67.

34 Ibid., 237.

35 "Krest'ianskoe pozemel'noe ustroistvo i vykup krestianskikh povinnostei v Lifliandii, Prussii i Avstrii," in *PIM*, vol. 11, Finansovaia Kommissiia po kresti'anskomu delu, *Proekt o vykupe krest'ianami pozemel'nykh ugodii* (St. Petersburg, 1860), prilozheniia, 134, 144, 160.

tion, 30 years or more, were most common. Both the size of provincial subsidies and the rates of capitalization rates varied. But in the end many peasants had annual loan payments as little as one-third of their former dues. In addition, converting the capitalized sum into a long-term debt was thought to be of benefit to the lords, as it provided them with a fixed annual income for a considerable period of time, although not always for the same number of years as the term of amortization on the loan to the peasants.

With one good eye on Austrian and German precedents, but with only a blurry image of rural Russia, here is what the Editing Commission decided and what was eventually enacted into law. It adopted as fundamental principles that serfs, attendant to land reform, were to receive their existing allotments, and, at worst, they were to continue to pay no more than their existing dues. For most serfs, a reduction in their dues was anticipated. The commission felt "with complete certainty" that the existing allotment, with few exceptions, was "the best and even the sole, correct, practical standard for that quantity of land, that corresponds to the real needs of the peasant." Keeping the existing allotment was described as "the cornerstone of the entire current question."[36] Similarly, the commission affirmed that *"existing dues* should serve as the main point of departure for determining peasant quitrents" upon being emancipated and then upon becoming property owners through the redemption operation.[37] In other words, as a substitute for a cadastre, the Editing Commission in estimating the size of peasants' dues and their land allotments took" *as a starting point, existing facts,* or the order of things, established under the influence of age-old experience," and claimed it had found "in the vast majority of cases, an accurate depiction of local needs and resources."[38]

The Editing Commission was well aware of the price it was paying for the empire's historic administrative underdevelopment. By taking existing allotments as the basis for determining the amount of land

---

[36] *PIM,* vol. 2, Report of the Economic Division no. 1, 22; *PIM,* vol. 4 (December 4, 1859), Supplement to the Report of the Economic Division, no. 5, 18. *PIM,* vol. 13. Report of the Economic Division (July 21, 1860), 27.

[37] *PIM,* vol. 1, p. 5 (March 5, 1859); *PIM,* vol. 6 (March 1, 1860) Supplement to the Report of Economic Division, no. 17, 120. Emphasis in the original.

[38] *PIM,* vol. 18, Obshchaia dokladnaia zapiska (October 10, 1860), 14. Emphasis in the original. See also *PIM,* vol. 13, 47.

the peasants were to receive and by using existing dues which, following German and Austrian practices, would then be capitalized at the prevailing rate of return on investment in agriculture, the Editing Commission admitted the peasants were not redeeming the value of their specific allotment based upon a careful valuation of their land. "In theory, recognizing as just the correspondence of dues with the value of land, the Economic Division [of the Editing Commission] has come to the conclusion that such a method of determining dues cannot be applied in practice," at least in part, "due to our lack of a cadastre.[39] In fact, "the establishment of such a correspondence, simultaneous with the promulgation of the [Emancipation] Statute, is impossible since implementing this on every estate would require a more or less protracted period of time."[40] The Economic Division stated clearly in September 1860 that "it does not make a secret of the fact that it does not seek a correspondence of dues with the value of the land ... because to achieve this goal would require decades and a land cadastre."[41] Finally, the Editing Commission reiterated in its final report: "In determining the right size of allotments and dues, the Editing Commission had in mind that the goal of the reform being undertaken consisted not in the strict application of some sort of abstract theory, based upon a mathematical relationship of the assessed needs of the peasants to the productivity of the soil, and the value of land in relation to its value in cash or in labor, but in resolving a paramount social problem: to improve the well-being of one estate with, to the degree possible, minimal losses for the other."[42] The commission stated it had one simple goal attendant to land reform, that "the compensation to the landowners stand in the greatest possible correspondence to the previous income of the serf owners, and the annual payments of the peasants after redemption be proportionate to their previous quitrent."[43]

In all this, the Editing Commission was being both pragmatic and realistic given the lack of reliable information on land prices in general, let alone for individual estates, and an inability to determine whether

---

39 *PIM*, vol. 3, Report of the Economic Division no. 17, 80-81. See also *PIM*, vol. 2, Report of the Economic Division no. 1, 22-29.

40 *PIM*, vol. 4, Supplement to the Report of the Economic Division no. 5, 13.

41 *PIM*, vol. 13 (September 6-7, 1860), 14.

42 *PIM*, vol. 18, "Obshchaia dokladnaia zapiska" (October 10, 1860), 14.

43 *PIM*, vol. 11 [Finance Commission], 158.

the peasants could even afford to pay these prices if they could be determined. Although this did not accord with the expressed wishes of the tsar and the Main Committee, in fact, much of the final legislation did not. Clearly, the Editing Commission tried, though in vain, to collect reliable data on land prices in an attempt to implement Imperial will. But in its reports the Editing Commission explained in detail the reasons behind the policies and procedures that were ultimately adopted, and the constraints which had forced it to do so. In Austria, the law clearly stated that peasant dues and services as recorded in the cadastre for each noble estate were the right of the lord, and were to be subject to redemption. In Russia, the emancipation legislation declared that the lords were not being compensated for the loss of serf labor. But precisely what the peasants were redeeming—their land, dues, or other assets—remained uncertain, as the commission had no way to evaluate them, as it readily admitted. The more carefully the law is read, the more obvious it becomes that much was intentionally left unsaid. Perhaps, in deference to the tsar and the Main Committee, the Editing Commission chose to be ambiguous, and nothing in the redemption process necessitated greater specificity. All the law stated was how the redemption sum granted to the lords and lent to the peasants was to be calculated, and that peasant allotments were to be considered collateral for this loan. In undertaking land reform, most states in Europe were involved in a complex balancing act and were constrained by manorial customs and administrative realities. However, the scales in Russia were crude, and matters could not be kept simple. In severing the relationship between the value of the specific lands the peasants were to receive and the compensation due the lord, the Editing Commission determined their levels independently, linked only by current practices. The commission was not overly concerned because as nearly as could be established from the information at hand, this relationship did not exist under serfdom either. Existing quitrents were determined under the conditions of serfdom, which included the right of the lord to fix them at any level.[44] Nothing in law or in practice required the lord to base the quitrent on the income from the land the peasants held as provision plots. In large parts of the empire serf off-farm earnings were considerable, and quitrents reflected serf income and not simply the value of the land the

[44] *PIM*, vol. 2, Report of the Economic Division no. 5, 14.

peasants used. Of this the commission had no doubt.[45] In contrast, in the view of the commission, many serfs uniformly labored three days a week for their lord regardless of the amount of land they were allotted to support themselves.

The commission examined in detail the factors that affected the size of peasant allotments. It understood that some lands were salty, sandy, or loamy, and had varying crop yields. Lands in the non-black earth region usually had to be manured, and thus peasants needed larger allotments to graze livestock and provide feed in order to obtain natural fertilizers.[46] The amount of land the lord owned, local population density, the potential for off-farm earnings, and the accessibility to markets all played a considerable role in determining peasant allotment sizes. Manorial policies also needed to be considered. If peasants were on quitrent, then generally there was no demesne, and all the land was turned over to the peasants for their use. Some of these peasants had quite large allotments, due to managerial neglect, absentee owners, an unwillingness or inability on the part of the lord to provide the requisite capital investment that direct farming necessitated, or any combination of these factors. How intensively the peasants cultivated some of these lands, if at all, is unknown. In contrast, peasants with labor obligations on manorial lands usually had smaller allotments, more uniform in size across estates, and generally more fertile. Overall, the Editing Commission was well aware of the spectrum of servile practices, but again, it needs to be emphasized, it did not know how these circumstances impacted any individual estate.

Administrative underdevelopment forced the commission into adopting what can only be described as fast and dirty practices to achieve its policy goals, if land reform were to be implemented in a timely manner. As has been made clear, the commission was overwhelmed with widely varying data on the amount of serf quitrents and the size of peasant allotments. It could not determine with any degree of certainty for an individual estate how much of the variation was due to local and regional conditions of ecology and economy, and how much to differing levels of manorial exploitation, that is, to estate policies and practices.

As a result, in a significant departure from land reform elsewhere in Europe, the commission computed averages, applied ranges, and

---

45 *PIM*, vol. 13 (September 6-7, 1860), 30.

46 *PIM*, vol. 3, Report of the Economic Division no. 15, 23-27.

sometimes just guessed. The commission used existing reality to establish broad regional norms on peasant dues and land allotments and did not fix the terms of freedom using the current practices and obligations for individual estates. In other words, it used the data available from the survey of serf estates to determine a *range* of allotment sizes and to compute *average* quitrents for broad geographic areas, and then applied the results to all estates within the region. Although not a perfect analogy, it is as if property assessors came into a new housing development and, being unable to determine the value of each home, computed average lot sizes and estimated average construction costs per square foot. Then the purchase price for each home was fixed (without negotiation) based upon these averages, subject to modest variation, but with little regard for the actual features in the home, the quality of the construction, or the neighborhood.

In the final legislation, the country was divided into regions, zones, and localities. Twenty-nine Great Russian provinces, 3 provinces of New Russia, Mogilev, and part of Vitebsk were divided into 3 zones (black earth, nonblack earth, and steppe), with a total of 29 localities. In the second major regional statute, the Little Russian provinces of Chernigov, Poltava, and part of Kharkov were divided into 9 localities. In the third regional statute, Kiev, Podolia, and Volynia provinces were also divided into 9 localities. Estates in Vilna, Grodno, Kovno, Minsk, and parts of Vitebsk provinces were divided into 2 zones, with the 4 districts of Vitebsk further subdivided into 9 categories based upon population densities. Special rules were written for Bessarabia and Siberia, and for Stavropol' province. Localities were to be established here, only if deemed necessary, as the emancipation was implemented. The Land of the Don Host *(Zemlia Voiska Donskago)* was split into four localities. In all, over 50 different localities were established, as the Editing Commission sought to capture the economic reality of the 130,000 serf estates in the empire.

The commission recognized that in numerous instances the norms established by the emancipation law poorly reflected local circumstances. There was no alternative, however. For example, locality number 1 in the non-black earth zone under the Great Russian provinces and New Russia statute included territory from 26 districts in 9 provinces, from St. Petersburg in the north to Tambov in the south, with approximately 850,000 serfs living as much as 1,000 kilometers apart.

In the end, while making allowances for the varied nature of serfdom, but lacking the specificity of a cadastre, the emancipation law became complicated indeed. As regards the amount of land allotted to the peasants, for 69 percent of all serfs, that is, those living in zone 1 and 2 of the first regional statute and all those covered under second regional statute, a minimum and maximum allotment size was established for each of 26 localities. Peasants with existing allotments below the minimum were to have them increased; those over the maximum, reduced to the statutory maximum. Peasants who held allotments between the minimum and maximum were to keep their current allotments. However, for serfs living in zone 3 of the first regional statute, just under 4 percent of all serfs, a single fixed allotment was specified, without any minimum or maximum, for each of the 12 localities.

Just under 12 percent of the serfs lived in Kiev, Podolia, and Volynia provinces, which were covered under the third regional statute. Here, by the laws of May 26, 1847, and December 29, 1848, inventories imposed by the autocracy regulated the terms of peasant servitude. Inventories "defined the size of the holdings of the peasants and fixed the amount of dues that had to be paid for them."[47] The emancipation law specified that these serfs were to keep all the land held under the terms of the inventories, unless they wished otherwise. Inventories that had recently been compiled, although not universally implemented, were also used for the provinces of Grodno, Vil'na, Kovna, and Minsk and 4 districts of Vitebsk province with approximately 8 percent of all serfs, who were covered by the fourth major regional statute. Serfs here were to receive all the lands held under the terms of inventories.[48]

The inventories for the Western provinces made drafting the terms of emancipation considerably easier than elsewhere in the empire. The

---

[47] Jerome Blum, *Lord and Peasant in Russia from the Ninth to the Nineteenth Century* (Princeton, NJ, 1961), 460-61.

[48] Four additional laws covered serfs of special status. The first related to household serfs, who comprised approximately 7 percent of the total serf population, over 1.4 million peasants. In spite of this designation, household serfs were rarely in service, but lived on landed estates, serving as masters, apprentices, skilled laborers, and overseers. Other laws related to the half million serfs assigned to private factories, mines, and the salt industry; and to the 340,000 peasants living on so-called *melkopomestnye* estates, that is, serf estates with fewer than 21 male souls and who belonged to 43,000 different serf owners.

Editing Commission, having agreed to use the inventories, found little need to pay additional attention to the region. In contrast, for the vast majority of serfs, those living in Russia proper, the situation was quite different. In its early discussions the Editing Commission hoped that for most serfs their current allotments would fall within the minimum and maximum specified for the locality in which they lived.[49] However, a maximum size was required because some allotments "have a fortuitous basis." In the northern non-black-earth zone, in particular, where direct estate farming was less common, peasants often had very large allotments with "land they do not use and do not need."[50] Thus, the Editing Commission stated allotments must have upper limits "in order to protect the interests of the lords, having in mind that on many extremely land-rich quitrent estates, all the land is shown as being in peasant use, although part of it finds no agricultural application whatsoever." In the opinion of the commission, specifying a maximum allotment in these instances did not amount to a reduction in the peasants' allotment, but simply "a demarcation of peasant land from estate [land]." Moreover, the commission recognized that peasant well-being depended not solely on the size of the allotment, but on the availability of working capital and labor. Allotments on land-rich quitrent estates that did not correspond with the availability of labor and livestock "add nothing to [a peasant's] well-being and bring him negligible benefit." Even in fertile grain producing areas, the commission recognized that the availability and intensity of peasant labor was a significant factor affecting output, independent of allotment size.[51] Finally, the commission felt that some lords had been overly "generous" to their serfs in allotting them land. In the interest of "fairness," such lords were not to be penalized for their past generosity. Overall, the commission felt that the maximum allotment for each locality should be set such that "the cutting off of surplus peasant land could not become a common occurrence, but would always retain only the character of *an exception*."[52]

---

[49] *PIM*, vol. 2, p. 27 Report of the Economic Division no. 1 (June 9, 1859); *PIM*, vol. 3, Report of the Economic Division no. 15, 2, 13-16.

[50] *PIM*, vol. 3, Report of the Economic Division no. 15, 27.

[51] *PIM*, vol. 2, Report of the Economic Division no. 9, 26-27.

[52] *PIM*, vol. 3, Report of the Economic Division no. 15, p. 2. Emphasis in the original. *PIM*, vol. 16, III. See also *PIM*, vol. 2, Report of the Economic Division, no. 1, 22-29.

A minimum allotment was required to ensure the peasants a livelihood. The commission emphasized it did not wish for serfs, upon being freed, to be turned into landless laborers, entirely dependent on their lords for a livelihood. Rather, the intent was to make them property owners with adequate resources to subsist.[53] Originally, the Editing Commission proposed that the minimum allotment for serfs living in the territory covered by the Great Russia and New Russia statute be set at 40 percent of the maximum. This was based on results computed from the information on estates with over 100 serfs that had been analyzed by the commission. But upon subsequent examination of the data for estates with less than 100 serfs, it became evident that they often had less land per capita. As a result, in the final legislation the minimum was reduced to one-third of the maximum.[54] In the black-earth zone, the commission expected that a reduction in the size of the peasant allotment would occur on no more than 25 percent of all serf estates.[55] In the north, the commission estimated that between a quarter and a third, although occasionally as many as half, of all serf estates in each non-black earth locality had allotments over the statutory maximum.[56]

New Russia created special challenges. Raising livestock was an important component of the peasant economy, and the serfs often had access to vast amounts of land for grazing. Most of these lands were unsurveyed. On lands that were cultivated, a variety of long-fallow rotation systems were used, and generally the serfs used as much land as they needed. These circumstances made it impossible for the commission to determine the range in size of serf allotments. As a result, all the commission did was specify a single, fixed allotment for each locality.[57]

Special circumstances also applied to Chemigov, Poltava, and parts of Kharkov provinces. With improved opportunities to market grain and other agricultural products through Black Sea ports, many serf owners had found it profitable to expand the demesne at the expense of peasant land. By the late 1850s, almost a third of the serfs in this region had no

---

[53] *PIM*, vol. 1, pp. 47-53; *PIM*, vol. 15, III.

[54] *PIM*, vol. 3, Report of the Economic Division no. 15, 34-35.

[55] *PIM*, vol. 3, Report of the Economic Division no. 15, 16.

[56] *PIM*, vol. 3, Report of the Economic Division no. 34-35 and *prilozhenie*, 4-15.

[57] *PIM*, vol. 6, p. 2 (January 29, 1860), *PIM*, vol. 15, "Poverochnyia raboty," II.

land at all; many held only a household plot. The commission sought to rectify this problem and place the peasants on a comparable economic footing to those in the Great Russian provinces. Thus, specifying a minimum allotment was intended to improve the well-being of a considerable portion of the serfs.[58] The minimum size for a land allotment was defined as half of the maximum.

The fact that the emancipation law seemingly resulted in a reduction in the size of the allotments held by many peasants prior to 1861 has been one of the most criticized aspects of the land reform. Nevertheless, it is important to note that generally speaking (for there would be exceptions) only peasants with allotments over the maximum had them reduced, and their allotments were reduced to the maximum allowed under the regional statute for their locality. As we shall see, the law was designed so that those serfs who had the largest pre-reform allotments had the most land cut off, and that in fact is what resulted. Within a locality, the peasants with the most land per capita prior to emancipation suffered the most; but after reform they still had more land than many of their neighbors.

The actual figures on allotment size were a matter of considerable discussion in the Editing Commission. In late August 1859 the Economic Division of the Editing Commission issued a preliminary report with recommendations specifying the size of the maximum allotment for each locality. Subsequently, 20 members of the commission, each with responsibility for one to three provinces, were assigned the task to analyze in depth the data from the survey of all serf owners in the empire. Using the results, they were then to determine the impact on each locality if three different land allotment maxima were used. They were also to assess the effect of different maxima on estates with less than 100 serfs, data which were not available when the preliminary report was written. In addition, they were to provide more information about the division of the empire into zones and localities, and to make recommendations for adjustments. These reports and accompanying tables total over 1,150 pages.[59] They are not organized in a uniform format and are often rather confusing. Most compilers limited themselves to the narrow question before them, the impact of different maxima. A hand-

[58] *PIM*, vol. 3, Supplement to the Report of the Economic Division no. 15, 1-15.
[59] *PIM*, vols. 15 and 16.

ful of reports, however, provide more detailed information and make it possible to examine how the maxima were intended to work.

As can be seen from the information below, the maximum allotment specified in the emancipation legislation for Tambov province in all but two districts was set higher than the size of the mean pre-reform allotment, thus ensuring that the serfs to be subjected to a reduction in their allotment would still hold an amount above the mean.[60] For the other two districts, the maximum was set at the pre-reform mean.

Table 1

District	Average Pre-Reform Allotment (desiatinas)	Maximum Allotment under 1861 Legislation (desiatinas)	Of Three Proposed Maxima Actually Used	Percent to be Subject to a Reduction of All Estates	Serfs
Tambov	2.98	3.25	middle	32	27
Borisoglebsk	3.50	3.50	largest	28	44
Elat'ma	2.73	3.00	smallest	27	28
Kirsanov	2.92	3.50	largest	13	23
Kozlov	2.81	3.00	largest	29	35
Lebedian	2.26	3.00	largest	20	15
Lipets	2.51	3.00	largest	19	24
Morshansk	2.60	3.00	smallest	26	21
Spassk	2.99	3.00	smallest	30	44
Temnikov	2.49	3.00	smallest	18	19
Usman	3.00	3.25	middle	22	35
Shatsk	2.74	3.00	smallest	19	24

Similarly, in Kursk province, based upon information available to the commission, in 9 districts the maximum allotment was set higher than the average pre-reform allotment, at the average in 4 districts, and in 2, slightly below.[61] For Tula province, for which a pre-reform modal allotment was calculated, in 8 districts the maximum specified in the reform legislation was above the mode; in 1, at the mode, and in 1, be-

[60] *PIM*, vol. 15, 152, data compiled by P. P. Semenov.
[61] *PIM*, vol. 15, 383.

low the mode.[62] In all 11 districts of Mogilev province, the maximum as specified in the law exceeded the pre-reform average.[63] For the 10 districts of Penza province, the statutory maximum was in excess of the pre-reform mean in 6 and at the mean in 2 others. For 2 districts, those with the highest average pre-reform allotments, the maximum was set just below the mean.[64] In Saratov, the land reform maximum exceeded the pre-reform modal allotment in all districts, although in 3 districts the pre-reform average was above the statutory maximum.[65] In Kaluga and Kazan, in all but 2 of the 23 total districts the statutory maximum exceeded the average pre-reform allotment.[66] Further north, in the non-black earth province of Tver', the statutory maximum was over the pre-reform mean in 4 districts, at the mean in 3, and below the mean in 5.[67] Similar circumstances pertained in Pskov. Generally, in the non-black earth areas, there was considerably more dispersion around the mean in pre-reform allotment size than elsewhere. Pre-reform averages here were skewed toward the high end, distorted by those land-rich quitrent estates mentioned previously, that is, those on which there was no demesne. The Editing Commission was fully aware that the mean was not always the most appropriate measure in determining the size of the maximum allotment and made adjustments when necessary. Data on the modal or most common size of pre-reform allotments would have been more helpful, but were calculated only rarely. Using the mode, however, would have resulted in smaller allotments.

Ultimately, in spite of all the misrepresentations and inaccuracies in the information available, all the Editing Commission could do was hope that the averages it computed on the size of pre-reform allotments and the establishment of a wide minimum and maximum range for each locality would eliminate the distortions in the figures reported by individual serf owners and the provincial committees, and make it possible to draft legislation that would account for outliers and exceptions. In general, the reform legislation established maximum allotment sizes

---

62 *PIM*, vol. 15, 419-21. For two districts, as parts of each which were in different localities, results could not be calculated.

63 *PIM*, vol. 15, 576.

64 *PIM*, vol. 15, 608-09.

65 *PIM*, vol. 16, 26.

66 *PIM*, vol. 16, 266, 322, 333.

67 *PIM*, vol. 16, 429.

above pre-reform averages unless there were compelling reasons to do otherwise, usually because the average for some reason did not accurately reflect local circumstances. In the vast majority of cases, the maximum statutory allotment provided in the reform legislation exceeded the pre-reform average by five to 15 percent. From a statistical point of view, all this was an eminently reasonable policy given the intent of the commission and the absence of more reliable data.

Computing average pre-reform quitrents for each locality based upon the information from serf owners proved to be more problematic. Excluding the western provinces, where the inventories were used, the commission felt it had sufficient data to calculate meaningful averages for only 1.1 million male serfs.[68] But, for the over 6 million male serfs living in the black-earth and steppe regions; in the provinces of Mogilev, Perm, Viatsk, and Olonets; and parts of Pskov, Smolensk, Ore l, Penza, Tambov, Kazan', and Vitebsk, the commission admitted that "to determine existing quitrents accurately is impossible," as most serfs only performed labor obligations. Rejecting again "any artificial system or formula" for determining the size of post-reform money dues, the commission essentially guessed and comforted itself using the following logic.[69] First, in the law the *average* pre-reform quitrent was used to set a *maximum* post-reform quitrent that a peasant would pay for receiving the *maximum* statutory allotment.[70] In other words, and other words are needed, after reform, the peasants would pay an average quitrent for an above average allotment. Second, the emancipation law specified that no peasant could have his pre-reform quitrent increased. Third, in determining what constituted quitrent, the Editing Commission did not include any requisitions in kind that many lords required of their serfs or any time they spent in the fields guarding crops or on the estate protecting other property. Fourth, quitrent payments were fixed in the statute for a period of 20 years. The commission desired that any benefits of inflation accrue to the peasants and not the lords.[71]

The combined effect of these regulations meant that however off the mark or inflated the averages were, they could only be used to reduce

68 *PIM*, vol. 16, part II, "Vyvody o denezhnykh povinnostiakh," 5-8.
69 *PIM*, vol. 6, 120, 124.
70 *PIM*, vol. 3, Report of the Economic Division no. 17, 88.
71 *PIM*, vol. 2, Report of the Economic Division no. 9, 20-24.

peasant quitrents or keep them at the same level; quitrents could not be increased. And for many peasants, a substantial reduction would result. In those areas where pre-reform quitrents did reflect the value of the land the serfs held as provision plots, for the post-reform maximum allotment, they would pay only the average quitrent.

The commission reasoned that quitrents existed in fertile grain producing areas only on estates with high population densities. Here, demesne farming had become unproductive as the lord had been forced to allocate more and more land to the peasants for their subsistence needs. As it was well-known that direct estate farming was more profitable in this area, which is why it was so widespread, serf owners who had been forced to shift to quitrent had a lower income from their estate. Thus, using the limited data available on pre-reform quitrents for the black-earth and steppe area would yield averages on the low end to the benefits of the peasants.[72] Averages were then applied to extraordinarily wide geographic areas. For 52 percent of all serfs in the empire, a 9-ruble maximum quitrent was established.[73] For those living in Moscow and Iaroslavl' provinces, in St. Petersburg province more than 25 *versts* (16.6 miles) from the city, in four districts of Vladimir province, and in parts of Nizhegorod province, altogether slightly over 6 percent of all serfs in the Empire, a maximum quitrent of 10 rubles was set. In contrast, peasants in Mogilev, Viatsk, Vitebsk, and Olonets provinces and parts of Kazan', Orel, Pskov, Penza, Smolensk, and Tambov, about 10 percent of all serfs, were to pay only 8 rubles. The handful of serfs living close to St. Petersburg (and not in service) were subject to a maximum quitrent of 12 rubles. In Chernigov, Poltava, and parts of Kharkov provinces with about 5 percent of the serf population, the quitrent varied between 8 and 12 rubles. Most other serfs in the western provinces were covered by the inventories.

From the information provided by serf owners, the commission felt it had sufficient data to calculate reliably average quitrents for only 12 provinces. For Moscow province, the pre-reform average was 9.12 rubles; for Iaroslavl', 10.84; for four districts of Vladimir at 9.93; and St. Petersburg (exclusive of the area close to the city), about 11 rubles.

---

[72] *PIM*, vol. 16, part II, 9-10.

[73] *PIM*, vol. 6, Supplement to the Report of the Economic Division, no. 17 (February 29, 1860), 120 and 124. See also *PIM*, vol. 3, no. 17, 96.

Setting a *maximum* quitrent of 10 rubles for this region ensured a reduction for a considerable portion of the peasants. A 9-ruble maximum quitrent was set for Vologda where the pre-reform average quitrent was 8.54 rubles; Kaluga, 8.90 rubles; Kostroma, 9.71 rubles; Novgorod, 8.89 rubles; Riazan', 8.07 rubles; Tver', 9.26 rubles; nine districts of Vladimir, 8.74 rubles; and four districts of Smolensk, 8.14 rubles. Again, a substantial portion of these serfs would have their quitrents reduced, although in all likelihood a smaller number than those living in the 10-ruble zone.[74] For all remaining provinces, the commission simply imposed a 9-ruble maximum, unless a lower amount seemed appropriate from what was known of the peasant economy generally. The commission really had no other alternative, although it was not satisfied with its own results.[75]

The Editing Commission as well as many serf owners felt that peasant labor obligations were the most onerous aspect of serfdom. But establishing their cash value to permit their commutation into quitrent proved, yet again, impossible. "There is no doubt," the commission wrote, "that if there were a rational relationship between the two major forms of dues—cash and labor services—such a relationship would greatly facilitate converting one kind of dues into the other."[76] But the commission admitted that based upon the information available it could not establish any relationship. Thus, the levels of "peasant dues, cash or labor services," were "to be determined independently of each other."[77]

The commission was of the view that while there were "extremely varied average quitrents for different localities," peasant labor obligations were "uniform for all of Russia."[78] The commission assumed one peasant *tiaglo*, usually a husband and wife work-team supporting on average three dependents, worked 3 days per week for the lord, each adult laboring a total of 150 days on the estate or 60 days per capita (approximately 300 work days/five peasants). In reality, most female serfs worked somewhat less. To discourage the continuation of obligatory labor relations after emancipation, the final legislation provided

74 *PIM*, vol. 16, part II, 21-28.

75 *PIM*, vol. 16, part II, "Vyvody o denezhnykh povinnostiakh," 13.

76 *PIM*, vol. 3, Report of the Economic Division no. 10, 28-29. See also *PIM*, vol. 3, Report of the Economic Division, no. 5, 30.

77 *PIM*, vol. 3, Report of the Economic Division no. 10, 40.

78 *PIM*, vol.3, Report of the Economic Division no. 5, 30.

for a substantial reduction in peasant labor services. The statute set a maximum of 40 male work days per capita per year, a one-third reduction. Females could not work more than 30 days per year, half of the presumed pre-reform level. Peasants were required to provide draft animals and use their own equipment, as the work required. In addition, the emancipation law specified that only males aged 18-55 and females aged 17-50 were required to work for the lord. Although, prior to reform, policies varied from estate to estate regarding the age adults were required to carry *tiaglo* obligations, "generally it ran from 15-18 to 50-60 years of age for men, and from marriage to 50 for women," suggesting an even further reduction in peasant labor services after emancipation, especially for men.[79] In addition, the law stated that peasants who were ill, and women near childbirth and for six weeks after birth, could not be sent out to work. Although their obligations were to be carried out by other household members, in reality, this would not always be possible. The reduction in peasant labor obligations mandated by emancipation was very considerable indeed.[80]

The intent of the commission was to regulate *existing* dues and allotment sizes, and to see that peasant well-being was improved. The regulations enacted into law fulfilled these goals. In sum, here is how it worked: a maximum number of work days by gender, set substantially below the pre-reform level, was equated with the maximum regional quitrent which, in turn, was based upon the average pre-reform quitrent. Both were tied to the maximum statutory allotment, which was usually higher than the pre-reform mean. Each of these variables had been determined independently, governed by the principle of current practice. Stated more simply, for a maximum allotment, peasants were either to work a smaller number of days for the lord or pay the average pre-reform quitrent, unless, of course, their quitrent had been lower, in which case it could not be increased.

For serfs holding pre-reform allotments below the statutory maximum provided in the law, but above the minimum, their obligations,

[79] Blum, *Lord and Peasant*, 513.

[80] For Chernigov, Poltava, and Kharkov provinces covered by the second regional statute, serf corvee obligations were reduced by essentially the same amount, although they were calculated somewhat differently. See *Polnoe sobranie zakonov Rossiiskoi Imperii* (*PSZ II*), series II (St. Petersburg, 1830-84), vol. 36, no. 36663, article 195 and *prilozheniia*, 49.

whether in cash or in labor, did not decrease proportionately. Rather, two gradation systems were used. This was done because even though the commission was unable to determine the price of the land the peasants held as serfs, it was clear that peasant farmsteads, that is, developed lands with peasant buildings, adjacent service areas, kitchen gardens, and orchards, were considerably more valuable than grain fields and pasture land. In non-black earth areas, where natural fertilizers were commonly used, manured fields were, of course, valued more highly than other arable lands. Location also mattered, especially the proximity to sources of off-farm income.

In the first or non-black earth zone under the Great Russian, New Russian and White Russian statute, a three-step graded valuation was used. Depending upon the locality, of which there were nine, maximum quitrents of 8, 9, 10, or 12 rubles were imposed. Maximum allotment sizes under the statute varied from three to seven desiatinas. As stated, peasant labor services were fixed at the 40 male and 30 female workdays, without respect to zone or locality. If peasants received less than the maximum allotment, on the first desiatina of land they were to pay half of the total obrok—4.00, 4.50, 5.00, or 6.00 rubles. This was compensation for the more valuable farmstead and adjacent manured land. On the second desiatina, a quarter of the total quitrent, or 2.00, 2.25, 2.50, or 3.00 rubles was assessed. This land was deemed more valuable as, along with any arable land included in the first desiatina, it was more likely to have been manured as well. In fact, the emancipation law prohibited lords from cutting off manured land, if there were to be a reduction in the size of the peasants' allotments (article 54) unless no other lands were available. The remaining quitrent (2.00, 2.25, 2.50, or 3.00 rubles) was then equally assessed on the remaining land (which varied from one to four additional desiatinas) based upon the maximum statutory allotment.

Work days were calculated differently. For the minimum statutory allotment, which varied between 1 and 2.33 desiatinas, peasants were to work half of the maximum number of workdays, 20 for males and 15 for females. The range between the minimum and maximum allotment was then divided into 20 equal units, and for each additional unit of land the peasants received, males worked an additional day; females, three-quarters of a day. Table 2 below illustrates more clearly what all this means. Peasants living in a locality for which 9 rubles was specified as the maximum quitrent allowed (which is assumed throughout the table), but receiving only two-thirds of the maximum allotment, had to perform either 75 percent of the maximum number of work days or pay between 75 percent and 86 percent of the maximum quitrent, depending upon the locality. In the worst case, peasants receiving the minimum allotment (one-third of the maximum) were required to work half the maximum number of days or pay a quitrent between half and three-quarters of the maximum, again depending upon the locality. Finally, it needs to be emphasized that in all cases, if the money dues as calculated using the procedures described above resulted in a quitrent higher than the amount the serfs currently paid, they were to continue to pay the lower amount without any reduction in their land allotment.

Table 2

	Non-Black Earth Zone			Black Earth Zone, Steppe and New Russia		
Percent of Maximum Total Allotment	Total Number of Workdays (male/ female)	Quitrent (rubles)	Percent of Maximum Quitrent	Total Number of Workdays (male/ female)	Quitrent (rubles)	Percent of Maximum Quitrent
100	40/30	9.00	100	40/30	9.00	100
67	30/22.5	6.75-7.74	75-86	30/22.5	6.23-7.15	69-79
33	20/15	4.50-6.75	50-75	20/15	3.32-5.35	37-59

For all of the black-earth and steppe region, that is, zones 2 and 3 of this same statute, with 20 localities altogether, a simpler, two-step gradation system was imposed. A single maximum quitrent of 9 rubles was applied everywhere. The maximum number of work days was the same, 40 for males, 30 for females. But the maximum allotment varied from 2.5 to 6 desiatinas in the black-earth region, 6 to 12 desiatinas in the steppe region, and 3 to 7 desiatinas in New Russia. If peasants received less than the maximum, on the first desiatina they paid a 4-ruble quitrent or 44 percent of the totaL All the other desiatinas were said to be of equal value, as natural fertilizers were not used and location, especially the potential for outside earnings, was of considerably less import. The 5-ruble balance was therefore equally apportioned among them. To continue the example above, peasants receiving two-thirds of the maximum allotment either had to work 75 percent of the maximum number of days for their former owner or pay a quitrent which varied by locality from 69 to 79 percent of the maximum. Peasants receiving the minimum allotment had to work half the maximum number of work days, as above, or pay a quitrent between 37 and 59 percent of the maximum.

In the nine localities covered under the second regional statute (Chernigov, Poltava, and part of Kharkov provinces), a two-step graded valuation was also used. Maximum allotments varied between 2.75 and 4.5 desiatinas. But different procedures were used to assess quitrents and workdays, making the calculations rather more complex. On each desiatina of peasant homestead 5.10 rubles was assessed and had to be paid in cash by every peasant household. Most peasant homesteads were substantially less than a desiatina in size, so that only a fraction of this assessment was actually due. Dues on field lands could be paid in cash or in labor and were all evaluated equally. On these lands, quitrents varied between 1.40 and 2.80 rubles per desiatina among the localities. Labor obligations were assessed on males only and varied between 12 and 21 workdays per desiatina. For the maximum allotment, a peasant was required to work approximately 50 days. In contrast to the first regional statute, obligatory female labor was prohibited, and the lord was not allowed to require the peasants to provide draft animals. Overall, the intent of the Editing Commission and the statutes as enacted gave peasants here a settlement comparable to those covered under the Great Russia, New Russia, and White Russia law.

In the southwestern provinces of Kiev, Podolia, and Volynia, the same system was used to assess the obligations on peasant homesteads. Field lands were assessed between 1.35 and 3.30 rubles per desiatina, or 8.5 to 20 workdays. If the balance were paid in labor, again only male workdays were allowed, and the lord could not require the use of peasant draft animals. The precise level of peasant obligations depended on their holdings under the inventories.

The fourth regional statute covered Vilensk, Grodno, Minsk, Kovna, and four districts (uezds) of Vitebsk. First and foremost, lords here were not allowed to reduce peasant allotments by more than one-sixth. For the first four provinces, with the introduction of the land charter agreements, all peasants were to receive a 10 percent reduction in their labor services based upon their pre-reform inventories. In addition, a maximum of 23 work days, male and female combined, was imposed for each peasant allotment of land (not per unit of land). A maximum quitrent was set at three rubles per desiatina. For Vitebsk, special rules were written based upon the population density of an estate. Nine gradations were established. For peasants on estates with less than seven males per 40 desiatinas of peasant allotment, the least densely settled, a maximum quitrent of 1.65 rubles per desiatina was established. On estates with double the density, a maximum quitrent of 3.00 rubles per desiatina was specified. Seven other gradations fell between these two. The maximum number of workdays varied between from 12 to 23, for both sexes combined.

Finally, for the 128,000 males serfs living in the Land of the Don Host, another two-step gradation system was used, but with half the total quitrent assessed on the first desiatina. The remaining lands, as in the black-earth and steppe region, were equally valued. The maximum quitrent was set at eight rubles, but the maximum number of work days was lower than elsewhere, 36 days for males and 27 for females.

It is often claimed that under these systems of gradation peasants in the non-black earth area, especially those 3.75 million male serfs living in zone 1 under the first regional statute, where farming was less productive, were forced to pay more per unit of land.[81] And on this basis, it is alleged these peasants were forced to pay not only for the land they were to redeem, but to compensate the lord for their personal freedom. This is a serious misreading of both the intent of the Editing Commission and the consequences of the policy. Location is a major consideration in virtually all real estate transactions. For example, the opportunities for off-farm earnings often made peasant farmsteads in the non-black earth area more valuable by virtue of their location.[82] Similarly, the widespread use of natural fertilizers resulted in less uniformity in land quality and value. Quite simply, farmsteads and immediately adjacent arable lands were more valuable relative to the rest of a peasant's holdings in the non-black earth region than elsewhere. An independent study undertaken by the Ministry of State Domains in the mid-1850s had noted that in all the northern non-black earth provinces, there was

---

[81] Robinson, *Rural Russia*, 83; Blum, *Lord and Peasant*, 595.

[82] *PIM*, vol. 11, 5-6.

less uniformity in land prices than elsewhere as there were sharp differences between lands that had been routinely manured and those that had not.[83] The Editing Commission, quite rightly, felt obligated to take this into consideration.

To all this, five exceptions need to be noted. First, in spite of all that has been said above, lords covered under the first, second, and fourth regional statutes were entitled to keep up to one-third of their total land, as long as the peasant allotments after emancipation still remained above the statutory minimum. In zone 3 of the first regional statute, the steppe, they were allowed to keep half of their landholdings. The intent was to leave every lord with an economically viable estate, and these petty nobles, it was felt, had often been forced by circumstances to be the most innovative. In actuality, this regulation rarely came into play. Only a handful of very small estates were impacted, and lords in these circumstances rarely exercised their option, as it lowered the size of their redemption grant.

Second, the first regional statute permitted lords to petition the newly established Provincial Office for Peasant Affairs for a one-ruble increase in the maximum quitrent if they could demonstrate that the peasants had access to especially valuable water-meadows, lived within 3.3 miles of a city of more than 20,000 inhabitants that provided significant commercial benefit, resided in a village in which river commerce was particularly advantageous, subsisted primarily from fishing, or had any other special sources of income which might justify an increase. This provision appears to have affected approximately one percent of all serfs, primarily those living close to the provincial capitals in the northern part of European Russia.[84] Under the second and third regional statutes, lords could petition for a 10 or 15 percent increase in the maximum quitrent respectively, but at the request of the peasants the Provincial Bureau for Peasant Affairs had the right to lower the maximum quitrent by an equal amount, if considered appropriate. In the fourth regional statute, lords could petition for an increase in the quitrent to the level specified in the inventory, but the government could also lower it.

---

83 "Svedeniia o prodazhnykh tsenakh na zemli Iaroslavskoi gubernii," *Materialy dlia statistiki Rossii,* 1: 119-21.

84 Degtiarev, *Novgorodskaia derevnia*, 147-98.

Third, well after the Editing Commission completed its work and only eight days prior to the promulgation of the emancipation law, a special provision was added. It allowed a lord covered by the first two regional statutes upon mutual agreement with the peasants to grant them a so-called "gift allotment."[85] Peasants were to be allotted only one-quarter of the maximum for the locality, but they were free of all dues forever. The lord received no compensation. Although often cited as a last minute concession to defenders of serfdom and dubbed a beggar's allotment, only 6 percent of all serfs ever accepted the offer. Moreover, far from being the most unfortunate of peasants, as is often alleged, it is now clear that most *darstvenniki,* as they were called, were quite well off. Generally, they agreed to these small, free allotments because they lived where land was plentiful and cheap to rent or buy. Accepting the terms for acquiring land under the emancipation's redemption law would have been less advantageous.[86]

Fourth, a special statute covered *dvorovye liudi,* who comprised just under 7 percent of all serfs in the empire. Although frequently translated as "household serfs," most were not in domestic service, but worked rather as bailiffs, scribes, masters, and skilled laborers on noble estates. Those *dvorovye* who held an allotment of land prior to March 2, 1858, if they wished, were to be included under the general terms of land reform. Many, however, did not farm and did not desire or need an allotment. The statute allowed these serfs to stay in their current status with the same obligations, although a maximum quitrent was imposed, for a period of no more than two years. Lords were required to provide them with the same level of support. After two years, or before if certain conditions were met, all obligatory relations were to end. Lords received no compensation for this loss of serf labor, and the peasants were free to take up any rural or urban status, though in one instance permission of the community was required.

Fifth, special rules were established to address a variety of unique circumstances. Serfs who lived on estates with less than 21 male serfs *and*

85 *PSZ II*, no. 36,662, art. 123; no. 36,663, art. 116.

86 Daniel Field, *The End of Serfdom: Nobility and Bureacracy in Russia,* 1855-1861 (Cambridge, MA, 1976), 353-54; O. N. Burdina, *Krest'iane darstvenniki v Rossii, 1861-1907* (Moscow, 1996), 8-9, 45, and 190-91; N. Druzhinin, "Likvidatsiia feodal'noi sistemy v russkoi pomeshchich'ei derevne (1862-1882 gg.)," *Voprosy istorii,* no. 12 (1968): 3-34.

possessed allotments felt to be inadequate *(melkopomestnye krest'iane)* were in most cases to be resettled on state lands. Lords were permitted to keep all their land, but their holdings were quite small. In all, over 13 percent of all estates (17,500 estates), but only 180,000 male serfs fell under this provision. In addition, approximately 258,000 male serfs, living primarily in Perm' and Orenburg provinces, were assigned to private factories and mines or were under the authority of various state or private agencies. Nevertheless, most of these peasants had land allotments as provision plots and in this regard fell under the terms of the general and regional statutes. The special regulations either related to those serfs who did not farm at all, usually skilled workers and masters, or they detailed different procedures, more in accord with a factory regime, on the transition from labor obligations to quitrent.

From the final legislation on emancipation and redemption, it is clear that the autocracy was unable to conceptualize a vision of modernity and define a future for the society it sought to reform. It failed to enact freedoms based upon principles, reflecting its ambivalence as a modernizing state. More humbly and cautiously, current circumstances motivated the autocracy and drove reform policy. The great reformers seemed far more comfortable in modifying Western precedents and resolving complex technical questions than in undertaking a thoroughgoing agrarian reform. The Editing Commission in particular thought pragmatically, in terms of what the serfs paid and what the lords received. As was emphasized, the Editing Commission never claimed to have sought a correspondence between the value of the land the peasants were to acquire and their post-reform payments. Rather, the goal was to bring about an immediate improvement in peasant well-being. Lords were to be provided with a steady income, but only a portion of what they had received in the past. Again, in so doing, the commission was following closely the precedents of land reform in Austria and the German states, but no more.

In sum, concerned that the data available for those regions not covered by the inventories reflected serf owner biases, but governed by a strong commitment to improve peasant well-being, the Editing Commission used ranges and averages to solve its problem. For serfs on quitrent as well as those who chose to commute their labor obligations into cash payments after emancipation, as was common, a major improvement was assured because the *average* quitrent as calculated for each locality became under the law the *maximum* quitrent that the peasant could be charged for the *maximum* statutory allotment. Within the very broad geographic regions and zones, the general principle followed was that no peasant after emancipation would pay more than the average quitrent, although many would hold an allotment in excess of the pre-reform average. Lords who had been generous to their serfs in the past by imposing low quitrents simply lost out. While the commission was aware that some serfs might still seem to be disadvantaged—those who had their allotmentsreduced proportionately more than their quitrent—most of them lived either in areas with substantial off-farm earnings or where land was abundant and rental or purchase prices would be low. Thus, they would not be worse off in reality. For peasants who continued to perform labor services, with the substantial reduction in total number of work days per year mandated in the emancipation legislation, the benefits would be more uniform and even greater. On balance, the commission was correct in its claim that its policies served "to lighten dues such as is necessary for a significant improvement in peasant well-being," while still being able to state that it had minimized losses for the lords.[87]

As we look at the scales more carefully, however, the emancipation legislation proved to be far more beneficial to the peasantry than has been perceived.

[87] *PIM,* vol. 3, Report of the Economic Division no. 17, 81-82.

Index

C

D

www.ingramcontent.com/pod-product-compliance
Ingram Content Group UK Ltd.
Pitfield, Milton Keynes, MK11 3LW, UK
UKHW020059210526
471278UK00004B/115

9 781618 114280